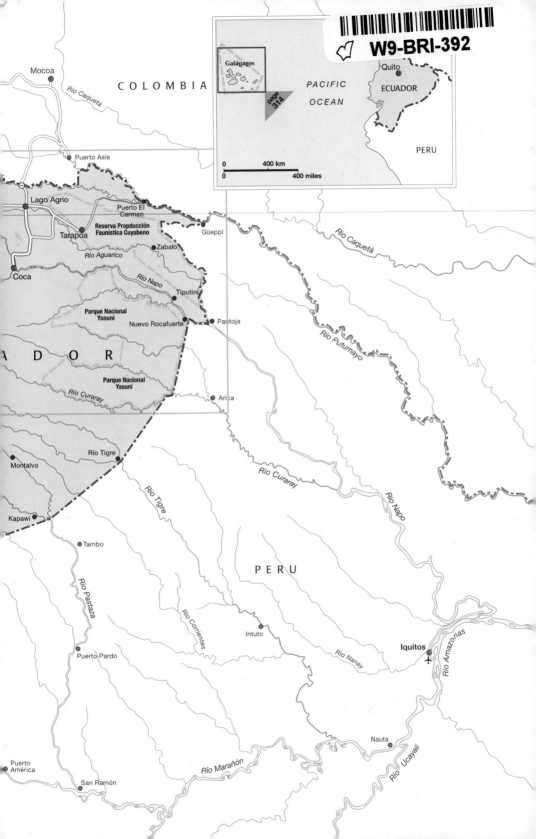

INSIGHT GUIDES
ECUADOR
& GALÁPAGOS

APA PUBLICATIONS L

Part of the Langenscheidt Publishing Group

LEFT: sinuous tributary of the Amazon.

journalist who writes for several English-landguage publications including *The Economist* and *Bloomberg*. He also updated the Best of Ecuador section, compiling a brand new Top Attractions feature, and the Galápagos Islands chapters. Kueffner wrote the fascinating feature on The Last Hidden Tribes.

The Places and Travel Tips sections were updated by **Gabi Mocatta**, a freelance journalist who writes and photographs for newspapers, magazines, and travel guides. She first fell in love with South America volunteering on eco-tourism development projects in Venezuela. She's since traveled extensively in Ecuador and Peru, and currently works with remote Andean communities on sustainable development projects.

Other contributors whose work is retained from previous editions include **Sally Burch**, **Mary Dempsey**, **Sean Doyle**, **Rob Rachowiecki**, **Betsy Wagenhauser**, **Jane Letham**, and **Mark Thurber**.

The principal photographer for the book was **Corrie Wingate**, who has contributed to several of Insight's Latin America titles, but many other talented photographers contributed their work, including **Eduardo Gil** and **Peter Frost**.

The text was copy-edited by **Naomi Peck** and proofread by **Sue Pearson**. The index was compiled by **Helen Peters**.

tion of essential practical information. There is also a handy Spanish phrasebook with tips on grammar and pronunciation. An easy-to-find contents list for Travel Tips is printed on the back flap, which also serves as a bookmark.

◆ The **photographs** are chosen not only to illustrate the Ecuadorean landscape, and the beauty of its cities, nature reserves, and beaches, but also to convey its cultural diversity.

The contributors

This new edition was commissioned and edited by **Rachel Lawrence**, and builds on previous versions edited by **Pam Barrett**, **Christina Park**, and **Tony Perrottet**, and updated by **Dominic Hamilton**, **Nicholas Gill**, and **Andrew Eames**.

The introduction, History, and Features sections were updated by **Stephan Kueffner**, a Quito-based

Map Legend

▬ ▬ ▬ ・▬	International Boundary
▬ ▬ ▬ ▬	Province Boundary
⊖	Border Crossing
▬ • ▬	National Park/Reserve
▬ ▬ ▬ ▬	Ferry Route
✈ ✈	Airport: International/Regional
🚌	Bus Station
❶	Tourist Information
🏛 † ⛪	Church/Ruins
†	Monastery
⌂	Hacienda
🏰 🏚	Castle/Ruins
☾	Mosque
✡	Synagogue
∴	Archaeological Site
∩	Cave
1	Statue/Monument
★	Place of Interest
✉	Post Office

The main places of interest in the Places section are coordinated by number with a full-colour map (eg ❶), and a symbol at the top of every right-hand page tells you where to find the map.

Contents

LEFT: rural farmstead in the Central Highlands.

Travel Tips

THE BEST OF ECUADOR: TOP ATTRACTIONS

From the Galápagos Islands to colonial gems and sandy beaches to snow-capped volcanoes, here is a shortlist of Ecuador's most spectacular attractions

△ Culture does not get more Andean than in **Otavalo**, with its excellent textile market. Nearby lakes, haciendas, and colonial Ibarra round off the experience. *See pages 177–84.*

△ Snow-capped peaks along Ecuador's Andean spine form the **Avenue of the Volcanoes**. Hike and climb at the top of the world, as measured from the earth's center. *See pages 187–201.*

▽ Cupolas of the 19th-century Catedral Nueva blend in with the older buildings of **Cuenca**, a Unesco World Heritage Site, and one of Latin America's best-preserved colonial Spanish cities. *See pages 205–9.*

◁ The historic Old Town of **Quito**, one of the biggest in the Americas, is studded with Baroque churches, such as La Compañía de Jesús. *See pages 147–58.*

△ **Pacific coast beaches** offer leaping whales, water sports, and some of the oldest archeological remains in the Americas. *See pages 251–68.*

◁ Marvels of isolated evolution, the **Galápagos Islands** boast unique wildlife, approachable like nowhere else on the planet. Swim with sea lions, and dive with sharks and marine iguanas. *See pages 293–320.*

▽ Possibly a temple for sun worship, fortress-like **Ingapirca** is Ecuador's best-preserved pre-Colonial monument, built by the Inca Tupac Yupanqui in the late 15th century in imperial Inca style. *See pages 213–14.*

▷ Frigid but spectacular, the **Páramo del Ángel**'s unique flora seems extra-terrestrial; wander the expanse amid frailejón flowers the size of small palm trees. *See page 184.*

▷ Just a hop away by plane and canoe, **Amazon lodges** offer a doorway to the world's most diverse ecosystem. *See page 224.*

THE BEST OF ECUADOR: EDITOR'S CHOICE

Wildlife, adventure sports, and handicrafts are just some of the attractions of this small but diverse country. Here, at a glance, are the editor's top tips for making the most of your visit

BEST WILDLIFE-WATCHING

- **The Galápagos Islands** The most famous wildlife reserve in the world and the place where Charles Darwin formed his theory of evolution. See page 293.
- **Parque Nacional Machalilla** Most visitors come for the whale-watching around Isla de la Plata, but you can also see frigate birds and blue-footed boobies on Isla de la Plata. See page 267.
- **Parque Nacional Yasuní** Ecuador's largest nature reserve is home to the elusive jaguar and the vocal howler monkey. See page 55.

ABOVE: sea lions taking a break on the Galápagos.
RIGHT: blue-footed boobies, Galápagos Islands.
BELOW: *La Familia* (The Family) by Oswaldo Guayasamín.

BEST ART MUSEUMS

- **Capilla del Hombre** Guayasamín's masterpiece in the Bellavista district of Quito is perhaps the most stunning example of Modernist Latin American art on the continent. See page 162.
- **Centro Cultural Libertador Simón Bolívar** On Guayaquil's Malecón 2000, this modern museum has some of the best contemporary art in the country, along with a fascinating anthropological collection. See page 278.
- **Museo del Banco Central** This art museum in Quito showcases a wide range of Ecuadorian art, from pre-Columbian artifacts to contemporary pieces. See page 160.

BEST FOR FAMILIES

● **Salinas** The most complete beach resort on Ecuador's coast. See page 283.

● **Teleférico** Quito's cable car whisks you to the top of a hill, beside an active volcano, for awe-inspiring views of the city.

See page 150.

● **Museo Solar Inti Ñan** Located right on the equator, this small museum to the north of Quito has interactive exhibits that will keep kids of all ages amused. See page 169.

BEST ADVENTURES

● **Hiking the Inca Trail to Ingapirca** This three-day trek is not nearly as crowded as its Peruvian cousin, but it takes you

to a magnificent Inca ruin just the same. See page 213.

● **Climbing Mount Cotopaxi** Over ice and snow, the 5–8-hour ascent takes you to the top of one of the world's highest active volcanoes. See page 188.

● **Surfing in Montañita** Hang ten in this all-encompassing surfing resort on the Pacific coast. See page 268.

● **White-water rafting in the Andes** Take a multiple-day rafting trip down the Class III and IV rapids at the eastern edge of the Andes mountains right into the heart of the Amazon jungle. See page 228.

BEST MARKETS

● **Otavalo** The largest Saturday market in the Andes now runs almost every day. This is the place to pick up handmade clothes and bags, pottery, and other crafts. See page 177.

● **Saquisilí** Pens of llamas and sheep, produce, and various animal parts and products are all for sale at what is generally considered to be Ecuador's most important indigenous market. See page 191.

ABOVE LEFT: balancing an egg on the equator line, Museo Solar Inti Ñan. **ABOVE:** ceramic *ranchero* bus.

BEST CHURCHES

● **La Compañía de Jésus** With gold-plated walls and ceilings, this cathedral in Quito is one of the most impressive churches in Latin America. See page 153.

● **El Sagrario and Catedral de la Inmaculada Concepción** Cuenca's "old" and "new" cathedrals dominate the main plaza. The first dates back to the mid-16th century, while the second was built in the late 19th century and contains a famous crowned image of the Virgin. See page 206.

BELOW LEFT: a wall of ice on Volcán Cotopaxi in the Avenue of the Volcanoes. **BELOW:** ornate facade of the Baroque church La Compañía de Jesús, Quito.

LATITUDE 0° 00'

Small but spectacular, Ecuador is one of Latin America's most attractive destinations, with fabulous diversity in both culture and nature

In 1736 Charles-Marie de la Condamine and Pierre Bouguer headed a pioneering expedition mounted by the French Academy of Science to study the equatorial line at its highest points. Close to a century later, the founders of the Republic of Ecuador chose the invisible line in the Andes as its namesake, already well aware of the geographical diversity of its territories.

Among the world's most biodiverse countries – 1 hectare (2½ acres) of Amazon forest holds more tree species than all of North America, and one in three bird species is found in Ecuador – the country has drawn explorers and researchers for more than 300 years, from German explorer Alexander von Humboldt and Charles Darwin in the 19th century, to modern biologists who still discover previously unde-scribed species. Although only slightly larger than Color-ado and somewhat larger than Britain, Ecuador contains the snow-capped Andes, the wide, largely deserted beaches of the Pacific coast, and expanses of steamy Amazon jungle.

Historically one of Latin America's least stable countries, Ecuador has had well over 100 presidents since full inde-pendence in 1830, amid a succession of minor civil wars through the early 20th century, and numerous coups and defenestrations of leaders at the hands of the people or the military. Yet these events have been short-lived, and Ecua-dor has almost entirely escaped the brutal violence that has haunted so many of its Latin American neighbors. Hence it is also among the safest in which to travel, though pickpocketing and instances of armed robbery are on the increase in some tourist areas.

Ecuador is not, and has never been, a prosperous country, but it has largely avoided the most bitter extremes of poverty that afflict other Andean countries. Ecuadorians remain approachable and easygoing, including the close to a dozen indigenous groups, many of whom still speak Quichua and maintain traditions from Inca times and earlier.

With its fascinating natural and cultural diversity, it is easy to see why Ecuador has become one of the most popular destinations in South America. ❑

PRECEDING PAGES: herding alpacas in the Sierra; La Ronda street scene, Quito; Thursday market at Guamote, Chimborazo province. **LEFT:** Local girls in their finery near Cotacachi. **ABOVE:** butterfly in Parque Nacional Machalilla on the Pacific coast.

COAST, SIERRA, AND JUNGLE

Sandy beaches, snowy volcanoes, Amazon rainforests, the Galápagos Islands... Ecuador's vivid diversity is one of its greatest attractions

Straddling the Andes on the most westerly point of South America, Ecuador is half the size of France (271,000 sq km/103,000 sq miles), making it the smallest of the Andean countries. The Andean mountain chain divides the country into three distinct regions: the coastal plain, or Costa, the mountains themselves, or Sierra, and the Amazon jungle, or Oriente. A fourth region, the Galápagos Islands, is a volcanic archipelago in the Pacific Ocean some 1,000km (620 miles) west of the mainland.

Contrasting ecosystems

The gently rolling hills of the Costa lie between sea and mountains. Frequent seasonal flooding makes access to some low-lying areas difficult in the rainy season. Much of this area was virgin coastal rainforest at the turn of the 20th century, but now it is devoted primarily to agriculture. The shoreline offers long stretches of sandy palm-lined beaches, and the sea is warm all year round. The river estuaries harbor man-

> The term "Avenue of the Volcanoes" was coined by the German explorer Alexander von Humboldt in 1802. At its northern end lies Mount Cotopaxi, the world's highest active volcano.

grove swamps, many of which are used for shrimp-ranching; inland there are plantations of bananas, sugarcane, cacao, and rice.

The Andes consist of an eastern and western range, joined at intervals by transverse foothills.

LEFT: Volcán El Altar near Riobamba.
RIGHT: *indígena* girl minding sheep near Guamote.

Nestling between the ranges are valleys with highly productive volcanic soils that have been farmed for several thousand years. From the valley floors, a patchwork quilt of small fields climbs far up the mountainsides, using every available centimeter of land. The Quichua communities who own this land produce a variety of crops, including potatoes, corn, beans, wheat, barley, and carrots.

The northern half of the Ecuadorian Andes is dominated by 10 volcanoes that tower to over 5,000 meters (16,000ft). These peaks are covered by ice and snow that draw mountaineers from all over the world, while trekkers are enchanted by the surrounding sub-Alpine grasslands known locally as *páramo*, and host wildlife such as the Andean condor, Andean fox, and spectacled bear, as well as hundreds of wildflowers.

The Amazon rainforest of the Oriente begins in the foothills of the eastern Andes. River systems flowing from this rainy wilderness become tributaries of the Amazon, the longest being the Río Napo (855km/530 miles). Settlement, previously limited to the banks of these rivers, is rapidly being changed by an expanding road network begun by the oil industry in the early 1970s. Settlers and agricultural interests are converting once virgin rainforest into pastures and croplands, but for the moment, much of the

original forest survives and offers both magnificent scenery and ideal terrain for adventure.

The Galápagos Islands, home to the famous giant tortoises, blue-footed boobies, and marine iguanas, consist of 13 islands (the biggest, Isabela, measures over 4,000 sq km/1,520 sq miles) and 40 to 50 islets. Since this archipelago was never directly connected to the mainland, the wildlife that exists here evolved in isolation, and many species are endemic. The area is biologically unique, and all of the islands are protected both by a national park and a marine reserve.

Land of sun and rain

Being right on the equator, Ecuador lacks the four seasons of the temperate zones. Every location in the country generally has a wet (winter) and dry (summer) season, but it is difficult to predict the weather on a day-to-day basis, especially during an El Niño year, when much of the country gets drenched by heavy rains.

The rainy season for the Costa is between January and June. It rains most of the time in the Oriente, though December to February are usually drier. Both these regions are hot (above 25°C/80°F) all year round. The Galápagos Islands are hot and arid. Weather patterns in the Sierra are complex, and each region has its own microclimate. Generally, the central valleys are rainy between February and May, while the rest of the year is drier, with a short wet season in October and November. The climate overall is mild, and Quiteños brag about their perpetual spring, where gardens bloom all year round.

A dynamic landscape

The forces of tectonic plates, volcanoes, and water have sculpted an exquisite array of landscapes, but have also caused devastating natural disasters throughout Ecuador's history. In 1996 an earthquake shook the province of Cotopaxi, causing 30 deaths and leaving thousands homeless.

In 1660, a century after the colonial city of Quito was founded, the nearby volcano of Guagua Pichincha erupted catastrophically, dumping several feet of ash onto the city. It began erupting again in 1999, causing the evacuation of villages near the crater. However, Quito is safe from lava and pyroclastic flows: the crater opens to the west away from the city, and another lower, dormant crater, Rucu Pichincha, blocks any potential flows. Further south, Tungurahua started spitting out ash and incandescent rocks soon after Guagua and is still restless.

Demographics

The country is divided into 24 provinces, many named after mountains or rivers. The population of Ecuador is more than 14 million, two-thirds of whom live in the cities. The capital, Quito, has about 1.8 million inhabitants. but Guayaquil is the largest city, with a population of over 2 million, and Ecuador's commercial hub. ❑

ABOVE: traveling by boat along the Río Napo, the longest tributary of the Amazon.
RIGHT: sea lion sleeping, Galápagos Islands.

DECISIVE DATES

PRE-CERAMIC 30,000–6000 BC
Hunter-gatherers using stone axes inhabit the Andes.

FORMATIVE PERIOD 3500–500 BC
First permanent settlements and communities. Surviving pottery testifies to the sophistication of the society.

3500 BC
Earliest Valdivian site, called Loma Alta, is established.

1500 BC
Ceremonial temples are built in Real Alto.

REGIONAL CULTURES 6TH CENTURY BC–16TH CENTURY AD
Distinct cultural hubs develop along the coast (Manteño culture), the northern Andes (Quitu-Caras) and the central-southern Andes (Puruháes, Cañaris), with metallurgy, pottery, and textile production.

1460–1520
Inca conquest under Tupac Yupanqui amid fierce resistance (Quitu taken in 1492). Forced resettlement and construction of Ingapirca under Huayna Cápac.

1527–32
Civil war between Atahualpa, heir to the Kingdom of Quito, and his half-brother Huascar ends with Huascar's defeat.

SPANISH COLONY AND EARLY INDEPENDENCE

1526
First *conquistadores*, under Bartolomé Ruiz, land near Esmeraldas.

1530
Francisco Pizarro lands near Manabí.

1532
Atahualpa captured and killed.

1534
Pedro de Alvarado lands in Manta. An army led by Simón de Benalcázar defeats the Incas when thousands of members of the Inca army stage a mutiny. Benalcázar founds San Francisco de Quito on the ruins of the city burned by Inca leader Rumiñahui.

1535
Guayaquil is founded.

1549
The Spanish conquest is completed, but the *conquistadores* fight over gold until subdued by the Spanish crown in 1554.

1550s
The land is divided up among the Spaniards and worked under a form of serfdom on huge estates (*encomiendas*). *Obrajes* (textiles workshops) using forced labor are established in Otavalo.

1563
Quito becomes the seat of a *Real Audiencia* (royal court).

17th century
Seminaries and universities are established in Quito.

1720
Encomiendas are abolished, but indigenous peoples become serfs on large *haciendas* under the *wasipungo*, or debt peonage, system.

1736
Expedition by the French Academy of Sciences measures a degree of the meridian near the equator and determines the circumference of the earth.

18th century
Enlightenment ideals reach Ecuador. Eugenio Espejo (1747–95) campaigns against colonial rule and dies in prison.

1801–3
Alexander von Humboldt travels through Ecuador.

1809–22
Ecuadorian fight for independ-

ence from Spain culminates in the Battle of Pichincha on May 24, 1822: the forces of Antonio José de Sucre defeat the royalist army and liberate Quito.

1823
Simón Bolívar's Gran Colombia, incorporating Ecuador, Venezuela, and Colombia, is formed, but lasts only seven years.

1830
General Juan José Flores announces the creation of the Republic of Ecuador. Sucre is assassinated, and Bolívar later dies in exile.

1835
Charles Darwin spends five weeks on the Galápagos Islands, where he makes many of the observations underpinning his theories of evolution.

1858–75
After years of instability, Gabriel García Moreno imposes an ultra-Catholic dictatorship, yet begins amid a boom in cocoa exports. He is assassinated in 1875.

PRECEDING PAGES: mural near the market in Saraguro. TOP LEFT: pre-Columbian Manabí pottery. LEFT: Francisco Pizarro. ABOVE: Simón Bolívar monument, Quito. TOP RIGHT: member of the palace guard, Quito.

THE 20TH CENTURY

1895–1912
Liberal Revolution under Eloy Alfraro. Completion of railway, separation of Church and state.

1925–9
Instability amid decline in cocoa exports, introduction of habeas corpus and women's right to vote.

1933–72
José María Velasco Ibarra elected president five times, but fails to end a term in office.

1941
Border war with Peru ends with loss of almost half of Ecuador's claimed Amazon territory.

1950s
Crisis in the *hacienda* system triggers intermittent military dictatorships.

1964
Land reform gives *indígenas* title to their plots of land.

1972–82
Oil becomes main export under military dictatorship. Center-left government of Jaime Roldós begins period of democracy, Succeeded by Osvaldo Hurtado amid El Niño floods crisis.

1984–92
Conservative León Febres Cordero violently represses small guerrilla movement.

1987–8
Earthquake shuts down oil pipeline. Febres Cordero succeeded by Social Democrat Rodrigo Borja.

1995
Border war with Peru; border treaty signed in 1999.

1996
Conservative Sixto Durán Ballén is last president to end constitutional term.

1997
Ousting of Abdalá Bucaram starts decade of instability amid widespread allegations of corruption. All three presidents elected between 1997 and 2002 are toppled amid a deep crisis brought on by renewed El Niño flooding and the collapse of oil prices and the banking system.

2000
US dollar replaces sucre.

2006
President Alfredo Palacio declines to sign a Free Trade Agreement with the US and expels US oil company Occidental Petroleum. Rafael Correa wins presidential elections.

2008–9
Correa allies rewrite the Constitution, approved by voters in a referendum. Correa wins early re-election for a term through 2013, promising to accelerate his "Citizens' Revolution."

LOST WORLDS

Ancient civilizations bequeathed a rich variety of cultural remains that continue to intrigue both archeologists and visitors

The archeology of the Americas shines, in the public mind, with a few especially bright stars: the Incas of Peru, the Aztecs of central Mexico, and the Maya of southern Mexico and Guatemala. The many pre-Columbian cultures beyond those centers are still relatively unknown, in spite of some astonishing recent discoveries.

Ecuador comprises one of those *tierras incognitas*, even though it has a fabulously rich archeological heritage. Because of the close proximity between coast, Sierra, and Amazonia, experts are able to study the movements that shaped civilization on the entire continent. It is becoming clear that many key developments defining pre-Columbian South America took place in Ecuador. The oldest pottery in all of the Americas has been found here. Cultures have been discovered that worked in platinum, a metal unknown in Europe until the 1850s. Ancient trade links have been established between Ecuador, Mexico, and Amazonia. And it seems likely that pre-Columbian Ecuadorians sailed to and explored the Galápagos Islands.

The remote past

The first human beings who came to Ecuador were hunters and gatherers. The approximate period of their arrival is still debated, but it is certain that human beings have been in the Andes for 15,000 years, probably 30,000 years, and perhaps even for as long as 50,000 years. But the crucial question in Ecuador itself surrounds the gradual, all-important transformation from the hunting and gathering way of life to what archeologists call the "formative period."

LEFT: pre-Columbian ceramic figure, Museo del Banco Central, Quito. RIGHT: necklaces at MAAC, Guayaquil.

While hunters and gatherers led a nomadic existence, formative cultures featured permanent settlements. This transformation in the Americas occurred over a 2,000- or 3,000-year period, beginning around 3000 BC in the most advanced areas. To the great surprise of many archeologists, the earliest pottery and other evidence of formative cultures in the whole of South America has been found on the coast of Ecuador, from a culture known as Valdivia.

The Valdivian culture stretched along the Ecuadorian coast of modern-day Manabí province, with its extensive, ecologically rich mangrove swamps, reaching inland to the drier hilly country. The earliest Valdivian site, dating back perhaps to 3500 BC, is called Loma Alta. A range of extraordinary pottery has been found at this site, decorated with different carved motifs and a variety of colored clays. The Valdivian potters also formed multicolored female figurines that turn up in late strata in the archeological sites.

In Real Alto, a large Valdivian town continuously inhabited for over 2,000 years, archeologists have found the remains of over 100 household structures, each of which may have housed 20 or more people. By 1500 BC, the Real Alto people had built ceremonial temples on the tops of hills in the center of their town, where complex rituals obviously took place.

For archeologists, the biggest puzzle surrounding the Valdivian culture, with highly developed pottery, agricultural cultivation, and social organization firmly under its belt, is that it could not have appeared out of nowhere. There must have been a long series of precursors, of trial-and-error development that led up to these cultural achievements. Conclusive evidence to show that these developments occurred on the coast of Ecuador hasn't been found.

The daring and well-publicized voyages of Thor Heyerdahl encouraged such archeologists as Emilio Estrada (*see panel, below*) to link Valdivia to prehistoric Japan. Indeed, visitors to the Museo del Banco Central, Quito's most important archeological museum, may still encounter this theory as if it were a proven fact. Decorative motifs common to both Valdivia and Japan's Jomon cultures are, however, found all over the world, because the techniques that produced them are precisely those which potters choose almost automatically when they experiment with the results of applying a finger, a bone tool, a leaf, or a stone to the wet clay.

Origins in the Amazon

In the Oriente region of Ecuador, as elsewhere in Amazonia, the persistent presence of hunting and gathering peoples has led many observers to regard Amazonia as a historical backwater, incapable of supporting large populations and advanced civilizations. The first hint that this could not be the case came from agricultural scientists investigating the domestication of manioc, which they concluded had taken place in the Amazon basin at least 8,000 years ago.

Archeologists believe that large cities of more than 10,000 people, supported by manioc cultivation, grew up on the Amazon's fertile floodplain as well as in the jungles on the eastern slope of the Ecuadorian and Peruvian Andes. The cultures of the Amazonian cities, which archeologists are now starting to find in Ecuador and Peru, may, according to some, have given pottery and manioc to South America. Manioc, along with corn (which came to Ecuador from Central America by way of trade), formed the agricultural foundation for a series of advanced coastal cultures, starting with Valdivia, according to some archeologists.

An important site near Cuenca, called Cerro Narrio, sits at the crossroads of a route following the drainages of the Pastaza and Paute rivers.

From around 2000 BC, Cerro Narrio may have been a key trading center, where exchanges of technologies, products, and ideas from the coast, Amazonia, and the Sierra took place. Ceramics bearing unmistakably similar designs to those of coastal cultures have been found at Cerro Narrio, but archeologists are unable to determine whether these pots were imported from the coast or were made at Cerro Narrio by potters who had come from the coast to live in the Sierra.

A number of important items were traded between coast, Sierra, and jungle. Coastal societies collected spondylus shells, which were processed into beads in the Sierra and traded

networks, stretching from Mexico to Peru and from the Amazon to the coast, archeologists describe a period of "regional development" (500 BC–AD 500) followed by a period of "integration" (AD 500–1500). The final period culminated in the conquest of all of present-day Ecuador by the Inca Empire, which undertook an extensive program of city-building and artistic creativity, before being itself destroyed by the Spaniards. A grand flowering of cultural activity preceded the Inca conquest of Ecuador, and the abundance of distinctive phases, especially on the coast, is overwhelming. The extraordinary achievement of these coastal cultures is

in Amazonia, where the shell design appears on much of the pottery that has been discovered. The Sierran societies cultivated the potato – used for trade – as well as coca, crucially important in rituals and ceremonies in the area. Meanwhile, Amazonian societies were renowned for their ritual vessels, made for more than 3,000 years, and for their hallucinogenic potions.

Flowering of coastal activity

Following the establishment of formative cultures and of wide-ranging trade and exchange

LEFT: pre-Columbian ceramic figurine at MAAC, Guayaquil. **ABOVE:** pre-Columbian copper pieces which have been found in the Sierra.

FINDING NEW DIGS

Hundreds of new sites have been uncovered or revisited early this century in Ecuador, particularly in Moroni-Santiago, where the Santa Ana-La Florida site has turned up evidence of a complex Amazon society 4,500 years old. In Manabí, sites like Cerro de Hojas – bigger than Machu Picchu – and the underwater remains of the city of the Caras are being investigated. Restoration and reconstruction projects are under way at the Cochasquí pyramids and Pambamarca fortresses north of Quito, and much of the Tulipe site of the Yumbo culture northwest of the city has been restored as has Cuenca's Pumapungo Inca site.

embodied in the goldwork and sculpture of the La Tolita and Manta civilizations.

La Tolita civilization

The La Tolita culture reached its zenith around 300 BC, and its star shone for perhaps 700 years on the coast of northern Ecuador and southwestern Colombia. The key site is a small, swampy island in the coastal province of Esmeraldas. Now inhabited by Afro-Ecuadorian fisherfolk, La Tolita came to the attention of Westerners in the 1920s, when several European explorers announced the discovery of unprecedented numbers of finely crafted gold objects.

The merciless pillage of these priceless objects went on for years, and was even industrialized by prospectors, who mechanized the milling of thousands of tons of sand, from which gold artifacts were extracted and then melted down into ingots. Despite this, many gold objects are still found on La Tolita, such as the magnificent mask of the Sun God, with its ornately detailed fan of sun rays, and the symbol of Ecuador's Banco Central. So much gold has been uncovered there that archeologists believe that the island was a sacred place, a pre-Columbian Mecca or Jerusalem, a city of goldsmiths, devoted to the production of holy images. It may have been the destination of pilgrims from the coast, the Sierra, and possibly Amazonia, who went there

to obtain the sacred symbols of an ancient cult that influenced most of what is now Ecuador.

The quality and beauty of La Tolita goldwork is matched by the sculpture found on the island. The free-standing, detailed figures in active poses make La Tolita sculpture unique in pre-Columbian art. The sculptures depict both deities and mortals, the latter displaying deformities and diseases, or experiencing emotions of joy, sadness, or surprise.

La Tolita artisans also excelled in a form of metalcraft unknown in Europe until the 1850s. Smiths on the island worked in platinum, creating intricate masks, pendants, pectorals, and nose-rings in a metal with a very high melting point. Archeologists have puzzled over how they were able to do this, with only rudimentary tools and technology. One theory is that by combining pure platinum with bits of gold, which melts at a much lower temperature, the smiths created an alloy with which they could work.

The Manta culture

The Manta culture, in the modern province of Manabí, flowered during the period of integration, and also produced objects of outstanding beauty in gold, silver, cotton textiles, pottery, and stone. The great city of Manta housed more than 20,000 people, and by including the population of outlying villages, archeologists have arrived at very high numbers of people who lived during the Manta culture. There is evidence that the Manta people settled extensive coastal areas, and traded with the coastal peoples of western Mexico and central Peru.

There is an intriguing theory held by some archeologists that Manteño mariners, along with pre-Columbian Peruvian sailors, discovered the Galápagos Islands. A quantity of ceramic shards, almost certainly of pre-Columbian vintage, have been uncovered on three of the islands; the presence of cotton plants, cultivated on the continent, also indicates some sort of contact between the islands and the mainland. Whether the contacts were only occasional, whether the islands were used as a seasonal fishing outpost, as Thor Heyerdahl and others favor, or whether they were settled by groups of Manteños, as a few archeologists assert, has yet to be established. ❑

LEFT: Jama Coaque drinking cup. **RIGHT:** Manabí pottery figurine, Museo del Banco Central, Bahía de Caráquez.

HUB OF TWO EMPIRES

Fought over and dominated by the Incas and the *conquistadores*, Ecuador became a key center for both of their empires

Within the space of a century, successive invaders – the Incas and the Spaniards – swept across the country in great waves of destruction, each seeking to remake it in their own image. Their impact is reflected in the varied ethnicity of the Ecuadorian people – 7 to 10 percent indigenous, 78 percent mestizos (mixed European-indigenous blood), 11 percent criollos (locally born Europeans), and 5 percent the descendants of black Africans. Their legacy of brutal exploitation constitutes an ongoing struggle for modern Ecuadorians.

Sierra cultures

The land that is now Ecuador was first brought under one rule when the Incas of Peru invaded in the middle of the 15th century. By this time, the dazzling cultures of Manta and La Tolita on the Ecuadorian coast had flowered and faded, while an increasingly powerful series of agricultural societies had divided the region's highlands among them.

The Incas made battle drums from the stomachs of their enemies. By 1492, they had conquered much of present-day Ecuador, ending with the epic battle that gave Yahuarcocha, or blood lake, near Ibarra its name.

The greatest were the Cañaris, who inhabited the present-day towns of Cuenca, Chordaleg, Gualaceo, and Cañar. Theirs was a rigidly

LEFT: Alexander von Humboldt and his fellow traveler Aimé Bonpland. **RIGHT:** a fanciful European depiction of the Inca Atahualpa.

hierarchical society. Only the Cañari elite were allowed to wear the fine, elaborate gold and silver produced by their metalsmiths. Among the Cañari artifacts, figures of jaguars, caymans, and other jungle animals predominate, showing their strong links with Amazonian groups.

In the north, archeological evidence points to a more fragmented rule, though often still called "the Kingdom of Quito." Research has all but dispelled the existence of the legendary Shyri and Duchicela dynasties. Rather than a centralized state, local chieftains formed periodical military alliances, possibly giving the attacking Incas the impression of centralized rule under the Quitu-Cara tribe based around

Quitu, particularly in light of their fierce defense of their independence. The city was already an established commercial center on the site of present-day Quito,

Tribes in the area included the Yumbos, traders between the Andes and the coast, Cochasquies, Cayambis, Otavaleños, and the Pasto on the present-day border with Colombia. The pre-Inca Cochasquí pyramids north of Quito are among Ecuador's most important archeological ruins. Locals were well aware of the equator as "the path of the sun." Their economy was based on spinning and weaving wool, and there was a traveling class of merchants who traded with tribes in the

The Cañaris fought valiantly against all odds for several years before being subdued by the Inca Tupac Yupanqui. His revenge severely depleted the indigenous male population: when the Spanish chronicler Cieza de León visited Cañari territory in 1547, he found 15 women to every man. Inca occupation was focused on the construction of a major city called Tomebamba on the site of present-day Cuenca. It was intended to rival the Inca capital of Cuzco, from where stonemasons were summoned to build a massive temple of the sun and splendid palaces with walls of gold.

But by the time Cieza de León arrived, Tomebamba was already a ghost town. He found

Amazon Oriente. Further south, the Puruháes, ferocious warriors based around Ambato, were more closely related to the Cañaris.

The Inca invasion

Into this landscape of tribal identity marched the Incas – literally, "Children of the Sun" – who were to be the short-lived precursors of the Spaniards. Although established in the Peruvian Andes from the 11th century, it was not until about 1460 that they attacked the Cañaris, with the ultimate objective of subjugating the Kingdom of Quitu. Ecuador became brutally embroiled in imperial ambitions as armies dispatched from distant capitals turned the country into a battlefield.

LEGENDARY DYNASTIES

According to local lore, the Caras – who, it is thought, arrived in the Andes by traveling upriver from the areas around Esmeraldas and Bahía de Caráquez on the coast – were under the rule of the Shyri ("lord") dynasty. They then conquered an area including Cayambe and Otavalo in the north down to Latcunga and Ambato in the south. The Puruháes, ruled by the Duchicela family, intermarried with the Shyri in the 14th century, so creating a "Kingdom of Quito," the core of a pre-Hispanic Ecuadorian nation. Belief in this realm is still widespread, though historians as early as the 19th century began to question its very existence.

enormous warehouses stocked with grain, barracks for the imperial troops, and houses formerly occupied by "more than two hundred virgins, who were very beautiful, dedicated to the service of the sun." At nearby Ingapirca, the best-preserved pre-Hispanic site in Ecuador, the Incas built an imposing complex that also served as temple, storehouse, and observatory.

Inca conquest along the spine of the Andes continued inexorably. Quitu, which had fallen by 1492, became a garrison town on the empire's northern frontier and, like Tomebamba, the focus of ostentatious construction. Battles continued to rage: for 17 years the Caras resisted the Inca onslaught before Huayna Cápac, Tupac's son, captured the Caras' capital, Caranqui, and massacred thousands.

The Incas at war were a fearsome sight. Dressed in quilted armor and cane or woolen helmets, and armed with spears, *champis* (headsplitters), slingshots, and shields, they attacked with blood-curdling cries. Prisoners taken in battle were led to a sun temple and slaughtered. The heads of enemy chieftains became ceremonial drinking cups, and their bodies were stuffed and paraded through the streets.

Imposing the new order

The Incas introduced their impressive irrigation methods and some new crops – sweet potatoes, coca, and peanuts – as well as the llama, a sturdy beast of burden and an excellent source of wool. The chewing of coca, previously unknown in highland Ecuador, soon became a popular habit. The Imperial Highway was extended to Quitu, which – although 1,980km (1,230 miles) from Cuzco – could be reached by a team of relay runners in eight days. Inca colonization also brought large numbers of loyal Quechua subjects from southern Peru, and many Cañaris and Caras were in turn shipped to Peru as so-called *mitimaes*. Loyalty to the Inca, with his mandate from the sun, was exacted through the system of *mita* – imperial work or service – rather than taxation. As large areas came under centralized control for the first time, a nascent sense of unity stirred; but it was an alien and oppressive regime, attracting little genuine loyalty.

LEFT: famous Inca masonry at the ruins of Ingapirca.
RIGHT: the capture of Huascar during the Incas' bitter civil war.

The Ecuadorian natives who suffered Inca domination were proud, handsome peoples. Cieza de León spoke of the Cañaris as "good-looking and well grown," and the native Quiteños as "more gentle and better disposed, and with fewer vices than all Indians of Peru." Tupac Yupanqui married a Cañari princess, and Huayna Cápac, in turn, the daughter of a Quitu aristocrat. This was to play a crucial part in the collapse of the empire, for Huayna Cápac, seeking to unite his domain through marriage, achieved just the opposite.

Huayna Cápac had been born and raised in Tomebamba; his favorite son, Atahualpa, was

the offspring of the Quitu marriage and heir to the northern quarter of the empire. Atahualpa's half-brother Huascar was descended from Inca lineage on both sides, and thus the legitimate heir. In 1527, Huascar ascended the Cuzco throne, dividing the empire. Civil war soon broke out, and continued for five years before Atahualpa defeated and imprisoned Huascar after a major battle near Ambato.

Atahualpa, an able and intelligent leader, established the new capital of Cajamarca in northern Peru. But the war had severely weakened both the infrastructure and the will of the Incas, and by a remarkable historical coincidence, it was only a matter of months before their death-knell sounded.

Into the Amazon

A sign on Quito's cathedral and a monument in front of the church at Guápulo honors Ecuador's proud discovery of the Amazon basin.

Once Quito had been settled, the *conquistadores* began to seek new lands and adventures. Tales of El Dorado and Canelos (the Land of Cinnamon, supposedly to the east) filled the air. Fran-

cisco Pizarro appointed his brother Gonzalo to lead an expedition to find these magical destinations.

The search for El Dorado

On Christmas Day, 1539, Gonzalo Pizarro left Quito with 340 soldiers, 4,000 *indígenas*, 150 horses, a flock of llamas, 4,000 swine, 900 dogs, and plentiful supplies of food and water. Surviving an earthquake and an attack by hostile natives, the expedition descended the Cordillera. At Sumaco on the Río Coca they were joined by Francisco de Orellana, who had been called from his governorship of Guayaquil to be Gonzalo's lieutenant.

Hacking their way through dense, swampy undergrowth, and hampered by incessant heavy rain, they were reduced to eating roots, berries, herbs, frogs, and snakes. The first group of natives they met denied all knowledge of El Dorado, so Gonzalo had them burned alive and torn to pieces by dogs. They met another group who spoke of a city, supposedly rich in provisions and gold, just 10 days' march away at the junction of the Coca and Napo rivers.

A large raft was constructed, and 50 soldiers under Orellana's command were dispatched to find the city and return with food: already 2,000 natives and scores of Spaniards had starved to death. Hearing nothing of the advance party after two months, Gonzalo trekked to the junction, but there was no city. The pragmatic natives had very sensibly lied to save their skins. In early June, 1542, the 80 surviving Spaniards from Pizarro's group staggered into Quito, "naked and barefooted." By then, Francisco de Orellana was far away. The brigantine's provisions were exhausted by the time the party reached the river junction: sailing back upstream against the current was impossible, and the difficulties of blazing a jungle trail would have killed the weary men. Hearing the call of destiny and whispers of El Dorado across the wilderness, Orellana sailed on.

For nine months the expedition drifted on the current. Crude wooden crosses were erected as they progressed, purporting to claim the lands in the name of the Spanish king. They encountered many indigenous tribes: some gave them food and ornaments of gold and silver; others attacked them with spears and poisoned arrows, claiming many Spanish lives. On one occasion 10,000 natives are said to have attacked them from the river banks and from canoes, but the Spaniards' arquebuses soon repelled them. They heard frequent reports of a tribe of fearsome women known as "Amazons," who lived in gold-plated houses. Near Obidos, the "Amazons" attacked. They were "very tall, robust, fair, with long hair twisted over their heads, skins round their loins, and bows and arrows in their hands." From this report, the great South American river and jungle area took its name.

Finally, in a lowland area with many inhabited islands, Orellana noticed signs of the ebb of the tide and, in August 1541, sailed into the open sea. For the first time, Europeans had traversed South America. Today, if you want to emulate this experience in style and comfort, you can take a cruise aboard the *Manatee Amazon Explorer*, a comfortable riverboat which began operating in 2002 on the Río Napo from the town of Francisco de Orellana, colloquially known as Coca. ❏

LEFT: *conquistadores* abuse one of their porters.

The bearded white strangers

Rarely have the pages of history been stalked by such a greedy, treacherous, bloodthirsty band of villains as the Spanish *conquistadores*. With their homeland ravaged by 700 years of war with the Moors, the Spanish believed they had paid a heavy price for saving Christian Europe from Muslim domination. When news reached Spain of the glittering Aztec treasury, snatched by Cortés in 1521, it fired the imaginations of desperate owners of ruined lands – and the Church – and spawned dreams of other such empires in the New World.

The first *conquistadores* to set foot on Ecuado-

Emperor) and the title of governor and captain-general of Peru, Pizarro – this time with 180 men and 27 horses – landed in the Bay of San Mateo near Manabí.

For two years the *conquistadores* battled against the native peoples and against the treacherous terrain of mosquito-infested swamps and jungles, and frozen, cloud-buffeted mountain passes. Arriving exhausted in Cajamarca in November 1532, they formulated a plan to trap the Inca Atahualpa. At a pre-arranged meeting, the Inca and several thousand followers – many of them unarmed – entered the great square of Cajamarca. A Spanish priest outlined the tenets

rian soil landed near Esmeraldas in September 1526. They had been dispatched from Colombia by Francisco Pizarro to explore lands to the south. The party, led by Bartolomé Ruiz, discovered several villages of friendly natives wearing splendid objects of gold and silver, news of which prompted Pizarro himself, with just 13 men, to follow a year or so later. Near Tumbes, he found an indigenous settlement whose inhabitants were similarly adorned, and so planned a full-scale invasion. Late in 1530, having traveled to Spain to secure the patronage of King Charles I (or Charles V, Holy Roman

of Christianity to Atahualpa, calling upon him to embrace the faith and accept the sovereignty of Charles I. Predictably, Atahualpa refused, flinging the priest's Bible to the ground; Pizarro and his men rushed out from the surrounding buildings and set upon the astonished Incas. Of the Spaniards, only Pizarro himself was wounded when he seized Atahualpa, while the Incas were cut down in their hundreds.

Atahualpa was imprisoned and a ransom demanded: a roomful of gold and silver weighing 24 tons was amassed, but the Inca was not freed. He was held for nine months, during which time he learned Spanish and mastered the arts of writing, chess, and cards. His authority was never questioned: female attendants

ABOVE: 16th-century depiction of the Spanish advance during the conquest.

dressed him in robes of vampire-bat fur, fed him, and ceremoniously burned everything he used. The Spaniards melted down the finely wrought treasures, and accused Atahualpa of treason. Curiously, Pizarro baptized him "Fransisco," and then garroted him with an iron collar.

Two worlds collide

To the Incas, the Spanish conquest was an apocalyptic reversal of the natural order. In the eyes of a 16th-century native chronicler, Waman Puma, these strangers were "all enshrouded from head to foot, with their faces completely covered in wool... men who never sleep."

LAMENT FOR ATAHUALPA

An elegiac lament was composed by the Incas upon Atahualpa's death: "Hail is falling/Lightning strikes/The sun is sinking/It has become forever night." Atahualpa is still considered by many people to have been the first great Ecuadorian. Curiously, Pizarro baptized him with his own Christian name, Francisco, before garroting him with an iron collar.

There are indigenous people today, in the Saraguro region, who are said to wear their habitual somber black and indigo ponchos and dresses because they are still in mourning for the death of Atahualpa, nearly 500 years ago.

The Incas had no monetary system and no concept of private wealth: they believed the only possible explanation for the Spaniards' craving for gold was that they either ate precious metals, or suffered from a disease that could be cured only by gold. Their horses were "beasts who wear sandals of silver."

Conversely, the conquerors perceived the natives as semi-naked barbarians who worshiped false gods and were good for nothing; Cieza de León's positive remarks (see page 35) only illustrate his unusual fair-mindedness.

While Pizarro continued southward toward Cuzco, his lieutenant, Sebastián de Benalcázar, was dispatched to Piura to ship the Inca booty to Panama. But rumors of these treasures had traveled north, and Pedro de Alvarado, another Spaniard in search of riches, set out from Guatemala to conquer Quitu. With 500 men and 120 horses, he landed at Manta in early 1534, and during an epic trek slaughtered all the coastal natives who crossed his path.

Hearing of this, Benalcázar quickly mounted his own expedition to capture Quitu. Approaching Riobamba in May, he encountered a massive Quiteño army under the Inca general Quisquis. Fifty thousand natives, the largest Inca force ever assembled, were deployed, hopelessly outnumbering the Spaniards. But the natives, owing no loyalty to the Incas, mutinied and dispersed, and the best opportunity to defeat the Spanish was lost. Alvarado was paid a handsome sum by Pizarro to abandon his Ecuadorian excursion and return quietly to Guatemala.

Benalcázar marched northward with thousands of Cañaris and Puruháes in his ranks, for both tribes sought revenge on the brutal Incas. Arriving in Quitu in December, 1534, he found the city in ruins; Rumiñahui, the Inca general, had destroyed and evacuated it rather than lose it intact. Atop Cara and Inca rubble, with a mere 206 inhabitants, the Villa de San Francisco de Quito was founded on December 6, and Guayaquil the following year. Rumiñahui launched a counter-attack a month later, but was captured, tortured, and executed.

By 1549, the conquest was complete: a mere 2,000 Spaniards had subjugated an estimated 500,000 natives. The number of casualties is impossible to ascertain, but tens of thousands died in this 15-year period, through starvation, disease, and suicide, as well as in battle.

The Spanish yoke

With the restless natives quieted, the *conquistadores* fought each other for the prizes: not until 1554 did the Spanish crown finally subdue them. In 1539, Pizarro appointed his brother Gonzalo governor of Quito, but when the first viceroy to Peru passed through shortly thereafter, he found the colonists in revolt. Gonzalo fought off the viceroy's forces in 1546, only to be deposed and executed by another official army two years later. During Gonzalo's governorship, an expedition was mounted to explore the lands east of Quito. The undertaking was a disaster *(see Into the Amazon, page 36)*, but

The Avenue of the Volcanoes, the strip of land 40 to 60km (25 to 40 miles) wide running the length of Ecuador between two towering rows of volcanoes, was ideal farmland. In addition, workshops were established to produce textiles, and slaves were brought from Africa to man the coastal cacao plantations. Ecuador escaped the grim excesses of mining that befell Peru and Bolivia, as the Spanish, to their disappointment, found few precious metals here.

As well as horses, pigs and cattle were introduced, and Ecuador nurtured the first crops of bananas and wheat in South America. The Spaniards also imported diseases such as small-

under the renegade leadership of Francisco de Orellana, the first transcontinental journey by Europeans was made in 1541.

When Cortés cried, "I don't want land; give me gold!" he spoke for all *conquistadores*. But the immediately available treasures were soon exhausted. The land and its inhabitants were divided among the *conquistadores*, and the first settlers soon followed. Of the Quito region, in contrast to the damp, ghostly barrenness of Lima, Cieza de León wrote: "The country is very pleasant, and particularly resembles Spain in its pastures and climate."

Left: Francisco Pizarro, the conqueror.
Above: the construction of San Francisco in Quito.

pox, influenza, measles, and cholera. But with much of the highlands and all of the Oriente so inaccessible, Spanish settlement was relatively light, so geography saved the natives from extermination, if not from subjugation.

Colonial administration was based on the twin pillars of the Church and the *encomienda* system, where *encomenderos* (landowners) were given tracts of land and the right to unpaid native labor, and in return were responsible for the religious conversion of their laborers. The natives were obliged to bring tribute, in the form of animals, vegetables, and blankets, to their new masters, as they had to the Incas. It was a brutally efficient form of feudalism whereby the Spanish crown not only pacified the *conquistadores* with a life of luxury, but also gained an empire at no risk or expense. For centuries, the main landowner was the Church, as dying *encomenderos* donated their estates, in the hope of gaining salvation. Pragmatically, *indígenas* accepted the new faith, embellishing it with their own beliefs and rituals. Days after Benalcázar founded Quito, the cornerstone of the first major place of Christian worship, the church of San Francisco, was laid. Franciscans were followed by Jesuits and Dominicans, each group of missionaries enriching themselves at the natives' expense.

Methods of conversion could be brutal: children were separated from their families to

lar uprisings and nascent cries of "Liberty!" As early as 1592, the lower clergy supported merchants and workers in the Alcabalas Revolution, protesting against increased taxes on food and fabrics. The authorities put an end to the agitation by executing 24 conspirators and displaying their heads in iron cages.

During the 1700s, the ideas of the European Enlightenment crept slowly toward Quito University. The works of Voltaire, Leibnitz, Descartes, and Rousseau, and the revolutions in the United States and France, gave intellectual succor to colonial libertarians. The physician-journalist Eugenio Espejo, born in 1747 of an

receive the catechism; lapsing converts were imprisoned, flogged, and their heads were shaved. Some priests took native women as mistresses, and their children contributed to the number of mestizos, people of mixed Spanish-native blood. Quito – seat of a Viceregal Court or *Audiencia* from 1563 – grew into a religious and intellectual center during the 17th century as seminaries, libraries, and universities were established. Art, particularly painting and sculpture, flourished in Quito and was exported to other parts of the Spanish Empire.

Push for independence

In reaction to the Spaniards' oppressive socio-economic actions there sprouted violent popu-

indigenous father and a mulatto (Afro-Hispanic) mother, emerged as the anti-imperialists' leader.

Espejo was a fearless humanist. He published satirical, bitterly combative books on Spanish colonialism; and as founding editor of the liberal newspaper *Primicias de la Cultura de Quito*, was probably the first American journalist. He was repeatedly jailed, exiled to Bogotá for four years, and finally died, aged 48, in a Quito dungeon. From his cell, he wrote to the President of the *Audiencia*: "I have produced writings for the happiness of the country, as yet a barbarian one." ❑

ABOVE: a contemporary depiction of the quayside at Guayaquil.

Von Humboldt: The First Travel Writer

According to the German scientist, Ecuadorians sleep calmly under active volcanoes, live in poverty atop riches, and are cheered by sad music. This still rings true.

Simón Bolívar described Humboldt as "the true discoverer of America, because his work has produced more benefit to our people than all the *conquistadores*." Praise indeed from the liberator of the Americas. But how did this wealthy Prussian mineralogist come to play such a vital role in the history of the continent?

Alexander von Humboldt was born in Berlin in 1769. As a young man he studied botany, chemistry, astronomy, and mineralogy, and traveled with Georg Forster, who had accompanied Captain James Cook on his second world voyage. At the age of 27 he received a legacy large enough to finance a scientific expedition, and made such an impression on Charles IV of Spain that he received special permission to travel to South America.

Humbolt's expedition

With his companion Aimé Bonpland, Humboldt set off for Caracas in November 1799. During their five-year expedition the two men covered some 9,600km (6,000 miles) on foot, horseback, and by canoe; suffered from malaria; and were reduced to a diet of ground cacao beans when damp and insects destroyed their supplies. Following the course of the Orinoco and Casiquiare rivers, they established that the Casiquiare channel linked the Orinoco and the Amazon. In 1802 they reached Quito, where Humboldt climbed Chimborazo, failing to attain the summit but setting a world record (unbroken for 30 years) by reaching almost 6,000 meters (19,500ft). He coined the name "Avenue of the Volcanoes" and, after suffering from altitude sickness, was the first to realize its connection with a lack of oxygen. Between ascents he studied the role of eruptive forces in the development of the earth's crust, establishing that Latin America was not, as had been believed, a geologically young country.

RIGHT: the young Humboldt, who received a legacy at the age of 27, enabling him to finance his research.

A man of many interests

While in Ecuador, Humboldt began assembling notes for his *Essays on the Geography of Plants*, pioneering investigations into the relationship between a region's geography and its flora and fauna. He claimed another first by listing many of the indigenous, pre-conquest species; and he was responsible for the birth of the guano industry, after he sent samples of the substance back to Europe for analysis.

Humboldt's contributions seem endless: off the west coast he studied the oceanic current, which was named after him; his work on isotherms and isobars laid the foundation for the science of climatology; he invented the term "magnetic

storms," and as a result of his interest the Royal Society in London promoted the establishment of observatories, which led to the correlation of such storms with sunspot activity.

He was also deeply interested in social and economic issues and was adamantly opposed to slavery, which he considered "the greatest evil that afflicts human nature." Goethe, a close friend, found him "exceedingly interesting and stimulating," a man who "overwhelms one with intellectual treasure"; while Charles Darwin had been inspired by Humboldt's earlier journey to Tenerife, in the Canary Islands, and his description of the volcanic Pico de Teide and the dragon tree. Darwin respectfully described him as "the parent of a grand progeny of scientific travellers." ❑

INDEPENDENCE AND AFTER

From the battle for independence to recent oil exploitation in the Amazon, the history of modern Ecuador has been turbulent

A s the crown's grip on its colonies began to loosen, the ghost of the *conquistadores* stirred from its slumber. From the beginning of the Spanish era, money and muscle had meant power; laws, constitutions, and governments were subject to the greed of reckless individuals. Cortés and Orellana disobeyed orders and attained greatness, and Pizarro answered to no one.

The ethos they bequeathed to those who came after them was devoid of ideas and morality. Through the age of *caudillos* – warlords – in the 19th century, and of military dictators in the 20th, Ecuador was viewed as a treasure, like Inca gold, conveniently there for the taking.

The road to freedom

Ecuador's first step toward independence was also its first coup. In response to the fall of Spain to Napoleon in 1808, a new wave of repressive measures was enforced in the colonies, prompting members of the criollo oligarchy to seize power in Quito in August, 1809, and imprison the president of the *Audiencia*. Within a month, loyalist troops from Bogotá and Lima had displaced the usurpers, but the subsequent reprisals were so harsh that they prompted a second rebellion two years later. This time, a constitution for an independent state was formulated, but the uprising remained confined to Quito, and so was easily suppressed.

But the whole continent was moving inexorably toward liberation. With English support, Simón Bolívar – "El Libertador" – had taken on

the Spanish loyalists in his native Venezuela, where he became dictator, and then in Colombia. In October, 1820, Guayaquil ousted the local authorities and established a revolutionary junta; and following the Battle of Pichincha in May, 1822, when forces led by Antonio José de Sucre resoundingly defeated the royalist army, Quito was liberated.

A few weeks later, Bolívar arrived in Quito. He was the archetypal criollo – ambitious, paternalistic, impatient, never doubting his methods or goals. His brilliance sprang from the singular intensity of his vision, which brought liberation to a continent, but he failed to appreciate the dynamics of the new nations.

PRECEDING PAGES: mural celebrating the annual Pendoneros festival. **LEFT:** a worker overlooking the Quito of the 1890s. **RIGHT:** Simón Bolívar, "El Libertador".

His Argentine counterpart, José de San Martín, was stoic, taciturn, and self-effacing, Bolívar's ideal complement. But at their only meeting, in Guayaquil in July, 1822, to plot the future of a proposed Gran Colombia, they had a fundamental disagreement: Bolívar wanted a republic, while San Martín envisaged a monarchy. What happened at that meeting is not known, but Bolívar triumphed, and San Martín went into self-imposed exile in Europe.

Gran Colombia was formed in 1823, incorporating Ecuador, Colombia, and Venezuela. But the new, united nation lasted just seven years: in September, 1830, the military commander of

False freedom

The inequalities of the colonial social structure were preserved with ruthless duplicity by the new Ecuadorian elite. While cries of "Fatherland" and "Freedom" echoed across the country, the poor remained enslaved in workshops, on haciendas and plantations. National power was up for grabs, and the struggle between the Conservatives of Quito and the Liberals of Guayaquil began immediately. Flores made a deal with the opposition Liberal leader, Vicente Rocafuerte, to alternate the presidency, with Flores retaining military control, but in 1843 he refused to step down from his second term and

Quito, General Juan José Flores – a Venezuelan who had married into the Quiteño aristocracy – announced the creation of the Republic of Ecuador. The new republic's population now stood at approximately 700,000 and its ill-defined borders were based on those of the colonial *Audiencia*.

That same year, Sucre – Bolívar's chosen successor – was assassinated en route from Bogotá to his home in Quito, prompting Bolívar to grieve, "They have slain Abel." On the northern shores of the continent that he had transformed, *El Libertador* died a broken man: overcome with frustration, he said of his life's work, "Those who serve the revolution plough the sea."

was bribed into exile. Flores held power for two more years before being toppled by the Liberals.

In the subsequent period of chronic political disorder, the next 15 years saw 11 governments and three constitutions come and go, while the economy stagnated. Border disputes sprang up with both Peru and Colombia. This morass was tidied up by strongman Gabriel García Moreno, who had risen from humble origins to the rectorship of the University of Quito. During his decade in power, the nation became a theocracy where only practicing Catholics could vote. He frequently indulged in acts of self-humiliation: photographs capture him carrying a heavy wooden cross through the streets, followed by his cabinet.

Freedom of speech was non-existent, and political opponents were imprisoned or exiled. But there was progress too: hospitals, roads, and railways were constructed; schools were opened to natives and women; Guayaquil's port facilities were improved; and new crops enhanced

> Eloy Alfaro (1842–1912) completed the railway started by García Moreno but was his complete ideological adversary. Dubbed the "Old Fighter," he led a revolution that made Ecuador an early adopter of divorce and civil marriage.

separate Church and state before an incensed pro-clerical mob tore him to pieces. His liberal reforms, however, mostly remained in place.

War in the Amazon

Ecuador was originally more than double its present size, but Brazil, Colombia, and Peru have each taken generously from its portion of Amazonia. In 1941, Peru snatched almost half of Ecuador's territory in an invasion that was largely uncontested, as President Carlos Alberto Arroyo del Río, fearing a coup, kept most of his troops in Quito while much of El Oro, a region rich in gold, bananas, and coffee, was occupied.

agricultural productivity. García Moreno's critics were many, but they trod a dangerous path, all too aware of the fate that awaited enemies of the regime. Quiteño journalist and leading intellectual Juan Montalvo railed against the president's tyrannical clericalism. From his exile in Colombia, he rejoiced on hearing of the president's assassination in 1875, declaring: "My pen has killed him."

As the century turned, the Liberal President Eloy managed to improve the lot of the indigenous peoples, modernize the legal code, and

---

LEFT: the victorious Marshal Sucre signing the Act of Independence in 1822. **ABOVE:** workers on a banana plantation in the 1880s.

Ecuador subsequently reneged on the Rio de Janeiro Protocol of 1942, which imposed the new boundary, but de facto had to accept that its Amazon territory included only a small part of the river's headwaters. Several skirmishes broke out over the following years. One conflict in 1995 lasted three months, cost both sides several hundreds of casualties and had a damaging effect on the economy. A ceasefire finally took place, with Ecuador reluctantly accepting the border imposed in 1942.

In 1998 the leaders of Ecuador and Peru, both anxious for a real solution, agreed to submit the unresolved issues to arbitration by the guarantor countries of Brazil, Argentina, and Chile. In October, the historic Acta de Brasília Peace

Treaty was signed, the conflict zone demilitarized and bi-national development plans put into place. Since then relations have improved dramatically between the two countries.

The economy has expanded from its original bases of textiles, Panama hats, and cacao to include coffee, shrimp farming, fresh flowers, tourism, and, particularly, oil and bananas. Under the iron fist of the Boston-based United Fruit Company, Ecuador became, and remains, the world's leading exporter of bananas. Rampant capitalism produced a crisis in the archaic hacienda system in the 1950s as, for the first time, money spread beyond the few hundred

four times, last by the military that grabbed control of the new oil wealth.

The dictators were comparatively weak, however, and Ecuador in 1978 was the first Latin American country to restore democracy, soon after Spain. The center-left government of Jaime Roldós, elected the following year, launched massive literacy and housing programs. Emphasizing issues instead of personalities, the government increased workers' wages and encouraged the emergence of a politically articulate middle class, and of mass-based organizations such as peasant co-operatives and labor unions. But an economic crisis eventually loomed as oil prices

dominant criollo families. The long-overdue land reforms of 1964 further eroded traditional socio-economic ties, and the discovery of massive oil deposits in the Oriente has permanently shifted Ecuador's economic base away from agriculture, with oil now the leading industry, and mining showing major economic potential.

Democratic leaders

Over the 20th century, nepotism, populism, and instability have characterized the political landscape. José María Velasco Ibarra, a populist firebrand who appealed to the poor and on one occasion cried, "Give me a balcony and I will be president," was elected to five presidential terms between 1934 and 1972. But he was toppled

dropped and payments on foreign debt fell due, and for a while rumors of a military coup were rife.

In 1981, Roldós died in a plane crash. Vice-President Osvaldo Hurtado fulfilled his pledges to serve his full term, to continue Roldós's reforms, and to maintain civil liberties, despite the added difficulty of the great El Niño floods of late 1982, which ruined banana and rice crops and destroyed roads and railways. León Febres Cordero, a Conservative, won the 1984 elections. Febres Cordero oversaw sustained economic growth, but his rule was marred by charges of misuse of public funds, which he allegedly paid to an Israeli counter-insurgency adviser to help to dismantle a guerrilla movement, and human rights violations associated with the fight against the rebel movement. He overshadowed Ecuadorian politics until his death in 2008.

Elections in 1988 brought to power President Rodrigo Borja, a Social Democrat from Quito. He set an honest, competent political course: civil disturbances such as transport workers' strikes and student riots over price rises were handled leniently. Inflation fell, foreign debt was serviced regularly, and foreign investors continued to be attracted, both under Borja and under his successor, Sixto Durán Ballén of the Christian Social Party, who was elected in 1992. Sixto was not a popular president, although the border dispute with Peru did produce a temporary surge in support. One of his more unpopular policies was the introduction of a privatization program for telecommunications, electricity, and parts of Petroecuador, but Congress stalled the program. He was succeeded in 1996 by populist Abdalá Bucaram who set the stage for a decade of turmoil. Bucaram, a former mayor of Guayaquil nicknamed "El Loco" (the madman, a name he coined himself), as president recorded a CD which many government employees were "encouraged" to buy. The country soon tired of the show. Bucaram introduced rigorous economic measures that caused steep price increases and those already living in poverty – the people he had promised to help – found themselves worse off. Most serious though was his blatant corruption.

In February 1997 a two-day general strike in protest against Bucaram brought the country to a standstill. By the end of the second day, Congress conveniently found a clause in the constitution that enabled them to oust Bucaram on the grounds of mental incapacity. Confusion followed as both Vice-President Rosalia Arteaga and Fabián Alarcón, President of Congress, claimed the presidency. Finally Congress officially voted in Alarcón as interim president.

Mismanagement and corruption continued and reform was delayed until the new president, Jamil Mahuad, a Harvard-educated centrist, took office in August 1998. An economic slide was exacerbated by El Niño floods on the coast that destroyed crops of key agricultural exports.

With the price of oil collapsing, Mahuad's success in bringing about peace with Peru was overshadowed by his unpopular introduction of austere economic reforms to secure IMF loans and the collapse of the banking system still not completely resolved a decade later. The value of the sucre fell sharply as the central bank bailed out the banks, and in an attempt to halt speculation, Mahuad ordered banks to freeze all existing accounts for at least a year. At the end of 1999, Mahuad announced his plan to replace the sucre with the dollar. The aim was to curb the 60 percent inflation rate, bring down interest rates, and spur investment. Many

THE RISE OF THE NEW LEFT

Rafael Correa is one of a slew of left-of-center leaders elected president in Latin America since the late 1990s pledging wholesale transformation of their unequal societies. Among them, Correa has pursued a course to the left of Chile's Michelle Bachelet and Brazil's Lula, while pursuing a moderately more conservative course than Hugo Chávez in Venezuela and Evo Morales in Bolivia. After being re-elected in April 2009, he pledged to radicalize his "citizens' revolution." His government enjoys high levels of popularity but has kept Ecuador polarized. With success at the polls, there is little to indicate that he will abandon his brinkmanship.

LEFT: bananas for sale in Guamote market.
RIGHT: President Rafael Correa in August 2009 during the swearing-in ceremony for his second term in office.

sectors accepted the measure, but it incensed indigenous groups, who rallied together and marched to Quito in protest. On January 21, 2000, Mahuad was forced to flee as thousands of indigenous protesters stormed the Congress Building with the help of junior military officers, including Colonel Lucio Gutiérrez. US warnings of withdrawing financial aid pressured the military chief in command of the new junta to back down in a matter of hours.

Power passed to the vice-president, Gustavo Noboa, who faced the challenge of a radicalized indigenous movement amid a general distrust of politicians and the country's worst economic crisis in 70 years. He, however, presided over a transformation of Ecuador's economy, helped by declining inflation since dollarization and millions of dollars of foreign investment in oil exploration and production.

In late 2002, former coup leader Gutiérrez won the election, and soon secured IMF financing, but he lacked congressional support and became the third president in eight years to be toppled after inviting Bucaram home. He was replaced by Alfredo Palacio, his vice-president, under whom relations with the US deteriorated, as he refused to go ahead with a free trade agreement with US and expelled US oil company Occidental Petroleum. He was succeeded by Rafael Correa, whose political career began in a brief stint as Palacio's Finance Minister.

> Correa wants greater control of industries: as of mid 2009, the government had taken over a business conglomerate of two fugitive bankers, local assets of a Brazilian construction firm, and a French oil company.

Correa won on a platform of radical constitutional reform and economic equality. A former economics lecturer, he aped the model of Hugo Chávez of Venezuela, with whom he shares many ideological ties. Correa has won an unprecedented slew of elections as voters gave his party a majority in the constitutional assembly, approved the new charter that gives the government greater control of the economy, and re-elected him to a second term in early elections in 2009. Attacks on the privileged have been accompanied by harsh criticism of the media and the breaking of diplomatic ties with Colombia in the wake of an unauthorized Colombian raid on a rebel camp inside Ecuador in March 2008.

Despite the recent political turmoil, Ecuador's economy has grown by 6.5 percent in 2008, mainly due to high oil prices and the stability brought by dollarization. Economic performance, however, still hinges on the price of oil, and it remains to be seen if Correa's agenda of massive government spending produces lasting social and economic progress. ❏

ELUSIVE POLITICAL STABILITY

Ecuador's political fragmentation has not ended with Correa's dominance of the political landscape. His political movement, Alianza País, includes a wide range of disparate influences from the hard left to centrists. Correa's popularity did not allow the movement to secure an absolute majority in the legislative assembly which, thanks to Ecuador's highly complex election system, includes nine political parties with just one representative each. By late 2009, evidence of growing discontent emerged above all on the left wing of the political spectrum, with indigenous organizations declaring a rebellion to protect their rights to manage sources of water.

LEFT: protesters in Quito in October 2009 concerned about the effect of proposed legislation on indigenous lands. **RIGHT:** child and grandmother in Alausí.

ECONOMY AND ENVIRONMENT

Ecuador has a difficult balancing act to perform if it is to conserve the environment while accelerating growth that has been fueled largely by the oil industry

Agro-exporter Ecuador was transformed by the discovery of large petroleum reserves in the pristine Amazon rainforest of the Oriente by Texaco in 1968. The development of these oilfields spurred an economic boom in the 1970s – helped by a dramatic rise in world oil prices – but also resulted in profound damage to the rivers, rainforest, and the indigenous way of life. The government quadrupled its budget in three years, and public spending on social services was proportionally higher than in any other country in Latin America. Investments were made in education, health, and infrastructure that improved the lives of most Ecuadorians.

Oriente, the oil province

While oil money was raked in in Quito, in the Amazon settlers, large oil corporations, and indigenous peoples competed for land and resources. Little thought was given to the potential impact on the environment, and the native contingent had no concept of ownership, allowing oil companies to build roads and drill in exchange for gifts.

Settlers were awarded plots of land if they were willing to "improve" it, which meant clearing it for agriculture or pasture. As their land was usurped by settlers, the indigenous peoples in the Lago Agrio area were forced to enter the new Ecuadorian society, often at the lowest social rung as laborers, domestic workers, or prostitutes. Or they fled deeper into the rainforest, coming into conflict with other tribes. Additionally, thousands of Colombian refugees have entered from the war-torn north. Road construc-

tion continues, aiding the influx of settlers into remote regions and destroying the forest. However, settlers demand more roads as they provide access to basic healthcare and schools.

With the support of the environmental lobby in the 1980s, however, native groups began to raise awareness in Ecuador and abroad through protests, putting pressure on the government to recognize their land rights, and for the oil companies to clean up their act. Initially, oil production was solely in the hands of US company Texaco, that dumped 16 billion gallons of highly poisonous wastewater in a swathe of the northeast Amazon from 1971 to 1992, now the object of the biggest lawsuit in history *(see page 232)*.

LEFT: oil pipes in the Amazon. **RIGHT:** Huaorani protesters at trial proceedings in the Chevron/Texaco lawsuit.

Oil, agriculture, and development

The oil industry provides crucial income but few of the steady jobs Ecuador so desperately needs. The boom years of the early 21st century provided some $30 billion in revenue, and before President Correa refused to continue payments on a third of its foreign debt, Ecuador's debt levels were already among the lowest in Latin America. Oil accounted for more than 60 percent of Ecuador's exports at its peak price in July 2008, and it will remain a crucial source of foreign income in the foreseeable future.

Pressured by some international shareholders, oil companies have begun to improve their

act. The Correa administration has promised to beef up environmental standards, which currently are generally higher in the foreign oil industry than at state-owned PetroEcuador, which faces practically daily spills.

Development of rainforest is difficult to manage, and when done well, the oil industry is less damaging than the rampant illegal logging, which governments have done little to stop. Exotic hardwoods are smuggled to Colombia, Peru, and the US. Wide tracts of rainforest on both sides of the Andes are being cleared at an annual rate among the highest in Latin America (around 300,000 hectares/750,000 acres each year). Both subsistence farmers trying to eke out a meager living, clearing land for grazing and

planting, and large companies cutting down trees around Esmeraldas on the coast and in the Oriente to make way for a monoculture of African palms, are to blame. Agriculture accounts for 20 percent of foreign earnings, just behind petroleum in importance, and pesticides are used extensively to maximize production. The laws regulating pesticide use and residues on food are strict, but rarely enforced; most farmers have no training or protective equipment. The proper management of water is an important issue, too, and doubts about the country's reliability from a business perspective have slowed private foreign investment.

Tourism is one development option currently in vogue with the government. Supervision is still shaky, however, and travelers will do well to seek out eco-lodges meeting internationally recognized standards. Numerous high-quality lodges have sprung up in the Andean foothills northwest of Quito, all along the Andean chain, and in Oriente around places like Tena and east of Coca. The most famous of these is Kapawi on the jungle border with Peru, which established milestones for co-operative management with local communities, rewarding them for the protection of their environment and heritage.

Climate change

Since the early 1900s, annual rainfall has significantly decreased and glaciers have retreated on average 300 meters (950ft). In 1995–6 electricity was rationed because the Paute hydroelectric plant that provides 65 percent of the country's electricity was dry due to lack of rain as well as deforestation, which causes soil to absorb water less efficiently. Recurring El Niño weather patterns, however, have caused periodic widespread flooding and destruction, driving up prices for the poor and saddling the government with infrastructure costs.

Ecuador has large, undeveloped hydropower reserves, and several new hydroelectric plants are under construction. Planned, massive further investment faces controversy due to financing rather than environmental issues. However, more hydroelectric electricity will release Ecuador from the ridiculous amounts of money it spends to import diesel and gasoline, which it even subsidizes. ❑

LEFT: logging roads cut deep into the heart of the country's Choco rainforest.

National Parks

While protection on paper is better than nothing, much needs to be done to save Ecuador's hugely diverse ecology from destruction.

Ecuador's Ministry of the Environment currently manages and protects 32 national parks and protected areas that cover 28 percent of the total area of the country, concentrated in the Galápagos, the northeast Oriente, and the eastern slopes of the Andes.

The entrance fees to the most popular national parks (Galápagos, Cotopaxi, and Cotocachi-Cayapas) help subsidize some of the less visited and more threatened reserves. For instance, many coastal mangrove swamps, which are vital breeding grounds for marine fish species, have been destroyed in the past 20 years by the construction of expansive pools for "shrimp-ranching." The Cayapas-Mataje and the Manglares-Churute reserves were created to protect a small portion of these rapidly disappearing mangroves, but many locals are unaware that these reserves exist. There is a great need for community education on sustainable use of fish resources within these reserves.

The value of untouched forests

Cloud forests were being cleared from the Andean central valley long before the Spanish conquered Ecuador in the first half of the 16th century, but the Andean eastern slope has never been cut because it is so wet, rugged, and inaccessible. However, as more roads encroach into the Oriente and colonists begin to fell the old-growth mahoganies and alders, protected areas such as Cayambe-Coca Ecological Reserve, Llanganates and Sangay national parks become important refuges for rare species such as the Andean spectacled bear, wooly mountain tapir, and Andean condor. One of the latest additions to the park system is the bi-national Parque Nacional Cordillera del Cóndor, which escaped deforestation and development because it was located along the disputed border with Peru. Although it is still mined and not yet set up for tourism, scientists are beginning to catalog its biological diversity.

RIGHT: a jaguar, one of the creatures native to Ecuador that are in need of protection.

Yasuní National Park in the Oriente is considered the most biologically diverse place in the world, where over 900 different species of trees have been identified in a single 2-hectare (5-acre) plot. Even with Unesco Biosphere Reserve status, however, the howler monkeys and jaguars of Yasuní still have to share their habitat with oil companies and aggressively colonizing indigenous groups. Conservationists are extremely wary of this experiment, since the nearby Cuyabeno Reserve had its western half lopped off and the area is now filled with colonists and oil wells.

Mediating land-use conflicts perhaps presents the greatest challenge to the environmental

protection offices. Multiple and often environmentally damaging activities such as homesteading, timber harvest, grazing, water projects, mining, and oil production are permitted by other government agencies in the protected areas. The Correa administration is trying to reorganize the warren of overlapping authorities, and schemes such as the plan to protect parts of the Yasuní by selling carbon bonds may provide some much-needed funding.

Cynics often refer to Ecuadorian protected areas as "paper parks" since essential environmental policing is still lacking, but it is remarkable that a country with limited resources has had the foresight to sketch out so many natural areas that are worth saving in the future. ❑

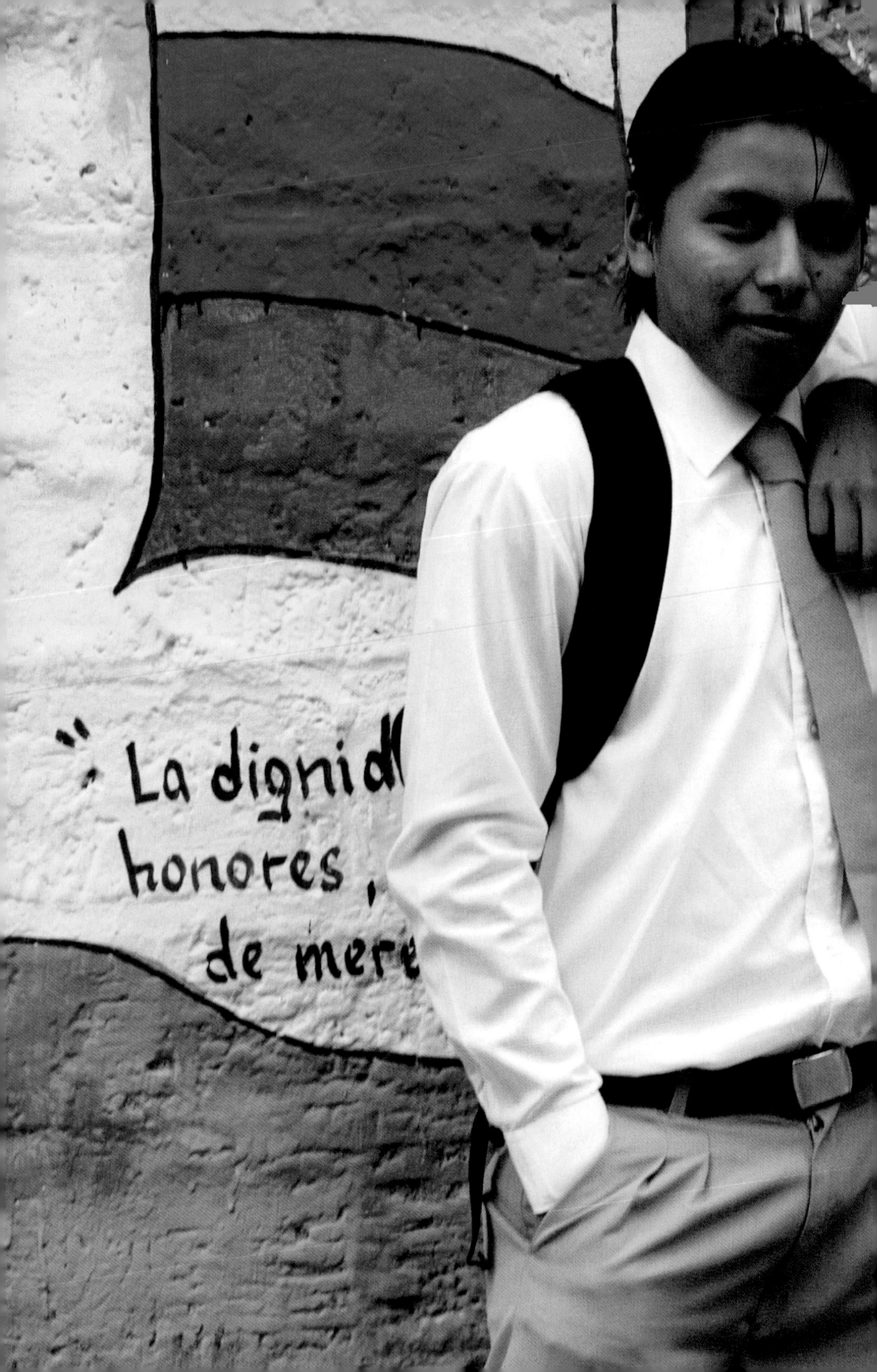
"La dignid
honores
de mere

THE ECUADORIANS

The people of Ecuador inhabit a relatively small land, but they are as diverse and colorful as the landscape with many of mixed heritage

Like other Andean countries, Ecuadorian society reflects divisions that can be traced back to the Spanish conquest of the early 16th century. But the people have been shaped as much by Ecuador's wild geography as its history: the racial make-up, accent, temperament, and outlook of Ecuadorians is radically different on the coast, in the Sierra, and in the jungle.

Until the discovery of oil in the early 1970s prompted an urban explosion, Ecuador was an almost completely rural society. To a large extent it still is: although more than two-thirds of the population live in towns or cities, how they behave and think is closely linked to their relationship with the land, and modern urban life conserves elements of traditional rural customs. To understand the differences between Ecuador's three regions, one should first look to village life.

Images from the countryside

The typical *campesino* (peasant) of the Sierra works hard to obtain a meager living from rocky, volcanic soil. Andean families live in a harsh environment, where bare mountains descend into shelving ravines and gentle valleys. The land is rarely flat, except on the valley bottom, which generally belongs to the rich landowners. The *campesino* must use ingenuity to terrace and cultivate the steep mountainsides on slopes with up to 60-degree angles, where the topsoil is easily washed away by rain.

In harmony with this environment, the typical *serrano* (mountain-dweller) tends to be tough, patient, frugal, and resigned to the difficulties

PRECEDING PAGES: Guamote market-goers; schoolboys in Puerto López. **LEFT:** children at Cañar's Sunday market. **ABOVE:** working in the fields around Guamote.

of life. Yet *serranos* can be vivacious when their imaginations are fired. Andean music, with its plaintive tones, melodic pipes, and sorrowful lyrics, expresses the *serrano* temperament.

The peasants of the Costa live in contact with the abundant nature of the green lowlands, where the warm climate and fertile soil make daily living easier. Like their environment, the *costeños* (coast-dwellers) tend to be easygoing and exuberant, but also quick-tempered, and unconcerned about what tomorrow may bring.

The Oriente is a case apart; it represents scarcely 4 percent of the population. Indigenous peoples have lived there for centuries in relative isolation, and their way of being is very different from that of the people of the Sierra who have suffered long years of discrimination. Light-hearted and self-confident, they are accustomed to a generous natural environment and a free lifestyle. This situation has begun to change with the presence of timber and oil companies that are endangering their environment, as well as encroaching colonization, which has brought about an accelerated process of assimilation.

Natural differences between the regions have been accentuated by slow, hazardous transport and difficult communications. But within each region, society is characterized by diverse racial and ethnic groups.

still exists in a few areas, though it was officially abolished in 1971.

Mestizos (of indigenous and Hispanic origin) were employed on haciendas as managers, stewards, or clerks. The power they wielded over those under their authority fueled racial animosity between natives and mestizos, generally.

The traditional social order of the Sierra began to disintegrate in the 1960s with the introduction of agrarian reform. In the face of rapid population growth and increasing unrest among the peasants, who were pressing for more land, the authorities passed legislation to break up the larger estates and

Traditional Andean society

The rigid social order that reigned in the Sierra from colonial times until the land reform of 1964 is the basis on which modern society was built. Cut off by the difficult mountain passes and under the strong influence of the Catholic Church, Andean society engendered a world of traditional values centered around the family.

The nucleus of rural life was the hacienda, or estate. These large properties were the main pole of production. Their owners were descendants of the Spanish *conquistadores* and later immigrants who controlled the country's economy and politics. They allowed indigenous families a small plot of land for their own subsistence in exchange for labor. This form of dependence

CONFLICTING VALUES

The typical Spanish settler in the Sierra considered the act of work to be degrading, whereas the indigenous population valued it and disapproved of laziness. This was a further element that exacerbated racial tension, since the Spaniard expected the native to work for him, but then despised him for doing so.

These perceptions – Spanish intolerance and native incomprehension – still survive in diluted forms today, particularly within the realm of public service. It is this lack of mutual understanding that is largely to blame for the fundamental disunity which is so characteristic of Ecuadorian society.

haciendas and hand over uncultivated land to the peasants.

Frontier settlements

While the Sierra has mainly produced food for local consumption, the Costa has been developed over the past 100 years for export cash crops. Cocoa, bananas and, more recently, cultivated shrimps have each had their boom period.

Landless peasants from the Sierra traveled to the coast in search of work on the plantations or a piece of undeveloped land to till. Thus, in the space of a century, the inhabitants of the Costa changed from being a small fraction to

The urban explosion

In the 1970s, following the discovery of petroleum deposits in the Oriente, Ecuador began to export oil, which meant more jobs and the promise of new opportunities in the cities. At the same time, those peasants who had been unable to obtain land under the agrarian reform of 1964 had to leave the haciendas, and many of them sought work in the towns.

In just two decades, a quarter of Ecuador's population uprooted from a lifetime of rural living to the noise and pace of towns and cities, causing an urban explosion that the country was unable to support. Housing, and water and

slightly more than half of the total population.

The owners of the haciendas on the Costa tended to be more business-minded and enterprising than their *serrano* counterparts, and generally did not mind dirtying their hands alongside their wage-earning farmhands. This helped to create a more liberal and egalitarian society, which was accelerated by greater contact with the outside world via the seaports.

Today the Ecuadorian Costa has a Caribbean flavor, which has led to Guayaquil being called "the last port of the Caribbean."

FAR LEFT: *indígena*, Guamote. **LEFT:** tending the land near Quilotoa. **ABOVE:** a farm on the Pacific coast. **ABOVE RIGHT:** woman and baby, Esmeraldas province.

Hundreds of thousands of Ecuadorians emigrated overseas after the 1999 economic crisis. Workers' remittances, mostly from the US and Spain, have provided important economic support but torn thousands of families apart.

electricity supplies, could not possibly keep up with the huge increase in demand. Today, Ecuador is short of an estimated 1 million homes; half of the existing houses lack running water and sewage facilities, and 20 percent have no electricity supply.

With the foreign debt crisis of the 1980s, unemployment increased dramatically. The new urban population had nowhere to turn, except to the streets to scrape together a living by their wits. Vendors of trinkets, clothes, or electrical goods of doubtful origin throng intersections, competing for the attention of passers-by. And on street corners, five-year-olds sell newspapers, shine shoes, or urge you to buy chewing gum in the hope of earning their daily meal or forced to do so by uncaring adults. Today, less than half the workforce has a steady full-time job; about 40 percent are in the informal sector of street vendors and self-employed craftsmen, and close to 10 percent are unemployed.

Meanwhile, the well-to-do find all the comforts of modern life in smart apartment blocks protected by armed guards. Shopping precincts display a broad variety of goods, and chauffeur-driven limos wait at the doors of luxury restaurants.

These contrasts are an expression of the erratic modernization of Ecuador, which has radically changed living and working conditions in scarcely three decades, without being able to answer the basic needs of more than half of its population. The most flagrant social contradictions are to be found in Guayaquil, center of the nation's wealth, which is surrounded by vast slum areas, the scene of abject poverty and rampant delinquency.

Chronic poverty

It is ironic that in Ecuador, a country rich in natural resources with its fertile valleys, abundant marine life, extensive forests, and reserves of oil and gold, most people face a daily struggle to scrape together the bare necessities. Since the US dollar replaced the sucre as Ecuador's currency in 2000, poverty rates have dropped to about 23 percent in the cities, where most people live, but remain very high at about 70 percent in rural areas. Ecuador traditionally has not been as badly off as Peru and Bolivia. The cost of living is relatively low, and as Ecuador produces most of its own food, few families are unable to get a square meal each day, and most do have a roof of some kind over their heads.

Hardship is not reserved to the towns. In rural areas, those who became small landowners cannot keep up with production costs, which rise faster than the price they receive for their crops, and they can rarely get cheap credit or adequate technical help. And once the paternalistic relations of the hacienda disappeared, the lack of social services became acute.

Successive governments have implemented social welfare programs in healthcare, aid to small farmers, food distribution, cheap housing, childcare, employment, and other needs, but there are never enough resources.

All the same, in spite of hardship, the Ecuadorian people are on the whole patient, peaceable, and honest. The violence that has become typical in Colombia and Peru is less common here, though the crisis has brought about a rise in delinquency and crime, above all in Guayaquil and Quito.

Indigenous groups

The visitor to Ecuador is readily seduced by the colorful costumes and skillful handicraft of the indigenous population: the women's embroidered blouses, the ponchos, the woven belts. But these are just the outward embodiment of a whole culture, an identity and a long history of resistance to assimilation by colonial society.

There are 10 different indigenous groups in Ecuador, each of which considers itself a distinct nationality, with its own language and culture. Together, they make up at least 10 percent of the population, with exact figures lacking. The most numerous are the Quichua, who live mainly in the Sierra and are related to the Quechuas of Peru and Bolivia.

In Ecuador, the terms *indígena* and *blanco* (indigenous person and white) are social and cultural rather than racial definitions. The term mestizo (mixed-blood) is not used frequently, although it is probably the most accurate description of the genetic heritage of most

Native organizations claim up to 4 million Ecuadorians are of indigenous origin. According to the 2001 census, the provinces with the largest proportion of indigenous people are Chimborazo, Cotopaxi, and Imbabura.

But these same children can return to their parents' community, and identify themselves as *indígenas* should they so choose.

Some Ecuadorian indigenous groups have been residents of the land for centuries, while others are descendants of people (called *mitmakuna*) who were moved around the Andes by the Incas: loyal Inca Quichua-speakers who were sent to recently conquered areas to serve as a teaching and garrison population, and people who were moved far from their homelands as a punishment for resistance to Inca rule.

Racism is deeply ingrained in Ecuadorian society. Native people who become "white" by

Ecuadorians. About 8 percent of the population are self-identified as indigenous, according to the 2001 census: people are considered *indígenas* if they live in an indigenous community, speak Quichua (or another indigenous language) and dress in a particular way.

Ethnicity in Ecuador is, to some degree, fluid. To an extent, over a generation or two, people can change their ethnic identity. An indigenous family can move to Quito, send their children to school dressed in Western-style clothes, and the children will generally be considered white.

leaving aside their traditional dress, language, and identity are often those who show the most virulently racist attitudes. "Stupid Indian" or "dirty Indian" are typical epithets used about people who for years were excluded from public education, while their cultural heritage and language were treated with disdain.

Many *indígenas* have defied attempts to integrate them into mestizo society, manifesting a tacit resistance to the ill-treatment and discrimination practiced against them. The survival of indigenous culture and identity despite the odds is witness to their endurance.

The Quichuas and the native Amazonians in the Oriente have retained their own identities

LEFT: street boys in Quito. **ABOVE:** Tsáchila man from the Western Lowlands. **ABOVE RIGHT:** modern footwear meets traditional embroidery.

more than most. They lived for centuries in almost complete isolation from the rest of the world, apart from a few missions that were established there. But when oil companies began to dig pipelines and build roads into the region, settlers soon followed, and the natives with whom they came into contact were rapidly assimilated into modern society.

Recently, with international campaigning for protection of the Amazonian forest, indigenous groups who are still seeking to preserve their environment and lifestyle have found a worldwide audience for their claims, which gives them greater leverage on governments. In the late 1990s CONAIE (the Confederation of Indian Nations of Ecuador) gathered steam in its fight for economic reform and has become the most cohesive and influential indigenous organization in South America. The storming of the Congressional Building by thousands of indigenous protestors in January 2000 and the subsequent overthrow of President Jamil Mahuad demonstrated the growing influence that these groups are finally having on national politics. For more details, contact Survival International in London; tel: +44 (0)20 7687 8700; website: www.survival-international.org.

Afro-Ecuadorians

Many coastal people have curly hair and darkish skin, revealing their descent from African slaves. But in two areas, the warm Chota Valley in the mountainous province of Imbabura, and the northwestern province of Esmeraldas, there is a predominantly black population. In both areas there is a strong African cultural heritage, which has mixed with indigenous culture. The people of the Chota Valley, for example, play the plaintive native music of the Sierra on African-type instruments, while the native Awa from north of Esmeraldas have adopted the marimba, which is of West African origin.

Immigrant groups

There has been little immigration to Ecuador, apart from an influx of Colombians in the north, and a substantial number of Chinese who settled in Guayaquil and Quevedo. The only other sizeable foreign ethnic group is the Lebanese, popularly known as "Turks," who came to Ecuador at the beginning of the 20th century and have accumulated considerable economic and political power.

Religious fervor

Since the arrival of the early missionaries, Ecuador has been under the strong influence of the Catholic Church. The word of the local priest or bishop still holds great weight, especially in the rural Sierra. However, since the end of the 19th century, when the anticlerical liberal movement of the Costa took power, state and Church have been separated. In state schools, the curriculum does not include religion.

In recent years, the Catholic Church in Latin America has reaffirmed its intention to work on behalf of the poor. Some Catholic groups

LEGACY OF SLAVERY

The origin of Ecuadorian blacks goes back to the slave trade. Historians believe that a Spanish frigate loaded with slaves was shipwrecked off the northern coast of Ecuador around the middle of the 17th century, and that the Africans who survived the wreck spread gradually across the province of Esmeraldas, living practically in isolation there for many years.

The black population of the Chota Valley, on the other hand, are the descendants of people who were brought to Ecuador to work on the sugarcane plantations at the height of the slave trade, and who were given their freedom when slavery was finally abolished in the region.

have taken this attitude further and are promoting political organization among the rural and urban slum populations as a means of seeking solutions to their grave problems.

Meanwhile, Protestant groups are engaged in active evangelization, particularly among the native population. Their success is due partly to the funding they provide for development projects and infrastructure, but also to the Protestant work ethic, which has been favorably received in many communities, as it has much in common with the indigenous belief in the dignity of labor. For several Protestant sects, however, the priority is to counter-

Ecuadorians are generally glad to share whatever they have with family and friends, whether there is abundance or scarcity. The kind of individualism typical in northern countries, such as wanting to live alone, is considered a strange and antisocial aberration.

But this sense of community operates only within the immediate group of family and acquaintances. Outside, in the cement jungle of the cities, the rule is everyone for himself.

The family unit

Middle-class families in Ecuador are typical of Latin countries: they value strong family ties

act the work of progressive sectors of the Catholic Church.

Community life

Native culture greatly values the community. For example, indigenous peoples advocate communal ownership of land, a concept that often comes into conflict with Ecuadorian tenancy laws. Another facet of the community spirit is the *minga* – a collective work effort inherited from Inca times via the hacienda system (*see page 76*).

LEFT: Ecuadorian of African descent from Bahía de Caráquez on the Pacific coast.
ABOVE: Holy Week Passion Play, Otavalo.

and the close supervision of womenfolk, while men tend to take their sexual freedom for granted, priding themselves on their gallantry and their *machismo*. Among the poorer urban classes, especially those in the Costa, family relations are often far more informal, and it is not unusual for a man to have several families with different women, with whom he lives in turn, rarely contributing much to their upkeep. Young indigenous couples often have a "trial marriage" before formalizing their relationship with wedding vows.

The status of women

Although Ecuador was the first country in South America to grant women the right to vote, it has been one of the slowest to embrace the principle of equality of the sexes in the workplace and at home. However, attitudes are beginning to shift. In 1989 a law prohibiting all forms of discrimination against women was introduced, and in 1995 an inter-American law against violence to women was written.

Another legal breakthrough has been the provision of free legal assistance to women when proceeding with charges of violence against them. However, domestic violence continues to occur at an alarming rate, with around 80 percent of women in relationships having suffered some form of violence. In Quito and

Guayaquil an average of 70 domestic abuse cases are reported daily.

The number of women's organizations working toward making the laws effective in practice is increasing. CEPAM (Center for the Promotion and Action of Ecuadorian Women) is one of the largest. Notably, there has been active participation of indigenous women in promoting such issues in the Sierra. The migration of more men than women from the Sierra to urban areas has led to indigenous women taking on new responsibilities in their communities. Organizations are focusing on providing education and healthcare for women.

Approximately 40 percent of women are now economically active. Many started work due to financial pressure, but as family size has decreased to an average of two or three children in urban areas, women are freer to pursue careers. They have entered most fields, although you will not see a female bus driver or welder. In 1990 women made up 5 percent of the police force. The number of women and men studying at university level is more or less equal.

Despite ingrained attitudes about traditional gender roles in Ecuadorian society, women are making inroads into national politics. The first female vice-president of Ecuador, Rosalia Arteaga, was elected in 1996. In a decisively pro-woman stance, President Correa named seven women to his first 17-strong cabinet, although, tragically, the new Minister of Defense, Guadalupe Larriva, died in a helicopter crash soon after taking office. Indigenous women are also gaining a political voice, both within and outside the indigenous movement. Correa in 2009 attended the funeral of Tránsito Amaguaña, born in 1909, who pioneered resistance and organization of agricultural workers in the Sierra.

Urban youth

Lifestyles in urban Ecuador are rapidly modernizing and changing the face of Ecuadorian culture. A middle-class teenager from Quito or Guayaquil probably identifies more with peers from the United States or Europe than with those in an isolated mountain village. These young people have access to cable TV, internet, and MP3s. Western rock and pop are often more popular than traditional Latin music.

Shopping malls have become popular meeting places for teenagers before a night out at one of the modern multi-screen cinemas. On weekends *discotecas* playing salsa and rock music are bursting at the seams until 3 or 4am.

The best jobs for young professionals are often with foreign companies. As a result, night schools are as full as the *discotecas*, with students studying English and computer programing. As Ecuadorian yuppies enjoy their symbols of success – cell phones, credit cards, espresso coffees, and copies of *Newsweek* – they are worlds away from the rural *campesino* who still earns about $5 a week. ❑

ABOVE: young Quiteñas in the capital's happening Mariscal Sucre district. **RIGHT:** stallholder at the Plaza de Ponchos in Otavalo market.

THE BRIGHT COLORS OF EVERYDAY WEAR

The distinctive clothes of Ecuador's indigenous peoples are not just worn on high days and holidays, but can be seen in any market or village street

The diversity of native dress in Ecuador is witness to the strong sense of identity which the various groups have retained throughout the centuries. Some of the clothes that the *indígenas* wear so proudly today are in fact adaptations of the 16th-century Spanish-style costumes that were once a kind of uniform, indicating which hacienda they belonged to.

Inca Inspiration

Some items go back much further: it is said that the indigo and black clothing of the Saraguro people is worn as a sign of perpetual mourning for the Inca Atahualpa, killed in 1533 at the beginning of the Spanish conquest. Hats, too, date back to before the colonial period. Even the Panama is an adaptation of the headgear worn by the Manabí people at the time of the conquest. Fragments of *ikat* tie-dyed textiles from the pre-Hispanic period have also been found.

Traveling around the many markets in Ecuador, you are bound to notice the wide variety of colors and styles of shawls, ponchos, and *macanas*, the ubiquitous carrying cloths which are used to carry various items from kindling to babies.

ABOVE: Otavalo women traditionally bind their long hair with brightly colored ribbons called *cintas*.
LEFT: a Cañari woman wearing a blue-trimmed white bowler hat.

ABOVE: the multi-colored clothing of women in Alausí, Chimborazo province, waiting for their turn with the bank teller.

BELOW: Shepherds of Cañar province, north of Cuenca, wear sheepskin chaps, along with deep red ponchos.

COLORS TO DYE FOR

The rich, vibrant colors of the ponchos, shawls, and scarves are the most striking thing about the dress of indigenous Ecuadorians.

Many of the shades come from natural dyes: the deep indigo blue worn by the Saraguro comes from the Indigofera, a tropical bean-producing plant; and the rich red of the scarves and wraps worn by *indígenas* of Salasaca is produced from cochineal, which is extracted from the crushed bodies of female insects *(Dactylopius coccus)* which live on the Opuntia cactus. *Ikat* textiles – made into ponchos, shawls, and belts – are also richly colored. They are created by a process of tying and dyeing before the garment is woven.

The indigo-dyed cotton shawls called *paños*, which are made around Gualaceo, are the best known of the *ikat* products. These shawls have macramé fringes which are an art form in themselves, as they can take many months to make.

LEFT: the women of Otavalo wear intricately embroidered cotton blouses, hand-spun shirts, and shoulder-wraps, with gold beaded necklaces. Their teeth are often capped with gold.

RIGHT: woman selling *shigra* bags at Guamote market. *Shigras* are brightly colored bags made of agave fiber, which are made by hand and only found in the central Sierra region and nowhere else in the Andes.

LIFE AND LORE IN THE SIERRA

Ancient values, traditional healers, and Christian festivals are all part of life in the Sierra, an area that has seen little change for hundreds of years

Every valley of the Ecuadorian highlands is populated by distinct indigenous groups, some descendants of original Ecuadorian tribes, others descendants of the Incas or of people imported by the Incas from other areas of the country. Any guidebook that assures you "the people lead lives unchanged since Inca times" should be tossed right out of the window, because indigenous Ecuadorians don't live in a static universe any more than others do.

Europeans and Ecuadorian *indígenas* have been in contact for nearly 500 years, with the former influencing he lives of the latter in profound ways. Language, clothing, food, housing, and religion all have a European imprint. The influence has also worked the other way round: for example, more than half the food crops consumed in the world today were domesticated in the Americas before the arrival of Europeans. Most significant are maize and potatoes, which were the economic foundation of the Inca Empire.

Distinctive subcultures

Indigenous people still retain a number of customs of pre-Hispanic origin. Although the various groups have distinctive subcultures, they share a number of traits. Some might argue that a poor, evangelical Protestant family in Chimborazo that ekes out a living on half an acre of bad land has nothing in common with a wealthy Catholic weaving family in Otavalo that has just finished the construction of a four-story apartment building in town. Yet both families consider themselves *indígenas*, both wear a dis-

tinctive dress that identifies them as members of a particular ethnic group, and both families speak Quichua inside their homes.

To paraphrase Sir Winston Churchill, the *indígenas* of Ecuador are separated by the barrier of a common language: Quichua or Runa Shimi (The People's Tongue). Quichua is part of the Quechua language family. There are several Quechua languages spoken today in Peru, and two or three different Quichua dialects spoken in Ecuador. This means that *indígenas* from different regions of Ecuador do not necessarily understand each other. The origins of Quechua are unknown, but we do know that the Chinchay, a trading group on the coast of Peru, spoke it around the time of

---

PRECEDING PAGES: bargaining often takes place in Quichua at Guamote animal market. **LEFT:** market day at Guamote. **RIGHT:** Easter procession in Cacha.

Christ. The Incas adopted Quechua from the Chinchay and spread it throughout the Andes as they expanded their empire in the 14th and 15th centuries. Then the church employed Quichua as a lingua franca to help them Christianize the *indígenas*, who resisted Spanish.

The Quechua language family is growing; more people speak it now than in Inca times, including in Ecuador. Today most *indígenas* are bilingual in Quichua and Spanish, but some older people, especially in remote communities, speak Quichua only.

Despite efforts, no standard version of Quichua or Quechua spelling has yet been set.

Various alphabets have been devised over the centuries, and this accounts for inconsistencies in spelling. The Quichua word for baby, for example, can be spelled *wawa*, *guagua*, or *huahua*.

Cooperative values

If there is a core value in indigenous society it is reciprocity, and naturally there are Quichua words that express this. One such word is *minga*, a collective work effort, which operates in various ways. In community *minga* the leaders organize an effort to repair the roads, or clean the irrigation channels, and every family must furnish several workers. If they fail to show up, some communities levy a fine.

Then there is a private *minga*. If a family needs to roof a house, for example, they invite the neighbors to a roofing *minga*, supplying copious quantities of food and *chicha* (a local beer made from corn and manioc or *yuca*) for the workers, and people come willingly because they know they will need help themselves one day.

In the same way, *compadres* (two couples who are ritual kin because they are godparents to one another's children) also know they can call upon each other for help, anything from a loan of money to working in the kitchen at a fiesta.

Before the Spanish conquest, money did not exist in indigenous societies. Items were bartered or labor was traded. Under the Incas, people paid their taxes in the form of labor (*mita*) or goods, and in return were taken care of with food from central storehouses in times of famine. In many places, reciprocity still means the exchange of goods or services rather than money. It is useful, as a tourist, to bear this in mind: for example, giving people photographs is much better than paying them to let you take their picture. However, this is not always applicable in public places such as markets, where you're likely to draw a huge crowd. Sharing food or gifts of food is culturally appropriate in most situations.

Sacred mountains

Indígenas throughout the Andes have worshiped mountains for millennia. In Ecuador, mountains are seen as male or female individuals, inhabited by powerful spirits. Mountains are also believed to control the rain and therefore the fertility and well-being of the entire region. The highest peak in any area was considered to be a *waka* (*huaca*) or sacred spot by the Incas. The Spanish decided to construct Catholic shrines over Inca sacred places, which is why you will see so many isolated chapels on hilltops.

Chimborazo, in the western cordillera of central Ecuador, is the highest mountain in the country, an enormous snow-cap that looms over the province like a giant ice cream. It is known as Taita (Father) Chimborazo, while slightly to the north and in the eastern cordillera is Mama Tungurahua. Lesser peaks in the region are also seen as male and female pairs. Offerings such as guinea pigs, *trago* (a fierce sugarcane liquor), or plants are sometimes made to the mountains to propitiate them.

In Imbabura province, Mama Cotacachi reigns to the west of Otavalo while Taita Imbabura dominates the east. When Cotacachi's peak is snow-capped the *indígenas* say it is because Taita Imbabura visited her during the night. Needless to say, this encounter resulted in a baby, Urcu (Mountain) Mojanda, which lies just to the south of Otavalo. The connection of mountains with fertility is obvious here, and many *indígenas* carry it even further. When, for example, people who live on the flanks of Imbabura plant crops they first ask Taita

Shamanism and healing

Virtually every Ecuadorian community has a man or woman who knows the healing properties of various plants, or who can diagnose and cure by correcting spiritual imbalances or undoing spells. Healers are known by various Spanish names: *curanderos* (curers), *brujos* (witches), or *hechiceros* (sorcerers, witches). In Quichua, traditional healers are called *yachaj mamas* or *yachaj taitas* (knowledgeable mothers or fathers). There are also midwives, who are known as *parteras*. The details of healing vary among the different ethnic groups, but in the Sierra people might go to a local healer for a

Imbabura to give them an abundant harvest. And when it rains in the region people say that Taita Imbabura is peeing on the valley below. If the mountains send the rain, Mother Earth (Allpa Mama or Pacha Mama) feeds the people by producing crops. It is customary to throw the last few drops of an alcoholic drink on the ground as an offering to her.

It was not uncommon for the Incas to sacrifice humans on the mountain tops, most often teenage girls who were told from a young age they were the chosen ones. The ritual was considered a great honor.

LEFT: Quilotoa woman. **ABOVE:** family winnowing grain in Guamote.

number of reasons: it might be because they have intestinal parasites, or because they believe an envious neighbor has cast a spell on them (*envidia*), or because they are looking for success in love or business. In addition, many people in the highlands have combined the Quichua belief in an inner and outer body, which must be kept in balance, with the medieval European belief in humoral medicine. This ancient tradition held that the body was composed of four humors: yellow bile, black bile, phlegm, and blood, whose relationships determined a person's disposition and health.

Today people believe that such illnesses as infant diarrhea occur because the baby has had a fright, which caused the inner and outer bodies to become unbalanced. If the inner body actually flees, then death can result, so the healer performs a ceremony known as "calling the soul" to bring back the baby's inner body. Bodies can also become diseased because of bad air (*wayrashka* in Quichua), known as *mal aire* in Spanish. *Mal aire* gave us our word malaria, because people initially believed that the disease came from swamp vapors rather than from the bites of mosquitoes that lived in the swamps.

Calling the soul involves a cleansing, in which the patient's body is rubbed with a raw egg. The egg is shaken, and the sounds it makes indicate that the bad air is being absorbed. After

the cleansing a child is sent to hide the eggs in the fields nearby. Calling the soul also includes prayers in Quichua to God the Father, Son, and Holy Spirit, the Virgin Mary and the saints. The healer tells the patient's heart to rise up (that is, to come back), passes alcohol to all present, and smokes cigarettes, blowing the smoke on the patient. Tobacco has long been used by indigenous groups for healing. There are many early Spanish accounts of its use among the Maya, and it is still used in healing and religious rituals throughout the Americas.

While most communities have their own healers, several areas are famous for their *curan-*

NATURAL REMEDIES

How effective are these spiritual healers? It depends entirely on your belief system and on what kind of results you expect.

A positive attitude is tremendously important in healing of any kind. Western doctors say that 80 percent of all illnesses are self-healing and it is the other 20 percent that need medical intervention. If local healers have an 80 percent success rate, that looks pretty impressive. We should also bear in mind that many Western drugs, such as cocaine, curare, and quinine, come from plants that local healers know well and have used in their remedies for hundreds of years.

deros. People in the Sierra believe that the Shuar people have special healing powers, as do the Tsáchila of Santo Domingo de los Tsáchilas (colloquially known as *colorados* because men dye their hair red) west of the Andes. The healers of Ilumán, outside Otavalo, are also famous, and people come from all over the highlands to be treated by them.

These healers rely on centuries of knowledge passed down from their ancestors. In *ayahuasca* rituals, a psychotropic plant is given to the patient, allowing the shaman to enter the sick person's body, find the illness, and cure it. These medicine men are well-respected members of their communities and are given credit for saving many tribes from death. The practice is making a comeback as Ecuadorians and international tourists frustrated with modern medicines look for alternative methods of treating disease and mental anguish.

A calendar full of fiestas

Latin America's reputation for partying and festivities has a long history. In pre-Hispanic times community fiestas were organized around the agricultural and solar cycle. After the Spanish conquest, the Church cleverly turned many traditional indigenous religious celebrations into Catholic feast days on the grounds that people were going to celebrate

time of the year wander into a town in the middle of a fiesta in honor of its patron saint. However, here are a few of the major Sierra fiestas that are well worth catching:

Carnival (February or March) is held during the week before Lent begins on Ash Wednesday. *Carnaval* is a transplant from Europe, and represents a last fling before the austerity of Lent. Carnival in Ecuador is not like the one in Rio. In the Sierra the main activity is throwing water, and it is definitely not fun to be hit in the back with a water balloon or to have a bucket of water dumped on your head in a chilly mountain village. Ambato, however, has

anyway, so they might as well observe a Christian occasion. Heavy drinking of *chicha* (local beer) is associated with nearly all Andean festivals, despite the Catholic Church's efforts to phase it out.

While a number of civic festivals are observed throughout the year in Ecuador, the most interesting fiestas by far are the traditional celebrations in the country. These mainly occur in the spring and summer, especially after the harvest and during the dry season. Every community has its own ritual calendar, so you might at any

outlawed water-throwing and has a fiesta of fruit and flowers that includes street dances and folkloric events. Hotels fill up early, but Ambato is reachable easily from Baños by bus, so it's possible to make a day trip out of it.

Holy Week (Semana Santa, the week before Easter) begins with Palm Sunday (Domingo de Ramos). Throughout Ecuador people buy palm fronds in the market, weave them into different shapes and take them to church. Four days later, on Maundy Thursday, families visit the cemetery and bring food and drink for the dead in an observance similar to that of the Day of the Dead (*see page 82*).

In Quito on Good Friday there is an enormous, spectacular procession through the

FAR LEFT: Tsáchila man with dyed red hair.
LEFT: shaman ritual near Cotacachi.
ABOVE: celebrating Semana Santa (Holy Week) in Quito.

streets of the city, complete with flagellants, men dragging huge wooden crosses, and penitents dressed in what look rather like purple Ku Klux Klan outfits. There are also impressive Good Friday processions, with costumed penitents in such Chimborazo towns as Yaruquíes, Tixán, Chambo, and Chunchi.

Corpus Christi, in honor of the Eucharist, is a movable feast, held on the Thursday after Trinity Sunday, usually in the first half of June. It is a major fiesta in the central Sierra, especially in Cotopaxi and Tungurahua provinces, but it is celebrated in many places, including some communities in Chimborazo province, in

and night are less dramatic, but astute indigenous astronomers still recognized them.

Today, **Saint John the Baptist** (San Juan Bautista, June 24) is the major fiesta in the Otavalo Valley and probably replaced an ancient, pre-Inca solstice festival.

Among the Otavaleños, San Juan is a male fiesta lasting the better part of a week. On the night of the 23rd, the male vespers (*la víspera*) dress up in costumes. The dancing begins after dark both in Otavalo and in the outlying towns.

The variety and ingenuity of the costumes is a sight to see, from Batman, Kalimán, and North American Plains Indians with feathered

Cuenca, and in Saraguro, Loja province. Dancers with ornate headdresses and spectacularly embroidered costumes are now found only in such communities as Pujilí, Cotopaxi, and San Antonio de Píllaro, Tungurahua. In Salasaca, the *indígenas* wear plaster masks, bright ribbons and feathers on their hats, and dance from Salasaca to the nearby town of Pelileo. In Cuenca, celebrations include tiny paper hot-air balloons, fireworks, and special sweets.

The winter solstice, Inti Raymi, celebrated on June 21, was once a major event in the Inca festival calendar. In the Cuzco area, south of the equator, the winter solstice is the shortest day and longest night of the year. Closer to the equator, the differences in the length of the day

RITUAL BATTLES

Also connected with the festival of San Juan is a ritual battle that involves rock-throwing, and takes place at the chapel of San Juan. The chapel is located on the west side of the Pan-American Highway, away from the town proper. Until the 1960s people were sometimes killed during these fights, and there are still some nasty injuries sustained. The point of spilling blood seems to be a payment or sacrifice to Mother Earth (Pacha Mama), in gratitude for the corn harvest.

Similar ritual battles (called *tinku*), fought with rocks and fists, still occur in the highlands of Peru and Bolivia, with corresponding casualties.

headdresses, to Mexicans with giant sombreros, women, and soldiers. Some *indígenas* even parody gringos by wearing blond wigs, down jackets, jeans and running shoes, and carrying backpacks. The dancing goes on each night for a week, with groups of musicians and dancers moving from house to house and dancing (actually stomping) in a circle, with sudden reversals of direction which may represent the movement of the sun.

Saints Peter and Paul (San Pedro y San Pablo, June 29) is a major fiesta that takes place in Imbabura province, and in many towns and villages the San Juan and San Pedro y Pablo festivities run together.

On the night of June 28 bonfires are lit in the streets throughout the province. This seems to be a combination of indigenous and Spanish customs. Young women who want to have a child are supposed to leap over the fires. San Pedro is especially important in Cotacachi, where there are also ritual fights, and in Cayambe. While San Juan is important to the Otavaleños, San Pedro is the big event for the other main ethnic group in Imbabura, the people who live on the east side of the mountain in the communities of Zuleta, Rinconada, La Esperanza, and Angochagua.

Because San Pedro is the patron saint of the canton of Cayambe, hundreds of *indígenas* come into town and parade under the banners of their communities. The groups dance down the streets, around the main plaza, and past a reviewing stand, where local officials award prizes to the best groups. Among the dancers are men and women carrying roosters in wooden cages or tied to poles for a ceremony called the *entrega de gallos* (delivery of roosters). In the days of *wasipungo* (serfdom) the indigenous people on the haciendas had to show their loyalty to the landowner by making a ceremonial gift of roosters at this time. Today the ceremony is most often performed for the indigenous sponsor (called the *prioste*) of local fiestas.

The feast of the **Virgin of Carmen** (La Virgen del Carmen, July 16) is a notably larger celebration in the southern provinces than in the north. There is a fair (*feria*) in front of the

church of that name in downtown Cuenca. In Chimborazo this fiesta is celebrated in Pumallacta and in Chambo.

Chambo, located just outside Riobamba, is the site of a miraculous shrine and fountain, one of those instances where a Catholic church was built on a mountain over what was undoubtedly a pre-conquest holy site. The shrine is dedicated to the Virgen de la Fuente del Carmelo de Catequilla. *Indígenas* from throughout Chimborazo, in their finest traditional dress, visit the shrine and chapel on July 16. There is also a small fair at the base of the springs where food, drink, candles, and holy items are sold.

Saint James (Santiago, July 25) is the patron saint of Spain, and his image (on horseback with a raised sword) was carried into battle by the Spanish. The Spanish had firearms, which were unknown to *indígenas*, who associated Santiago with the powerful Inca god of thunder and lightning (Illapa). Today Santiago is the patron of many communities, and there are many fiestas in his honor.

The feast of the **Virgin of Mercy** (La Virgen de la Merced, September 24) is a major two-day fiesta in Latacunga (Cotopaxi province), where a local dark-skinned statue of the Virgin is known as La Mamá Negra, the black mother. La Merced is also celebrated in Columbe (Chimborazo province).

LEFT: fiesta of San Pedro celebrated in Cayambe.
ABOVE: traditional dancing is a vital part of many Andean festivals.

All Saints' Day and the Day of the Dead (Todos Santos and Día de Difuntos, November 1 and 2). These two Catholic feast days are another example of the blending of Andean and European traditions. In pre-conquest burials, food and drink were placed in graves to feed the dead in the next life. Some people believe that the spirits of the dead return to earth for 24 hours and will be unhappy if they aren't remembered.

If you are in Quito in early December you will get swept along in the festivities that celebrate **The Founding of Quito** (December 6). There are parades, bullfights, dancing in the street, and general merriment.

Finally, there are many beautiful **Christmas** (Navidad, December 25) pageants and celebrations throughout Ecuador; it's a wonderful time of year to be traveling there. Christmas is the main religious holiday, though as commercial here as anywhere else, with stores

> *Commonly used for transportation in tropical areas, open-sided buses called* chivas *play a big role in Quito's fiesta, where they parade through the city day and night, with bands playing on the roof.*

SPIRITUAL FOOD

All over Ecuador, little human and animal figures are baked from bread dough and taken to the cemeteries on November 2, where they are placed on graves along with paper wreaths and other offerings of food and drink. It sounds as if it would be a very sad occasion, but in fact it is often quite cheerful and festive.

In a nice local variation on the theme of "waste not, want not," poor people often come to the cemeteries and offer prayers at each grave site in return for some of the food. It's a sensible idea, as they need the food more than the departed, and, of course, a few extra prayers never go amiss.

setting up Christmas displays as early as September. Among the local Christmas customs is the Pase del Niño (Presentation of the Christ Child). Families who own statues of the baby Jesus carry them in a street procession to the church, accompanied by musicians and by children dressed as Mary, Joseph, and other Nativity figures. The baby Jesus statues are blessed during a special Mass and then taken back to the household cribs.

The most famous Pase del Niño occurs in Cuenca, on the morning of December 24. It begins at the churches of San Sebastián and Corazón de Jesús and converges on the cathedral on the Plaza de Armas. Families from around the region bring their children, some dressed as *indígenas* and mounted on horseback, their horses decked with gifts of food, liquor, sweets, and fruits. Other children are on foot, dressed as Nativity figures or as gypsies, gauchos, or Moors, each group carrying its own statue of Jesus. Inside the cathedral the children are given *chicha* and bread, then the participants wind their way through the streets to celebrate Christmas at home. The Pase has grown so large, however, that its quality has declined over the years.

In Saraguro, Loja province, each indigenous community owns a statue of the Christ Child which is carried in a procession on Christmas Day from the main church to the home of the

Fiesta etiquette

There are appropriate and inappropriate ways to behave at fiestas, and everyone will have a better time if you know how to act. If you want to take photographs, for example, you will be less conspicuous and find it much easier at the larger and more public events. If you are the only outsider at a small village event, then circumspection is the word. Put your camera away, watch the festivities, talk to people, and then ask if you can photograph them. *Indígenas* have been pushed around by people for nearly 500 years, and they are pushing back. They resent the arrogance of some outsiders who assume

Christ Child's "godparents," the *marcan taita* and *marcan mama*. The procession is led by violinists and drummers and accompanied by costumed dancers. At the *marcan taita*'s house the statue is placed on a decorated altar, and the entire community assembles for a huge meal and an afternoon of music and dancing.

Other Christmas observances include the fiesta of the Holy Innocents (Santos Inocentes) on December 28 (in Quito), and the feast of Epiphany or Three Kings (Tres Reyes or Reyes Magos), on January 6.

they can photograph anything, anywhere without asking permission. Remember, you're a guest here, not Sebastián de Benalcázar.

Ritual drinking is customary at all fiestas, and by late in the day many participants are hopelessly intoxicated. It is insulting if you refuse to drink when the *trago* bottle is passed around, so join the revelers in a drink or two and throw the dregs on the ground as an offering to Pacha Mama. One of the best ways to enjoy a fiesta without causing or taking offense is to arrive fairly early in the morning and leave by about 2pm, before things get seriously out of hand and before you've shared so many drinks that you can't find your way back to the bus stop. ❏

LEFT: open-sided *chiva* bus taking indigenous Ecuadorians to market. **ABOVE:** Christmas procession in Quito's Old Town.

SOUNDS OF THE ANDES

Ecuador's diversity extends to its musical traditions: Andean pipes happily coexist with brass bands and salsa clubs. And then there are the weekend marimba parties...

A t fiestas in Ecuador, two kinds of music are usually played: traditional, indigenous music and Spanish (or more generally European) music. But after almost 500 years there has been much blending of the two.

You can hear traditional music groups (*grupos* or *conjuntos*) at many indigenous fiestas and in folk-music clubs (*peñas*). There are also local and national traditional music competitions, which are usually free to the public, with an amazing variety of talent (or lack thereof).

Ancient instruments

Pre-Hispanic vocal and instrumental music was based on a pentatonic (five-note) scale, which gives Andean music its distinctive haunting, melancholic sound. Pre-Hispanic instruments consisted of flutes, panpipes, conch shells, drums, and rattles and bells. Flute-like instruments used today include the seven-hole bamboo *quena*, a notched bamboo with six finger holes and a thumb hole, and a smaller flute (*pingullu*), which has three or four holes. The pre-Hispanic flutes are always held vertically; flutes (*flautas*) held horizontally are modeled on the European instrument.

The panpipe (*rondador*) goes back at least 2,000 years, and is typically made of varying lengths and widths of cane or bamboo tied together in one long row, the different lengths and diameters producing distinct tones. Many Ecuadorian musicians now use *zampoñas*, the panpipes typical of Peru and Bolivia, which are tuned differently from the *rondador* and usually have two rows of pipes lashed together,

which musicians say make it easier to play. The frequent use of Peruvian and Bolivian instruments by Ecuadorian musicians is indicative of the cross-fertilization that occurs as Ecuadorians travel in Peru and Bolivia, and southern Andean musicians (or their tape cassettes and compact discs) come north.

Percussion instruments include drums (*bombos*) and gourd rattles (*maracas*). Bells (*campanas*) are still used, especially by dancers. In Imbabura province, for example, 10 or 12 cowbells are attached to a piece of cowhide and are worn over the shoulder by dancers at the fiestas of San Juan and San Pedro (June 24 and June 29).

LEFT: making a bamboo panpipe. **RIGHT:** musican playing a traditional Ecuadorian panpipe and *charango*.

Spanish influences

Stringed instruments were introduced by the Spanish and were soon incorporated into the traditional repertoire. These instruments include the guitar *(guitarra)*, violin *(violín)*, mandolin *(bandolín)*, *charango*, and Andean harp *(arpa criolla)*. The *charango* originated in Bolivia and looks like a ukulele, but has five pairs of strings and eight frets. The body is sometimes made of wood, but more often from an armadillo shell. The Andean harp is a home-made version of the European harp, beautiful to listen to but difficult to make and transport, which is why few musicians use them.

After the Spanish introduced cattle into Ecuador, the indigenous peoples made a unique instrument from cow horns, called a *coroneta* or *bocina*. The tone of the *coroneta* depends on the number of horns used. The accordion *(acordeón)* and harmonica *(rondín)* were introduced in the 19th century. The most recent addition is the portable Yamaha organ.

Brass instruments are another European introduction, and it is traditional for brass bands to play at small-town fiestas and civic events, during which volume and enthusiasm often surpass musicianship. Another venerable musical tradition is the weekend concert in the park. Many towns have municipal bands which assemble on Sunday mornings and rouse the populace from their Saturday-night torpor. It's not exactly indigenous music: you are quite likely to get a rendition of the theme tune from the latest hit television series. In traditional music groups, men usually play musical instruments and sing, while women are only vocal-

> The anniversary of the founding of Quito is celebrated with bullfights and flamenco music. Alternative artistic events step away from this glorification of Spain, peaking in an annual rock festival dubbed Quitu Raymi.

ists. Some types of music, including the *wayñu* (or *wayno*) and the *yaraví*, were probably introduced by the Incas and are almost always sung in Quichua. But the most common is the *sanjuanito*, which qualifies as Ecuador's national dance music. *Sanjuanitos* can be both instrumental and vocal and are played by folk-music groups and modern bands at most fiestas.

At a *peña* a typical group will be composed of young men playing the guitar, mandolin, *charango*, violin, drum, *quena*, *pingullu*, *zampoña*, and *rondador*, and they will alternate purely instrumental music with songs with musical accompaniment. Many of the songs will be in Quichua. Some you will hear all over the country, others are specific to certain provinces.

Festival music

To foreign ears, much traditional fiesta music sounds like an obsession with one theme. The same refrain is repeated over and over, endlessly hypnotic and great to dance to. During San Juan, the musical groups literally dance all night (to *sanjuanitos* naturally), moving from house to house throughout the village.

Increasingly, traditional groups are being replaced by ones that use amplified instruments, especially for such occasions as weddings and other large parties. Into the house come the musicians in traditional dress, but instead of guitars and *quenas* they carry an electric sound system that will prevent any sleep in the *barrio* for days. The musicians will tune up and launch into "La Rasca Bonita," a *sanjuanito* with a catchy tune and upbeat tempo that qualifies as the national party melody. The band alternates *sanjuanitos* with *cumbias*, music of Afro-Caribbean origin from the coasts of Colombia and Ecuador. Everyone from grandparents to toddlers dances at these parties.

Marimba and salsa

In the Esmeraldas region dominated by Afro-Ecuadorians, marimba is still very much alive. The marimba instrument itself, the *chonta*, is similar to a xylophone and is made of local hardwood. It is accompanied by *bombos* (drums), *cununeros* (small tambourines), and *guasos* or bamboo stalks filled with seeds. In the villages near Borbón, every single house has its own marimba. At weekends and important holidays people head out to marimba parties. The local

business by the plethora of stores and shacks selling illegally copied MP3 CDs.

Rap, reggae, and Andean chill

In larger cities popular Latin music is more likely to be played, along with foreign and local rock and pop. Reggaeton is big in Ecuador, and a blend of rap and Latin pop music is what you are most likely to hear in a *discoteca*. Andean chill – a fusion of traditional songs, tunes and instruments with electronica – is one of the more respected genres to have emerged in the Andes in recent years, and Miki González is one of the genre's premier artists. ❑

firewater *(aguardiente)* is often thrown on the instrument itself, to signify the beginning of the marimba. Each song tells a story, moralizing, instructing, illustrating daily life, or recognizing death. The haunting, passionate music goes on until dawn and sometimes for several days. Salsa, merengue, and cumbia, essentially dance music from Caribbean countries, is particularly big on the coast. In shopping malls it is easy to find good recordings of salsa on CD. Music stores have rows of salsa compilations; however, many legitimate stores have been driven out of

LEFT: street musician playing the Andean harp, a local version of the European harp.
ABOVE: marimba players in Esmeraldas province.

TAKING PART

Segundo Quintero and Carmen González are two of the better-known marimba artists, but recordings of marimba are hard to find. The Centro Cultural Afro-Ecuatoriano, Tamayo 985 and Lizardo García, Quito, tel: 02-252 2318, has videos of some of these frantic dances and information about the bigger festivals.

If you have time, there are plenty of schools in Quito where you can learn to dance to the tropical rhythms of salsa and merengue, in individual or group lessons. Once you have learned the basics, head to Seseribó in Quito (Veintimilla and 12 de Octubre) on Thursday or Friday nights and join in.

PEOPLES OF THE AMAZON

The Amazonian people preserve many of the old ways,
but are learning how to live with changes, both good
and bad, that the modern world has introduced

W hen Westerners think of indigenous Amazonian peoples, they conjure up strings of age-old stereotypes. The popular image is of naked men and women slipping through the jungle with Stone Age tools, isolated until recently from history and the outside world. According to this school of thought, they have always hunted for their food rather than grown it, and often engaged in brutal wars, shrinking their enemies' heads and occasionally eating their flesh. Conversely, they are held to be ecological saints, protecting their delicate environment at all costs.

Not surprisingly, the image has little to do with reality, as anthropologists in the Ecuadorian Oriente are rapidly finding out.

Coping with change

Far from being unchanging, undeveloping societies – and therefore "idyllic" – all Amazonian peoples have their own histories, and very dynamic histories at that.

Because Amazonians did not possess writing systems and, even more importantly, because their rainforest home is particularly unconducive to preserving the remains of past civilizations, there is little data with which to reconstruct Amazonian history. However, archeologists can now show that human beings have lived in the Amazon since at least 10000 BC, and that major technological breakthroughs occurred in the Amazon basin.

Amazonians domesticated manioc around 8000 BC, and probably invented clay pottery around 4000 BC, before any other indigenous

cultures in South America. Migrations, new languages, and vast cultural and religious transformations characterize the history of the Amazon basin. Archeologists believe that cultural advances moved out of Amazonia into the Andes, not the reverse.

After the arrival of the *conquistadores*, Amazonian societies changed tremendously, whether they had direct contact with the invaders or not. Plagues of diseases to which indigenous peoples had no resistance moved in waves from the coast, over the Andes, into the rainforest, drastically reducing the population. Migrations of peoples away from regions conquered and colonized by the Spanish and Portuguese provoked chain

---

PRECEDING PAGES: Amazon paddle power. **LEFT:** Cofan tribesman. **ABOVE:** rainforest boy with bananas.

reactions of indigenous peoples being forced off their original lands into unfamiliar territories.

New technologies reached the Amazon as well, again brought by intermediaries, so that no direct contact occurred with Europeans. Steel tools and new foods (especially the banana, plantain, and papaya, which originated in Southeast Asia) were traded from one people to the next throughout the jungle, transforming the ways of life throughout the Amazon. In this way, the pressures created by the Spanish conquest of Ecuador and Peru transformed Amazonia, and the pre-conquest jungle lifestyle will for ever remain a mystery to modern man.

A range of jungle groups

The Ecuadorian Amazon is small compared with the vast jungles of Brazil, but it is nevertheless an important, even crucial, part of the region. It is inhabited by six major ethnic groups (the term "tribe," with its primitive implications, has been discarded). The largest grouping is the Quichua people (60,000), followed by the Shuar (40,000), Achuar (5,000), Huaorani (3,000), Siona-Secoya (650), and the Cofan (600).

The Huaorani people remain the most nomadic of Ecuador's indigenous Amazonians, and the least interested in cultivation, but during the 20th century they too partially adopted

MYTH AND REALITY

Although the popular Western image persists of Amazonians surviving by hunting wild game and gathering fruits and nuts, the truth is that most indigenous peoples are no longer true hunter-gatherers. In the 21st century they obtain nearly all their foodstuffs from cultivation.

They are either horticulturists, which means that they establish moderate-sized, temporary gardens; or agriculturalists, planting crops on a permanent basis and usually on a much larger scale. The only partial exception to this is the Huaorani group, the most nomadic of the Ecuadorian Amazonian peoples.

horticulture. Because they customarily went about naked, and relied so much on hunting and gathering wild foods, the Huaorani were originally called "Aucas," which means savages in the Quichua language. The Huaorani have rejected this name, which they, quite understandably, consider highly derogatory.

It appears almost certain that the Huaorani, who are composed of a number of discrete groups (Guequetairi, Pijemoiri, Baihuairi, Huepeiri, etc) are an amalgamation of survivors from many different groups diminished by disease, war, and migrations. For this reason, anthropologists view the sparse material culture of the Huaorani, not as evidence of "backwardness," but as the basic survival mechanisms of those forest cultures that endured the most intensive stresses.

The Amazonian Quichuas are closely related to the people of the same name who dominate the Andean highlands of Ecuador. Anthropologists surmise that Quichua-speakers migrated down into the rainforests after the Spanish conquered the highlands in the early 1500s. The most numerous of the indigenous Amazonians, the Quichuas are composed of two distinct ethnic groups, the Canelos and the Quijos. These peoples brought the knowledge of well-developed agricultural systems from the Andes to the jungle, although they had to learn how to

Siona-Secoya, a combination of two once separate groups with very similar customs that unified when their numbers dwindled drastically in the 20th century. These peoples practice what anthropologists call "slash and burn," a technique of creating small clearings in the forest which produces food for two or three consecutive years and then must be abandoned to replenish their fertility. The Siona-Secoya usually leave big trees standing, especially those that produce fruits, and they do not always burn off the vegetation they have cut, but sometimes allow it to rot and mulch the exposed earth.

grow very different crops in their new territory. Living in dispersed, permanent settlements on individually owned plots of land, the Quichua men clear land and plant crops, while the women maintain, weed, and harvest them. They use a rotation system, resting the plot for three years after approximately five years of cultivation.

In the northern Oriente

The small ethnic groups that live in the northern region of the Ecuadorian Amazon are the Cofan (who call themselves the A'I) and the

These peoples are semi-nomadic, which is to say that they move about within defined territories, abandoning old plots for new ones located in richer hunting grounds. They most frequently locate their gardens close to their houses, but sometimes plant smaller, less complex gardens at some distance from home. Siona-Secoya and Cofan farmers are women, and the profundity of their knowledge about soils and maintaining their fertility, about weather patterns, plant behavior and diseases, and crop combinations (beans and corn, or corn and manioc, for example) is truly astounding.

The Shuar people of the southern region of Ecuadorian Amazonia, and their closely related cousins the Achuar, practice a horticultural

LEFT: missionaries at work in the early 1900s.
ABOVE: Huaorani children outside their village home in a clearing in the Amazon jungle.

system heavily dependent upon one crop plant; sweet manioc. Women harvest the tuber a year or more after planting it, and, as they harvest, they re-sow small tuber cuttings. When manioc is mature, it can be left in the ground to continue growing without any risk of spoilage, which has obvious advantages in tropical Amazonia. The Shuar and Achuar may perhaps be described as semi-settled, rather than semi-nomadic. In recent years, Shuar and Achuar men have started raising cattle in increasing numbers, converting jungle to pasture. This income-earning strategy is probably not sustainable considering the fragile soil and subsoil

exclusively to indigenous men, who would have discussed their own activities, and not those of their womenfolk.

Another, more recent, myth held about indigenous Amazonians is that they never kill more than they need in the rainforest, that they revere the jungle's animals, and are attuned to the natural balances of their environment. There is some validity to this view, but much of it stems from the industrialized nations' recent awareness of how they themselves have abused the planet's ecology, coupled with an all-too romantic view of Amazonian life. In fact, it is fairly obvious that the indigenous people of the

ecology of the jungle, yet the Shuar and Achuar are finding increasingly sophisticated methods of planning their survival in the rainforest.

Movements through the forest

It is still true that hunting, gathering, and fishing determine the movements and rhythms of life for indigenous peoples. Anthropologists once assumed that hunting was the most important of these activities, but the gathering of wild fruits, honey, nuts, roots, grubs, and insects – a task performed exclusively by indigenous women – actually provides the largest part of the diet. The origin of the "hunting" myth was probably due to the fact that the mostly male Western anthropologists talked almost

BENEFICIAL TABOOS

The Shuar and Achuar people believe that deer, owls, and rabbits are the temporarily visible embodiments of the "true soul" of dead human beings, and therefore they do not hunt these animals.

The Siona-Secoya will never eat deer for similar reasons, and they prohibit the hunting of tree-sloths, black monkeys, opossums, and weasels. They also revere and fear the pink river dolphins, and never harm them.

The Quichua honor the jungle puma, a very rare feline, and would never shoot one. It is thanks to these beliefs that many of these creatures still flourish in Ecuador's jungles.

Oriente kill animals for food until those animals become scarce. Then they move on.

Yet the nomadic and semi-nomadic lifestyles of most indigenous Amazonians have prevented and continue to prevent the extermination of game animals upon which indigenous peoples depend. The horticultural groups have always placed an overwhelming social emphasis upon having small families with no more than two children. Population stability unlocks the door to ecological stability. Amazonian belief systems also encompass a number of iron-clad taboos against hunting and killing certain animals *(see panel, opposite)*.

smocks, called *cushmas*, which they dyed blue or red. The Quichuas adapted the forms of clothing their highland cousins wore. All of these peoples now usually wear trousers, shirts, and blouses, dresses, skirts, and shorts that are indistinguishable from those of other Ecuadorians.

Basket-weaving, a male craft, has survived a lot better than the production of clothes. Plastics simply do not perform as well as baskets made of natural materials in the tropics because they are much heavier, induce food to rot, and are not nearly so versatile. The normal carrying basket of the Amazon is a plaited, openwork cylinder, no more than a meter high, tightly woven and

Crafts of the Oriente

For all groups except the Huaorani (who wore nothing, though men would use string to tie their penises up by the foreskin), a major craft was clothes-making. Shuar men and Achuar women spun homegrown cotton, wove it into cloth and dyed it with vegetable dyes. The men wore wrap-around kilts, tied in place by bark string, and the women fastened their dresses over their right shoulders, using a belt around their waists. The Siona-Secoya and Cofan men wove ultra-lightweight knee-length cotton

---

LEFT: Cofan Indian woman collecting water being piped to the village of Dureno.
ABOVE: Cofan woman lighting a fire.

very sturdy. The finest baskets are woven by the Shuar, for holding personal ornaments and other finery; they are lined with smooth banana leaves, and have an attached cover.

The tourist market has almost completely transformed another craft, pottery, which has always been the domain of women. Quichua women make clay vessels for household use, as well as sacred vessels with ritual character. These vessels are meticulously executed, elaborate, and eggshell-thin, with geometric and zoomorphic shapes and motifs. Shuar women lavish intricate geometrical adornments on the jars used to boil and serve the hallucinogenic beverage *aya-huasca (see page 97)*. Tourist demand for Amazonian pottery has transformed its production into something resembling an assembly line, where duplicates are produced with patterns that have no significance. The income derived from the sale of ceramics is, relative to the overall monetary income of indigenous Amazonians, quite considerable, and has given women a degree of power over their lives in the midst of ongoing cultural transition.

Most fantastic of all Amazonian arts are the feather and beadwork crowns, necklaces, earrings, and other ornaments, which rely upon the plumage of magnificent birds like toucans, parrots, and hummingbirds. These stunningly beautiful works of art have always possessed enormous ritual and spiritual significance for Amazonian peoples, directly linked to their use in the *ayahuasca* ceremony *(see below)*. Today, tourist demand for such ornaments as souvenirs is encouraging indigenous Amazonians to kill the most colorful, and usually the most endangered, birds at an accelerated rate.

Amazonian shamans

It was in the realm of spiritual and mythical creativity that indigenous Amazonians made their greatest strides and their most momentous discoveries. Because the Amazonian storehouse of knowledge and wisdom has always been

DON'T EVEN THINK ABOUT IT

Don't buy anything made from the plumage of Amazonian birds.

Because the importation of products which cause the death of any endangered species is prohibited by the United States, Australia, and all of Western Europe, tourists who are irresponsible enough to attempt to take their "trinkets" home will inevitably have to surrender them at the customs office. This makes the death of these magnificent birds, and the devaluation of the traditions of Amazonian peoples, a tragic exercise in futility. The lower the demand for such souvenirs, the fewer birds will be killed.

transmitted orally, a great deal of the complexity has been lost. Indigenous spirituality has been mercilessly attacked by missionaries ever since the Spanish conquest. In recent years Protestant groups have worked to blot out the legacy of thousands of years, preventing the transmission of traditions from the old to the young. Nevertheless, the enduring center of that legacy, shamanism, survives among the six principal peoples, albeit by ever more slender threads.

Shamans are the individuals who preserve the oral histories, myths, legends, and other belief systems of their peoples. Among the Siona-Secoya, Quichua, and Cofan groups shamans are usually men, but female shamans are not unknown in the Shuar and Achuar cultures.

Many shamans devote their time to curing diseases through elaborate rituals. There are shamans who bewitch others, causing disease and misfortune to their enemies, or to the enemies of those who pay them to do so. Shamans enact the ceremonies of initiation, the rites of passage of young men and women into adulthood; and they train others to take on the role, passing on the knowledge and the rituals.

The tools they use vary. Quichua shamans own magical stones, which act as their familiars. The Shuar and Achuar shamans utilize magical darts called *tsentsak*, to bring about both healing and harm. But the most important tools

visions. This communion with their ancestral past and the supernatural is a continuous source of social and cultural cohesion for indigenous Amazonians, and has nothing in common with the often self-destructive use of drugs encountered in Western cultures.

The power of the family unit

In indigenous Amazonian society the most important organizational unit is the extended family. The rules of kinship define the individuals' rights of inheritance, whom they should marry, and where they should live.

The Huaorani, a society pared down to

they all employ are hallucinogenic substances extracted from jungle plants. The vine known as *ayahuasca*, Quichua for "vine of the soul," is the hallucinogen par excellence.

Using drum rhythms and other musical patterns, vocal incantations, the light of fires, and the colors provided by feather ornaments and body paint, the shamans guide those who have drunk potions derived from *ayahuasca* to see visions based on the symbolism and mythology of their cultures. The jaguar, anaconda, and harpy eagle recur over and over again in such

LEFT: Huaorani man gathers *curare* which contains a muscle-relaxant used to coat darts for hunting.
ABOVE: young Cofan *indígenas*.

essentials in its struggle to survive, have very loosely defined kinship rules that do not even insist on the authority of older people over younger. Cofan and Siona-Secoya men may only marry women allowed to them by a patrilineal system: couples live with the family of the man's father, or in a house built close to the father's home, and they inherit property and privileges from the man's father.

Shuar men initially live close to their wives' families, before moving to their own houses, but inherit through their fathers' line. Achuar men permanently reside near their wives' families, inherit through their mothers' lines, and marry women according to matrilineal relationships. The Quichua people possess a patrilineal system, but one which is broader and more complex, defining a kinship group called the *ayllu*, several of which compose a community.

Amazonian cultures have no single leader or chief. Instead, leadership has always been provided in crises by shamans and military men. While Quichua farmers did not wage wars or carry out raids as much as they suffered from them, the lives of all the other groups were defined by feuds, raids, and war. The Siona-Secoya, Cofan, and Huaorani raided to capture women and to avenge raids against them, but never for territory. For the Shuar and Achuar, warfare symbolized the spiritual quest for

power: by killing a designated enemy a man could gain the visionary magical soul called *arutam*, and possess the power to lead others.

The practice of severing an enemy's head, removing the skull, and shrinking the skin is a source of great notoriety for the Shuar and Achuar. As gruesome as this practice may seem and as perverse as it became in the early 1900s due to Westerners' fascination with it, the rituals associated with shrinking heads were an integral part of the shaman-leader complex that defined war and peace among these peoples. Today, far from shrinking heads, the Shuar and the Achuar have organized the most successful ethnic federation in the Amazon basin, a model for groups in Ecuador and other nations.

21st-century politics

Oil development over the past 40 years has changed the rainforest environment for ever. The indigenous Amazonians have no choice but to adapt and develop different strategies in order to survive.

The Federation of Shuar Centers fights for land rights and is involved in the protection of the environment in the southern region of the Ecuadorian Amazon. It has also published scores of books about Shuar and Achuar oral traditions, which will make them more accessible to future generations; and shamans now use their powers for health and community issues, rather than vengeful purposes.

For the Quichuas, organizational models are available from their highland cousins, who have become intensely political. The Quichua regional federations have helped to link indigenous Amazonians and the peoples of the highlands; as a result, an Amazonian and highlander confederation, CONAIE, has been formed at national level.

The Siona-Secoya community on the edge of the Cuyabeno Fauna Reserve has resisted oil development in its territory and worked with the Ministry of Environment in putting together a sustainable development plan for the reserve and buffer zones. This tribe is committed to maintaining its close relationship with and dependence on the rainforest.

Faced with the multinational oil companies and the subsequent influx of outsiders, a small number of the Cofan people, the tiniest of the groups, are developing their own survival mechanisms in the village of Zabalo. Meanwhile, working through CONAIE, the Huaorani have struggled to gain title to about 600,000 hectares (1½ million acres) of their former territory; theoretically, enough land to sustain a way of life that retains some elements of hunting and gathering. Although the Ecuadorian government maintains the right to exploit deposits of oil under some of these lands, much of the area near the Peruvian border was declared "untouchable" by an act of congress in 1999. The decree signed by President Palacio in 2007 creating a 809,000-hectare (2 million-acre) zone to the south of Yasuní National Park, goes someway to making up for the lack of protection from oil exploration. ❏

ABOVE: making a canoe in the Oriente.

The Last Hidden Tribes

Despite legislative protection, the outlook for Ecuador's few isolated Amazon tribes is bleak, due to the onslaught of the modern world.

At most, there are just 400 tribes believed to be living in Ecuador's northeast Amazon refusing contact with mainstream civilization. Most of the evidence known of these rainforest warriors still clinging to their Stone Age way of life stems from violent encounters. In 1987, as oil companies encroached on land inhabited by the Tagaeri, a group of Huaorani, Coca's Spanish-born bishop Alejandro Labaka sought to contact them in a last-ditch pitch for their survival. He and Inés Arango, a Colombian nun, gave their lives in the attempt as they were found dead. The ensuing media exposure, however, kept the oil industry at bay, as Labaka had hoped.

Nevertheless, conflicts continue. Many Huaorani today work for oil companies or in tourism; some also work with the loggers. Through 2008, poachers of rare rainforest woods were found dead, fatally wounded by the Huaorani's heavy spears. Encouraged by loggers and poachers, in March 2003 a group of Huaorani sought to avenge a Tagaeri "kidnapping" by killing up to 30 forest dwellers, including women and children, who were burned to death inside a large dwelling. But the dead were members of the previously unknown Taromenani who had moved into the jungle building abandoned by the Tagaeri. The judicial authorities did almost nothing to investigate the Taromenani killing.

Members of the two tribes are so few that they fit inside just a few homesteads, each of which can house some 60 people. While these can be widely dispersed amid the jungle, pressure from the 21st century is great from inside Ecuador and from across the border in Peru.

Protective measures

Aware of the race against the clock to save the two tribes, the Correa government has set up half a dozen control posts staffed with police and scientists to stop access to the "intangible zone" established for their protection in and around the southern part of the Yasuní National Park. The government also says it is doing more to control

RIGHT: gringo kayaker encounters a Quichua Indian boy.

the boom in the smuggling of hardwoods to the US and Colombia.

Most oil companies demand proof of vaccination and special permits from visitors in an attempt to protect the tribes from the common diseases that eradicated so many other natives since the arrival of the first Europeans. Contact with anyone from tourists to other tribes could wipe them out in one devastating epidemic. To the exasperation of the government, however, the "intangible zone" means nothing to the Tagaeri and Taromenani as they roam to hunt, and live in such proximity to the last outposts of mainstream society that they can steal machetes and axes from nearby tourist lodges and

illegal logging camps. Despite their recent "discovery," the modern world has already influenced the Taromenani, who use plastic string and bottle caps to decorate their spears and necklaces.

Environmentalists say that current steps to protect them are too little too late. Some advocate a more aggressive, pre-emptive attempt to vaccinate them against disease before a plague can break out. This, however, would end their isolation, exposing them to the cultural dislocation that has affected other peoples, particularly the Cofan and Huaorani, who also first encountered Western society only a few decades ago. Such is the pressure from the greedy outside world that their traditional way of life will almost certainly end in the foreseeable future, even if they are to survive. ❏

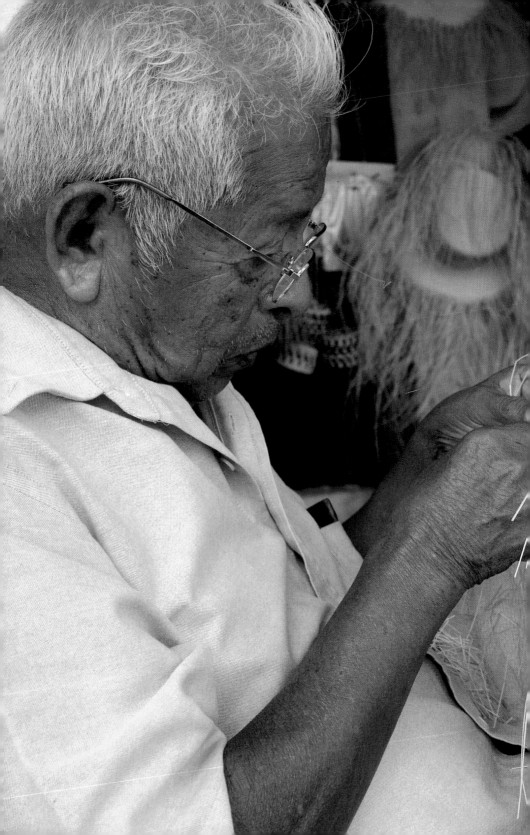

ARTESANÍAS

The ancient crafts traditions of the indigenous peoples of Ecuador have become much sought after by Western visitors

There are no words in the indigenous languages of Ecuador for art, nor is there a distinction between fine arts and crafts. Seduced by their beauty, Westerners have included many traditional Ecuadorian *artesanías* in their own category of fine art, particularly textiles, ceramics, and jewelry. If you have the time, there's something particularly satisfying about buying from the artisans themselves or shopping in the market, but products from throughout the country make their way into Quito and to the famous market in Otavalo.

Woven textiles

Four or five thousand years ago, some genius in the northern Andes invented the stick loom, which is still in use and generally called the backstrap loom (local names include *awana*, *macana*, and *telar*). This loom, sophisticated in concept and simple in form, is made of sticks and poles, with one end fastened to a stationary object and the other to the weaver's back.

When the Incas made a census of their empire they counted humans first, cameloids (llamas and alpacas) second, and textiles third, before precious metals, gemstones, ceramics, or food. The Spanish were amazed by their superb hand-woven cloth made of cotton, and cameloid wool.

Ecuador's damper climate has not been as conducive as Peru's to the preservation of organic materials, but the few pre-Hispanic textile fragments that exist suggest a tradition as venerable and as exquisite as that of Peru. The Spanish introduced the treadle loom, spinning wheel,

sheep, and silk; much later came electric looms and synthetic fibers. But an amazing number of weavers still use the stick loom. Even in Otavalo, where most weaving is done on the treadle loom, some ponchos and virtually all belts are made on the backstrap loom. In Saraguro, blankets (*cobijas*), grain sacks (*costales*), and most items of traditional dress are hand-spun on simple spindles of the kind you see throughout the Sierra, and hand-woven on the stick loom. These pieces are difficult to come by, but some are sold in Quito stores. In Ecuador, the majority of weavers are men, although many women also weave.

Azuay is famous for its *ikat* textiles. *Ikat* (*amarrado* or *watado*) is a dyeing rather than

---

PRECEDING PAGES: traditional Ecuadorian rugs; making panama hats in Montecristi. **LEFT:** hand-woven blankets. **RIGHT:** stallholder in Otavalo market.

weaving technique, where the warp threads are tied and dyed *before* the piece is woven. Pre-Hispanic *ikat* fragments have been found. The best-known *ikat* textiles are *paños*, indigo-dyed cotton shawls with elaborate macramé fringes; a newer style is black and red with a macraméd, embroidered fringe. It takes only hours to wrap the design, dye and weave the shawl, but up to three months to knot the fringe. *Paños* were traditionally worn by indigenous women, but young women no longer wear them, so fine ones are becoming rare. If you want to see the older women in their finery, proud as queens, visit the Sunday market at Gualaceo.

The skilled dyers and weavers now make *ikat* woolen belts, scarves, and shawls without fringes, usually dyed black or brown over red, blue, green or purple. Some of these shawls are made into high-fashion clothing, available in Quito.

Ikat carrying-cloths called *macanas* are made around Salcedo and in Chimborazo province. The Salcedo *macanas* are of deep indigo like the Cuenca *paños*, but the designs are coarser and they have a short fringe. *Macanas* are used throughout the Sierra as carrying-cloths, to haul everything from a baby to a load of firewood.

Ikat ponchos are made and worn in the Sierra from Cañar to Natabuela, north of Otavalo. The poncho is a post-conquest garment, an adaptation of the Inca tunic. Various kinds of plain

> When the Incas conducted a census they rated textiles more highly than food, precious metals, or gemstones. To measure inventories, their accounting system used multicolored and knotted wool strings, or quipus.

ponchos are woven for daily wear, while the *ikat* ones are reserved for weddings and fiestas. Especially beautiful *ikat* ponchos are made in Cañar, Chordeleg, Cacha Obraje (outside Riobamba), and Paniquindra. Like ponchos, *ikat* blankets are made in every highland province, but these are for daily (or nightly) use. A good one of hand-spun wool, woven in two sections and sewn together weighs 4.5kg (10lb).

Belts (*chumbis*) are woven on the backstrap loom. Double-faced belts with motifs ranging from Inca pots to farm animals are woven from hand-spun wool or commercial cotton thread in Cañar. These are among the finest belts made in Ecuador, rivaled only by those of Salasaca.

Salasaca belts are still made of hand-spun wool, and many are dyed with cochineal, a natural dye made from crushed female insects which live on the Opuntia cactus. Running a close race are a number of double- and single-faced belts with woven motifs made in Chimborazo and Bolívar provinces, followed by belts made in Otavalo and nearby Paniquindra.

Tapestries

In the late 1950s the Andean Mission embarked on a craft project that was a resounding success. Weavers from Salasaca and Otavalo were taught how to make tapestries (*tapices*) on the treadle loom. This technique, in which the weft threads interlock, gives tapestries a painterly quality. Today the stores around the main plaza in Salasaca and half the Otavalo market are filled with tapestries, including wall hangings, handbags (*bolsas*), and pillowcases (*cojines*).

Hand-knit clothing

While Ecuadorian women have been knitting since the colonial era, a Peace Corps project in the 1960s got the modern industry off the ground. Today sweaters (*chompas*), vests (*chalecos*), and hats (*gorros*) of hand-spun wool are made in Cuenca and in the northern towns of Ibarra, Mira, San Gabriel, San Isidro, and Atuntaqui. The highest-quality ones are usually sold in Quito or abroad, although some fine ones do show up in the Otavalo market. Wherever you buy a sweater, try it on. The knitter's idea of size may not necessarily be the same as yours.

Embroidery

If you look carefully in the Otavalo market you will see women from an ethnic group other than the Otavaleños, wearing pleated skirts and blouses with extremely fine, intricate embroidery on the bodice and sleeves. The women come from communities on the south and eastern sides of Imbabura Mountain, such as Zuleta, La Esperanza, San Isidro de Cajas, and Rinconada. You can buy these blouses in the Otavalo and

264). In the 1960s the Peace Corps introduced other items such as Nativity sets and Christmas tree ornaments to help tide the *paja* weavers over hard times in the hat industry.

Shigra means sack in Quichua. *Shigras* are made of *cabuya* (agave) fiber in the central Sierra provinces of Cotopaxi, Tungurahua, and Chimborazo. These bags, made by hand with a buttonhole stitch, are found nowhere else in the Andes. Tied over the shoulders, they serve as a carry-all for *indígena* men and women. While originally meant for local use, *shigras* found ready acceptance in the tourist and ethnic arts markets, and the best of them are true collec-

Ibarra markets. In addition, the women embroider a range of more commercial items, such as dresses, napkins, towels, and tablecloths.

Hats, baskets, and bags

Contrary to popular belief, Panama hats aren't made in Panama; they're made in southern Ecuador in and around Cuenca and in Montecristi on the coast, where they're called *sombreros de paja toquilla* after the palm fiber from which they are woven. They have been made here for more than a century, with the industry going through cycles of boom and bust (*see Panama Hats feature, page*

tors' items. Baskets (*canastas*) made from various plants including cane and *totora* reeds are made throughout Ecuador and found in every market. Giant ones with lids come from Cuenca, smaller ones from around Latacunga, and fine two-color baskets from the Oriente.

Leatherwork

Cotacachi is the main center for wallets, purses, knapsacks, and clothes made from leather (*cuero*). The main street of the town is lined with shops. Leather items can also be found in the Otavalo market and in many Quito shops. The leatherwork is usually good, but be sure to check the quality of zippers and clasps before you make a purchase.

LEFT: colorful woven bags in Guamote's Thursday market. **ABOVE:** *Otavaleña* embroidering by machine.

Jewelry

One look at the pre-Hispanic gold, silver, and platinum objects in the Museo del Banco Central in Quito and you know the ancient Ecuadorians were master metalworkers. In indigenous communities jewelers make silver, nickel, and brass shawl pins (*tupus*), with the finest coming from Saraguro. Contemporary gold and silver filigree jewelry is a specialty of Chordeleg, where jewelry stores (*joyerías*) line the road into town and the main plaza. The workmanship is excellent and the prices are reasonable. In pre-Hispanic times the Ecuadorian coastline was the source of the prized, coral-colored spondy-

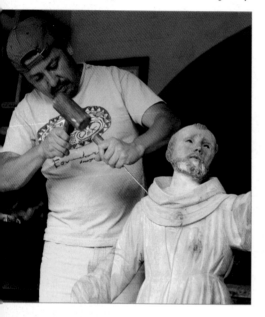

lus shell, traded throughout the Andes. Beads are still an essential part of women's traditional dress. The preference for red or coral-colored beads goes back to the days when spondylus was queen.

Ceramics

The most beautiful ceramics in Ecuador – perhaps in the entire upper Amazon – are made by the Canelos Quichua *indígenas*, or Sacha Runa (jungle people), who live between the Napo and Pastaza rivers in the Oriente. Women make the bowls and pots for household and ceremonial use, by hand-coiling. The finest pieces are eggshell-thin, with painted designs representing various aspects of their life and mythology.

Some beautiful ceramics are now also made for the ethnic arts market.

There are several ceramic factories with showrooms in Cuenca. The Cuenca *barrio* of Corazón de Jesús, and the towns of San Miguel and Chordeleg, are traditional producers of pottery, which is sold at the Cuenca market. These potters use the imported wheel, and in San Miguel and Chordeleg you can see their wares drying in the shade outside their houses. The Sierra around Latacunga and Saquisilí is another pottery center, where enormous Inca-style amphoras (*tinajas* or *ollas*) for making *chicha* are produced in the town of Tejar. Pujilí, noted for its Corpus Christi celebration, also has potters who make figurines of birds, animals, and fiesta scenes.

Woodcarving

There are two main centers of woodcarving: the Canelos Quichua region in the Amazon and San Antonio de Ibarra north of Otavalo. The former's woodcarvings of tropical birds and animals are designed expressly for the ethnic arts market. Most of the carvings are made from balsawood, painted, and lacquered.

Woodcarvings in San Antonio de Ibarra run the gamut from elaborate furniture to Nativity sets, boxes, wall plaques, and statues of the Virgin, saints, and beggars. Some are kitsch, but there are some treasures, and you can watch the carvers at work in the rear of their shops.

> Balsa trees thrive in the tropical Andean foothills. In Ecuador, Canelos Quichua craftsmen in the Oriente developed a carving industry producing brightly painted balsawood sculptures of tropical birds, fish, and other animals.

Bread figures

The productions of brightly dyed dough figures of humans and animals for sale and for export is a main industry in the community of Calderón at the northeast end of Quito. They are placed on graves as offerings to the dead on the feasts of All Saints (Todos Santos) and the Day of the Dead (Día de Difuntos) on November 1 and 2 respectively. ❑

ABOVE: carving a religious statue, San Antonio.
RIGHT: Otavalo woman wearing typical jewelry.

A NATION OF PAINTERS

Quito has a thriving artistic scene that may yet rival
the accomplishments of its 16th-century precursor,
though today, the subject matter is often Ecuador's
indigenous population rather than Christian motifs

Until early in the 20th century, art in Ecuador was mainly associated with the colonial School of Quito (*see page 165*), but
the first three decades of the 1900s saw the rise
of a school called *indígenismo* (indigenism).

As Ecuadorian artists have not been isolated
from currents in the international art world and
many of them have studied or traveled in Europe
and North America, the unifying factor of the
indigenist school has not been the style of painting, which ranges from Realist to Impressionist,
Cubist, and Surrealist, but the subject matter;
Ecuador's exploited indigenous population.

Inspired by a Sierra life

Eduardo Kingman is perhaps the prototypi-
cal indigenist. From the 1930s until his death
in 1998 he painted murals and canvases, and
illustrated books exploring social themes and
the use of color. *Juguetería* (Toy Store), an oil
painted in 1985, shows the back of a bare-
foot *indígena* girl peering into the window of
a brightly lit toy shop. The toys are rendered
in cheerful primary colors, while the girl out-

*Camilo Egas went through a Daliesque period
before he went on to become the most
indigenist of the Ecuadorian painters.*

side in the shadows, the picture of longing, is
painted in somber burgundy, black, and blue.

Such paintings as *Mujeres con Santo* (Women
with Saint), *El Maizal* (The Maize-Grower)

and *La Sed* (Thirst) are characteristic of Kingman's work: the indigenist subject matter and
highly stylized, semi-abstract human figures
with heavy facial features and huge, distorted
hands. These paintings convey powerful images
of oppression, sorrow, and suffering.

Camilo Egas, who died in 1961, lived in France
for long periods of time and moved through a
range of styles, from Surrealist to Realist, and
abstract Expressionist. In *Indios* (Indians),
painted in the 1950s, three longhaired men lean
diagonally into the picture, using ropes to haul
an unseen burden. The painting is executed in
a few bright, clear colors: blue sky, black hair,
brown skin, red, white, and yellow clothing.

LEFT: Oswaldo Guayasamín, Ecuador's most famous
painter. **ABOVE:** detail of painting by Jaime Romero.

Neither the bodies nor the features of the men are abstract or distorted, and the impression conveyed is one of dignity and strength rather than misery. He also produced *El Indio Mariano*, a beautiful profile portrait in the same idiom.

Manuel Rendón was a prolific painter who produced a remarkably diverse body of work. Rendón spent his youth in Paris, where his father was the Ecuadorian ambassador, and he was greatly influenced by the modern art movement in France. Rendón is considered an indigenist artist, but he is equally well known for his Cubist-style paintings of men and women in the 1920s and for a series on the *Sagrada Familia*

gnarled hands have become parodies of the genre. Make up your own mind by visiting the Museo Guayasamín in Quito *(see panel opposite)*.

Anyone familiar with the graphic paintings and statues of Christ, agonized and bleeding, in Spanish colonial churches can trace this theme of suffering in Guayasamín's work, although his figures are secular rather than religious.

One of his early works, the 1942 painting *Los Trabajadores* (The Workers) is realistic in a manner similar to that of the Mexican muralist José Clemente Orozco. The similarity is more than coincidental, as Guayasamín worked with Orozco in Mexico. Guayasamín went on

(Holy Family) in the 1940s. He also painted pointillistic figurative and abstract works, and did many sketches in pencil and pen and ink.

Ecuadorian maestro

Oswaldo Guayasamín, who died in 1999, is the best known of the generation of artists who came of age in the 1930s and 1940s. His father was an *indígena*, and Guayasamín consistently and proudly emphasized his indigenous heritage. Few people are neutral about Guayasamín's work, with its message of social protest. His admirers see him as a gifted artistic visionary and social critic, while his detractors see him as a third-rate Picasso imitator whose innumerable paintings of *indígenas* with coarse features and

to develop a style influenced by Cubism, with its chopped-up and oddly reassembled images, notably in his series of monumental paintings *La Edad de la Ira* (The Age of Anger), *Los Torturados* (The Tortured), and *Cabezas* (Heads).

In 1988 Guayasamín continued to make visual political statements with his enormous mural in the meeting hall of the Ecuadorian Congress in Quito, in which 23 panels convey episodes from Ecuador's history; Guayasamín produced anything but a romanticized picture. Nineteen of the panels are in color, four are in black and white. The latter depict the first Ecuadorian president to enslave the *indígenas*, Ecuador's civilian and military dictators, and a skeletal face wearing a Nazi helmet emblazoned with the letters "CIA."

While Ecuadorians took the mural in their stride, the United States was outraged. The US ambassador called for the letters to be painted out and various US congressmen discussed cutting off economic aid to Ecuador. Guayasamín regarded this as exactly the kind of bullying that he was protesting against, and the panel has remained unchanged.

Perhaps what will become his most famous work was only finished after his death at the insistence of his family. *La Capilla del Hombre*, in the Bellavista neighborhood of Quito, is rapidly becoming known as his masterpiece. The stone temple resembles an ancient pre-Columbian one on the outside, but inside it is very modern, with fine woodwork and architectural design. A mural depicts the Latin American man from pre-Columbian times to the present. An eternal flame marks the altar on the lower level, which burns for peace and human rights. The minimalist chapel shows the dreams, fears, anguish, inspirations, and love of this great artist.

An artistic immigrant

Olga Fisch arrived in the country more than half a century ago as a refugee fleeing from Hitler, bringing with her a background in the visual arts. Fisch was among the first to recognize the value of Ecuadorian *artesanías* as art, and the design potential of traditional motifs. A talented painter, Fisch is best known for her work in textile design, especially rugs and tapestries, based on her interpretations of pottery, embroidery and weaving motifs. She also designed clothing and jewelry, available at her two stores in Quito (*see Travel Tips, page 345, for details*).

Modern-day artists

The younger generation of painters has moved away from *indigenismo* to more personal, idiosyncratic themes and subject matter. In the 1970s Ramiro Jácome was part of the neo-Figurative movement, a return to works with recognizable figures. In the early 1980s he changed his style, painting a series of abstract oils, characterized by deep, rich colors. Later in the 1980s he returned to figurative works. In *Barrio* (Neighborhood), painted in 1989, three semi-abstract people are delineated by swift, black brushstrokes. They lean against storefronts in what looks like a seedy downtown neighborhood, and the use of yellows and reds contributes to a carnival-like atmosphere. Jácome's 1990 oil *A la Cola* (To the End of the Line) depicts a slashing rainstorm in which three bright-yellow taxis outlined in black divide the canvas diagonally. They are balanced by a mass of frantic people in the upper left, rendered in swirling lines of black and white. The painting effectively conveys the feeling of desperation familiar to anyone who has ever tried to catch a taxi in Quito in the rain. ❑

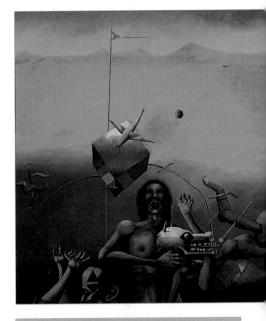

WHERE TO SEE IT

The Casa de la Cultura on Avenidas Patria and 12 de Octubre in Quito has a good collection of modern art, with 20th-century sculptures on the lawn outside. The Museo y Taller Guayasamín, at Calle Bosmediano 543, is devoted solely to Guayasamín's work. La Capilla del Hombre is five blocks up from the Museo Guayasamín at Lorenzo Chávez EA18-143 and Mariano Calvache. The Centro Cultural Metropolitano, at García Moreno and Espejo, and the Museo de Arte Contemporánea, at Luis Dávila y Venezuela in the San Juan neighborhood, have exhibitions. Ecuador's largest international art exposition is the Cuenca Bienal, held in that city late in odd-numbered years.

LEFT: an example of the indigenist painting style, by Eduardo Kingman. **ABOVE:** detail of a canvas by Washington Iza.

OUTDOOR ADVENTURES

Climbing, trekking, rafting, or biking; the astonishing variety of terrain in Ecuador is a big attraction for many sports enthusiasts

Outdoor enthusiasts have discovered that Ecuador's diverse topography provides an ideal environment for "adventure travel." The country's small size makes getting around easy: nothing is too far away from anything else, and there are roads to almost everywhere.

Yet, for its size, Ecuador has an amazing assortment of terrain, while the climate is favorable for almost year-round excursions. Except for February and March, when it seems to be raining everywhere, good weather can be found in one region or another throughout the year.

Trekking in the Sierra

Trekking is one of the most popular adventure activities. A number of national parks offer uninhabited areas for days of wandering, while the populated highlands of the Sierra are dotted with small villages whose inhabitants usually offer a welcome to backpacking gringos.

One of the most popular treks in Ecuador is the easy three-day hike to the ruins of Ingapirca,

Buy topographical maps at the Military Geographical Institute (IGM) in Quito (see page 351). Its website (www.geoportaligm.gov.ec) has many maps, although their quality is inferior to those on paper.

the finest example of Inca stonework in the country. The hike begins in the charming village of Achupallas, north of Cuenca, 15km (9

miles) off the Pan-American Highway. A dirt track eventually gives way to a cobbled footpath leading to a pass. You have to squeeze through a small cave to get to the other side. After a brief descent, the trail starts to climb again and traverses a mountain slope above the green valley of the Río Cadrul. An excellent site for the first night's camp is beside the sparkling waters of the high mountain lake Laguna Las Tres Cruces (Lake of the Three Crosses).

After about a half-day walk on the second day – crossing rocky ridges and skirting boggy valleys – the trail drops below the peak of Quilloloma. The remains of the old Inca road appear in the valley below. There is an excellent

PRECEDING PAGES: climbing Pichincha volcano near Quito. **LEFT:** a climber at the summit of Mount Chimborazo. **RIGHT:** view from Cotopaxi.

place to camp near Laguna Culebrillas and some minor Inca ruins, aptly named Paredones ("ruined walls") because of the surviving crude stonework. A final three- to four-hour hike on the third day follows the grassy Inca road to the ruins of Ingapirca (*see pages 213–14*).

National parks

Several national parks within the highland region of Ecuador are especially popular with trekkers because of the ease of accessibility, established trail systems, and marvelous scenery. In most cases, day hikes supplant longer treks for those who prefer to see the sights with a

lighter load. Parks can be visited at any time of year, but facilities within them are at a minimum, if they exist at all. A small park entrance fee is usually charged.

Cotopaxi National Park not only attracts climbers who come to scale the Cotopaxi volcano, but also its wide open *páramo*, which is ideal for cross-country treks. The lower slopes (called the Arenal – a word that comes from the Spanish *arena* meaning sand) are an interesting landscape of volcanic sand and boulders from an eruption and associated mud flows in the late 19th century. The Trek of the Condor is a three- to four-day hike from the village of Papallacta to the base of Cotopaxi. It passes several mountain lakes harboring Andean teal,

Andean lapwing, *caricari*, and wild horses. The glaciers off Antisana loom over the *páramo*, and condors can sometimes be seen soaring around Sincholagua.

Parque Nacional El Cajas lies about 32km (20 miles) west of Cuenca. Within its 30,000 hectares (74,000 acres) there is a huge variety of landscapes, ranging from granite rock outcrops to barely penetrable cloud forests, where mountain toucans and tropical woodpeckers make their home. With the exception of day-hike trails around the ranger station, most of the area is totally without marked trails, yet a cross-country trek of several days is quite feasible. The region is dotted with some 250 lakes of various sizes and colors, and fishing for trout is encouraged.

Parque Nacional Podocarpus, south of Loja, is very popular with hikers. The area is largely cloud forest and is home to the reticent spectacled bear, the flamboyant Andean cock-of-the-rock, and the mountain tanager. A trail system includes several day hikes from the park headquarters, and there are various options for overnight camping. Conservation group Arcoiris, www.arcoiris.org.ec offers further information.

Mountaineering

The Andean mountain range in Ecuador comprises one of the largest concentrations of volcanoes in the world. It is possible to gain valuable high-altitude experience on moderate routes that do not require technical ice-climbing skill. With proper acclimatization, most peaks can be conquered over a weekend. Huts, or *refugios*, have been constructed on many of the higher and more popular climbs. Some of the huts are equipped with bunks (bring a sleeping bag), a communal kitchen with gas stove, and the services of a hut guardian who knows the present conditions and route descriptions. Bringing your own stove during peak climbing periods is a good idea, as the huts can get crowded and the communal kitchen overused. Water is available at the *refugios*, but must be treated with purification tablets or boiled before drinking.

Good climbing weather is possible almost year-round, but normally the best months are June through September and during a short dry spell in December and January. Being a tropical mountain range at the equator, the Ecuadorian Andes generate unusual weather conditions. One part of the cordillera may be inundated with rain, while the next section will have clear skies and perfect conditions. This, at least, makes for plenty of options.

Proper equipment is essential for safe climbing, regardless of how straightforward most routes may appear. Any climbs which involve ice or glacier travel are considered to be technical and require special equipment and knowledge of its use. Crampons, an ice axe, and rope are necessary, along with the warm clothing demanded by high-altitude mountain conditions.

A rucksack with plenty of water, food, and extra-warm clothing is vital for a sum-

best way to accustom your system to altitude is to stay in a relatively high city or town, and take a few day hikes to higher elevations. Quito is a good choice, and there are several strenuous hikes that can help the climber get in shape. Pasachoa makes an ideal warm-up hike as far as the rock face at 4,100 meters (13,400ft), and on a clear day gives you fabulous views over the Valley of the Volcanoes.

Easier climbs

Climbers recently arrived have several options for warm-up peaks. The most popular was Tungurahua until it erupted in 1999. Now Iliniza

mit attempt. Flag markers, or wands, are used during the ascent for route-finding, as cloudy conditions will often obscure the descent. In addition, a good headlamp with spare batteries is essential, since all climbing begins in the early hours of the morning. All mountaineering gear can be hired in Quito, but, as with the trekking equipment, quality can vary.

Many climbs are so short that the need for proper acclimatization is often underestimated, but with major peaks above 5,700 meters (18,000ft), it should not be overlooked. The

LEFT: climbers descending Mount Cotopaxi at dawn.
ABOVE: aerial view of Cayambe volcano to the north of Quito.

YOU GET WHAT YOU PAY FOR

Mountain guides are available for inexperienced climbers, but caution in selecting the proper guide is strongly recommended. There are people who claim to be guides when they do not have the appropriate experience, and the result is potentially dangerous. A decent guide charges a decent price, and it is not something that you should economize on.

It is best to go with an adventure outfitter or agency which specializes in mountain excursions, or you could hire a guide recommended by one of the climbing shops or the South American Explorers Club in Quito (see page 123 for more details).

Norte, Corazón, Atacazo, and Imbabura are where climbers go to get acclimatized. Iliniza Norte is a rocky 5,126-meter (6,800ft) peak about 55km (34 miles) southwest of Quito, which can be scaled in two days, and the climb is straightforward when the going is dry. A truck can be hired in Machachi or El Chaupi to get up to the parking area called La Virgen, named after a blue statue of the Virgin Mary. There is a three- to four-hour hike to the refuge. Climbers first follow a rutted road onto an exposed ridge, then up a sandy slope to the saddle where the refuge sits between the two Iliniza peaks. The refuge is basic, but has a stove and bunks.

bers of climbers set out at the same time, and the flickering light from their headlamps is all that is visible as they ascend through the darkness.

Cayambe is the most difficult of the three peaks, but also perhaps the most beautiful, with its rugged glacial terrain and views of the Oriente rainforest.

Mount Cotopaxi has gentle, curving snow slopes and the massive rock wall of Yanasacha just below the summit. It's a pleasurable ascent as the dawn rays of the sun set the whole glacier sparkling. The summit crater seems perfectly formed against the deep blue Andean sky.

The next morning, around sunrise, climbers head up the rocky ridge to a cliff. There is a traverse named Paso de la Muerte (Death Pass), which is as difficult as it sounds, and a final scramble on loose rock to the summit.

Mountain highs

For climbers with greater technical experience, the volcanoes of Cayambe, at 5,790 meters (almost 19,000ft), Cotopaxi (5,900 meters/19,340ft), and Chimborazo (6,310 meters/20,700ft), are the main attractions. At weekends during the peak season, the *refugios* are packed with climbers preparing for the rigors of the climb ahead.

Start the climb at around midnight for a round trip of about 10 hours. Often large num-

Chimborazo holds the attraction of being Ecuador's highest peak, and, because of the equatorial bulge, it is the highest spot on earth, as measured from the center of the planet. After several hours of negotiating one steep slope after another, the process becomes something of a slog, and one begins to wonder if the summit will ever appear. In the end, the persistent achieve their goal, and the final summit views are well worth the effort.

White-water rafting

The attraction of running untamed rivers draws world-class rafters and kayakers to Ecuador. Those with little or no experience can also safely enjoy the thrill of white water with the growing number of travel adventure companies operating out of Quito, Tena, and Baños.

Many of Ecuador's rivers can be run year-round, while some of the more technically difficult ones are possible only during certain seasons. The most accessible and commonly run ones are the Río Toachi and the Río Blanco, both two to three hours from Quito. These rivers traverse the Western Cordillera, passing through forested canyons interspersed with small farming villages. The best time to go is from February to May.

A popular Class III rafting trip, suitable for both beginners and experienced rafters, is along the upper Río Napo. It starts near Tena and is a fun trip through tropical rainforest descending the upper slopes of the Amazon basin and passing several indigenous Quichua communities. The trip is possible all year round, but the best months to do it are between March and October.

For the experienced rafter and kayaker Ecuador has many challenging Class IV and V rivers. One of the most exciting is the Río Misahuallí, but beware of the Casanova Falls. The river can be run safely only from October to March in the low-water season when, after a set of Class IV rapids, rafters must be able to stop themselves before the falls.

It is a beautiful trip through virgin rainforest; parrots, oropendulas, and other tropical birds abound. The combination of spectacular natural scenery and a strong feeling of isolation makes the adventure all the more exciting. Trips down the Río Misahuallí are organized out of Tena.

Horseback riding

Horseback riding across the lush valleys and hills of the Sierra has become a popular leisure activity throughout Ecuador. Several agencies offer organized trips out of Otavalo, Baños, and Cuenca (see Travel Tips, pages 353–4). Ride Andes offers a wide range of trips, including one-day rides around Quito as well as hacienda tours, cattle round-ups, and volcano treks. Longer trips can be arranged into the Podocarpus Reserve in the very south of Ecuador from the village of Vilcabamba. Make sure the agency knows what your experience is, particularly if you are a beginner.

LEFT: horses carrying trekking equipment.
ABOVE: cycling in Quito's Parque Metropolitano.

Mountain biking

The best way to get off the beaten track is on a mountain bike exploring the extensive dirt and cobbled roads that pass through villages rarely visited by tourists. The high elevation, hilly terrain, and poor road conditions are challenging, but the views and the colorful local communities make cycling well worth the effort.

If you stay off the main paved roads such as the Pan-American Highway – the Ecuadorians are known for their unsafe driving – the unpaved routes selected from a good topographical map will usually offer solitude and pleasant surprises.

A good place to get acclimatized to the elevation is the market town of Otavalo, from where day trips can be made to the surrounding small villages known for their artesanías. Several outfitters in town will rent you bikes for the day and give advice about some good routes to follow. A more ambitious ride takes you 600 meters (2,000ft) up a paved road to the Laguna de Cuicocha, a spectacular collapsed volcanic caldera now filled with water. A labyrinth of unpaved roads leads back to Otavalo.

A popular day trip is a mostly downhill ride from Baños, where bikes of dubious quality can be rented, to the jungle town of Puyo. You follow the cliff-hugging road along the gorge of the Río Pastaza, passing several waterfalls. In Río Verde town, bikes may be left with a local shopkeeper while you visit local waterfalls. Buses pass at half-hourly intervals: put your bike on top of the bus and avoid the long climb back to Baños.

A popular three- to five-day ride takes you past the volcanic crater lake of Laguna de

> *Baños is the place to go for extreme sports. Try rafting, canyoning, or even puenting – bungee-jumping from bridges. There are six sets of hot pools to soak tired muscles, as well as some luxury spas.*

Quilotoa. A long climb (or bus ride) from the Pan-American Highway to the indigenous village of Zumbahua is rewarded by views of a volcanic landscape decorated by wheat fields. A dirt track leads to the lake. The next day, after a cold night on the crater rim, you wind along the edge of a deeply eroded pumice plain to the town of Siglos, where a bus can be taken back to Quito.

Paragliding

The topography of Ecuador is well suited for paragliding. One popular launch site is at the refuge (4,200 meters/13,800ft) on Mount Cotopaxi, where you can ride thermals to the top of the highest volcano in the world. The best time of year to fly is December. Equally exciting is a flight from La Crucita on the coast, catching winds off the ocean, and following a ridgeline nearly 10km (6 miles) long, staying airborne for three to five hours. Some enthusiasts take off from the slopes of Mount Pichincha and soar over the city of Quito. The best times to fly are during August and September. There is a paragliding school with an excellent safety record (*see Travel Tips, page 347*).

Surfing

Ecuador has much to offer as a surfing destination thanks to the Pacific storms which send waves directly towards its coast. In 2004, the country hosted the World Surfing Championships, in which more than 27 countries participated. Kite-surfing has also become established.

Montañita, in Guayas province, is Ecuador's surfing mecca and a popular backpacker hangout. In the north, Mompiche (Esmeraldas province) is renowned for its north break and 300-meter (985ft) ride. South breaks can be caught from June to October, while the north-facing breaks are better from December to April.

The Galápagos Islands are another well-known surf spot. On San Cristóbal the waves are best from November to March, while Santa Cruz is best between April and August.

Scuba-diving

Ecuador is home to some of the world's best diving sites. In the Parque Nacional Machalilla, the coral is in good condition here and attracts porcupinefish, parrotfish, and broomtail groupers, as well as eels, rays, starfish, sea cucumbers, and green turtles. The waters of the park are best explored from June to September, as the drop in water temperature allows for greater visibility. Humpback whales can be seen around the Isla de la Plata at this time when they come to mate and give birth.

Diving in the Galápagos Islands is an unforgettable experience. The reefs around Wolf and Darwin islands are home to dolphins, marine turtles, hammerhead and whale sharks, and moray eels, while schools of tropical fish can be seen at the Devil's Crown on Floreana. At Estrada Point on Santa Cruz, it is possible to see marine iguanas, sea lions, white-fin reef sharks, and at the nearby Caamaño islet pods of friendly sea lions. ❏

ABOVE: catching the waves at Montañita.

South American Explorers

Finding the right tour in Quito can be bewildering, with an overwhelming amount of travel offers. The South American Explorers will help you make an informed choice.

The Quito Clubhouse of the South American Explorers (SAE) is a valuable information center for travelers, outdoor enthusiasts, and members of scientific expeditions. If your ambition is to climb Cotopaxi, look at orchids, find a reliable boat to the Galápagos Islands, go white-water rafting, or simply to meet up with compatible hiking companions, then this is the place to come.

The club was founded by Don Montague and Linda Rojas in Lima, Peru, in 1977. Following its huge success, the Quito club was opened in 1989. New clubhouses were built in Cuzco, Peru, in 1999 and Buenos Aires, Argentina, in 2006. Montague still runs the US headquarters and edits a quarterly journal, *The South American Explorer*, an informative and topical magazine. Articles range from archeology, anthropology, and geology to mountaineering, indigenous peoples, and languages.

Everything you want to know

The non-profit club is funded by membership dues. Just $60 a year ($90 for a couple) allows you use of all its facilities in all of its clubhouses. You have access to an extensive library, equipment storage, book exchange, email, postal mail, phone message services, and bulletin boards. There are also first-hand trip reports written by members, which provide personal accounts of hotels, transport, guides, and agencies, plus advice and directions for a proposed trip, trek, climb, or any other activity; and there are plenty of useful books and maps for sale. The Quito club also holds bimonthly pub quizzes, yoga classes, and organizes visits to area prisons.

Besides the general services for its members, the club's mission is to support scientific field exploration and research in the social and natural sciences. Its aim is to awaken greater interest in and appreciation for wilderness conservation and wildlife protection. With this aim in mind it invites guest speakers to give presentations on their specialist subjects and encourages follow-up activities. Talks

range from the intellectual property rights in relation to medicinal plants, to climbing the active volcanoes of South America, or giving detailed information about wildlife in the Galápagos.

Over the years the club and its members have built up close ties with orphanages, environmental organizations, and community aid projects. If you are interested in volunteering for one of these projects, check out the club's Volunteers Resources Desk. You'll find a mine of information on the types of opportunities available, how to get in touch, and a realistic idea of what the projects involve.

If you join the SAE before you head to Ecuador you will have the advantage of being able to ask for

specialist advice on planning your trip. For a small fee to cover the cost of photocopies and postage, the staff at the Ithaca headquarters will recommend, select, and mail trip reports to members. The club also has its own catalog, offering books, maps, CDs, language tapes, and handicrafts, with discounts for members.

Before you go, contact SAE headquarters in the US at 126 Indian Creek Road, Ithaca, NY 14850, tel: 607-277 0488, fax: 607-277 6122 or visit www.saexplorers.org. The Quito Clubhouse (Jorge Washington 311 and Leónidas Plaza, Mon–Fri 9.30am–5pm, Sat 9.30am–noon), is located in Quito's Mariscal district. The mailing address is Apartado 17-21-431, Eloy Alfaro, Quito; or email quitoclub@saexplorers.org. ❑

ABOVE: climbers descending Cotopaxi.

FOOD

There's no escaping bananas. But Ecuador's topography has led to the development of some very distinctive dishes in different regions

There is no single Ecuadorian cuisine, but several ones that correspond to Ecuador's geographical regions: Costa, Sierra, and Oriente. And what you will find in good restaurants is quite different from what most people eat in rural areas and what you will find in market booths and small cafés throughout the country.

Bananas, however, are everywhere. Several varieties are grown on the coast and in the Oriente, from tiny finger bananas *(oritas)* to large, green cooking plantains *(plátanos* or *verdes)*. The yellow bananas of the kind Westerners are accustomed to are called *guineos* in Ecuador. Short, fat red bananas called *maqueños* are also good to eat raw. Bananas and plantains are trucked up to every highland town and market, so you'll have no trouble finding them.

Staple foods

Rice *(arroz)* is not an indigenous food, but it is ubiquitous, although potatoes *(papas)* are more of a highland staple. You can count on one or the other to come with every meal. And sometimes, for a complete carbohydrate overload,

Ecuador was the original banana republic. For many years bananas were its principal export, and the country is still among the world's largest exporters.

noodles *(fideos)*, potatoes, rice, *yuca* (a white starchy tuber), and *plátanos* will be served, and

---

PRECEDING PAGES: Pacific coast market produce.
LEFT: ceviche can be made from a variety of seafood.
RIGHT: tempting fresh fruit juice for sale, Sua Beach.

that's the meal. This is poor people's food, and a partial explanation of why many Ecuadorians are short in stature: besides a genetic component, they do not consume much protein.

Ecuador is overflowing with fruit, from enormous papayas to more exotic treats like passion fruit *(ayatacso, maracuyá,* and *granadilla* are just a few varieties), sweet custard apples *(chirimoyas)* and tart tamarinds *(tamarindos)*. The *naranjilla*, a tiny fruit that looks like a fuzzy, orangey-greenish crab apple, makes a strange-colored but tasty drink that is often served instead of orange juice. If you are uncertain about how to eat a fruit, try it as a juice *(jugo)*. You can ask for juice without water *(sin agua)* and without sugar *(sin azúcar)*.

Visit a market as soon as possible after your arrival. Do not be intimidated by the strange-looking array. Instead, buy every fruit you've never seen before, then go back to your hotel or *hostal* and ask the owner to share them with you and tell you the names of the different varieties. You'll discover some delicious fruits, which you can then enjoy for the rest of your trip.

Pacific flavors

Many of the coastal dishes are typical of the entire Pacific coast from Chile to Mexico. They include ceviche, which is fish (*pescados*) or various types of seafood (*mariscos*) marinated in

lemon or lime juice, onions, and chili peppers. The dish has been around since Inca times, when they marinated raw fish in *chicha*. Ecuadorian ceviche is quite soupy, uses oil and tomatoes, and is served with popcorn on the side.

Ecuador's superb sea bass is served a number of ways, including fried (*frito*), breaded and fried (*apanado*), and filleted and grilled (*a la plancha*). Try any seafood cooked in *agua de coco* (coconut milk), including clams (*almejas* or *conchas*), grouper (*cherna*), mackerel (*sierra*), marlin (*picudo*), snapper (*pargo*), tuna (*atún*), and squid (*calamares*). The *dorado*, or dolphinfish, which is not a mammal like the true dolphin, is also popular and not to be missed.

A thoughtful Ecuadorian custom for regulating the spiciness of food is to serve hot sauce (*salsa picante*) made from chili peppers (*ají*) in a little side dish so that you can add as much or as little as you like.

Tastes of the Oriente

Coastal and Oriente foods are similar because of the two regions' low elevation and tropical climate, although there is more game-hunting in the jungle (everything from monkeys to tapir and *paca*, a large rodent) and freshwater fish instead of seafood. In both places you'll find lots of *plátanos*, *yuca*, rice, and fried fish. There are several dishes served exclusively in the Oriente, however. One is piranha, although it surprises many visitors that the notorious carnivorous fish is itself good for eating. The Oriente rivers also have lots of catfish (*challua* or *bagre*), which people make into a stew with plantains, chili peppers, and *cilantro* (leaf coriander).

For a jungle salad, try *palmitos* (palm hearts) or chonta palm fruits (*frutas de chonta*), both considered delicacies. *Chucula* is a tasty drink made with boiled and mashed plantains, which resembles a banana milkshake.

Serrano cuisine

As we climb to the highlands, a word about the tuber, that traditional mainstay of indigenous Andean life. There are a lot of tubers in the Andes, beginning with dozens of varieties of potatoes. The potato was cultivated around Lake Titicaca, the region that still has the most varieties, some of which are so specialized they grow only at altitudes above 2,400 meters (8,000ft). Potatoes are served with almost every meal in the highlands, usually boiled, but sometimes cut up and added

ANDEAN FESTIVAL DISHES

Andean festivals are a great place to try local foods. *Fanesca* is an incredibly rich soup served only during Holy Week (the week before Easter). You name it and *fanesca* has it: fish, eggs (*huevos*), cheese (*queso*), corn, and every imaginable grain and vegetable, but no meat. *Cuy*, or guinea pig, is often eaten on special occasions, and you can almost always find it in some form during Andean festivals. Whether it's fried, roasted with potatoes, or in a spicy sauce, *cuy* is a delicacy. *Yahuarlocro* is a hearty potato soup made with sheep's innards seasoned with oregano and peanuts and served with avocado, chopped red onion, and tomato.

to thick soups. If you don't like potatoes you're in trouble in Ecuador. They are the food of the common people, and, as in Inca times, everyone plants and eats them. The great Inca terraces, however, used to be reserved for another crop, corn, which was usually made into *chicha*.

Besides regular white potatoes in many sizes and varieties, you will come across the sweet potato (*camote*) as well as the *oca*, which looks like a long, skinny, lumpy potato. One Ecuadorian potato specialty is *llapingachos*, potato pancakes made with potatoes, cheese, and onions and eaten with fried eggs and spicy sausage. A better lunch cannot be had.

cook. One of the most common *locros* is called *yaguar locro* (blood soup) that contains the heart, liver, and other internal organs (which is to say tripe, or *mondongo*) of a cow (*vaca* or *res*), pig (*chancho*), or sheep (*borrego*); the soup is sprinkled with blood sausage or the animal's dried blood.

Mazamorra is a thick soup made with a ground corn base and cabbage, potatoes, onions, and spices. *Sancocho* is a stew made with *plátanos* and corn. Most soups and stews are liberally seasoned with *cilantro* and many are given a yellow or orange color by the addition of *achiote* seeds.

Soups are the essence of meals in the Sierra. Before the Spanish conquest *indígenas* did not have ovens for baking, which meant that most food was boiled, a custom that survives today. Soup is called *caldo*, *sopa*, *chupe*, or *locra*. Generally, a *sopa* or a *caldo* is a thin soup with potatoes and various unidentified floating objects of the faunal variety. A *locro* or *chupe* is a thick, creamy soup. *Sopa seca* or just plain *seco* (which means dry) is more of a stew than a soup, with meat and vegetables added according to the budget and whim of the

LEFT: some of the ingredients for making *ceviche*.
ABOVE: chilis and limes for sale in Cuenca.
ABOVE RIGHT: corn is one of Ecuador's staple foods.

Corn (*maíz* or *sara*) is another staple, especially in the Sierra. Unlike in Mexico and Central America, corn in the Andes is not ground and made into tortillas. In northern Ecuador corn is most commonly served on the cob (*choclo*). Ecuadorian corn has enormous, sweet kernels arranged irregularly, and it's the best corn-on-the-cob imaginable. In the north, corn is also eaten as parched kernels (*kamcha*) or as popcorn (*canguil*). In southern Ecuador it is commonly served as boiled kernels (*muti* or *mote*). *Humitas* are corn *tamales*: cornmeal seasoned and steamed in the leaf. Don't eat the leaf – unwrap it and eat what's inside. *Tostadas de maíz* are corn pancakes that make a good breakfast or snack.

Miracle grain

Other grains grown locally include *quinoa*, wheat (*trigo*), and barley (*cebada*). *Quinoa* is native to the Andes. This tiny, round grain is an amazingly nutritious food, consisting of 15 percent complete protein, 55 percent carbohydrate, and only 4 percent fat. The Incas regarded *quinoa* as sacred, and it was their second-most important food crop. *Quinoa* is usually served in soup, but it can also be eaten as a side dish, in the same way as rice. The grain has become a staple in Novo Andina, New Andean food which blends traditional Andean recipes with contemporary cooking methods. *Quinoa* is

In search of meat dishes

You should ask for *lomo* or *bifstec*, or *chuleta* if you want a chop. *Parrilladas* are steakhouses or grills, where the meat is sometimes charcoal-grilled at your table. *A la parrilla* means grilled, and *churrasco* or *lomo montado* is meat (usually beef) topped with fried eggs. You can also order veal (*ternera*), lamb (*cordero*), or pork (*puerco* or *chanco*; *kuchi* in Quichua). *Lechón* is suckling pig. *Salchicha* means sausage, while *chorizo* refers to pork sausage. Bacon is called *tocino*, ham is *jamón*.

Asado, which means roasted, always refers to whole roasted pig in Ecuador, unless otherwise

often served as a risotto or used to encrust a fish or meat.

Most barley is ground up and used in soup, but wheat flour is used to make a variety of good breads and rolls (*pan* and *panecitos*) and *empanadas*, which are baked pastries filled with cheese or meat. Around Latacunga you'll hear women at street stalls calling *allullas*, *allullas* (pronounced "azhúzhas"). These are homemade rolls, good when hot and fresh, but hard when they get cold.

Broad beans are called *habas*. These beans, which are much larger than you may have seen at home, are boiled and served hot, dipped in salty *campo* cheese, or cold in a salad dressed with butter and lemon juice.

FROM PET TO POT

If you'll settle for something smaller than a sirloin, try guinea pig *(cuy)*. Until the arrival of the Europeans, *cuy* was the main source of meat in the Andes. Every family had guinea pigs running around the kitchen, and some still do.

Cuy is eaten only on special occasions, when one is scooped up, killed, gutted, cleaned, rubbed with lard and spices, put on a spit, and roasted in the fire or baked in the oven. If you can bring yourself to try *cuy*, you will find that there's not much meat, but what there is is delicious, and, as the Ecuadorians put it, what else are guinea pigs good for?

modified. *Fritada* (fried pork) is cooked in large copper and brass *pailas* (wok-like pans) and *chicharrón* is fried pork skin, crispy and delicious.

Other sources of dietary protein include chicken *(pollo)* or hen *(gallina)*, and eggs served

> The Quichua language has contributed one word to English: "jerky," derived from charqui, meaning dried meat. Made from any form of meat, it is normally sun-dried and often "rehydrated" for use in empanadas.

in the usual ways, as well as pasteurized cow's milk *(leche)*, which is sold in unwieldy liter-sized plastic bags, and excellent cheese *(queso)*, the quality of which has soared in recent years with the arrival of Swiss and Italian immigrants who have introduced European varieties. As for fish, in the Sierra many streams and lakes have been stocked with tasty, if rather bony, trout *(trucha)*.

Slaking your thirst

Bebidas is the term for beverages in general, alcoholic or otherwise. Ecuadorian wine *(vino)* is unlikely to win any international awards, although occasionally bottles can be quite good. Argentinian and Chilean wines are often excellent, but expensive. You're better off sticking to soft drinks *(gaseosas)*, mineral water *(agua mineral)*, among which Güitig (pronounced wee-tig) is the most common brand, or beer *(cerveza)*. There are a number of locally brewed beers, the most common of which is Pilsener.

There is also tea *(té)*, herb tea *(agua aromática)*, hot chocolate *(chocolate caliente* or *cocóa)*, and coffee *(café)*. This last is usually boiled until it becomes a sludge, then set on the table in a small carafe. Known as *esencia* (essence), it looks just like soy sauce and causes some interesting confusion in Chinese restaurants *(chifas)*. The *esencia* is poured in your cup and hot water or milk is added; its taste is similar to instant coffee. Black coffee is *tinto*, coffee with milk is *café con leche*, and coffee with hot water and milk is *pintado* ("painted"). *Api* is a thick, hot drink made from ground corn; *chicha morada* is a sweet, non-alcoholic drink made from purple corn.

When it comes to liquor, what you get is the most potent intoxicant with the highest imaginable octane rating: a distilled sugarcane liquor known as *trago* or *puntas*, which burns with a clear blue flame. Local brands include Cristal and Sinchi Shungu ("strong heart"); there are several nameless varieties that are produced without sanitary regulation in the countryside. *Hervidas* are hot drinks served at every fiesta, consisting of *trago* mixed with honey and *naranjilla* or blackberry juice; *guayusa* is *trago* mixed with sugar and hot *guayusa* tea, while *canelazo* is *trago* spiced with cinnamon, sugar, and lime. As they say in Ecuador: *¡Buen provecho!* ❏

A Very Special Specialty

One jungle specialty is *chicha* (or *aswá*), a fermented beer made from *yuca*, which is also known as manioc *(mucuna)*. In order to make the *chicha* ferment, women chew the manioc, spit it into a large jar, and add water – the enzymes in the saliva cause the fermentation. In the highlands, however, *chicha* is not made by mastication; instead yeast and sugar are added to make it ferment.

Generally, the drink will only be offered to you in people's homes, so if you find the thought of it unpalatable you needn't worry about encountering *chicha* in the course of ordinary travel, unless your tour includes remote rainforest homes.

Far Left: spit-roast pig is popular street food in Ecuador. **Left:** cooking *cuy* (guinea pig) in Baños. **Above:** freshly squeezed juice for sale.

PLACES

A detailed guide to the entire country,
with principal sites cross-referenced
by number to the maps

Ecuador is the smallest of South America's Andean republics and without doubt the easiest to explore. The capital city, Quito, is the perfect base for travelers; situated 24km (15 miles) south of the equator at an altitude of 2,800 meters (9,180ft), it has a pleasant, spring-like climate all year round. Unlike other Latin American capitals, Quito has not been engulfed by a population explosion: its elegant colonial heart preserves the streets and buildings of the 18th century, while the modern "New Town" offers every comfort of the 21st.

The classic excursion from Quito, and one of the country's most famous attractions, is the short hop north for the Saturday handicraft market in Otavalo. Then, stretching south of the city, is the lush mountain valley that the German scientist Alexander von Humboldt dubbed "the Avenue of the Volcanoes." The city of Cuenca, considered Ecuador's most beautiful colonial treasure, marks the beginning of the Southern Sierra, a remote and strongly traditional region that has some of the country's most distinctive *indígena* (indigenous) communities and its most important Inca ruins.

But Ecuador offers much more than *serrano* (highland) cultures and the spectacle of ice on the equator. Just 20 minutes west of Quito by air

is the Pacific coast. Moving to a more languid rhythm of life than the highlands, the coast is dotted with comfortable resorts and washed by warm sea currents from the northern Pacific. Travelers often head to the coast directly rather than passing through tropical Guayaquil, Ecuador's largest city and its often chaotic commercial heart.

Twenty minutes by air east of Quito is the Oriente region within the Amazon basin. Comfortable jungle lodges abound, and boat or canoe trips can take you to the farthest reaches of this threatened region, which is fast becoming one of the continent's greatest travel attractions.

Finally, the Galápagos archipelago is in a class of its own. Easily visited on a tour or independently, this naturalists' paradise alone can justify a visit to Ecuador. A journey here is an expensive treat, but it remains one of the world's unforgettable travel experiences. ❑

PRECEDING PAGES: Guamote market; fishing boats at Las Playas; the blue domes of Cuenca's Nueva Catedral; Valley of the Volcanoes. **LEFT:** Salasca market. **ABOVE RIGHT:** Mount Cotopaxi. **ABOVE LEFT:** boats on the beach at Puerto López.

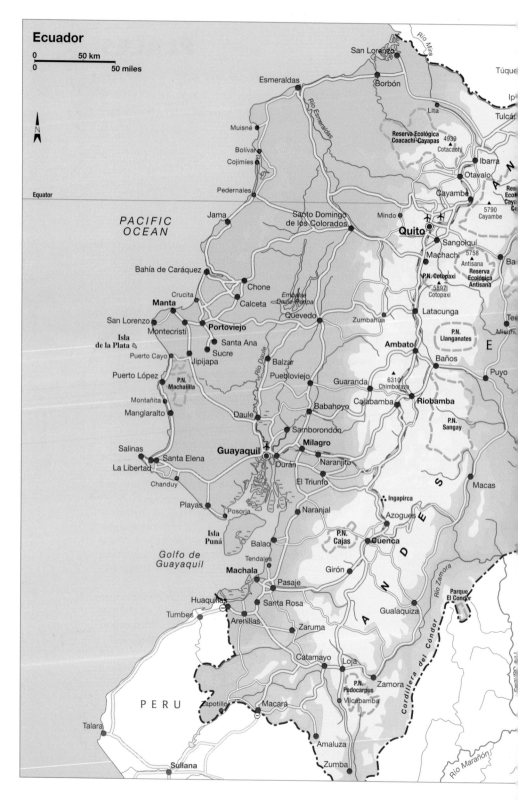

Ecuador

0   50 km
0   50 miles

N

**PACIFIC
OCEAN**

Equator

San Lorenzo
Esmeraldas
Borbón
Muisné
Bolívar
Cojimíes
Pedernales
Jama
Bahía de Caráquez
Crucita
Chone
Manta
Calceta
San Lorenzo
Montecristi
Portoviejo
Isla
de la Plata
Santa Ana
Sucre
Puerto Cayo
Jipijapa
Puerto López
P.N.
Machalilla
Montañita
Manglaralto
Daule
Salinas
Santa Elena
La Libertad
Chanduy
Playas
Posorja
Isla
Puná
Balao
Tendales
Machala
Pasaje
Huaquillas
Santa Rosa
Tumbes
Arenillas
Zaruma

Lita
Túque
Ip
Tulcár
Reserva Ecológica
Coacachi-Cayapas
4939
Cotacachi
Ibarra
Otavalo
Res
Ecol
Caya
Cayambe
5790
Cayambe
Mindo
Quito
Sangolquí
Machachi
5758
Antisana
Reserva
Ecológica
Antisana
P.N. Cotopaxi
5897
Cotopaxi
Ba
Santo Domingo
de los Colorados
Quevedo
Embalse
Daule-Peripa
Zumbahúa
Latacunga
P.N.
Llanganates
Te
Misahi
Ambato
Baños
Puyo
E
Guaranda
6310
Chimborazo
Balzar
Puebloviejo
Cajabamba
Riobamba
Babahoyo
P.N.
Sangay
Samborondón
Milagro
Guayaquil
Durán
Naranjito
El Triunfo
Macas
Naranjal
Ingapirca
Azogues
P.N.
Cajas
Cuenca
Girón
Catamayo
Loja
Zamora
P.N.
Podocarpus
Vilcabamba
Gualaquiza
Río Zamora
Parque
El Cóndor
Cordillera del Cóndor
Río Janira

**Golfo de
Guayaquil**

P E R U

Zapotillo
Macará
Talara
Sullana
Amaluza
Zumba

Río Mira
Río Esmeraldas
Río Daule

A
N
D
E
S

Río Marañón

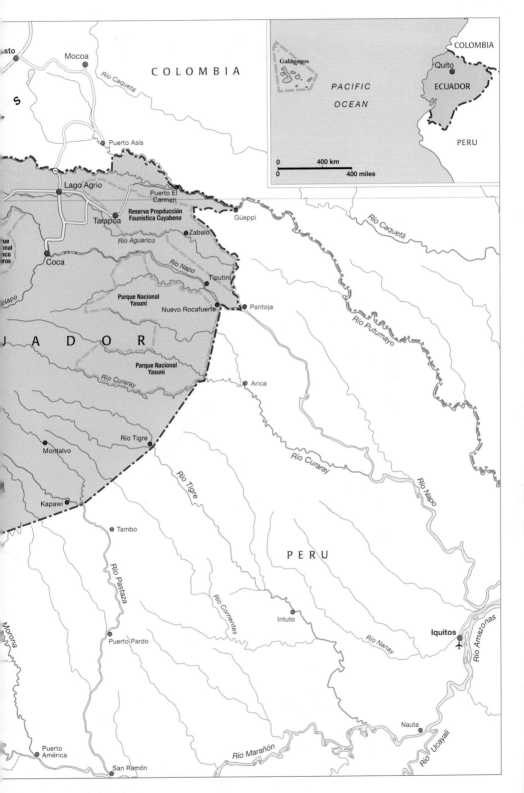

QUITO

Latin America's most beautiful church is here, along with splendid colonial buildings and some bargain shopping. A grid system makes it easy to find your way around

Surrounded by snow-capped volcanoes but only 24km (15 miles) from the equator, Quito is a strange and beautiful city with a year-round spring-like climate. Although an important city in Inca and pre-Inca times, its original buildings have been erased, and today it is divided between the colonial architecture and sculpture of its Spanish conquest days and the clean lines of its modern section. This combination of superb, well-preserved colonial churches and convents, shining glass, and sleek contemporary architecture makes Quito one of the most beautiful cities in the whole of Latin America.

Nestled at the foot of 4,696-meter (15,402ft) high Rucu Pichincha volcano, Ecuador's capital owes its name to the Quitua tribe. When the Inca Empire spread as far as Ecuador under the leadership of Huayna Capac, the indigenous Indians living in what is now Quito put up impressive resistance to the invaders from Cuzco (in modern-day Peru). But, in the end, Huayna Capac not only added the area to the empire but married a beautiful princess from the conquered tribe and set up the Incas' northern capital in Quito. A road was built to link Cuzco with Quito, from which Huayna Capac preferred to rule.

His decision to divide the Inca kingdom into northern and southern regions – and his fathering of sons in both – were key factors in the downfall of the empire. When Huayna Capac died, his legitimate heir in Cuzco, Huascar, claimed the throne at the same time as the leader's illegitimate (but some say favorite) son, Atahualpa, declared himself Inca in Quito. The rights to the throne were clouded, too, by the Inca line of succession – which was not based solely on birth order. In many instances, the first son of an Inca was passed over for younger siblings who showed greater leadership skills, wisdom, and courage. And, in the case of Huascar and Atahualpa, their

Main attractions
CERRO PANECILLO
TELEFÉRICO
LA COMPAÑÍA DE JESÚS
LA RONDA
TEATRO BOLÍVAR
LA BASÍLICA
MUSEO GUAYASAMÍN
CAPILLA DEL HOMBRE

PRECEDING PAGES: view across Quito towards Cotopaxi. **LEFT:** the Virgin of the Americas. **BELOW:** street in the colonial Old Town.

Looking up to the Cerro Panecillo from the Old Town. The hill is dominated by the statue of the Virgin of the Americas.

subjects at each end of the kingdom supported the local son.

A razed city

A year after Francisco Pizarro had Atahualpa executed on the main plaza of Cajamarca, now in northern Peru, Sebastián de Benalcázar, accompanied by *conquistador* Diego de Almagro, arrived to claim Quito for the Spanish crown. They skirmished with Atahualpa's general, Rumiñahui (Face of Stone), and when it became clear he would be overcome, he angrily set the Inca palace on fire. The flames spread and the city the Spanish finally claimed was razed. (Rumiñahui, meanwhile, was captured and executed.) For that reason Quito has no Inca structures; all that remained of those magnificent buildings perched on the city's beautiful high plain were massive rock foundations. On those bases, the Spanish conquerors built churches, convents, and palaces in the exuberant style of the Latin American Baroque.

By the end of the 16th century, the new colonial city's population reached 1,500 and it was declared the seat of the royal *Audiencia*, a legal subdivision of the New World colony. The proliferation of churches, convents, and monasteries won Quito the nickname "The Cloister of America" and, in 1978, the same colonial buildings prompted the United Nations to declare the city a Unesco World Heritage Site.

In early colonial Quito, changes came slowly but steadily as wheat farming was introduced; the indigenous

Quito Old Town

population was converted to Christianity; and colonial rule and laws replaced the native culture. In the centuries that followed, Quito became a center for art and sculpture in the New World, with the School of Quito (see page 165) producing an art form characterized by violent Christian themes, such as saints drawing their last breath in horrifying and bloody scenes of martyrdom, painted in rich dark colors and gold brushwork, a style similiar to the work of the School of Cuzco in Peru.

The growth and development of Quito was not problem-free. There was a bloody rebellion against a royal sales tax in 1592 and another in 1765, when a rumor spread that government-dispensed rum had been poisoned to eliminate the poorer classes. But things remained relatively peaceful until full-scale insurrection occurred when the winds of independence spreading across the continent reached this city. In August of 1809 the first sparks of revolution ignited in Quito and, on May 24, 1822, the city fell into the hands of the independence troops, led by Marshal Sucre, after a bloody battle in the foothills of Pichincha shadowing the city. May 24 is now a national holiday. For eight years Ecuador was part of La Gran Colombia – modern-day Colombia, Venezuela, and Ecuador united under a single government – but, in 1830, separated itself to become independent under the presidency of Juan José Flores.

Modern city, modern problems

While the Old Town – the Centro Histórico – with its churches, convents, and whitewashed houses with red-tile roofs, has not changed much physically since colonial times, in contrast, northern Quito now boasts huge business centers, banks on every corner, shopping arcades, embassies, and smart government buildings. This part of Quito is where upper-class residential areas are concentrated. Quito's poorest areas are largely on the city's south side,

together with the factories and heavy industry that stretches along the Pan-American Highway, known simply as the *Panamericana*.

Quito today extends far beyond the Old Town's borders, even spreading up the slopes of Pichincha on the west side. The city has grown to a length of 35km (22 miles), with a width of just 3–5km (2–3 miles). On the eastern side of the city is the **Los Chillos** valley, which has experienced considerable urban development in recent years due to a new highway connecting it with the city.

Despite its growing population of over 1.5 million, the city has managed to avoid the sprawling squatter settlements common to many other large cities on the South American continent. However, there are plenty of areas where the housing is at best basic and electricity and water supply erratic; and street crime has become a problem even in the smartest areas of Quito. Traffic jams on ancient cobbled streets never designed to carry cars and choking pollution from vehicles also contribute to Quito's problems.

Quito flies the flag.

Riches, Poverty, Inequality... Equals Crime

Like many Latin American cities, Quito is a mix of extremes. There are still historic mansions, staffed by servants, that house luxury cars in their garages, boasting manicured gardens and equally manicured owners. The well off in Quito enjoy a comparatively luxurious lifestyle, and there is a growing middle class that is increasingly able to enjoy some of the upper echelons' way of living.

For the majority of the city's population, however, life is hard. Some of the poorest Quiteños are recent migrants from the countryside who have come here in search of work. The few jobs available to them are basic and poorly paid and most families struggle to make ends meet in a city that is expensive, particularly since dollarization in 2000 which has increased the cost of living considerably for ordinary Ecuadorians.

The result is a large wealth discrepancy between the haves and have-nots; a gap that has led to a rise in street crime in recent years. Quiteños are quite aware of it, and visitors need to be circumspect too: take common-sense precautions like carrying minimal cash in an internal pocket and only carrying your credit cards or passport when you need them. Take care, particularly after dark, in the Mariscal Sucre area, late at night in the Old Town, and watch your belongings if you travel on public transport. The Terminal Terrestre bus station is also a notorious hotspot for theft.

Quito from above

In order to get an idea of the city's layout before you start exploring, it's a good idea to go to a spot that offers a fine panoramic view of Quito and the surrounding volcanoes. **Cerro Panecillo**, a hill dominating the Old Town and topped by a statue of the Virgin of the Americas and an observation deck, lures those who want to survey the basin in which Quito sits. A series of steps and paths from García Moreno and Ambato enables you to walk up the hill but assaults are frequent and visitors are strongly advised to ascend El Panecillo only by taxi. The hill is where an Inca site for sun worship was once located. An even more splendid view is available from the **Cima de la Libertad**. Founded on the site of the 1822 Battle of Pichincha, this spot has a **museum** dedicated to the independence era in Quito. The museum exhibits flags, weapons, a model of this pivotal battle, and a sarcophagus containing the remains of its heroes. Dramatically, their tomb is guarded by an eternally burning flame.

On the east side of Quito's Centro Histórico, **Parque Itchimbia** at 2,910 meters (9,544ft) is another prime spot for views, with excellent panoramas of the volcanoes on clear days. There are frequent art exhibitions in the beautiful **Palacio de Cristal** cultural center, children's playgrounds, and plenty of green space with a network of walking tracks. The best views over the Old Town from here are at dusk, when you can watch the city's lights come on. Some of the restaurants at the base of the park (*see Travel Tips, page 337*) have balconies that hang spectacularly right over the city: a prime spot for an evening drink on your first night in Quito.

Quito's loftiest attraction, the **Teleférico** (Mon–Thur 10am–7pm, Fri until 10pm, Sat 9am–10pm, Sun 9am–8pm; charge), starts at the base of Volcán Pichincha and transports visitors by cable car to the top of Cruz Loma at an altitude of 4,270 meters (14,000ft). The views over Quito and of the surrounding mountains are breathtaking, as is the altitude itself. From Cruz Loma, you can hike to the summit of Rucu

BELOW: view from Cima de la Libertad, the site of the 1822 Battle of Pichincha.
BELOW RIGHT: Quito's Teleférico.

Pichincha and back in five to six hours. Be prepared for the cold, and take things slowly in the thin air: the oxygen bar at Cruz Loma is not just for fun. Back at the cable car's base, the slightly tacky Volcano Park has a number of restaurants, a disco, gift shops, and a small amusement park that is good for children. The line to get on the cable cars tends to grow as the day goes on, so try to get there early.

Strolling through the past

Quito's Centro Histórico was made a Unesco World Heritage Site in 1978 and, thanks to a large-scale restoration project, it is now one of the most attractive colonial centers in Latin America. Much of the area's former grandeur has been restored, and boutique hotels, restaurants, and galleries continue to appear. Walking around the hilly, narrow streets is the best way to see Old Quito, and perhaps the best introduction to the Old Town is to take one of the guided walks of the historic center (10am, 11am, 2pm, and 7pm; charge) offered by Quito Visitors' Bureau in conjunction with the Tourism Unit

of the Metropolitain Police force. The walks follow various routes and leave from the visitor information center on the main plaza.

The heart of the historic center is the **Plaza de la Independencia Ⓐ**. Also known locally as the Plaza Grande, this garden-graced square is dominated by **La Catedral Metropolitana Ⓑ** (Metropolitan Cathedral; daily, except during Mass; charge). The other sides of the plaza are flanked by the Palacio de Gobierno *(see page 152)*, the Palacio Arzobispal (the Archbishop's Palace), and the Edificio de la Administración Urbana (City Hall), which was erected in 1978, sadly replacing another colonial jewel. At the center of the plaza is a bronze and marble monument celebrating Ecuador's first declaration of independence against its Spanish conquerors, in 1809.

Quito's cathedral is believed to have existed first as a wood and adobe structure before the official church was built on the site in 1565. Earthquake damage has forced restoration on three occasions. The cathedral is filled with paintings by some of Ecuador's finest early

The four corners of the Plaza de la Independencia are planted with flora from different parts of the word: tropical palm trees, European fruit trees that blossom in spring, an Australian eucalypt, and even an araucaria from southern Chile. It's a marvel how this diverse international collection can survive at an altitude of 2,800 meters (9,240ft), and almost on the equator.

BELOW: taking it easy in the Plaza de la Independencia.

Detail from a Kingman painting.

artists from what became known as the School of Quito (*see page 165*). Outstanding amongst the cathedral's artworks is the sculpture known as the *Descent from the Cross*, by indigenous artist Caspicara. Like many churches built in Quito (and Cuenca) during the 16th and 17th centuries, the cathedral shows Moorish influences: its wooden ceiling is distinctive of the geometric-patterned *Mudéjar* style. One of the side altars contains the remains of Venezuelan-born Marshal Antonio José de Sucre, leader of the liberation army. Left of the main altar is a statue of Ecuador's first president, Juan José Flores, and behind the altar is a plaque showing where President Gabriel García Moreno died on August 6, 1875, from gunshot wounds he received while returning to the Presidential Palace after Mass. He was carried back across the street to the church, but attempts to save his life were futile.

BELOW: guards outside the Palacio de Gobierno.

Around the corner from the cathedral on Calle García Moreno is **El Sagrario** , built between 1657 and 1706 as the cathedral's main chapel but now used as a separate church. In the cupola are some restored frescoes painted by Francisco de Alban.

Back in the Plaza Grande, the **City Hall** is worth a visit to see the huge brightly colored naïf murals of Quito life by one of Ecuador's great artists of the 20th century, Eduardo Kingman.

Roller-coaster politics

On the northwest side of the plaza is the **Palacio de Gobierno** (Government Palace), also known as the **Palacio de Carondelet**. The entrance is flanked by guards in red, blue, and gold 19th-century-style uniforms, which seem somewhat anachronistic in contrast with the automatic rifles they carry, and which were used during the attempted coup in 1976. This building has seen a great deal of activity, especially in the early days of the republic. From 1901 to 1948 alone, Ecuador had 39 governments and four constitutions, and at one point

there were four presidents in a span of 26 days.

Guided tours of the palace (Tue–Sun 9–11.45am and 1–4.15pm, departing every 15 mins; free, ID must be produced) have been possible since 2006 when Rafael Correa first came to power. Visitors are shown the interior patios, ornate with fountains, iron balconies and columns, and some of the halls of government if they are not in use. One of the palace's treasures is Oswaldo Guayasamín's famous mosaic mural depicting explorer Francisco de Orellana's voyage to the Amazon. Nearly 400 years old, the palace is an unusual mix of formal and informal, and must be one of the world's few presidential offices where the street-level floor has been converted into small shops that sell souvenirs.

Half a block from the plaza, at Eugenio Espejo 1147, is the **Centro Cultural Metropolitano** Ⓔ, commonly known as the Museo Alberto Mena Caamaño (Tue–Sun 9am–4.30pm; charge). This museum is set in an early Jesuit house that later served as barracks for the royal Spanish troops

in Quito and was the old headquarters of the Royal Audencia. The stone column in the patio was the pillory, and underneath it is the dungeon where 36 revolutionaries of the 1809 uprising were imprisoned for nine months before being executed. Wax figures in the museum graphically illustrate their deaths. The museum contains ecclesiastical art from the 16th and 17th centuries, as well as works from the 1900s.

Latin America's most beautiful church

Almost next door to the museum is the impressive 16th-century church of **La Compañía de Jesús** Ⓕ (Mon–Fri 10am–5pm, Sat 10am–4pm, Sun noon–4pm; charge). This Jesuit church took 163 years to finish and is the most ornate in the country. It was severely damaged by the 1987 earthquake, but FONSAL, the Cultural Heritage Protection Fund, finished extensive restoration in 2002. Richly intricate both inside and out, it is a masterpiece of Baroque and Quiteño Colonial art: its altars are covered in gold leaf and the fine paintings on its vaulted

Sacred Hearts on a church door in Quito's Old Town.

BELOW LEFT: ornate exterior of La Compañía de Jesús.
BELOW: La Compañía de Jesús's gilded altar and ceiling.

BELOW:
evangelist praying
outside Iglesia
Santo Domingo.
BELOW RIGHT:
Santo Domingo's
beautiful *Mudéjar*
ceiling.

ceiling have earned it the nickname "Quito's Sistine Chapel." The walls are covered with School of Quito murals. The designs on the columns inside the church clearly show a Moorish influence, and the columns themselves are said to be copies of those by Bernini in the Vatican; they are reproduced in the main altar. However, the church's most precious treasures, including an emerald- and gold-laden painting of the *Virgen Dolorosa* (Our Lady of Sorrow), are kept in the country's Central Bank vaults and taken out only for special religious festivals. And the church's original holdings were far, far richer than what remains now. In 1767, when a decree banned the Jesuits from Spanish domains, the treasures in La Compañía were put into 36 boxes and shipped to Spain to pay war debts. What remained – mostly silver – was put up for sale but the devout Quiteños refused to buy it, saying that the items in question belonged to God.

At the foot of the altar in La Compañía are the remains of Saint Mariana de Jesús. In 1645, a combination of measles and diphtheria epidemics and an earthquake killed 14,000 people in Quito, prompting a frantic attempt to break the city's streak of bad luck. It was then that 26-year-old Mariana de Jesús stepped in. The orphaned daughter of an aristocratic family, she had already given all her wealth to the poor and was said to have miraculously healed the sick. Now she made a bargain with God, offering him her own life if the rest of the city's population could be saved. As the story goes, she fell ill immediately and, with her death, the plagues on the city ended. Just before she died, doctors bled her – as was the custom – and threw the blood into the garden of her home. It was said that a lily grew where the blood touched the earth and, for that reason, when the Pope canonized Mariana, he called her the "Lily of Quito."

When you come out of La Compañía, turn right, then immediately left down Avenida de Mariscal Sucre and between the streets of García Moreno and Venezuela you will find the **Museo Histórico Casa de Sucre** ❻ (Tue–Thur 9am–5pm, Fri–Sat 10am–2pm; charge), once the home of Marshal Antonio José de Sucre. The museum

houses a collection of weapons, clothing, furniture, and documents both belonging to Sucre and from the independence era. A statue of Sucre, pointing in the direction of Pichincha where he led independence troops to victory in 1822, is two blocks away at Bolívar and Guayaquil on the busy little Plaza Santo Domingo. Also in this square is the **Iglesia de Santo Domingo** ⓗ (daily; free), a church that is especially attractive in the evening when its domes are illuminated against the sky. FONSAL has completed the restoration of the church, including the beautiful wooden *Mudéjar* coffered ceiling. Santo Domingo has fine religious sculptures, especially those of the Virgen del Rosario, donated by Spanish King Charles I.

The Dominican **Museo Fray Pedro Bedón** (Mon–Sat 8.30am–5pm, Sun 9am–4pm; charge), attached to the church, also has an impressive collection of art (the friar himself was a painter). The museum is home to the astonishing silver throne used to carry the Virgen del Rosario during religious processions.

Roaming La Ronda

From Plaza Santo Domingo, turn down Guayaquil to Calle Juan de Dios Morales. This street is more commonly known as **La Ronda**, and is the most romantic slice of colonial Quito, with its bright white houses trimmed with ornate balconies and geraniums, and brightly painted window frames and doors opening out onto the narrow, cobbled street. Restored around 2005, La Ronda has become a mix of old-time artisans selling items such as ornate church candles and Panama hats; historic, working-class inner-city housing; and popular cafés and restaurants with a bohemian feel. La Ronda's name comes from the guitar serenades *(rondas)* that drew crowds here during colonial days. At intervals along the way are portraits of famous Ecuadorian musicians and composers. Due to poverty, theft has become something of a problem in the area around La Ronda. Take care here at night, when only the guard-patrolled street of La Ronda itself is safe.

From La Ronda it is only three blocks to the Plaza San Francisco, but en route

BELOW LEFT: *canelazo*, a mix of hot spiced orange juice and *aguardiente*, for sale on La Ronda.
BELOW: view down colonial La Ronda.

you will pass Calle García Moreno. The **Museo de la Ciudad**  (tel: 02-228 3882; Tue–Sun 9.30am–5.30pm; charge) opened in 1995 at Rocafuerte 572 and García Moreno. The building, with two large courtyards, functioned as the San Juan de Dios Hospital from 1565 until 1973 and has since been beautifully restored. Exhibits show the stages of Quito's development and daily life from the pre-Hispanic era to the present day.

On the same block, at the corner of Calle Rocafuerte and García Moreno, the former home of Santa Mariana de Jesús (commemorated in La Compañía) houses the nuns of the **Monasterio del Carmen Alto** . This is a closed order: nuns who join never leave the building until they depart this world. The nuns are industrious, however, and make a range of products including shampoos, hand creams, natural remedies, honey, and biscuits, which can be bought by means of a revolving hatch to preserve the nuns' isolation. The church here is being restored and may be open to the public in the future.

BELOW: one of the courtyards at the Museo de la Ciudad.

Grand tribute to a patron saint

The expansive **Plaza San Francisco** is named for its monastery church, **El Monasterio de San Francisco** , honoring Quito's patron saint. The Flemish missionary Fray Jodocko Ricke directed construction of the church and monastery on the site of an Inca palace only 50 days after the city's 1534 founding, making this the American continent's oldest church.

The San Francisco religious complex is the largest structure in colonial Quito, with a sumptuous Spanish Baroque interior. The indigenous heritage of Quito is also represented in this Christian enclave; the church ceiling is decorated with images of the sun, the Inca divinity. The church's main altar is spectacularly carved and the side aisles are banked with paintings by School of Quito masters, including the *Virgen Inmaculada de Quito* by Bernardo de Legarda. This is reportedly the only winged image of the Virgin Mary to be found in either Europe or the Americas. The church itself is currently closed for archeological excavations and restoration until at least late 2010, but the complex's finest artwork, including paintings, sculptures, and furniture from the 16th and 17th centuries, can still be viewed in the interesting **Museo Franciscano** (Mon–Sat 9am–6pm, Sun 9am–noon; charge, guided tours available) to the right of the church's main entrance.

The museum is housed in a building that was originally established by Fray Ricke as a school of art and religious instruction for indigenous children. Note the details of the intricately wrought furniture: some pieces have thousands of mother-of-pearl mosaics in their construction. To one side of the San Francisco atrium is the **Cantuña Chapel**, built by the indigenous Cantuña, a Christian convert, and financed by treasures from the Inca Empire. Cantuña's remains lie in the church. The chapel has a magnificent carved altar – the work of Bernardo de Legarda – and its walls display finely carved wood.

A block and a half away from Plaza San Francisco on Calle García Moreno is **Casa Museo Maria Augusta Urrutia** **M** (Tue–Sat 10am–6pm, Sun 9.30am–5pm; charge). This beautiful 19th-century mansion became a museum in 1987 after the death of the former owner, Doña Urrutia. It offers a wonderful glimpse of high-society Quito of the Republican era, with its European furniture, sewing rooms, sophisticated drawing rooms, graceful courtyards, and salons.

Not far away is another of Quito's glorious churches – there are more than 80 in all. This one is **La Merced** **N**, located at the corner of calles Cuenca and Chile. Its monastery contains the city's oldest clock, built in 1817, and a striking statue of Neptune, which sits on the fountain in the cloister's main patio. The castle-like La Merced – constructed from 1700 to 1734 – was one of the last churches built during Quito's colonial period, and it has the Old Town's tallest tower

(47 meters/154ft) and its largest bell. The walls are decorated with pink and white reliefs displaying more than three dozen gilt-framed School of Quito paintings, among them several with unusual scenes of erupting volcanoes and an ash-covered city. Bernardo de Legarda carved the main altarpiece in this serenely beautiful church.

Quito's gold convent

Turn down Calle Mejía when you leave the museum, and at the corner of calles Mejía and Flores you will find the **Monasterio de San Agustín** **O** (Mon–Sat 7am–noon and 1–6pm; charge), where Ecuador's first (short-lived) Act of Independence was signed in August 1809. Inside its flower-filled patio, robed monks pray against a backdrop of oil paintings by Miguel de Santiago, who spent most of his life in the monastery illustrating the life of St Augustine. The third floor of one wing of the cloister, which is open to the public, houses restoration workshops of the Cultural Heritage Institute. The room where the

Decorated door, Monasterio de San Francisco.

BELOW LEFT: the extraordinary main altar of Monasterio de San Francisco. **BELOW:** flowers for the altar.

Quito's modern trolley system is 11km (6 miles) long with 40 stops, and carries 14,000 passengers an hour.

independence document was signed is called the Sala Capitular and contains a portable altar in 18th-century Baroque style attributed to the indigenous artist Pampite. The remains of the leaders of the 1809 uprising are interred in San Agustín's catacombs.

Northeast along Calle Flores (toward the New Town) is the **Teatro Nacional Sucre** , the city's most beautiful theater, where concerts and plays are staged. This is the home of the National Symphony Orchestra; extensive renovations were finally completed in 2003.

Also on Calle Flores, four blocks back toward the Old Town is the **Teatro Bolívar** . This gorgeous Art Deco theater was inaugurated in 1933, and soon became the setting for the very best operas, ballets, concerts, and theater pieces seen in Ecuador, as well as a meeting place for high society. The theatre suffered a disastrous fire in 1999, but a painstaking restoration has returned it to its former glory and it is now once again home to the best of Ecuadorian performing arts. Guided visits (Mon–Fri 11am–3.30pm; charge)

reveal the plush, red main auditorium as well as taking fascinating peeks behind the scenes.

Where old meets new

From here, Calle Guayaquil, with its 19th-century buildings, leads toward the area where the past is left behind. The **Monasterio de San Blas** is one of the last colonial complexes before you come to modern Quito lying ahead at the point where the two parts of the city meet. Before entering the New Town, however, make a slight detour two blocks west to view what is arguably the city's most magnificent church. **La Basílica** (daily 9am–5pm; charge) took over 100 years to build and was not completed until the mid-20th century. This largest Gothic basilica in Latin America is intricately decorated with gargoyles inspired by Ecuadorian fauna, and has a soaring 114-meter (376ft) spire that you can climb for expansive views over both Old and New towns.

Heading for the New Town, wander through triangular **Parque La Alameda**, with its impressive monu-

BELOW: La Basílica, Latin America's largest Gothic basilica, looming over the Old Town.

ment of the liberation leader Simón Bolívar. The park contains a number of other busts and statues in honor of famous Latin Americans, among them Manuelita Saenz, the Quito-born woman who was Bolívar's companion throughout the revolution.

It was in 1598 that Spanish officials in Quito obtained permission to build the Alameda, an area for recreation, brightened by well-tended gardens, flowers, and shade trees. The natural lagoon here is nowadays used for boating: the rowing boats for hire are a popular attraction on weekends. At the center of the park is South America's oldest observatory, the **Observatorio Astronómico** ❺ (Mon–Fri 9am–noon, 2.30–5.30pm; charge), begun in 1864 and still used by meteorologists and astronomers today.

The small church of **El Belén** ❶ (daily; free) on the park's north side is a favorite subject of Quito's artists. It marks the site where the first Mass in Quito was said after the city was taken over by the Spanish. Simple and graceful, this church's lone nave contains a magnificent Christ believed to be the work of indigenous artist Caspicara. Two blocks up Avenida 6 de Diciembre and right on Calle Montalvo is the **Palacio Legislativo** ❶, a new government building with the history of Ecuador immortalized in carved stone along its north side. If you take Avenida Gran Colombia from here to Avenida Paz and Calle Miño, you can see the hill-top home of the **Instituto Geográfico Militar** ❶ (Geographical Military Institute; Tue–Fri 8am–4pm; charge). There is a museum, and the planetarium (Mon–Fri 9am–3pm, Sat 9–11am) – distinguishable by its white dome – has shows lasting for about half an hour that take place several times a day. If you turn right, however, from the Palacio Legislativo, and continue up Calle 6 de Diciembre, you will come to the **Parque El Ejido** (Communal Park). This park, the largest in central Quito, is a favorite spot – especially at weekends – for picnickers, soccer players, couples out for a stroll, energetic children, and street vendors seeking the park's shady trees as respite from the warm sun. Women carry huge trays of food balanced on their heads, offering for sale *fritada, papas, y mote* (grilled meat, potatoes, and corn). On weekends there is a large art market, popular with tourists.

Banks, boutiques, and bargains

At the north end of El Ejido, from Avenida Patria to Colón, lies Quito's modern tourist and business area with hotels, offices, banks, and restaurants. **Avenida Amazonas** is home to travel agencies, art galleries, money exchangers, outdoor cafés and artisan boutiques. This is a popular spot for strolling and shopping, with stops for cool drinks or snacks at the many restaurants and pastry shops along the route. Shopping bargains range from well-made handicrafts to clothing in shops carrying the latest fashions. You should also follow the parallel street, Juan León Mera, another good place

Setting up a stall at the weekend art market in the Parque El Ejido.

BELOW: climbing sphere in Parque El Arbolito near the Casa de la Cultura.

for cafés and shopping, restaurants and book stores. Many stores in this part of Quito close on Saturday afternoons and Sundays.

Officially a part of Mariscal Sucre, the area north of Veintimilla and south of Luís Cordero is nicknamed "Gringolandia" because of the number of backpacker hostels and tour operators there. Many of the city's most lively discos are found here, filled with a mix of locals and tourists almost every night of the week. On the eastern edge, Plaza de Quinde (more commonly known as Plaza Foch) underwent a major renovation and is now home to the city's trendiest cafés, restaurants, and bars.

Head east from the park, along Avenida Patria, to the **Casa de la Cultura Ecuatoriana**, a large circular glass building that houses the **Museo del Banco Central** Ⓦ (Tue–Fri 9am–5pm, Sat–Sun 10am–4pm; charge). This stylish presentation of Ecuadorian history should not be missed. The spacious museum includes five connected salons, devoted respectively to archeology, gold, colonial art, republican art, and modern art.

As you walk through the collections in chronological order you will gain a sense of Ecuador's priceless artistic heritage. Each of the pre-Columbian cultures is represented by artifacts – including pottery, tools, and jewelry – and well-constructed dioramas. The highlight of the gold room is a ceremonial mask fashioned from gold and silver. The museum also contains works of art from the Quito School, including one of only two known sculptures of the pregnant Virgin Mary.

The republican art collection has wonderful paintings of mountain and jungle landscapes, as well as themes exploring national identity and social change. The indigenous peoples' struggle for freedom is forcefully presented in the paintings of Eduardo Kingman in the modern collection. The museum also displays many works by Camilo Egas, one of Ecuador's best-known contemporary artists (see *A Nation of Painters, page 111*). Another salon is reserved for presentations of works that are rotated every month; it's certainly worth checking what is on while you are in the city. Written explanations

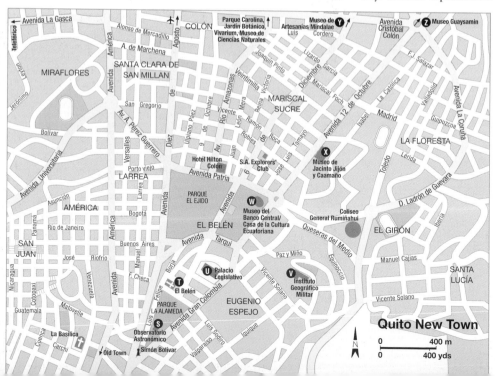

Quito New Town

throughout the museum are in Spanish and English; guided tours are also available in Spanish and English, as well as German, and French, by arrangement.

The **Museo de la Casa de la Cultura Ecuatoriana** (hours as for the Museo del Banco Central, above) is housed in the same building, and contains art from the colonial period to modern times. A separate room of the museum displays musical instruments, many of them several centuries old, gathered from all over the world. There is also a display of traditional dress from various indigenous cultures.

Just two blocks away, another fine art, archeology, and ethnographic museum is run by the Universidad Católica on Avenida 12 de Octubre. The **Museo de Jacinto Jijón y Caamaño ❌** (Mon–Fri 8.30am–1pm and 2–4pm; charge) contains the private collection donated by the family of the aristocratic archeologist after his death. It was the work of Jijón y Caamaño that provided the basis for the modern-day theories on how pre-Hispanic peoples lived in Ecuador; his books on the subject are valuable rarities.

The museum's collection includes *aribalos*, the graceful fluted-mouthed jars with pointed bottoms that are synonymous with pre-Inca cultures throughout the Andes, as well as a wide assortment of religious idols, masks, weapons, and shell and bone works. The museum also houses a small collection of colonial art.

Art and artifacts

One of Quito's newest museums is the **Museo de Artesanías Mindalae ❨Y❩** (Mon–Sat 9am–4pm, Sun 10am–5pm; charge), located on Calle La Niña, just off Avenida Reina Victoria in the north of Mariscal Sucre. The museum gives an insight into the cultural and historical background to Ecuador's astounding range of handicrafts. Come here for a fascinating education in Ecuadorian folk art before you buy your souvenirs. There's also a good fairtrade shop that sells top-quality handicrafts from all over the country.

The **Museo Guayasamín ❨Z❩** (Mon–Fri 10am–5pm; charge), at Calle Bosmediano 543 in the Bellavista district, is located in one of the city's most

Religious art in the Museo Banco Central.

BELOW LEFT: pre-Columbian statue, Museo Banco Central.
BELOW: reflections on the Casa de la Cultura.

Inside the Capilla del Hombre an eternal flame burns in defense of peace and human rights.

RIGHT: *Lidice,* by Oswaldo Guayasamín, in the Capilla del Hombre.

beautiful modern houses, perched on a hillside overlooking Quito. The museum contains perhaps the most intriguing colonial art collection in the city. Set up by artist Oswaldo Guayasamín, the complex is divided into three parts: a colonial art gallery (housing Guayasamín's own collection); the artist's gallery, where he displayed and sold his artworks, and a studio used by himself and his students. Provocative and political, Guayasamín's art made him the country's best-known artist, and the gallery of his works is considered a national treasure. Guayasamín was born of an indigenous father and mestizo mother, and much of his work represents the struggles and sufferings of indigenous people (*see A Nation of Painters, page 112*). A fine collection of sculpture is displayed on the flower-splashed tile roof.

The artist began what would later be considered his masterpiece in 1995, and it was finished after his death in 1999 at the insistence of his heirs. The **Capilla del Hombre** (Pasaje Lorenzo Chávez and Mariano Calvache; Tue–Sun 10am–5pm; charge) is located a few blocks away and is one of the most exciting contributions to Latin American art in recent years. There is a large collection of the artist's work including paintings, sculptures, and an eternal flame set in the center in defense of peace and human rights. The museum, modeled on an Inca temple, is dedicated to the values of the pre-Columbian man and his struggle against colonization. Set in picturesque gardens, the chapel overlooks the city. If you plan to visit the Museo Guayasamín as well, it is best to take a taxi here first and then walk the five blocks to the museum. After your visit to the museum, take a stroll through the fragrant eucalyptus forests in the **Parque Metropolitano**, which has splendid views of Quito and the nearby volcanic peaks of Cotopaxi and Cayambe.

To see what Quiteños do in their spare time, wander back down Bosmediano to the large **Parque Carolina**, located just off Avenida Eloy Alfaro. The green spaces here are crowded with soccer and volleyball players, runners, and groups of picnickers on weekends. Every Sunday in August, outdoor concerts are held here. The **Museo de Ciencias Naturales** (Natural History Museum; Mon–Fri 8.30am–4.30pm, Sat 10am–2pm; charge) is on the south side of the park, at the corner of Rumipamba and Los Shyris. It has a good collection of endemic fauna and is worth a visit before you go to see the flora and fauna in the wild. Also in the park, Quito's wonderful **Vivarium** (Tue–Sun 9.30am–5.30pm; charge) houses a large live collection of reptiles and amphibians, and explains some of the threats that face this aspect of Ecuador's spectacular wildlife. At the park's **Jardín Botánico** (Botanical Garden; daily 9am–5pm; charge), some of Ecuador's amazing plant life is on display: a stroll through the gardens gives a glimpse of the mind-boggling variety that makes this country one of the world's biodiversity hotspots. ❏

Quito's New Airport

Flying into Quito's Aeropuerto Internacional Mariscal Sucre is an adventure: you plunge out of the clouds and appear to be headed straight for a mountainside before the pilot miraculously alights the plane on a modest runway hemmed in by apartment blocks and busy suburban life.

For years, Ecuador's main international airport has effectively been inside the city, with planes landing simply too close to Quiteños for comfort, and with noise and air pollution to boot. Because of the city's high altitude (Mariscal Sucre airport is at 2,850 meters/9348ft), and short runway length, many planes are only able to take off at 60 percent capacity, and the largest planes are unable to fly here at all. It's been clear for many years that a new airport was needed. That is set to become a reality some time in 2010 when Quito's new $600 million international airport opens some 20km (12 miles) east of the city on the Tababela Plateau. Set at a lower altitude of 2,400 meters (7,872ft), away from urban development, and with a longer runway, the new airport will be able to handle larger planes at 90 percent capacity and greater fuel loads, so enhancing opportunities for cheaper, non-stop travel, improved imports/exports, and freeing Quito's residents from the ever-present threat of planes literally encroaching upon their lives.

COLONIAL ARCHITECTURE

Catholic concepts, indigenous motifs, and inspiration blend with Arabic influences to create the colonial style that has been carefully preserved in Quito and Cuenca

When the Spanish conquered Ecuador they brought with them priests from different monastic orders: Franciscans, Augustinians, and Dominicans, and later the Jesuits. Within 50 days of the foundation of Quito in 1534 the Franciscan monks had begun constructing their own church. This was the first classic example of colonial architecture.

Each religious order was assigned land by the Spanish crown and each competed against the others in the construction of churches, convents, and plazas. Brother Jodocko Ricke, a Flemish Franciscan, set up an informal school for indigenous children to teach them religion and art. It was the first school of fine arts in South America.

The Franciscans discovered the creative skills of the indigenous people and also brought over talented converted Muslims. Sun motifs (the Sun being the principal Inca god) are commonly found alongside Madonna and Child representations, and ceilings often show *Mudéjar* influence. This blend of European and indigenous ideas created the Quiteño school of art and architecture.

The Jesuits strengthened the arts movement when they arrived in 1586. In the following 250 years ornate churches with richly adorned sacristies, carved choirs, and fine paintings flourished. Workshops and guilds were established and by the middle of the 18th century: 30 guilds in Quito controlled all artistic production.

ABOVE: the ornate Baroque facade of the Jesuit church La Compañía in Quito, best seen in early morning light. Unesco considers it one of the world's 100 most exceptional buildings.

LEFT: neo-gothic stained-glass depiction of "the father of the church," St Augustine, in Cuenca's new cathedral.

THE SCHOOL OF QUITO

The niches of early colonial altarpieces were first decorated with paintings, but polychrome statues became dominant later additions. When the first colonial buildings were constructed, statues were shipped over to Ecuador from Andalucía in Spain. However, by the 18th century a distinct style of Quiteño art had emerged.

Baroque, Rococo, and neoclassical styles from Europe reached Quito and were interpreted in a new way. Artists used different mediums: stone, ivory, tagua, clay, porcelain, and metal, but polychrome statues made from wood were the most popular.

Native cedarwood and sometimes alder from the hills surrounding Quito were used. Smaller figurines were usually made from balsawood. Trees were cut only at the full moon so that the sap would have risen to the highest level possible, making the wood stronger for carving. First the artists primed the statues and then painted directly on them with bright primary colors. They developed attention to detail and realism, reddening the cheeks, using false eyelashes and nails, and glass eyes. The figures were sometimes dressed from head to toe in sumptuous fabrics with floral designs.

ABOVE: seen from the Plaza Grande, green tiled domes and Baroque statuary adorn the exterior of Quito's cathedral, begun in 1560.

RIGHT: a Baroque polychrome head of an angel from the Quito school of sculpture, displayed in Quito's Museo de la Ciudad.

BELOW: late afternoon light bathes the glazed cupulas and unfinished towers of Cuenca's new cathedral, begun in 1885 and completed only in the late 20th century.

DAY TRIPS FROM QUITO

Mountains, forests, thermal springs, and wildlife sanctuaries are all within easy reach of the capital, and the Virgin of El Quinche is renowned for her miracles

Quito makes a good starting point for many day-long excursions into the surrounding Andean Sierra. By hiring a car, taking a tour, or using public transport or taxis, you can discover a region crowded with mountains, waterfalls, thermal baths, and peaceful villages.

Buses to the Equatorial Line Monument, **La Mitad del Mundo ❶**, run about every half-hour on Avenida América, near the junction with Avenida Colón in the New Town. The monument is about a half-hour trip (22km/14 miles) to the north of Quito, located on latitude 0°, and provides an irresistible opportunity to straddle both hemispheres. It is a very popular spot, particularly at the equinoxes (March 21 and September 21), when the sun is directly overhead and neither monument nor visitors cast a shadow. The monument forms the focal point of a park and leisure area with gift shops and restaurants, and there is a good museum inside (Mon–Thur 9am–6pm, Fri–Sun 9am–7pm; charge). An elevator leads to the top for fine views. Close by is the quirky **Museo Solar Inti Ñan ❷** (daily 9.30am–5pm; charge), which claims to mark the true spot of the equator as measured by GPS. Fun, interactive exhibits include demonstrations of how water drains in different directions on either side of the Equator, as well as sun clocks, ethnographic displays, and best of all, some incredible 150-year-old shrunken

heads: ask the administration to show you if they are not on display.

About 4km (2 miles) farther on, toward the village of Calacalí, is the **Reserva Geobotánica Pululahua ❸**, centered on what is reputedly the biggest volcanic crater in South America. A rough path leads down from the rim, and the interior of the crater has its own microclimate, with rich vegetation and diverse birdlife. Nearby is the excellent El Crater restaurant and art gallery, with fantastic views. Also to the north of Quito is the **Reserva Maquipucuna ❹**

Main attractions
LA MITAD DEL MUNDO
MUSEO SOLAR INTI ÑAN
MUSEO DE SITIO TULIPE
BOSQUE MINDO-NAMBILLO
PARQUE ARQUEOLÓGICO
  RUMIBAMBA
PAPALLACTA THERMAL SPRINGS

PRECEDING PAGES: Guápulo church. **LEFT:** tourists at La Mitad del Mundo. **BELOW:** the eccentric Museo Solar Inti Ñan.

As well as hummingbirds, the Bosque Mindo-Nambillo is home to cock-of-the-rocks and several species of quetzals.

(contact the Quito office at Baquerizo 238 and Tamayo; tel: 02-250 7200; www.maqui.org): take the coast road through Calacalí to Nanegalito (61km/35 miles) and at the village follow the signposts for 19km (12 miles). The reserve consists of steeply sloping cloud forest, with a great diversity of fauna and flora.

Farther along the Calacalí–La Independencia road is the recently opened **Museo de Sitio Tulipe ❺** (Tulipe Archeological Site Museum, tel: 02-285 0635; Wed–Sun 9am–4pm; charge), which is situated between Nangelito and Gualea. The site has some 2,000 pyramids and mounds, constructed by the pre-Inca Yumbo people who inhabited the valleys north of Quito *c*. AD 800–1660. The ruins are thought to have been the Yumbo's main ceremonial site, with water being of great importance to rituals here, as shown by the remains of several chanels and pools.

Further west, the **Bosque Mindo-Nambillo ❻**, near Mindo, is a protected reserve that is home to birds, orchids, and bromeliads. The 20,000-hectare (49,400-acre) forest covers land of varying altitudes, which makes for a very diverse ecosystem, supporting some 325 species of bird. Tour operators in Quito offer all sorts of day excursions and longer trips to the forest, and there are several good lodges here *(see Travel Tips, page 346)* which make Mindo a popular break from the city for nature-spotting and relaxation.

Back closer to Quito, the **Parque Arqueológico Rumibamba ❼** (Thur–Sun 10am–4pm; charge) is making a stir. Located on the western edge of the city, the site was uncovered by excavators preparing to build a new housing project. The digging revealed Inca walls and thousands of artifacts from the Yumbo civilization. It is now all protected in this 32-hectare (79-acre) site, with an excellent museum in a restored hacienda as its centerpiece.

On the opposite side of Quito, the city's eastern fringes, lies the tiny village of **Guápulo** with its 400-year-old church containing works by the country's best-known 17th-century artists: this was the founding spot of the School of Quito *(see page 165)*. This church and former convent has a pulpit carved by indigenous sculptor Juan

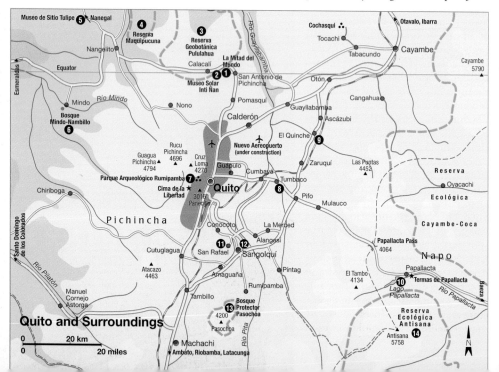

Quito and Surroundings

Menacho that is unquestionably the loveliest in Quito. From here, you pass through the district of Cumbayá, into the valley of Los Chillos, and through the countryside along the winding Río San Pedro. The settlement of **Tumbaco** ❽ is a green oasis close to the city and has many weekend houses and good restaurants, as well as a famous bungee-jump from the bridge at Chice.

Miracles and hot springs

The road through the Tumbaco valley passes through the sanctuary of **El Quinche** ❾, which attracts pilgrims from all over the northern Sierra. The Virgin of El Quinche is renowned for her miracles, and is a favorite among drivers and transport workers. Many make the yearly pilgrimage to Oyacachi, where the Virgin Mary statue originated. This small isolated community has some hot springs set in a lush valley at 3,200 meters (10,500ft) in the Cayambe Coca Reserve, just beneath the *páramo (see page 20)* It is connected to Cayambe and Quito via Cangahua.

Descend the main road (unpaved but well maintained) from El Quinche to the south. The view is wonderful, and snow and subtropical forests lie close together. At Km 59, the small **Lago Papallacta** ❿ is renowned for trout fishing. At Km 60, a road branches off to the springs of Huanonumpa, commonly known as the thermal springs of Papallacta and the most attractively developed hot springs in Ecuador. Stay overnight in the comfortable Termas de Papallacta hotel (*see Travel Tips, pages 330)* and go for a dip in one of its private pools. The public pools by the restaurant are crowded on weekends.

The **Valle de los Chillos**, another area of thermal springs, lies some 30 minutes' drive east of Quito. There is a fine descent into the valley on the Via Oriental and the Autopista de Los Chillos. The highway crosses the valley's main road in **San Rafael** ⓫ (12km/8 miles). Stop here to visit **La Casa de Kingman Museo** (tel: 02-86 1065; Thur–Sun 10am–4pm; charge),

the former home of the artist Eduardo Kingman (*see page 111)*. It now displays his works alongside other notable colonial and modern art. Ahead lies the village of **Sangolquí** ⓬, known for its Sunday market. Nearby, at La Merced and El Tingo, are some more thermal springs (turn left at San Rafael).

To the south of Sangolquí is the village of **Amaguaña**, which can be reached by bus from Quito (about an hour's drive). A few kilometers from Amaguaña, set around an extinct volcano, is the **Bosque Protector Pasochoa** ⓭, a sanctuary for birds and native plants (orchids bloom from February to May). For excursions, contact Fundación Natura (*see Travel Tips, page 347)*. The road to **Volcán Antisana** goes through Pintag. The volcano, which is protected in the **Reserva Ecológica Antisana** ⓮, has four snowy peaks, which are very difficult to climb. To use the road you must get the permission of the Fundación Antisana in Quito (Avenida Mariana de Jesús and La Isla; tel: 02-243 3851). In the surrounding reserve condors, rainbow ducks, and other birds can be seen. ❏

The rather clumsy-looking monument at La Mitad del Mundo marks the equator. Visitors can take the elevator to the top of the monument for some fine views.

BELOW:
relaxing at the Papallacta springs.

GOING NORTH

From Otavalo, home to Ecuador's greatest market, to the surrounding lakes and artisans' villages and up to the Colombian border

The province of **Imbabura**, just a short step north of Quito, is one of Ecuador's most popular destinations. Its numerous volcanoes, lakes, and valleys combine to create a landscape of extraordinary beauty, while the variety of local indigenous groups makes the northern Sierra one of Ecuador's most culturally vibrant regions. Even more beguiling for many travelers is that Imbabura province is a rich source of handicrafts: it is home to the woodcarvers of San Antonio, the leatherworkers of Cotacachi, and, most famously, the weavers of Otavalo.

Beyond the capital

Leaving **Quito ❶** behind, most visitors take the shortest route to Imbabura, some 100km (60 miles) along the paved Pan-American Highway. For those who have time to explore, there are a number of ways of reaching the province and several places worth visiting en route. There are buses from Quito to the towns numbered on the map on page 176. Getting to some of the villages takes a little more ingenuity if you do not have your own transport, but many are walkable from the nearest town, and round-trip taxi journeys are not expensive.

The main road passes through the **Guayllabamba** Valley, which is warm and fertile, and famous for its orchards and local fruit, such as the *chirimoya* (custard apple) and the local variety of avocado, which is small,

roundish, and black-skinned. Visitors are pressed to buy the produce, and local women compete by offering a *yapa* (one extra for the same price). A local specialty is the tasty *locro de cueros* (potato soup with pork rind) with avocados on the side.

Guayallabamba is home to the excellent **Zoológico de Guayalla-bamba** (tel: 02-236 8898; Tue–Fri 9am–5pm, Sat–Sun 9.30am–5pm; charge), which has over 50 species of native fauna representing all the diverse ecological regions of Ecuador.

Main attractions
GUAYALLABAMBA ZOO
OTAVALO MARKET
PARQUE CONDOR
LAGUNA CUICOCHA
INDIGENOUS HOMESTAY WITH RUNA TUPARI
HACIENDA ZULETA
RESERVA ECOLÓGICA EL ÁNGEL

PRECEDING PAGES:
Otavalo market wares. **LEFT:** selling woven cloth.
BELOW: the road to Ilumán near Otavalo.

Here, you can get close to rarely seen wildlife such as jaguars, moor wolves, Andean spectacled bears, ocelots, and sloths, along with a kaleidoscope of birds, monkeys, and squirrels. If you are not going to the Galápagos, you can see the remarkable Galápagos giant tortoise here, and you can also admire what is perhaps the country's most emblematic creature: the magnificent Andean condor. The zoo has a strong conservation ethos and several of its animals have been rescued from the illegal pet and fur trade.

Two roads lead out of Guayllabamba toward Cayambe: the left-hand one, via **Tabacundo**, follows a deep ravine, with curious rock formations. After crossing the Río Guayllabamba it is possible to make a detour along the riverside down to the tranquil villages of **Puellaro** and **Perucho**, where oranges grow and little seems to have changed for decades.

Another option is a visit to the archeological site of **Cochasquí**, on the southern slopes of **Mount Mojanda**, a short distance from Tabacundo. Some 15 flat-topped pyramids and 30 mounds are believed to have been built by the Caranqui around the 13th century, although some date from as early as AD 900. Take a guided tour from the resident guardian, and learn about religious and funeral practices, living styles, and even the astronomical discoveries made in that era.

The small town of **Cayambe**, under the perpetual vigilance of the extinct volcano of the same name, is worth a stopover to try its famous local cheese, especially *queso de hoja*, and the *biscochos*, a savory shortbread.

A few kilometers south of Cayambe is the well-known **Hostería Guachalá** (tel: 02-236 3042; www.guachala.com), the oldest hacienda in Ecuador, dating from 1580. Set in pleasant grounds with a swimming pool and opportunities nearby for horseback riding, it is an attractive place where it is easy to conjure up the rich history that its owner, Diego Boniface, is more than willing to reveal to you.

Going north from Cayambe, a turn in the main road unexpectedly brings into view Laguna San Pablo and, towering behind it, **Volcán Imbabura**,

BELOW: the heart of Otavalo market.

with its concave slopes covered in tiny fields. Opposite is its sister mountain, **Cotacachi**, and on the flat valley floor between the two, known as "the valley of the dawn," lies Otavalo.

Ecuador's greatest market

At dawn on Saturday mornings, the market square (called the Poncho Plaza) in **Otavalo** ❷ gets busy as the stallholders set up their displays. Handicraft workers from the outlying districts come to negotiate their wares with traders before the tourists arrive. By 9am the square is a feast of colors and textures: bolts of cloth; thick blankets; tapestry wall hangings; embroidered blouses and dresses; chunky hand-knitted sweaters; long patterned belts (*fajas*) that indigenous women wind round their waists; and *cintas* or tapes, with which they bind their long hair. The square is a maze of stands and narrow alleys with just enough room to pass.

Tourists making day trips from Quito arrive by bus at around 10am, and the haggling begins. The *indígenas* are experienced in business, can size up their customer, and know just how far to lower their price: several speak English.

Despite the crowds, the atmosphere is calm and relaxed; muffled, perhaps, by the walls of cloth. Most of the handicrafts are tailored to foreign tastes, although some of the designs are reworkings of traditional motifs. There is plenty to choose from: Otavaleño work is usually well made, at prices that seem a dream to most foreigners.

Saturday is also market day for the local population. At the north end of Poncho Plaza you will find hot prepared food and a corner market for such animals as *cuyes* (guinea pigs) and rabbits. The market plaza for the larger farm animals is at the western edge of town. Just follow the unmistakable evidence left by these animals along Calle Morales and across the Pan-American Highway.

In parts of Poncho Plaza and along Calle Jaramillo, vendors sell every item of Otavaleño traditional dress, including the intricate hand embroidery of the indigenous women's blouses, as well as fleece, yarn, loom parts, aniline

Finishing off a woven bag in Otavalo market.

BELOW: multi-colored fleece and yarn for sale in the Plaza de Poncho, Otavalo.

The Weavers of Otavalo

Demand by Ecuadorians for good-quality fabrics has safeguarded the livelihoods of many households in the Otavalo region.

Ecuadorians have kept their traditional dress, but some can now afford more luxurious fabrics. The weaving families of Otavalo have transformed this demand into an impressive business.

For as far back as anyone knows, the people of the high, green Otavalo Valley have been spinners, weavers, and textile merchants. Because Ecuador lacks the mineral wealth of Peru and Bolivia, the Spanish were quick to exploit the country's human resources, and this included their textile skills. Under the *encomienda* system the colonizers were given the right to use forced indigenous labor in return for christening the workers, and by mid-1550s an *obraje* (textile workshop) using forced indigenous labor was established in Otavalo.

Between 1690 and 1720 the *encomiendas* were abolished by the Spanish crown, but native land fell into white hands, and many *indígenas* entered into a system of debt peonage (*wasipungo*) whereby they were virtual serfs on large haciendas, many of which continued to operate weaving workshops. In 1964 the Agrarian Reform Law outlawed debt peonage and granted *wasipungeros* title to their plots of land, leaving *indígenas* free to weave at home or to hire out their labor. Many of the most prosperous contemporary weaving families are descendants of the *wasipungeros*.

The Agrarian Reform Law coincided with an increase in tourism to the region. In 1966 there was one crafts store in Otavalo; by 1990 there were about 80, most of them *indígena*-owned and operated. It's a mistake, however, to think that the textile industry is mainly dependent on tourism; most Ecuadorians own something from Otavalo, and most textiles are sold to other South Americans. There is also a substantial export business to North America, Europe, and Japan, which brings several million dollars a year into the region.

A creative majority

About 85 percent of the estimated 45,000 Otavaleños in the valley are involved in the textile industry either full or part time. Almost all families have at least one spinning wheel or loom in the house. Involvement ranges from women who spin 2kg (5lb) of yarn a week, to families weaving a few ponchos a month on a backstrap loom, to the Tejidos Rumiñahui company in Otavalo, which produces up to 300 ponchos a day on electric looms.

Increased prosperity has not meant the abandonment of traditional dress, but the use of more luxurious fabrics. The women's skirt wraps (*anakus*) and shoulder wraps (*fachalinas*) were traditionally made of hand-spun wool or cotton; today wealthy women wear velvet. The women's dress, incidentally, is one of the closest in form to the costume of Inca women worn anywhere in the Andes today. The men's dress is less conservative, being a mixture of colonial and modern elements, although the custom of wearing long hair and the use of *alpargatas* (espadrilles) are pre-Hispanic.

Although some older *indígenas* and residents of remote communities only speak Quichua, most *indígenas* are bilingual in Quichua and Spanish, and a few will surprise you by speaking fluent English, French, German, or Portuguese at the market (*feria*). The famous market is the high point of the week, not only for visitors, but for the thousands of *indígenas* who come to buy, sell, and socialize, and maintain the great tradition of the Otavalo weavers. ❑

LEFT: traditional designs by Otavaleño weavers.

dyes, and carders. Vendors also sell clothing worn by other indigenous groups in Imbabura province and by mestizos and criollos. Although Saturday is the largest and busiest market day in Otavalo – when prices tend to be higher – its popularity has led to there being some sort of tourist market every day of the week.

The incredible food market

Calle Jaramillo runs south into the permanent food market, which overflows on Saturdays with a mind-boggling array of vendors and food. There's every kind of fruit, vegetable, grain, and meat imaginable, but don't become so engrossed in your shopping spree in Poncho Plaza that you miss the food market, because if weaving represents one important means of subsistence, agriculture represents the other.

Hacienda country

While day tours to Otavalo from Quito are popular, many independent travelers arrive on the Friday night before the market and stay for the weekend to explore the lush surrounding country. The area around Otavalo is hacienda country: there are several historic estates which now provide luxurious accommodation for visitors and staying at one of these is an unforgettable experience.

Closest to Otavalo – just 10 minutes by taxi north of town – the elegantly restored **Hacienda Pinsaquí** (tel: 06-2946 116; www.haciendapinsaqui.com; *see Travel Tips, page 331*) dates from 1790. Once dedicated to textile manufacturing, Pinsaquí had workshops that employed 1,000 local people. Now, this beautiful stately home set in graceful gardens welcomes guests to its polished halls. Dinners are set under chandeliers in rooms elegantly furnished with French and Spanish antiques, and are served by hotel staff in traditional Otavaleño dress. Out on the estate there is excellent horseback riding to be had on one of the hacienda's beautiful steeds.

Also restored to its former splendor is the 17th-century **Hacienda Cusín** (tel: 06-291 8013; www.haciendacusin. com; *see Travel Tips, page 331*) near the picturesque – but very cold – Laguna

BELOW: mouth-watering fruit for sale in Otavalo.

BELOW: the crater lake of Laguna Cuicocha, near Cotacachi.

San Pablo. The rooms are crowded with antique religious paintings, wooden armchairs, and candelabras, while outside are elegant gardens, with ponds and banks of glorious flowers. All sorts of activities and excursions are offered, including riding and volcano climbing. One of the best is surely a visit to **Parque Condor** (Tue–Sun 9.30am–5pm; charge) located, amidst panoramic views, at 2,800 meters (9,184ft) on top of a hill called Pucara de Curilloma near the hacienda and not far from Otavalo. This excellent park displays rescued birds of prey, owls, and several magnificent condors, and highlights their importance in the ecosystem. The climax of a visit here is to watch the birds soaring high in one of the free flight demonstrations which are given daily at 11.30am and 4.30pm.

For more fabulous views of the Otavalo area and Cotacachi and Imbabura volcanoes, visit the ecologically oriented inn and farm **Casa Mojanda** (tel: 09-973 1737; www.casamojanda.com; *see Travel Tips, page 331*). Its friendly family atmosphere and excellent home cooking make it ideal for relaxing in a tranquil natural setting. Further up are the beautiful **Lagunas de Mojanda** and the peak of **Fuya Fuya**, about 18km (11 miles) south of Otavalo. A dirt road leads to the lakes, divided by hills inhabited by wild rabbits. Go in a group, as robberies have become a problem near the lake.

Artists at work

The villages close to Otavalo provide a chance to see another aspect of the handicraft trade: the craftsmen themselves at work. In nearby **Carabuela** **Ⓐ**, they make scarves, woolen gloves, ponchos, and belts, some still using the pre-Hispanic loom. Other craftsmen here specialize in making Andean harps. The village of **Peguche Ⓑ**, too, has its weavers, and is well worth a stop. Peguche is about 3km (2 miles) northeast of Otavalo, and is the home of several indigenous musical groups.

About 3km (2 miles) east of Peguche, **Agato Ⓒ** is worth a visit if you are interested in textiles. The Tahuantinsuyo Workshop uses traditional looms and natural dyes, and makes some

lovely items, which are often for sale at the Hostería Cusín. You can reach Agato by bus or taxi from Otavalo.

Another nearby village of artisans is **Ilumán**  (there are occasional buses, or it's a short taxi ride from Otavalo). The inhabitants make double-sided ponchos, felt hats, and tapestries. Ilumán is also famous for its traditional healers or *curanderos*, who use guinea pigs, candles, and ritual stones, as well as herbs and alcohol, to diagnose sicknesses and chase away evil spirits or negative energy.

Master leatherworkers

About 15km (10 miles) north of Otavalo is the village of **Cotacachi** **E**, Ecuador's leatherwork center. Predominantly made of tough cowhide, the goods are mostly top-quality, and there is an excellent choice, including jackets, skirts, boots, briefcases, bags, riding equipment, and wallets.

While visiting, try Cotacachi's traditional *carne colorada*, made of sun-dried and fried pork or beef, colored with *achiote* (a red seed), and served with avocados, jacket potatoes, a cheese, onion, and egg sauce, and corn.

A project called **Runa Tupari** (meaning "meeting the Indians" in Quichua; tel: 06-292 5985; www.runa tupari.com) has built simple guest accommodation in several indigenous communities around Cotacachi. Visitors can stay and experience the daily life of families: helping out in the fields or kitchen, learning weaving and handicraft production, taking meals with the family, and perhaps even visiting the village shaman. Indigenous guides also take guests on explorations of nearby lakes and volcanoes, or on horseback rides. This is a fantastic way to deepen one's understanding of indigenous life in Ecuador: the families are delightful, the guest cabins cozy, and the whole experience unforgettable.

West of Cotacachi lies **Laguna Cuicocha**, a sparkling blue crater lake

Peguche is home to several indigenous music groups.

Otavalo and Surroundings

Reserva Ecológica
Cotacachi-Cayapas

Apuela
Laguna Cuicocha
Quiroga
Cotacachi **E**
Ibarra Atuntaqui
Hacienda Zuleta

Hacienda Pinsaqui
Ilumán **D**
Imbabura

Carabuela **A**
Quinchuquí

Peguche **B**
Imbabura ▲ 4609

Selva Alegre
Quichinche
Poncho Plaza
Cascadas de Peguche
Agato **C**
Parque Cóndor

Otavalo
Club de Tiro, Caza y Pesca

Eugenio Espejo
Laguna San Pablo
San Pablo del Lago
El Monasterio
Hacienda Cusín

N

Pichincha

González Suárez

0   2 km
0   2 miles
Lagunas de Mojanda
Quito

*Making water ice
(helados de paila) in
a copper paila at the
Rosalía Suárez ice-
cream parlor in Ibarra.*

BELOW: adding the
finishing touches in
San Antonio, a
village of expert
woodcarvers.

situated at the southern end of the Reserva Ecológica Cotacachi-Cayapas. A well-marked hiking trail circles the lake; it takes 4–5 hours to complete the circuit. Take a taxi here from Otavalo and arrange pickup later in the day, or walk the scenic route back to Otavalo through unspoiled Andean villages and farmland. It is advisable to visit the lake in groups, however, as robberies have occurred in the area.

Further north

The highway northward from Otavalo curves around Volcán Imbabura and descends toward Ibarra, passing through **Atuntaqui**, which reputedly serves the best *fritada* (deep-fried pork) in the region. Just before Ibarra, a right-hand turn leads into **San Anto-**nio, home to expert woodcarvers. You can watch the craftsmen at work and buy the finished articles.

A shorter, much slower, but very attractive route to Ibarra is along the old Pan-American Highway from Cayambe, heading around the far side of Volcán Imbabura via the villages of **Olmedo** and **Zuleta**. This narrow cobbled road, full of potholes, winds through several of the region's oldest haciendas. Along the way, it presents an image of the traditional rural structure of Ecuador, mixed with modern farming techniques.

At Zuleta, you will find the incredibly beautiful **Hacienda Zuleta** (tel: 06-2662 182; www.zuleta.com; *see Travel Tips, page 331*), completed in 1691, and steeped in four centuries of colonial history. This 2,000-hectare (4,000-acre) working farm belongs to one of Ecuador's most illustrious families. Two presidents of the republic have come from here: Leónidas Plaza (1901–5) and Galo Plaza Lasso (1948–52). Today the presidents' descendants welcome guests to their 15 beautiful guestrooms in the exquisitely maintained colonial

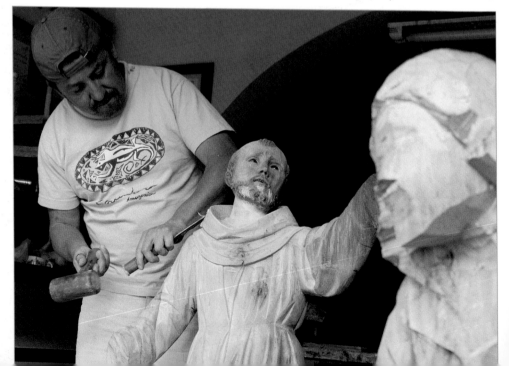

homestead. Meals are taken with the owners, the dinner conversation – in several languages – is fascinating, and out on the aesthetically gorgeous estate there are well-groomed horses to ride, condors to view, and long walks to take.

The white city

The provincial town of **Ibarra** ❸, about 22km (13 miles) north of Otavalo, has a population of 140,000, and enjoys one of the best climates of the Sierra due to its moderate altitude of 2,225 meters (around 7,000ft). Despite severe damage in at least two earthquakes, Ibarra has retained a colonial style. Its streets are cobbled, and the town's low, red-roofed buildings all have white-painted walls, which has earned Ibarra the nickname of "the white city." The population is a cultural mix of *indígenas*, *morenos*, and mestizos. Typical dishes made in the area include *arrope de mora* (blackberry syrup) and *nogadas* (a sweet made with walnuts). *Helados de paila* (water ices) can be found at the Rosalía Suárez ice-cream parlor on Calle Oviedo at Olmedo.

These are made by continuously beating fruit juice in a copper *paila* or round-bottomed pan, while it sits on a pile of ice.

Close to Ibarra is **Lago Yaguarcocha**. Its name means "blood lake" in Quichua, because in the 15th century the tough inhabitants of this region held out against the Inca invaders for some 16 years, until they were finally defeated and massacred on the shore. Today the lake is sometimes used for sailing, but is mainly known for the motor-racing track that surrounds it. Car races take place on this circuit during the September festival celebrations.

Sugarcane valley

On the other side of the mountain lies the warm **Chota Valley**, the lowest point in the northern Sierra, where sugarcane, vines, and tropical fruits grow. There are several thermal springs in this valley, such as **Chachimbiro**, though the road to them is somewhat arduous.

The Chota Valley is the only zone of the Sierra that has a predominantly black population. Today they are farmers, but

You may hear Ibarra's nickname, "the white city," translated into Spanish as La Ciudad Blanca.

BELOW LEFT: Parque Pedro Moncayo, Ibarra. **BELOW:** colonial Ibarra.

BELOW: topiary at the Tulcán cemetery.
RIGHT: embroidery adorns the clothes of Otavalo women.

the older inhabitants tell tales of their ancestors who fought against slavery on the plantations of Colombia. In the village of **Chota** (about an hour's drive from Ibarra), a concert hall regularly presents the *bomba negra* music of the local black population, which is a mixture of the music of the Sierra with African-style instruments and rhythms. One of the typical "instruments" is played by blowing tunes on a leaf held between the hands.

On the Colombian border

The highway north from the Chota Valley climbs steeply with twists and turns into the province of **Carchi**, over the high pass of **El Ángel**, and down to the frontier town of Tulcán. The **Reserva Ecológica El Ángel**, 15km (9 miles) north of El Ángel, preserves over 15,000 hectares (37,000 acres) of this region, encompassing a remarkably varied ecosystem where foxes, deer, armadillos, hummingbirds, and condors can often be seen. In some sheltered pockets of this well-watered *páramo* environment, montane forest supplants grasses, and there are dense

thickets of polylepis trees draped ethereally with mosses, orchids, and bromeliads. The reserve's crystal-clear lakes are also popular with anglers. Access is by taxi from El Ángel, or you can stay in the rustic stone cottages at **Polylepis Lodge** (tel: 06-295 4009; www.polylepislodge.com; *see Travel Tips, page 331*) 1km (½ mile) from the entry checkpoint.

About 40km (25 miles) before the border with Colombia is Carchi's sanctuary, the **Grotto of La Paz**, near the village of **San Gabriel ❹**, where pilgrims visit the statue of the Virgin sheltered in a natural cave. There are two splendid waterfalls just outside the village. In the border town of **Tulcán ❺**, the main attraction is the topiary garden in the cemetery, where huge cypress hedges are clipped into the shapes of animals, houses, and geometric figures. It is sensible to take extra care when visiting Tulcán as the proximity to the border means there are both guerrillas and drug-trafficking in town. It is best not to be on the streets after 10pm, and always carry your passport as there are frequent police checks. ❏

THE AVENUE OF THE VOLCANOES

The "spine" of Ecuador has hot springs and markets as well as a long line of breathtaking snow-capped mountains

The Andes are often thought of as the spine of Ecuador, but a ladder is a better analogy. Think of the Eastern and Western cordilleras as the sides of the ladder, with the lower east–west connecting mountains (called *nudos* or knots) as the rungs. Between each rung is an intermontane valley at about 2,300 to 3,000 meters (7,000 to 9,000ft) in elevation, with fertile volcanic soil.

The valleys are heavily settled and farmed today and were the territory of different ethnic groups in pre-Inca times. Both the Pan-American Highway and the railroad run north–south between the cordilleras, bobbing up and down over the *nudos* past fields, farms, and startled cows beneath a range of dormant and active volcanoes, some of which have snow all year round.

In 1802 the German explorer Alexander von Humboldt named this route the "Avenue of the Volcanoes." Ecuador's position on the equator means that you can travel through the avenue past orchids and palm trees, but with tundra vegetation, glaciers, and snow visible in the mountains above. By leaving the valley and hiking or climbing upwards, you can pass through all the earth's ecological zones from subtropical to Alpine.

A splendid way of traveling down the "avenue" is by rail, but you will need to check which lines are running. If open, the railroad does allow you to get an intimate look at life along the tracks, traveling through people's back yards, so to speak, rather than down the main road. The route suggested in this chapter, however, takes the Pan-American Highway, with detours and side roads to places of interest on the way.

The road south

Leaving **Quito ❶** by car or bus for the south can seem to take for ever, as the streets leading to the Pan-American Highway are usually jammed. However, there is a bypass, the Nuevo

Main attractions
PARQUE NACIONAL COTOPAXI
HACIENDA EL PORVENIR
THERMAL WATERS AT BAÑOS
VOLCÁN CHIMBORAZO
ALAUSÍ

LEFT: a *chiva* bus driving through the Avenue of the Volcanoes near Quilotoa. **BELOW:** Mount Cotopaxi is Ecuador's highest active volcano.

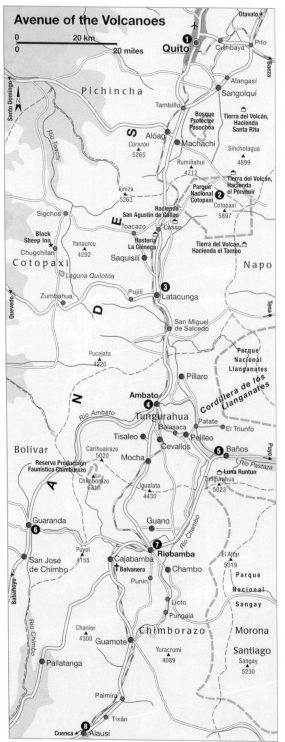

Avenue of the Volcanoes

Oriental, which connects with the Pan-American Highway on the outskirts of south Quito, and makes driving much less stressful. The road goes through the **Valle de los Chillos** and connects with the main highway about 8km (5 miles) farther south. The traffic eases a bit as you wind down off the Quito Plateau and into the first intermontane valley. Way off to the east the snowy peak of **Volcán Antisana** (5,750 meters/18,720ft) can be seen.

Looming over the region is **Volcán Cotopaxi** (5,897 meters/19,347ft), Ecuador's second-highest peak and one of the world's highest active volcanoes. On a clear day you can see its symmetrical, snow-capped cone from Quito. In the Western Cordillera, almost directly across from Cotopaxi, is **Volcán Illiniza** (5,265 meters/17,280ft), or the Illinizas as they are called, for there are actually two peaks. The lower, northern peak is a satisfying climb for non-technical climbers and hikers, while the southern one, Illiniza Sur, is only for those with experience.

Some 32km (20 miles) beyond Machachi, just over the first pass, is the

Fiesta de la Mamá Negra

Latacunga's festival of the Virgin of the Mercedes, commonly known as the Fiesta de la Mamá Negra (the Festival of the Black Mother) takes place on September 23 and 24. It's a lively event with obvious indigenous influences, despite its Christian name and outward trappings, which of course include paying homage to the figure of the black-faced Virgin Mary.

There are huge street parades with allegorical figures, often making satirical social or political points; masquerades; local bands; noisy firework displays; and dancing in the streets until all hours of the night. There is also a solemn Midnight Mass *(misa del gallo)* although some of the celebrants are a little less than solemn. It is one of the best-known such fiestas in the country and well worth seeing, if your visit happens to coincide with these dates.

entrance to the magnificent **Parque Nacional Cotopaxi ❷**.

Both sides of the highway are covered by a forest of Monterrey pines, many of them unfortunately dying from a fungal disease. The pines are not native; they were introduced from California for a forestry project and are a textbook example of the dangers of monoculture: the pines have crowded out the indigenous vegetation and the fungus has spread rapidly from tree to tree.

The national park centers on Cotopaxi, of course, but there are several other peaks that attract rock climbers, including **Rumiñahui** (4,712 meters/15,430ft), and there is also a great variety of wildlife, ranging from falcons and highland hummingbirds to tiny deer and the endangered, and rarely seen, Andean puma.

Haciendas and markets

As elsewhere in Latin America, the prime agricultural land in the valley was taken from the indigenous population soon after the Spanish conquest and turned into large Spanish-owned haciendas (estates), many of which still exist and include vast landholdings, despite the Agrarian Reform of 1964.

Several haciendas are also found in the less productive, windswept high *páramo*. Of these, the closest to Cotopaxi is **Hacienda el Porvenir** (tel: 02-223 1806; www.tierradelvolcan. com). This is the perfect base for some high-altitude acclimatization: there are wonderful walks and bike rides on the property, as well as adventurous horseback riding into the national park. Guided ascents of the volcano can also be arranged. The same company also owns remote, rustic **Hacienda El Tambo**, on the far side of Cotopaxi, and Hacienda Santa Maria, where there is a complex of aerial zip lines to take you flying over forest and river.

Very close by, just south of Machachi, is possibly one of Ecuador's most distinctive haciendas, **San Agustín de Callao** (tel: 03-271 9160; www.incahacienda. com). San Agustín is built on the site of an Inca palace, one of the two most important Inca constructions in Ecuador, and its dining room and chapel are built entirely within the original

The origin of the Quichua name Cotopaxi is not clear, and has had several different interpretations. Some translate it as the combination of two Quichua words: kotto, *meaning peak or mountain, and* paksi, *denoting shining. Another interpretation comes from the words* cutu, *meaning neck, and* pachi, *broken – which sees Cotopaxi as a headless neck with a white poncho of snow. Yet another translation denotes it, rather evocatively, as the "neck of the moon."*

BELOW: parading through the streets of Latacunga during the Mamá Negra festival.

The cathedral of Latacunga.

Inca stonework. Stay here amongst the antiques, murals and whispering masonry walls, and you will feel deeply immersed in history. There's also a whole program of activities, including hikes to the top of Cotopaxi, visits to some secret angling spots, or horseback rides across the *páramo* on one of the hacienda's beautiful steeds.

Further south, towards Latacunga is the small town of **Lasso**. Turn off west here for **Hostería La Ciénega** (tel: 03-271 9052). Now a hotel and restaurant, its main house – a stone mansion with huge windows, stonecobbled patios and Moorish-style fountains – was built in the mid-1600s for the Marquis de Maenza and was occupied by his family for more than 300 years. The stone chapel has a bell, still rung on Sunday mornings, which was installed in 1768 in thanksgiving when Cotopaxi ended 20 years of devastating eruptions. Von Humboldt stayed here in 1802 when he surveyed Cotopaxi, and the de Maenza-Lasso family plotted Ecuador's independence from Spain on this site in the 1800s. The comfortable rooms are beautifully furnished with antiques and chandeliers. Besides opportunities for excellent bird-watching in the gardens, you can ride horseback from here and make day trips to Cotopaxi National Park.

The little towns in the valley, and the larger city of **Latacunga** ❸ (pop. 50,000), are interesting primarily for their fiestas and market days. Some 90km (54 miles) from Quito, Latacunga is somnolent and pleasant, with a number of buildings constructed from local gray volcanic rock. It was founded in 1534 on the site of an Inca urban center and fortress. There are busy Saturday and Tuesday markets, where crafts are sold, especially *shigras* (bags), baskets, and ponchos.

Latacunga's *municipio* (town hall) and cathedral are on the main plaza, the Parque Vicente León, which has topiary and a well-maintained garden. Behind the cathedral is a colonial building housing an arcade with shops, offices, and an art gallery. Five blocks west down Calle Maldonado at Calle Vela is the **Casa de la Cultura** (Tue–Fri 8am–noon and 2–6pm, Sat 8am–3pm;

charge), built on the remains of a Jesuit monastery and the old Montserrat watermill. The museum houses pre-Columbian ceramics and weavings, and a library, theater, and gallery. Some 10km (6 miles) west of Latacunga is **Pujilí**, which has a lively market on Sunday, and colorful Corpus Christi festivities in June.

A wild and scenic loop west of Latacunga takes you through the market towns of Zumbagua, Chugchilan, Sigchos, and Saquisilí, then back to Latacunga. Zumbagua's market on Saturday is stocked with a kaleidoscopic array of fresh produce. Half an hour's drive farther on is Lake Quilotoa, an azure, water-filled volcanic crater, still considered active. Indigenous people from the Tigua Valley nearby sell naïve, brightly colored enamel paintings on sheepskin at the crater rim. On the way north from here to the village of Chugchilan is the Black Sheep Inn (tel: 03-281 4587; www.blacksheepinn. com), an ecological farm with delicious home cooking and great views over the sierra. The whole loop back takes several hours along mainly dirt roads,

so a stop here is a welcome break. **Saquisilí** only comes out of its torpor on Thursday market day. The market is an economic hub for the surrounding region, with *indígenas* buying and selling everything from cattle to cotton. The market is decidedly a local, rather than tourist, affair and a favorite with many travelers for that reason.

Another 10km (6 miles) farther south you cross the provincial boundary and enter Tungurahua province, named after the area's dominant volcano. The region is known for its relatively mild climate and production of vegetables, grain, and fruit, including peaches, apricots, apples, pears, and strawberries, and you will encounter roadside vendors along the highway on both sides of Ambato.

Provincial center

Some 128km (80 miles) from Quito, **Ambato** ❹ is the capital of Tungurahua province. Arriving in the city brings you abruptly face to face with the 21st century. Ambato was almost totally destroyed by an earthquake in 1949 and then rebuilt, so virtually

Sheep for sale in Saquisilí market.

BELOW: Quilotoa crater lake.

TIP

The Manto de la Novia, San Miguel, San Pedro, and Inés María waterfalls near Baños can all be reached by *chiva* bus tours.

nothing of the colonial town remains. With a population of about 150,000, the city is the sixth-largest in Ecuador. Industries include some textiles (especially rug-weaving), leather goods, food-processing, and distilling, but the most interesting aspect of Ambato is its enormous Monday market, the largest in Ecuador. Thousands of *indígenas* and country people come into town for the different activities, which take place in various parts of the city. Several plazas contain nothing but produce vendors, while the streets are lined with kiosks selling goods of all kinds. To reach the textiles, dyes, and crafts (ponchos, *ikat* blankets and shawls, *shigras* bags, belts, beads, hats, and embroidered blouses), follow Calle Bolívar or Cevallos about 10 blocks north from the center of town to the area around Calle Abdón Calderón.

Ambato's attractive central plaza is **Parque Montalvo**, named for the writer Juan Montalvo (1833–99). Montalvo's house, at calles Bolívar and Montalvo nearby, is open to the public. On the north side of the plaza is Ambato's modern **cathedral**, and opposite is the post office. The **Parque Cevallos**, a few blocks to the northwest, is green and tree-lined, and is the site of the **Museo de Ciencias Naturales** (Natural Science Museum; tel: 03-282 7395; Mon–Fri 8am–noon and 2–5.30pm; charge), packed with stuffed animals and birds of the region. The Río Ambato flows through a gorge to the west of the town center. A paved road leads out of Ambato to the east, past Volcán Tungurahua and down into the Oriente, forming one of the main east–west links between the jungle and Sierra.

From Ambato, catch a bus or truck 20km (12 miles) northeast to the small town of **Píllaro**. This is the way to get to the **Parque Nacional Llanganates**, which is perpetually wrapped in fog and covered with virtually impenetrable cloud-forest vegetation. These remote mountains appeal to the Indiana Jones in all of us because of various accounts of General Rumiñahui hiding Quito's gold here, before Benalcázar and the *conquistadores* could get to it.

BELOW: *indígena* in Salasca market.
BELOW RIGHT: traditional woven rugs for sale in Salasca.

Defiant and distinctive

About 14km (8 miles) east of Ambato on the road to Baños is **Salasaca**, the home of a small, beleaguered indigenous group, thought to be of Bolivian origin, which is struggling to hold on to its land and maintain its customs in the face of enormous pressure from criollos in the surrounding communities. This group is thought to be *mitmakuna*, living here as a result of the Incas' policy of forcibly moving whole tribes from their homelands to distant foreign territories as punishment for uprising or the threat of it.

Salasaca men wear black and white ponchos and handmade white felt hats with broad, upturned brims at the front and back. Unique to Salasaca are the men's purple or deep-red scarves dyed with cochineal, a natural dye that comes from the female insects that live on the Opuntia (prickly pear) cactus. Salasaca women wear the same hats as the men, brown or black *anakus*, cochineal-dyed shoulder wraps, hand-woven belts with motifs, and necklaces of red, Venetian glass beads.

A few kilometers past Salasaca is **Pelileo**, a little town where you would not want to invest in property: it has been leveled by earthquakes four times in the past 300 years. As the last quake was in 1949, the present Pelileo is an entirely modern town. There is a small Saturday market, which is attended by many *indígenas* from Salasaca. It is also Ecuador's major production center for blue jeans.

Subtropical climate

Beyond Pelileo the highway drops 850 meters (2,780ft) to Baños in only 24km (15 miles), following various tributaries and then the Río Pastaza itself in its headlong rush to the Amazon basin. The region produces sugarcane for distilled alcohol, and many kinds of fruits and vegetables.

Baños ❺ has always been famous for its thermal hot springs bubbling out of the side of the wild and unruly **Volcán Tungurahua** (5,023 meters/17,154ft). In 1999 the volcano started erupting again, and the 25,000 townsfolk were evacuated. Residents fought their way back in at the beginning of 2000 at

EAT

In typical holiday town style, Baños does a roaring trade in sweet treats. Most visible is the manufacture of *melcocha*, a hard toffee made from cane sugar that has to be pulled and shaped in long straps while warm. *Melcocheros* work the malleable sugar with a deft twisting and throwing action. If you stand and watch long enough, you might be given a bit to try.

BELOW LEFT: street stalls in front of the basilica of Nuestra Señora del Agua Santa, Baños.
BELOW RIGHT: Salasaca market traders.

their own risk, even with the volcano spewing hot rocks and ash only 7km (4 miles) away. Another major eruption took place in August 2006 accompanied by a 10km (6-mile) high ash cloud and pyroclastic flows resulting in seven deaths and destroying hamlets and roads on the western and northwestern slopes of Tungurahua. The volcano continued its activity through 2008 and 2009; geologists are still keeping a close watch on the peak and will evacuate the town again if activity increases. Tourist operators in town offer night-time volcano-viewing tours: but check if there are actually any pyrotechnics going on at the time you visit, before signing up.

Baños has become something of an adventure hub for backpackers. Streets full of tour operators tout four-wheel drive buggy tours, mountain biking, bungee-jumping, rafting, canyoning, and discount jungle visits. One of the classic routes in this area (for bicycle, scooter, or by 4WD bike) is to head along the road between Baños and Puyo skirting the deep canyon of the Río Pastaza, surrounded on all sides by cloud-forest-cloaked mountains, and waterfalls. Take care not to enter the many unlit road tunnels, though: there is an unpaved detour round each of them which is safer for pedestrians and cyclists. Some of the waterfalls along this route are spectacular, especially near Río Verde, where the plume-like Pailón del Diablo, about 20km (12 miles) from Baños, should not be missed.

The gentle, subtropical climate of Baños (altitude 1,800 meters/5,904ft) is another draw, and it makes the region a hiker's paradise. There are short trails in the hills directly above the town, and nearby, there are the little-explored national parks of **Los Llanganates** and **Sangay**, two of the most biologically diverse areas in the world. With luck and patience, four kinds of monkey, spectacled bears, mountain tapirs, and birds such as the cock-of-the-rock and black and chestnut eagle can be seen in the forests here. The area is also home to an exceptionally high diversity of plants, many still unknown to science. A recent study of just one genus of orchid has turned up 14 new species.

While foreign travelers come to Baños for the hot springs, hiking, and adventure activities, many Ecuadorians come here to pay homage to the Virgin of Baños, known as **Nuestra Señora del Agua Santa** (Our Lady of the Holy Water), whose statue is housed in the basilica in the center of town. The Virgin is credited with many miracles, including delivering people from certain death in a fire in Guayaquil, and saving the lives of travelers when a bridge over the Pastaza River collapsed. The walls of the basilica are hung with paintings depicting these events. The basilica grounds have a small museum with moldering stuffed tropical birds and the Virgin's changes of clothing.

The highest peak

From Baños, return to Ambato (buses are frequent and the journey takes

BELOW: the town of Baños attracts both visitors from Ecuador and foreign travelers.

about an hour) and make a trip to the west. A paved road circles around **Volcán Carihuairazo** (5,020 meters/16,470ft) and **Volcán Chimborazo** (6,310 meters/20,571ft) and heads for Guaranda and the coast. Chimborazo is the highest peak in Ecuador, and it looms over the provinces of Chimborazo, Bolívar, and southern Tungurahua like a giant ice cream, dominating the landscape (*see Travel Tips, page 347 for climbing information*). The **Reserva Producción Faunística Chimborazo** (Chimborazo Fauna Reserve), which surrounds the mountain, is the place to visit for views, high-altitude hiking, and to see some of the way of life of the remote, chilly indigenous villages in the area. The reserve covers a vast 56,560 hectares (139,703 acres) between 3,800 meters (12,540ft) above sea level to the summit of Chimborazo, and is home to vicuña, llama and alpaca; the last are also prized livestock for local people. Foxes and deer are also seen here, condors often soar overhead, and this is one of the few places to see the giant hummingbird (*Patagonia gigas*), which due to its cold-

temperature habitat, hibernates at night and wakes up with the sun. High-altitude polylepis forests are also a fascinating feature of the park, as are the pre-Inca sites of worship on the mountain's flanks, where local villagers still make ritual offerings.

The Western Cordillera outside Ambato is the land of emerald mountains. Every inch of the hillsides is farmed by the Chibuleo *indígenas*, turning the land into a patchwork quilt of every shade of green. Every so often, either Carihairazo or Chimborazo pokes its snowy head out above the clouds. The road climbs to the *páramo* above 4,000 meters (13,000ft), with some superb views of Chimborazo, then drops again to Guaranda, which is 85km (53 miles) from Ambato. Midway through the journey you enter Bolívar province.

Art and fireworks

About 90km (55 miles) from Ambato, the capital of Bolívar province, **Guaranda** ❻ (2,670 meters/8,725ft) is a small, sleepy town of 21,000 people that comes alive on Saturday with the

The statue of Nuestra Señora del Agua Santa, housed in her own basilica in Baños.

BELOW LEFT: Las Piscinas de la Virgen baths, waterfalls.

The Trees at the Top of the World

The amazing polylepis tree is found growing in sparse patches in the high Andes; indeed, it has the unique distinction of being the tree that grows at the highest elevations in the world. Stands of this ancient, gnarled, slow-growing tree with its bark as flaky as paper (hence the Greek name, meaning "many scales") are found between 3,800 and 4,600 meters (12,000–15,000ft) above sea level. This is remarkable because the natural treeline of the Andes (above which other trees cannot grow) is much lower: 3,200–3,500 meters (10,000–11,000ft) above sea level.

Polylepis trees usually grow in sheltered, inaccessible gulleys in high-altitude grasslands such as the Ecuadorian *páramo*, but researchers believe they may once have covered much more extensive swathes of the Andean range, and that existing forests are just the remnants that remain after millennia of being used for fuel and construction material. Many polylepis species (there are thought to be 28) are now protected.

Ecuador's ancient forests are also an important habitat for other endangered plant, bird and animal species, Furthermore, they help to prevent erosion on steep mountainsides and are the source of many medicinal plants.

TIP

One of the great experiences in this region is to soar down the side of Chimborazo from its Carrel Refuge (4,800 meters/15,744ft) on a bike. Several companies offer this thrilling 55km (33-mile) descent, but the best is Riobamba bike tour operator ProBici (tel: 03-295 1760; see Travel Tips, page 347).

BELOW: Riobamba's cathedral.

weekly market. The town is set among seven hills, one of which, Cruz Loma (Cross Ridge), has a giant statue of an indigenous chief, **El Indio de Guarango**, a *mirador* (lookout), and a small, circular museum with pre-Hispanic and colonial artifacts. There are three other small museums in the town with mixed collections, including colonial art and ethnographic material: the **Museo Municipal**, the **Museo de la Casa de la Cultura Ecuatoriana**, and the **Museo del Colegio Pedro Carbo**. Opening hours are variable: check on arrival at the tourist information office located on García Moreno (Mon–Fri 8am–noon and 2–6pm). The **Parque Central** has a monument to Simón Bolívar, which was a gift from the government of Venezuela. Guaranda is the market center for the **Chimbo Valley**, a rich agricultural region that produces wheat *(trigo)* and corn *(maíz)*. A 16km (10-mile) ride through the valley south from Guaranda takes you to **San José de Chimbo**, an ancient town with colonial architecture and two thriving craft centers. The *barrio* (neighborhood) of Ayurco specializes in fine

guitars, handmade from high-quality wood grown in the province. Tambán *barrio* produces hunting guns and fireworks, but these are not just any old fireworks. Bamboo frames (*castillos*, or castles) are fabricated in the shape of giant birds, huge towers, or enormous animals, with fireworks attached. They are set off to striking effect at fiestas throughout the country. It is not uncommon for the *castillo* to fall over, shooting sky rockets directly into the crowd. Gringos generally jump for cover behind the plaza fountain, but the Ecuadorians love it.

Ancient center

Riobamba ❼ is the capital of Chimborazo province. In 1541 the Spanish chronicler Pedro de Cieza de León began an epic 17-year horseback journey in Pasto, Colombia, riding south along the Royal Inca Highway through Ecuador, Peru, and Bolivia. By 1545 Cieza de León was in central Ecuador heading for Riobamba. "Leaving Mocha," he wrote, "one comes to the lodgings of Riobamba, which are no less impressive than those of Mocha.

They are situated in the province of the Puruhás in beautiful fair fields, whose climate, vegetation, flowers, and other features resemble those of Spain." Chimborazo is still primarily an agricultural province, growing crops such as wheat, barley, potatoes, and carrots, with some grazing land for small herds of sheep, llama, and cattle.

Although at 2,750 meters (8,993ft) Riobamba is only 180 meters (589ft) higher than Ambato, it feels much colder, perhaps because of the wind sweeping down off the glaciers of Chimborazo. The original Riobamba was founded by the Spanish on the site of a major Inca settlement 21km (13 miles) away, where the modern town of Cajabamba stands, but the old town was flattened by an earthquake in 1797 and a new location was chosen. The new Riobamba (pop. 150,000) retains much of its 18th-century architecture and is a relatively sleepy town, except on Saturday, which is market day.

Indigenous peoples

Chimborazo province was the pre-Inca territory of the Puruhá tribe. Mod-ern towns such as Guano, Chambo, Pungalá, Licto, Punin, Yaruquíes, Alausí, Chunchi, and Chimbo were all originally Puruhá settlements. But, as elsewhere, the Incas moved people around: they settled *indígenas* from Cajamarca and Huamachuco, Peru, in the Chimbo region and moved many Puruhá people to the south.

Today, Chimborazo has an amazing mixture of people who wear different kinds of traditional dress, although there aren't necessarily special names for all these groups. Chimborazo was the site of many *obrajes* (textile sweatshops) in colonial times and after independence. The indigenous population became increasingly impoverished and marginalized through succeeding centuries as they were pushed by new settlers into the mountains or became attached to the country haciendas as *wasipungeros* (serfs).

Street scene in the largely 18th-century Riobamba.

BELOW LEFT: ornate ironwork, Riobamba.
BELOW: mural depicting the history of Riobamba in the Parque 21 de Abril.

The Chimborazo *indígenas* did not take mistreatment and injustice lying down. There have been many revolts over the centuries, including an uprising of 8,000 *indígenas* around Riobamba in 1764, a revolt in Guano in 1778, and a rebellion in Columbe and Guamote in 1803. Land shortages are still a problem, and men from many communities frequently migrate temporarily to the larger cities in search of work. Chimborazo has also seen intensive Protestant evangelical activity, which has often exacerbated tensions.

The most obvious ethnic marker in Chimborazo is hats. While *indígenas* are increasingly using dark, commercially made fedoras, a large number still wear the handmade white felt hats, especially for fiestas and other special occasions. In the Guamote market you can spot as many as 15 different kinds of white, handmade hat being worn. Such variations as the size and shape of the brim and crown and the color and length of the streamers, tassels, or other decorations all indicate the wearer's community or ethnic group.

Two areas of the Riobamba market are of particular interest to visitors. Traditional indigenous garments, including such items as hats, belts, ponchos, *ikat* shawls, fabric, *shigras*, hats, and old jewelry (beautiful beads, earrings, and shawl pins) are sold in the **Plaza de la Concepción** on Orozco and 5 de Junio, along with baskets and *ikat* blankets. In one corner of this plaza people set up their treadle sewing machines and mend clothes or sew the collars on ponchos, while other vendors sell aniline (synthetic) dyes. Just south of this plaza on Calle Orozco is a small cooperative store selling crafts made by the *indígenas* of Cacha.

Another important craft of the Riobamba region is *tagua* nut carving. The egg-sized seeds of the lowland *tagua* palm are soft when first exposed to air but then harden to an ivory-like consistency. *Tagua* is carved into jewelry, chess sets, buttons, rings, busts, and tiny kitchen utensils. Stores selling *tagua* crafts are found opposite the train station on Avenida Primera Constituyente (Avenue of the First Constitution). The street acquired its name

BELOW: different colored dyes for sale in Riobamba market.
BELOW RIGHT: sewing the collar on a poncho in the Plaza de la Concepctión, Riobamba.

because, after winning independence from Spain, Ecuador's first constitution was written and signed in Riobamba on August 14, 1830.

About eight blocks northeast of the *artesanías* plaza is the **Plaza Dávalos**, where cabuya fiber (made from the *Agave americana* cactus, the century plant) and products are sold. *Cabuya* crafts have been an important local industry in the region since colonial times. *Indígena* women spin the fiber into cordage, used for the soles of espadrilles, rope, sacks, and saddlebags.

After the market has finished, the town empties rapidly and lapses into somnolence for another week. This is your opportunity to visit the **Museo de Arte Religioso** (tel: 03-296 5212; Tue–Sat 9am–noon and 3–6pm; charge), housed in the Convento de la Concepción on Calle Argentina. Among the items on display are statues, vestments, and a fabulous gold monstrance encrusted with diamonds and pearls.

There is also the museum in the **Colegio Nacional Pedro Vicente Maldonado** (Tue–Sat 9am–noon, 3–6pm) at Avenida Primera Constituyente 2412, with natural history exhibits; the **Museo de la Casa de la Cultura** (Tue–Sat 9am–noon and 3–6pm) focuses on archeology; and the **Museo del Banco Central** (tel: 03-296 5501; Mon–Fri 8.30am–5pm, Sat 10am–4pm; charge) located in the bank building downtown, has ethnographic and modern art exhibitions. The **Museo de la Ciudad** (tel: 03-295 1906; Mon–Fri 8.30–5pm, Sat 9am–4pm) has temporary and permanent exhibits. Opening times for all these museums can be erratic, so it is worth checking at the tourist information office on Avenida Daniel León Borja, which is not far from the train station. Riobamba also has some majestic old churches, including the **cathedral** on 5 de Junio and Veloz and the circular **basilica** (the only one in Ecuador) on Veloz and Alvarado in the Parque La Libertad.

Climb to the top of the **Parque 21 de Abril** (located on Calle Argentinos north of the center of town) for views of Chimborazo, Carihuairaso, Tungurahua, and **Altar** (5,319 meters/

Artifact in the Museo de Arte Religioso in Riobamba.

BELOW: Riobambo lies in the shadow of Volcán Chimborazo.

Landscape near Alausí in Chimborazo province.

17,457ft). This brooding hulk to the south of the city in the Eastern Cordillera is known in Quichua as Capac Urcu (Great or Powerful Mountain). It is better not to visit at sunset, however, as there have been muggings in the vicinity at that time.

Exploring the region

Riobamba is a good base for excursions to the rest of Chimborazo province. For a day trip to buy rugs and visit the artisans at work, catch a bus or cab 12km (7 miles) north on a subsidiary road, not the Pan-American Highway, to **Guano**. The town is known for its cottage-industry production of fine rugs, hand-knotted on huge vertical-frame looms. Most shops have a workshop attached where you can watch the weavers at work. Just a kilometer or two beyond Guano (there is a bus ser-

vice) is the small town of **Santa Teresita**, which specializes in the production of carrot or potato sacks woven from *cabuya* fiber. Many of the weavers have enormous warping frames in their yards, with hundreds of meters of *cabuya* on them, and you may also see the woven yardage stretched out along the road. At the edge of town is the **Balneario Las Elenas**, with two cold-water swimming pools and one warmer pool – all fed by natural springs – and a cafeteria.

Most of Chimborazo province lies south of Riobamba, and it's a part of Ecuador worth exploring. The road to Licto climbs above Riobamba and offers views of the city and the volcanoes.

A quiet but extremely traditional Sunday market, drawing *indígenas* from the Laguna Colta area and the usual assortment of vendors, is held in **Cajabamba**, 13km (8 miles) south of Riobamba on the Pan-American Highway. This was the site of the old Riobamba, which was originally a Puruhá community, and then the Inca settlement of Liripamba when it had fine, mortarless stonework, including a

BELOW: Guamote's Thursday market draws *indígenas* from all over the region. **BELOW RIGHT:** guinea pigs for sale.

temple of the sun, a house of the chosen women, and a royal *tambo* (lodge).

The stones from the Inca buildings were then incorporated into the Spanish town, which in turn was destroyed in the 1797 earthquake and subsequent landslide. The only building surviving from the 18th century is the chapel.

About 2km (just over 1 mile) beyond Cajabamba is the tiny town of **Balvanera** (also spelled Balbanera), on the shores of **Laguna Colta**. Colta *indígenas* graze their cattle and sheep along the marshy shores of the lake, and use the totora reeds in the lake to make *esteras* (mats) and *canastas* (baskets). Locals claim that the town's little church, with its image of the Virgin of Balvanera, is the oldest in Ecuador, constructed by the *conquistador* Sebastián de Benalcázar and his troops after a victory over the Inca forces, but there is no documentary evidence to support this.

In **Guamote** (51km/32 miles south of Riobamba), the Thursday market is the major weekly fair for the southern part of the province. *Indígenas* on horseback or leading llamas laden with produce arrive from communities where no road reaches. At the animal market much of the bargaining takes place in Quichua, but at the food and clothing markets more vendors speak Spanish. You will see more *indígenas* in different kinds of traditional dress here than at any other market in Ecuador.

Switchback railroad

From here, the highway drops down past Tixan and into **Alausí** ❽ (2,356 meters/7,704ft). Alausí was once used as a resort to escape from the heat of Guayaquil, and has a charming feel, with impressive mountain views, and a quiet way of life except for market day on Sunday. Alausí is most famous for the legendary **Nariz del Diablo** (Devil's Nose) railroad that switchbacks between here and Sibambe, dropping precipitously, on its way between Quito and Sibambe. The railroad used to run all the way to Guayaquil, but many switchbacks were washed away in the El Niño storms of 1982–3. Only the part between Riobamba and Sibambe has been repaired. (*For more details, see page 203.*)   ❏

Railway lines running through the colonial town of Alausí, which was once a summer resort for residents of Guayaquil.

BELOW:
Guamote's
Thursday market.

RAILWAY JOURNEYS

In their heyday, Ecuador's railways were its lifeblood. Today, road travel is the main means of transportation, and much of the country's train tracks and rolling stock have fallen into disrepair

Ecuador has not turned its back on the glory days of rail of the early–mid-1900s, when the coast and the Andes were united by steam trains transporting goods and passengers.

The current president Rafael Correa is a self-proclaimed rail enthusiast, and in 2007 he declared a "Railway Emergency," announcing $283 million spending on the railways' rehabilitation. Plans are under way to have the country's main routes fully operational again: the first of these will be the original Quito–Durán (close to Guayaquil) line.

La Empresa de Ferrocarriles Ecuatorianos (EFE) – the state railway enterprise – currently only runs *autoferros* (diesel buses, converted to navigate the rails) on still functioning routes: none are regularly plied by trains. Roof-riding has also been prohibited. Despite these caveats, taking a rail journey in Ecuador is still a wonderful way to travel. Routes currently operating include: Quito–Latacunga–Quito; Riobamba–Alausí–Sibambe–Alausí; Ibarra–"Primer Paso"; and irregularly, San Lorenzo–El Progreso. There's comprehensive train information at EFE headquarters in Quito's Old Town on Bolívar and García Moreno (tel: 02-258 5710; www.efe.gov.ec).

Until the grand rolling stock of EFE begins to move again, private tourism operators do occasionally run their own charter trains on some lines. Those with a hankering for a real train experience can research what's on offer at: www.steaminecuador.com and www. ecuadortrain.com. There's also the Chiva Express (www. chivaexpress.com), which operates its own *autoferro*.

ABOVE: *autoferros* arrive in Alausí station with a loud blow of the horn. The smell of grease and diesel, the calls of the conductor, and the screeching of the rolling stock add to the atmosphere.

ABOVE: *autoferros* (converted diesel buses) are the only type of train currently running on Ecuador's railways. They usually stop a couple of times for photos along the Devil's Nose stretch of track.
TOP LEFT: the railway station bell at Alausí.
LEFT: the attractive railway town of Alausí clings to a steep hillside above the Nariz del Diablo, surrounded by highland landscapes.

RIGHT: sign outside Guamote station.
BELOW: Sibambe train station at the base of the Nariz del Diablo is being restored and is set to host passengers again.

GUAMOTE
ALTITUD 3.056,0 M.
A QUITO   A DURAN
270,7K   181,3K

GETTING UP THE DEVIL'S NOSE

Train travel in Ecuador began in 1908, when the first train chugged its way into the Ecuadorian capital from the second city, Guayaquil. The opening of the Quito–Guayaquil line was a momentous achievement that had taken 30 years, huge financial investment, and had cost many lives. The route was immediately acclaimed as one of the "great railway journeys of the world," reducing to two days a former nine-day trek along a mule path often impassable due to rain.

The most technically challenging part of this route – and the most thrilling part of the section that still operates today – is the rightfully world-famous Nariz del Diablo (the Devil's Nose, pictured above) between Alausí and Sibambe. This daredevil piece of engineering takes the train or *autoferro* (*see opposite*) plunging down the steep switchbacks of a precipitous descent crossing spindly bridges over heart-stoppingly deep ravines. There are frequent stops for passengers to get out and marvel at the spectacular views as well as the engineering. Several times the train has to reverse to negotiate a radical switchback. Clouds of diesel smoke add to the atmosphere.

The track from Simbambe to Guayaquil requires substantial work and investment after devastating floods and landslides destroyed much of it in the 1997–8 El Niño event.

RIGHT: conductors play a vital role on the *autoferros*, talking the driver around steep bends and waving back road traffic.

THE SOUTHERN SIERRA

Beautiful colonial Cuenca, the Inca ruins of
Ingapirca, and the valley of Vilcabamba are
just three of many reasons for visiting
Cañar, Azuay, and Loja provinces

The southern Sierra, consisting of Cañar, Azuay, and Loja provinces, was until recently the least visited part of the highlands, mainly for reasons of accessibility rather than for lack of attractions. Once a very isolated region, it is now a major stop on the gringo trail from Ecuador to Peru due to improved roads and an expanding tourist infrastructure. The Andes broaden and flatten out somewhat here, with none of the dramatic snow-caps of the central and northern highlands, but there are plenty of stunning green vistas and mountain roads guaranteed to give you an adrenaline rush.

Hub of the south

The jumping-off point for most trips in the south is **Cuenca ❶**, capital of Azuay province, with a population of 600,000, making it Ecuador's third-largest city. Until about 35 years ago, Cuenca was isolated from the rest of Ecuador by the lack of good roads, but now it is connected to both Guayaquil and the northern Sierra by paved highways, as well as by daily flights to Quito and Guayaquil.

The Cuenca basin is a major *artesanías* center, producing ceramics, *paja toquilla* (Panama) hats, baskets, and Christmas ornaments, gold and silver jewelry, and *ikat* shawls, ponchos, and blankets. Other industries include textiles, furniture, and automobile tires. The city is the economic and intellec-

tual center of the southern Sierra, with a state university and a long history as the birthplace of artists, writers, poets, and philosophers.

Cuenca is considered to be Ecuador's most beautiful city, and in 1999 it was declared a Unesco World Heritage Site. Cuenca means river basin or bowl in Spanish, and the city is situated at 2,549 meters (8,335ft) on the banks of the **Río Tomebamba**. It has retained its colonial architecture and feel, with new construction in a neo-colonial style that is compatible with existing

Main attractions
CUENCA
MUSEO DEL BANCO CENTRAL
PUMAPUNGO
PARQUE NACIONAL CAJAS
INGAPIRCA
VILCABAMBA

LEFT: the 19th-century Catedral Nueva dominates colonial Cuenca's skyline. **BELOW:** flower seller outside El Carmen de la Asunción church.

The bells for Cuenca's cathedral, donated by Germany, have remained at the entrance to the nave ever since construction of the towers had to be abandoned.

structures. The blue domes of the new cathedral dominate the skyline. Thanks to its cobblestone streets, interior patios, public plazas overflowing with flowers and greenery, and whitewashed buildings with huge wooden doors and ironwork balconies, Cuenca is a walker's delight.

Originally, Cuenca was a major Cañari settlement. After the Inca conquest, it became an important city called Tumipampa, the Plain of the Knife (Hispanicized as Tomebamba), intended to be the Cuzco of the north. Very little of that Inca city remains. If you follow Calle Larga southeast as it goes downhill along the Tomebamba River (near the junction of Calle Tomás Ordóñez with Calle Larga) you will come to the ruins of **Todos Santos**. This small site includes four perfect Inca trapezoidal mortarless stonework niches, and the remains of the colonial mill of Todos Santos, which was constructed with stones taken from Inca buildings. There are also remains of Inca walls on the hill side above the mill, where ceramics and other evidence of Inca occupation were excavated.

Colonial culture

In 1532 the Inca armies retreated north before the advancing forces of Sebastián de Benalcázar. Cuenca was founded on this site in 1557, and named Santa Ana de los Cuatro Ríos de Cuenca. As soon as the Spanish arrived in an area they built a church, and Cuenca was no exception. The **Catedral Vieja** (Old Cathedral) or **El Sagrario** Ⓐ on the east side of the main plaza, the Parque Abdón Calderón, was begun the year the city was founded. But the city outgrew this simple old church and construction on the **Catedral Nueva** (New Cathedral) or **Catedral de la Inmaculada Concepción** Ⓑ started in 1880. This new church was built to hold 10,000 celebrants during religious events and is located opposite the Old Cathedral on the Parque Calderón. The neo-Gothic New Cathedral was intended to be 42.5 meters (141ft) wide and 105 meters (351ft) tall, which would have made it the largest church in South America, but the architect miscalculated and designed bell towers too heavy for the structure to support, so work on the towers was halted

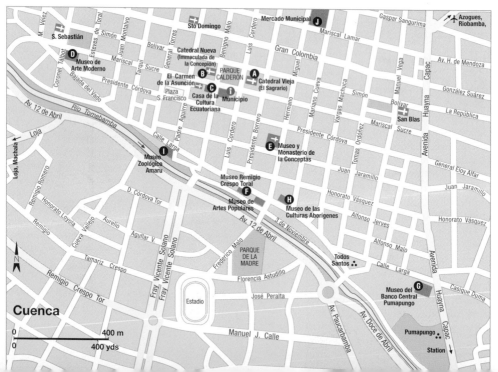

Cuenca

0   400 m
0   400 yds

before completion. It is constructed from alabaster and local marble with floors of pink marble imported from Carrara in Italy.

The **Parque Abdón Calderón** is Cuenca's main square, with the *municipio* (town hall) on the south side. The plaza is busy during the day with locals who come to relax on the many park benches amid the tall conifers, orchids, and other plant life. Just off the southwest corner of the square, on Calle Sucre, is the **Casa de la Cultura Ecuatoriana C** (Mon–Fri 9am–7, 8, or 9pm depending on events program). This small colonial-style building frequently has good exhibitions of local art. On the same block is the **Monasterio del Carmen de la Asunción**, founded in 1682. The church has a fine carved stone facade and the pulpit is gilded and embellished with mirrors. However, the building is often closed. A daily flower market is held in the tiny plaza in front of the church, and for a few coins you can brighten your hotel room considerably.

The **Museo de Arte Moderno D** (Modern Art Museum; tel: 07-283 1027; Mon–Fri 8.30am–1pm and 3–6.30pm, Sat–Sun 9am–1pm) is also on Calle Sucre, at Coronel Tálbot. This museum has rotating exhibitions of contemporary art as well as art workshops for children.

If you're not tired of churches (Cuenca has 27), go back along Calle Sucre and turn right at Calle Hermano Miguel to the **Museo y Monasterio de la Conceptas E** (Museum and Church of the Conception; Mon–Fri 9am–5.30pm, Sat 10am–1pm; charge). The entrance to the church contains 17th-century tombstones. The cloister, built 1682–1729, has been restored by the Banco Central. The cloister's museum contains an unusual collection of religious art, including toys presented to the convent by novices entering the order, a silver Nativity scene, and an altarpiece of carved wood and gold by the sculptor Manuel Machina. The museum houses a great collection of lithographs by Oswaldo Guayasamín (*see page 112*).

The **Museo Municipal Remigio Crespo Toral F** (Mon–Fri 9am–1pm and 3–6pm, Sat–Sun 9am–1pm; free),

The leafy main square, Parque Calderón, with the Catedral Nueva behind.

BELOW: the imposing marble entrance to the Catedral Nueva.

Bathing at Baños

As in many parts of Ecuador, geothermal activity is present near Cuenca. Happily for *Cuencaños* and visitors alike, that means deliciously hot water spilling from underground aquifers. The water at the thermal water resorts of Baños 8km (5 miles) southwest of the city (not to be confused with Baños in Tungurahua province, *see page 193*), emerge from the ground at a superheated 78°C (174°F), the highest temperature of any of the thermal waters in Ecuador. The water is channeled and cooled to a pleasant 38–40°C (100–104°F) before it can enter the pools and steam rooms of resorts at Baños. Its slightly milky appearance is due to the rich cocktail of health-giving minerals it contains.

The baths are said to be a cure for anything from rheumatism, psoriasis, kidney stones, and bronchial problems, to anemia, stress, and anxiety. Two recommended places to take the waters are Hostería Durán (tel: 07-283 2069; www.hosteriaduran.com; *see Travel Tips, page 332*) and the underground pools at Piedra de Agua Spa (tel: 07-289 2494; www.piedradeagua.com.ec). In addition to the thermal baths, both places offer Turkish-style baths and massage services, as well as on-site gourmet restaurants where guests can indulge themselves further.

TIP

One of the classic sights in Cuenca can be taken in on a stroll along the banks of the Río Tomebamba. The old, rambling houses on the north bank of the river are known as *barrancos* – or "hanging houses". These old mansions, mostly from the republican era, are built over five or six levels and hang precariously down the steep riverbank toward the water.

which is on Calle Larga 7–25 in front of Plazoleta La Merced, houses a wide selection of artifacts, from pre-Hispanic ceramics and goldwork of the Cañari and Chordeleg cultures to colonial paintings, furniture, and religious sculptures. The **Museo del Banco Central Pumapungo**  (Mon–Fri 9am–6pm, Sat 9am–1pm; charge) is located on Avenida Huayna Capac across Calle Larga, above the Pumapungo ruins where Inca and Cañari architecture and artifacts were unearthed. The museum has excellent exhibitions of colonial and republican art and historic photographs of Cuenca. There are interesting numismatic and ethnographic collections, too: the former fascinating for how it illustrates the freefall of the Ecuadorian currency, the Sucre, before dollarization, and the latter for its amazing shrunken heads. Allow time also to explore the outdoor Inca ruins on the edge of the river.

Also try the **Museo de las Culturas Aborígenes**  (tel: 07-283 9181; Mon–Fri 8.30am–12.30pm and 2.30–6.30pm, Sat 8.30am–12.30pm; charge)

at Avenida 10 de Agosto 4–70, close to the banks of the Río Tomebamba. It holds a fascinating collection of pre-Columbian archeological finds from various cultures throughout Ecuador.

Four blocks northeast, following Río Tomebamba upstream, lies the **Museo Zoológico Amaru**  (Mon–Fri 9am–1pm and 3–6pm, Sat–Sun 10am–5pm; charge). Cuenca's zoo displays more than 120 animal species, most of them native to Ecuador. The zoo puts an emphasis on the conservation of and research into fish, reptiles, and amphibians, and is an excellent place to visit, especially for those traveling with kids.

A blending of cultures

Many of the Cuenca Valley people are artisans and country people and occupy an intermediate position between *indígenas* and those of purely European origin. They represent a mixture of Inca, Cañari, and Spanish blood, although their rich mestizo culture is slowly disappearing as young people adopt modern-style clothing and move to the cities or go to work overseas.

BELOW: polychrome religious sculptures and altar in the Catedral Vieja.
BELOW RIGHT: Panama hats in all shapes and sizes.

In rural areas and especially at the markets in Sigsig, Gualaceo, Chordeleg, and sometimes in Cuenca you will still see people in traditional dress, which includes Panama hats for both men and women and colored ponchos, especially burgundy and red, for men. For fiestas, many of the local menfolk wear beautiful hand-woven *ikat* ponchos *(see chapter on Artesanías, page 106, for details)*. If you're in Cuenca for the weekly Thursday fair or for the smaller Saturday market, check out the plaza between Calle Mariscal Lamar and Sangurima off Calle Hermano Miguel, where *artesanías* including baskets, wool, and *ikat* shawls *(paños)* are sold.

Another interesting market to visit is the **Mercado Municipal ❶** on Calle Mariscal Lamar. Set over three levels, it contains hundreds of colorful stalls and is a veritable cornucopia of tropical fruits, cheeses, seafoods, meat, and baked products. This is a great hub of Cuenca life and commerce and the perfect spot for people-watching, accompanied by a coffee and a fresh bun at one of the stalls.

Excursions into the country

Gualaceo is about 36km (22 miles) from Cuenca on paved roads. Buses run regularly between the two places, heading north of Cuenca on the Pan-American highway, turning east at El Descanso and following the Río Paute. Gualaceo is a pretty town situated on the banks of the Río Gualaceo and has many *quintas* (summer homes) for people from Cuenca and Guayaquil. The slightly lower elevation makes it ideal for growing peaches, apricots, apples, cherries, guavas, and custard apples. There are several good restaurants along the river, and an inn, the Parador Turístico Gualaceo (tel: 07-255 110).

Chordeleg, a pre-Inca Cañari town, has artisans of all kinds: *ikat* poncho weavers, Panama hat and basket weavers, potters, embroiderers, and jewelers. The town is just a few kilometers up the mountain south of Gualaceo, a 10-minute trip in the local bus. The road leading into Chordeleg from Gualaceo is lined with stores selling silver and gold jewelry at very reasonable prices, in styles ranging from colonial

Selling textiles on Plaza San Francisco; a center for artesanías.

BELOW: crumbling colonial buildings in the center of Cuenca.

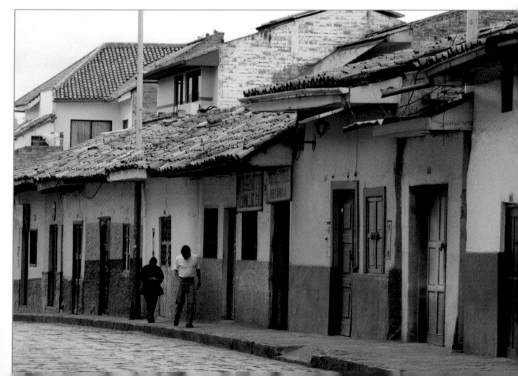

TIP

It is worth noting that entrance to the Parque Nacional Cajas costs $10, and a taxi from Cuenca to the information center in the heart of the park will set you back about $15–20.

BELOW: small lake in the Parque Nacional Cajas northwest of Cuenca.
BELOW RIGHT: Cañari *indígenas* at the Sunday market.

filigree to modern. Other local *artesanías* and textiles from Otavalo are sold in shops around the main plaza. There is a small but excellent ethnographic museum run by the Centro Interamericano de Artesanías y Artes Populares (CIDAP) on the plaza, with displays of local crafts and a gift shop. The exhibit showing the process used in making *ikat* textiles is especially informative.

There are pre-Inca ruins in the Chordeleg area, including an enormous snake-shaped stone walkway near the entrance to the town, and sites on nearby hilltops that have been excavated. Chordeleg has a small Sunday market, but most people from the town attend the larger market in Gualaceo. From the plaza in Chordeleg you can catch a bus to **Sigsig**, 20km (12 miles) farther south. Sigsig is a tiny colonial town with an equally tiny Sunday market, but the trip along the river is gorgeous. Two archeological sites, Chobshi and Shabalula, are close by; ask residents for directions.

If you are more interested in wilderness adventures, consider visiting **Parque Nacional Cajas**, 20km (12½ miles) northwest of Cuenca. The park has hundreds of clear, cold lakes, streams, and rivers at altitudes from 3,500 to 4,200 meters (9,000 to 13,000ft) on the *páramo* beneath jagged mountain cliffs. You can go swimming (if you're brave), or fishing for rainbow trout, and there are miles of good hiking trails, camping grounds, and even a small refuge.

Herds of llamas and alpacas have been brought in as part of a breeding program to reintroduce these animals to the southern highlands. It is also a wonderful spot for bird-watching, especially around the lakes, where numerous exotic species can be found, including hummingbirds and the occasional condor. Buses to Las Cajas (as the park is known) leave in the early morning from the church of San Sebastián, at calles Bolívar and Talbot in Cuenca, and return late in the afternoon. August to January is the best time to visit and it is a good idea to arrive early in the morning, as the afternoon tends to bring fog, mist, clouds, rain, and sometimes snow. Be sure to

bring a good map and compass: hikers who have come insufficiently prepared have lost their lives here.

Independent traditions

Cañar province, north of Cuenca, home of the Cañari *indígenas*, has the largest and the most complete accessible Inca ruins in Ecuador. While Cañar is considered a highland province, about one-third of its territory is in the western lowlands, where sugarcane, cocoa, bananas, and other tropical fruits are grown. In both the lowlands and the Sierra, extensive territory is given over to cattle that graze the large tracts of land owned by the big haciendas.

The Cañaris, who were once the principal indigenous group in southern Ecuador have suffered greatly since the arrival of the Incas in the 15th century. At first they resisted the Incas fiercely, at one time defeating them and driving them back to Saraguro. When civil war broke out in 1527 between two claimants to the throne, Atahualpa in Quito and Huascar in Cuzco, the Cañaris sided with Huascar. Atahualpa routed Huascar's army at Ambato and in revenge killed most of the men and boys of the Cañari tribe, despite their surrender. A year after the Spanish captured and killed Atahualpa in Cajamarca, a Spanish force under Sebastián de Benalcázar marched north to plunder Quito. When Benalcázar reached Tumipampa he was joined by 3,000 Cañari warriors, eager for revenge against the Quito Inca forces. The Cañaris fought with the Spanish throughout the conquest of Ecuador, but received scant recognition from the Spanish for their help. By 1544 many thousand Cañari men were working in the gold and silver mines of southern Ecuador, and the tribe was so reduced that in 1547 the Spanish chronicler Pedro de Cieza de León noted that the ratio of women to men was 15 to 1.

Currently there are about 40,000 Quichua-speaking Cañari *indígenas*

scattered throughout Cañar province. Most are farmers, but some are sheep- and cattle-herders. They are, on the whole, and perhaps understandably, averse to outsiders and have a reputation for being bellicose.

Cañari men's dress includes the *kushma*, a fine *ikat* poncho for fiesta use, black wool pants, a white cotton shirt with embroidery on the sleeves and collar and an extremely fine double-faced belt with motifs from local life. Like the men of Saraguro and Otavalo, Cañari men wear their hair in a long braid. The shepherds wear sheepskin chaps and carry a small whip with a wooden handle, which is worn over their shoulder. The typical Cañari hat, worn by both men and women, is handmade of white felt

TIP

When visiting Parque Nacional Cajas – even for a day trip – be sure to take warm, waterproof clothing: the origin for the name of this park is thought to be the Quichua word *caxas* – meaning cold.

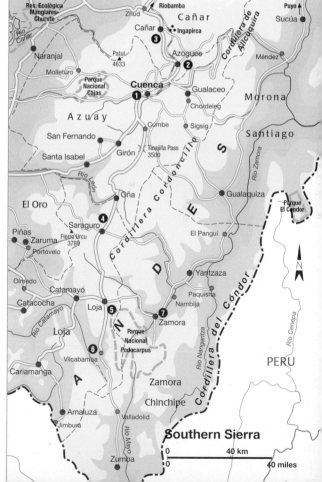

Southern Sierra

with a small round crown and narrow brim, turned up at the front. Cañari women wear an embroidered blouse, a shoulder wrap held shut with a *tupu* (shawl pin), and a woolen *pollera* skirt in various colors.

Exploring Cañar

The Pan-American Highway climbs out of Cuenca to **Azogues ❷**, the capital of Cañar province, with 28,000 inhabitants. Azogues has a quiet colonial air, with wooden balconies and shutters aslant on ancient whitewashed houses. *Azogue* means mercury, and the town was named after the nearby mercury mines. The **Convento de San Francisco** towers above Azogues on a hill to the southeast. The Spanish practice of building churches on pre-Hispanic Inca *huacas* (holy places), many of which were located on mountain tops, accounts for the large number of churches that are perched at ridiculous altitudes. If you need the exercise and want the view, it's a half-hour climb to the top.

Azogues has two museums: the **Museo Ignacio Neira** in the Colegio Julio María Matavalle has zoological, archeological, and mineralogical displays, but is open only on request; and the **Museo del Colegio de los Padres Franciscanos**, which houses religious art and archeological artifacts (opening times vary, check when you arrive; charge).

The Pan-American Highway winds past Azogues and into **Cañar ❸**, which is 65km (40 miles) from Cuenca and 36km (22 miles) from Azogues. Cañar is high and chilly at 3,104 meters (10,150ft); this is barley, potato, *quinua* (a highly nutritious grain), and cattle country. The town has a fascinating market on Sundays, when *indígenas*, including mounted Cañaris with *ikat* ponchos, whips *(chicotes)*, and sheepskin chaps *(zamarro)* come down off the *páramo* to buy, sell, and trade. The Cañari men's belts are beautifully made in a complex intermesh double-faced technique. The best place in town to buy belts is the jail (Centro de Rehabilitación Social), where *indígenas* doing time do not waste time, but spend it weaving. The jailer will unlock

BELOW:
livestock for sale
in Plaza de los
Animales in Cañar's
Sunday market.

the door and let you into the main patio where you will be besieged (in a friendly manner) by prisoners with belts and sometimes ponchos to sell.

Ecuador's greatest ruins

Many people visit Cañar for the market and then go on to **Ingapirca** (daily 8am–6pm; charge). There are several ways to reach the ruins. You can catch a bus from Cañar, take a bus or taxi from Cuenca (2 hours one way), rent your own vehicle, or go on an organized tour. A great alternative is to arrive at Ingapirca on foot. There is a hiking trail to the ruins *(see page 117)*, following the route of an Inca road, which takes three days through high-altitude *páramo* from Achupallas, east of Alausí. Ask at the iTur tourist information office in Alausí, which will be able to put you in touch with Achupallas-based guides. It is possible to do the hike without a guide, but you will need a detailed topographical map that you can only buy at the **Instituto Geográfico Militar** in Quito. Take care with the semi-wild *toros bravos* (fighting bulls) that you may encounter en route.

Ingapirca means "Inca stone wall"; the name was given to the site by the Cañaris. We know that the Inca Huayna Capac built Ingapirca in the 15th century on the royal highway that ran from Quito to Cuzco and stationed soldiers there to keep the Cañaris under control. Throughout the Inca Empire, outlying Inca settlements had multiple functions and were intended to be models of Cuzco on a much smaller scale. From what remains of Ingapirca, the site probably had storehouses, baths, a royal *tambo* or inn for the Inca, dwellings for soldiers and others, and a sun temple, the remains of which can be seen in the beautiful ellipse, made of green diorite and modeled after the Koricancha, the main temple in Cuzco. The high-quality stonework indicates that Ingapirca was a very important site.

The Incas often chose hilltops for their settlements, both for defensive reasons and to free up flat valley land for cultivation. Much of Ingapirca was dismantled over the centuries by local people who used the stones for domestic buildings.

Various other remains surround the main buildings. The Ingachungana, or Inca's playground, is a large rock with carved channels that may have been used for offerings or for divination, with water, *chicha* (a fermented drink, usually made out corn), or the blood of sacrificed llamas or guinea pigs poured in the channels. Near the Ingachungana is a chair or throne cut into the rock and called the **Sillón del Inca** (the Inca's Chair). Below in the gorge are several zoomorphic rock carvings – a couple appear to be a monkey and a turtle – and the **Cara del Inca** (the Inca's Face), a large stone outcropping that is probably natural, rather than carved. The site also houses a small museum (Mon–Sat) with ethnographic and archeological exhibits. The displays include such artifacts from the Cañari and Inca cultures as ceramics, jewelry,

Farmland in highland Cañar province.

BELOW:
Cañari women wearing the traditional white felt hat and embroidered woolen *pollera* skirt.

and textile fragments. Less than a mile away is the village of **Ingapirca**, which has a crafts cooperative store next to the church and a couple of basic restaurants. On Fridays the village plays host to a small but attractive indigenous market.

The far south

Tucked away deep in southern Ecuador between Azuay province and the border with Peru, Loja province is the least visited of the highland provinces, mainly because of its isolation. There are flights to the capital city, Loja, from Quito and Guayaquil, but not from Cuenca, so travelers heading directly south from Cuenca must go overland along the paved Pan-American Highway. Loja province is primarily rural and agricultural and there are only a few small towns along the road.

The highway south of Cuenca passes through rich, green land until **Cumbe** (14km/9 miles), where it begins to climb to **Tinajilla Pass** at 3,500 meters (11,445ft). It then traverses the *páramo* of **Gañadel**, which is usually misty and fogged in. In the middle of this wilderness, figures bundled in shawls and ponchos will appear out of the fog to flag down the bus.

The clouds sometimes part to surprise you with extensive views of the Western Cordillera and sunlight streaming through in the distance, a sight that looks like a Renaissance artist's idea of the dawn of creation.

From here the road twists a few miles to **Saraguro** ❹, a high, chilly town of about 19,000 inhabitants, mainly mestizos and whites. It is the social and commercial center for the Saraguro *indígenas*, relatively prosperous farmers and cattle traders who live in small communities (*barrios*) surrounding the town.

The Saragureños are said to be descendants of the Inca conquerors of Ecuador, who were brought to the region after the Inca Tupac Yupanqui's conquest of the area around 1455 and replaced the indigenous Palta people who were sent to Bolivia by the Incas. Under Inca rule, each ethnic group was required to retain its traditional costume, especially its headdress and hairstyle. The Spanish outlawed certain

BELOW: the ruins of Ingapirca, Ecuador's major Inca site. **BELOW RIGHT:** regular-shaped, coursed Inca masonry often uses no mortar.

kinds of Inca headgear and introduced brimmed hats, but in typically conservative fashion each ethnic group insisted on wearing a distinctive style, which accounts for the plethora of hat styles seen in the Andes today.

The *indígenas* of Saraguro were never serfs on the *haciendas* or laborers in textile sweatshops. They have survived as farmers and cattle traders, supplying much of the beef for southern Ecuador. Because of a shortage of pasture in the Saraguro region the Saragureños drive their cattle over the continental divide and down into the jungle around Yacuambi. The cattle are fattened and driven back up over the Andes to be sold at the Sunday Saraguro market. The people of Saraguro value education and are among the best-educated *indígenas* in Ecuador, with their own high school, and many young adults attending the universities in Cuenca and Quito.

Remembering the Inca

Saragureño dress is black or dark indigo-blue wool, which many *indígenas* say they wear in mourning for the death of the Inca Atahualpa. Most of the clothes are hand-spun and hand-woven, and everywhere you travel in the Saraguro region you will see women and girls with distaffs and spindles, spinning wool for their family clothing. Most striking, though, is the women's jewelry. Several jewelers in Saraguro specialize in making the large nickel or silver shawl pins *(tupus)* that women use to fasten their shoulder wraps. Fine silver *tupus* are heirlooms, passed down from mother to daughter, as are filigree earrings. Women also wear beaded necklaces. One style has rows of tiny seed beads strung in zigzags, and the colors of the beads and number of rows indicate the woman's community.

Saraguro has two very basic *pensiones* and a handful of restaurants catering to locals, but is worth visiting for the Sunday market. Some crafts, especially the traditional jewelry, are sold in small shops in the main market building and surrounding streets. The town was also an Inca settlement and extensive ruins, which are impossible to find without a guide: they are located outside the town in the forests

The village of Ingapirca has a small market on Fridays.

BELOW: fine Inca masonry at Ingapirca.

on the slopes of Mount Acacana. These ruins, called **Inca Iglesia** (Inca Church), are large but overgrown, and contain fine mortarless stonework walls and channels carved in the rock for the water system.

The Cuenca–Loja bus continues on to Loja after a stop in Saraguro to pick up passengers. If you decide to stay in Saraguro, a local Saraguro–Loja bus also makes the round trip between the two places several times a day. Loja is another 61km (38 miles) from Saraguro, a two-hour ride along a dizzying corkscrew road.

Colonial center

Loja ❺ is a bustling provincial city that is of most interest to visitors as a base for visiting the surrounding region, particularly the nearby Parque Nacional Podocarpus. Loja is the capital of the province of that name, and provincial it is: provincial and old. Because the Spanish invasion of Ecuador began in Piura on the north coast of Peru, Ecuador was conquered and settled from south to north. Loja was founded in 1548, which makes it one of the oldest cities in the country. The city has been rebuilt twice due to devastating earthquakes, the last being in the 1880s. Cieza de León commented on the prosperity of the region and on the vast herds of llamas, vicuñas, and guanacos when he rode through Loja on the Royal Inca Highway, but the Spanish conquerors soon hunted them to extinction. Loja has about 120,000 inhabitants and is nestled among the mountains at a pleasant 2,225 meters (7,275ft). Because it is so close to the Oriente it is a major entry point to the southern jungle and the province of Zamora-Chinchipe.

A short tourist circuit runs across the town. Begin at the Puerta de la Ciudad (the Door to the City), just north of the center. This castle-like structure was built in 1998 as a replica of a Spanish fortress that was built in Loja in 1571 but later torn down. A path leads from here down to the pleasant Parque Bolívar and from there to Parque Central, the city's main square.

The city has two universities, one of which has a law school and a music conservatory. A local branch of the

BELOW: the city of Loja, a gateway to the Oriente.

Museo del Banco Central (tel: 07-257 3004; Mon–Fri 9am–1pm and 2–5pm; charge) occupies a colonial mansion at 10 de Agosto and contains archeological, ethnographic, and colonial art collections. The **cathedral** and the churches of **San Martín** and **Santo Domingo** are Loja's most interesting religious buildings and have nicely painted interiors. The statue of the Virgin of Cisne is kept in the cathedral from August to November, while the fiesta of the Virgin takes place on September 8. The religious observances and the accompanying agricultural fair attract pilgrims from throughout northern Peru and the southern part of Ecuador. Further south, just past the Plaza de Independencia is Calle Lourdes, several blocks of which have been restored to highlight their wooden balconies and cobblestone patios. The buildings are home to a wide variety of artisans and galleries.

Valley of the ancients

Loja is the usual jumping off-point for beautiful **Vilcabamba** ❻, 62km (38 miles) due south. Vilcabamba gained a certain reputation in the 1970s as the valley of the ancients, where an unusual percentage of old people were said to live to be 100 to 120 years old. Disappointingly for those looking for the fountain of youth, these tales turned out to be exaggerated. One book on Vilcabamba, for example, contained a document purporting to be a birth certificate proving that one man was 128 years old. The document, on closer scrutiny, turned out to be a land title in his grandfather's name, which his descendant shared.

Vilcabamba is located at a comfortable, mild 1,500 meters (4,905ft) above sea level and is a visual delight: green, gentle, and pretty. In the past few years the town has become a popular retreat for visitors who want to slow down the pace of their travels and enjoy the tranquil surroundings. There are also plenty of opportunities for horseback riding and hiking up into the nearby **Parque Nacional Podocarpus** (charge), one of the most beautiful cloud-forest areas in Ecuador. The national park has out-

The Andean-cock-of-the-rock lives in the cloud forest: the male has brilliant orange and black plumage.

BELOW LEFT: Saraguro *indígena* with ornate *tupu* (brooch) and distinctive jewelry. **BELOW:** the Parque Nacional Podocarpus is named after the romerillo tree *(Podocarpus montanus).*

TIP

All is not tranquil in the quiet back blocks of Vilcabamba. There has been a phenomenon in recent years of well-off gringos buying up prime land around the town and building large, ostentatious houses, even *Dallas*-style ranches. The demand for land has driven prices up to a level no longer affordable to the people of Vilcabamba themselves, understandably engendering resentment among townspeople.

BELOW: trekking near Vilcabamba.
BELOW RIGHT: native orchid.
OPPOSITE: young cousins in Saraguro.

standingly diverse ecosystems, and is home to many rare species, including the Andean spectacled bear. It is also a paradise for bird-watching: Look out for Andean cock-of-the-rocks, toucans, hummingbirds, macaws, and jocotocos, which are endemic to the park. The park is named for the romerillo tree (*Podocarpus montanus*), a conifer that can grow upward of 40 meters (130ft) and lives for more than 1,000 years.

Several trekking and horseback-riding outfits that are based in Vilcabamba visit the park: just take a stroll around the tranquil main square and you will pass the doors of several recommended agencies.

Gold-rush outposts

Although strictly speaking part of the southern Oriente, **Zamora** ❼ is only 60km (40 miles) from Loja, but they are slow and bumpy miles. A colony was founded here by the Spanish in 1549 at about 970 meters (3,180ft) above sea level in the headwaters of the Río Zamora. This colony was wiped out by indigenous attacks but, undaunted, the Spaniards re-established it and pursued their feverish quest for gold. Around 1560 they refounded the colony, giving it the fanciful title of the Royal Mining Village of the Rich Hill of San Antonio of Zaruma. Gold was successfully extracted for some 70 years before the colony died out once more. Several attempts were subsequently made to re-establish Zamora, the most recent in 1869. It has held on to its existence somewhat precariously since then. In the 1930s there were fewer than a dozen buildings, but by 1953 it had become the capital of the isolated province of Zamora-Chinchipe, even though the only access was by mule. The first vehicle made it to Zamora in 1962.

In the 1980s, a new lode of gold was discovered some 15km (10 miles) northeast of Zamora, in the **Nambija** area, once the traditional mining grounds of the Incas. Ecuadorian prospectors, hoping to strike it rich, make their way to the Zamora region with their hopes as high as those of their predecessors. The urge to find gold is not something that goes out of fashion. ❑

THE ORIENTE

Reptiles, anacondas, piranhas, toucans, howler monkeys, and jumping spiders all await you in the Amazon basin. Your transportation can vary from floating hotel to dugout canoe

You may go to the Oriente only once in your life, so it is worth asking yourself what you want from your trip. How important is comfort? Do you need a specialist guide and are you more interested in wildlife, plants, or indigenous culture? Also, what impact is your visit going to have on the rainforest? When you've answered these questions, you can start making plans. Options include a wide range of jungle lodges, an Amazon riverboat, or the burgeoning number of "adventure tourism" groups. Trips can be organized from Quito or arranged in Misahuallí, Baños, Tena, or Coca. If you are looking for an expert guide or a comfortable lodge, it is best to organize the trip in Quito, although they can be cheaper elsewhere. *See Travel Tips, pages 353–4 for details of tour operators.*

River trips

For the adventurous, one of the best ways to experience primary tropical rainforest is to take a multi-day canoe trip down one of the rivers of the Oriente. Several qualified guides organize float trips on the Río Tiputini or in the Reserva Cuyabeno, where you can see wildlife close up. During the day you will see wooly and howler monkeys grazing in the trees, toucans or parrots in flight, or, if you are lucky, an anaconda lazing in the sun. At night you will be serenaded by a symphony of insects and an occasional unidentified animal.

Floating hotel

At the other end of the scale from canoe trips is the **Manatee Amazon Explorer**. Especially designed for cruises in the Ecuadorian rainforest on the Río Napo, the three-level riverboat allows travelers to dip into the rainforest and return to a certain amount of luxury. Small but comfortable cabins provide the amenities of a modern hotel, while the flotel has a bar, observation deck, and dining room where excellent meals are served. The slow but sure flotel visits different parts of the river, penetrating

Main attractions
SAN RAFAEL FALLS
RESERVA DE PRODUCCIÓN FAUNÍSTICA CUYABENO
VISIT TO A JUNGLE LODGE
JUNGLE RIVER TRIPS
WILDLIFE-SPOTTING
PIRANHA-FISHING

PRECEDING PAGES: tropical rainforest canopy in the morning mist. **LEFT:** giant ceiba tree. **BELOW:** a jungle river trip.

deep into the rainforest, and therefore offering more opportunities to see wildlife. Passengers are taken ashore to visit a local community, trek into the rainforest, and marvel at the birdlife from a jungle observation tower.

Jungle lodges

For those who prefer to be based in one location and make daily exploration forays, a jungle lodge is the way to go. These vary from rough-and-ready, shared accommodation that caters for backpackers, to lodges that would pass for five-star resorts. Those more distant from towns or settlements usually have better bird-watching and wildlife-viewing, though their facilities may be more limited. Some lodges have rainforest canopy walkways, which is usually the only way to get a treetop perspective. Whichever you go for, be sure to check that the lodge you choose offers some form of mosquito netting to protect you at night. Excursions offered at most of the lodges are similar: walks and canoe trips for wildlife-viewing, visits to indigenous settlements, and perhaps even some piranha-fishing.

Most people who have arranged river tours or visits to jungle lodges in advance will arrive by air, leaping suddenly from one climate to another. Daily flights dive from Quito to the towns of Lago Agrio and Coca deep in the jungle, covering in only 30 minutes the same distance that can take 12 grueling hours by land, as well as providing spectacular aerial views of the changing landscape. The dazzling white of the snow-capped Andes gives way to an endless mattress of green stretching into the horizon. Dozens of rivers snake beneath huge gray clouds, ready to drop their loads of moisture onto the rainforest.

The highway from Quito

Travelers who want to observe from the ground the subtle shifts in flora between the Sierra and Oriente gladly sacrifice comfort and speed for a bus window seat along the eastern highway. An hour east of Quito, the bus labors over the sometimes snow-covered **Papallacta Pass** – at 4,100 meters (13,400ft), one of the highest points in Ecuador that can be reached by public

transport. The narrow mountain road then plunges down in a series of ear-popping curves to the Oriente and the landscape alters dramatically.

The Oriente (the East), as Ecuador's Amazonian region is called, lies less than 100km (60 miles) from the Papallacta Pass as the condor glides. But the eastern slopes of the Andes tumble precipitously, and the road passes lush cloud forests full of giant Andean tree ferns, spiky bromeliads, delicate orchids, and brightly colored birds. This is the very rim of the Amazon basin, and the steepness of the terrain combines with the thick vegetation to make it almost impenetrable. The heavily forested subtropical slopes of this transitional area are the haunts of a variety of wildlife, including the spectacled bear. Birdlife is more conspicuous and colorful than wildlife in the cloud forest, with iridescent quetzals, glittering hummingbirds, and gaudy tanagers. Each elevation has its own distinct set of bird species, and the same occurs with the plants, resulting in a biological mosaic of unparalleled diversity. The northern Andean cloud forests have a total plant diversity as great as that of the entire Amazon basin, though they cover only a twentieth of the basin area.

Thirty minutes' drive past the Papallacta Pass is the town of **Papallacta** and its nearby hot springs, ideal for anyone in need of a little relaxation. The road drops toward the jungle taking the line of least resistance – a river valley. Amazonian climate patterns ensure heavy rainfall almost year-round, and there are hundreds of minor and major rivers flowing down the eastern Andes toward the Oriente. Although at this point they are only 240km (150 miles) away from the Pacific, these rivers will merge with the waters of the world's greatest river system and finally join the sea at the Atlantic 3,200km (2,000 miles) away.

An area of strategic importance

The road follows the valley of the Río Papallacta, and finally ends up in the first important Oriente town, **Baeza ❶**, near the Río Quijos (named for an indigenous tribe that lived in the

A vast part of what is now the Peruvian Amazon once belonged to Ecuador. Ecuador and Peru have fought bitter wars over this land, the most recent in 1941, followed by skirmishes in 1981 and 1995. The Rio de Janiero Protocol that ended the 1941 war ceded huge tracts of land to Peru, including land access to the Marañón and Amazon rivers. The border is still under dispute and is often shown as such on maps.

BELOW: hummingbird feeding at Papallacta springs.

The new road makes life a lot easier for travelers, but has had detrimental effects on the environment.

BELOW: children in Lago Agrio play in rivers highly contaminated by waste products of the oil industry.

region at the time of the conquest). Baeza is a small, ramshackle, subtropical outpost whose tin-roofed appearance belies its long and interesting history. Since before the Spanish conquest, lowland forest natives stopped here on their way to the highlands on trading expeditions. Recognizing the area's strategic importance, the Spaniards founded a missionary and trading outpost here in 1548, just 14 years after conquering Ecuador.

Perched on the edge of the Amazon basin at 1,400 meters (4,600ft) above sea level and 80km (50 miles) east of Quito, Baeza remained Ecuador's last outpost in the northern Oriente for more than four centuries. Today it is its gateway, and can also be reached by a popular road from Baños farther south, via the jungle town of **Puyo**. This is Ecuador's largest jungle town, with a bustling feel, but little to entice visitors other than some pleasant walks beside the Río Puyo, and on clear days, good views of the Sangay and Altar volcanoes. Indigenous community visits and adventurous jungle wildlife tours can usually be arranged from here.

Transformed by oil

Until the middle of the 20th century, this Andean rim of the Amazon basin was as far as colonists and travelers went. Wildlife and indigenous groups lived relatively undisturbed deeper in the Oriente's interior. This suddenly changed in the late 1960s with the discovery of oil in the jungle. Almost overnight, a good all-weather road was pushed from Quito beyond Baeza and deep into the heart of parts of the Oriente which until then could be reached only by difficult river travel or by light aircraft. The new 180km (110-mile) road stretches from Baeza to **Lago Agrio ❷** (literally "Sour Lake"), an oil town built in a trackless region in the middle of the jungle. For much of its length, the road to Lago Agrio parallels the trans-Ecuadorian pipeline, which pumps oil 495km (310 miles) from the oilfields of the Oriente, up across the Andes and down to the Pacific coast for processing and export. At irregular intervals along the pipeline, little communities have been created. Some are next to oil pumping stations, whilst others have been founded by colonists

near flat pieces of land that they have cleared.

The famous **San Rafael Falls** are on the Río Quijos, about halfway between Baeza and Lago Agrio. With a height of about 145 meters (475ft), they are the highest falls in the country. They can be glimpsed from the bus as it travels along the new road, but for an impressive close-up look you should get off at the NECEL electricity station at **Reventador**. From here, it is a 30-minute walk down an overgrown trail through lush forest to a viewpoint where, if the wind is right (or wrong, depending on your point of view) you can be sprayed by the light mist caused by the crashing water. Sometimes the spray can be so thick that it obliterates the view of the cascading river; at other times the mists clear for a magnificent sight of the falls. This is also a great place for bird-watching. Nearby Volcán Reventador, the most active volcano in the Cordillera Real, shows its peak above the cloud forest.

In November 2002, after 26 years of dormancy, Reventador erupted spectacularly, shooting a column of ash and rock 15km (9 miles) into the sky, which enshrouded Quito and the rest of central Ecuador. Smaller eruptions have occurred since then and heavy rainfall has caused ash deposits in the area to shift, in turn creating major landslides and causing damage to the oil pipeline. It is currently too dangerous to trek to or explore Reventador.

Lago Agrio itself is one of the fastest-growing places in Ecuador, although not much to look at. It is officially called Nueva Loja (New Loja), named by the first Ecuadorian colonists in the area who mainly came from the province of Loja in the south of the country. It was homesick North American oilmen working for Texaco who nicknamed the town Lago Agrio for the small Texan oil town of Sourlake, and despite what it says on the maps, that's what everyone calls it.

Lago Agrio was part of the huge jungle province of Napo, whose capital is Tena, an all-day drive away over ill-maintained roads. Tena is not an oil town, and the citizens of Lago felt that their very different interests were not represented. But Lago's importance

The rough-skinned green treefrog.

BELOW:
San Rafael Falls on Río Quijos is Ecuador's highest waterfall.

See Travel Tips, page 333 for details of the lodges mentioned in this chapter.

became apparent after an earthquake in 1987 isolated the town, cutting the oil flow and bringing the economy to a grinding halt. In 1989, Lago Agrio was made the capital of Sucumbios, while in 1998 the new province of Orellana was created to the south. A hot and humid climate pervades the town. Even the newest buildings begin to look decayed within a few months. The unpaved streets are often filled with mud, and rubber boots are the usual footwear. Yet it is a lively and progressive place; late-model jeeps churn the mud in the streets and the bustling market is thronged with shoppers. Sadly, it is also a frontier town that has suffered from the growth of drug-trafficking and armed groups in neighboring Colombia, and travelers are advised to make inquiries about the current safety situation before visiting the region.

Much quieter is the village of **Archidona**, south of Baeza. Archidona was originally a mission, founded in 1560, and still retains a pleasantly hushed air. The village center has a palm-shaded plaza that gets busy only

BELOW: whitewater kayaking on Río Tena.

on Sundays, when indigenous people from surrounding communities come in for the market. Just north of Archidona are the Cuevas de Jumandí, which have impressive stalactites and stalagmites, and need a good flashlight and sense of adventure to explore.

Tena lies 75km (47 miles) south of Baeza and is the kayak and rafting capital of Ecuador. The town straddles the Tena and Pano rivers, and you always have the feeling that the water is near. The charming main plaza overlooks the river, on the other side of which is the *malecón* (pier). Operators in town offer trips varying from wild whitewater (and white-knuckle) rides to gentle river floats, and taking one of these is a great way to see some of the beautiful jungle, canyons and cloud forest that surround the town. Visits to waterfalls and indigenous communities can also be arranged from Tena. Situated on an island right across from town is the **Parque Amazónico** (charge), reached by a thatched bridge, where there are great walking trails. You can see a number of species of monkeys in the trees, but sadly most of the animals, including a tapir, an ocelot, and a jaguarundi, are in cages.

About a one-hour bus ride and three-hour hike from the town brings you to the Comunidad Capirona (www. ricancie.nativeweb.org), a network of nine Quichua communities located within the Grand Sumaco National Park Biosphere Reserve, an extremely diverse and threatened area. There are opportunities to volunteer with development projects in the community.

Into the jungle

If there are no current security problems, it is well worth making the effort to get from Lago Agrio to the **Reserva de Producción Faunística Cuyabeno** ❸, up toward the Colombian border, where some 655,000 hectares (1.6 million acres) of incredibly bio-diverse territory, consisting mostly of flooded forest, have been turned into a national park. It's a full day's travel by bus and

motorized canoe along the Río Aguarico to reach the reserve itself.

The best of several lodges in or near the reserve is remote **Jamu Lodge**, located on the Río Cuyabeno, 15 minutes' motorized canoe ride downriver from Laguna Grande. Jamu has nine rustic, thatched *cabañas* on stilts, connected by raised walkways through the flooded jungle. The eco-conscious lodge is particularly atmospheric at night, when it's lit with kerosene lamps. Excursions include canoe trips, swimming in the black waters of nearby lagoons, and the opportunity to wade through flooded forests. There's also an chance to visit a Siona community in the reserve, and a very good chance of spotting an elusive pink river dolphin.

Close encounters with piranhas and caimans

On many jungle trips it is possible to try some piranha-fishing. Small pieces of raw red flesh are used as bait on handlines, bringing the infamous creatures out in their hundreds. These small fish are surprisingly easy to catch, although watch your fingers as you bring them

Despite their fearsome appearance, piranhas make a fine meal.

aboard: their small, triangular-shaped teeth are razor sharp.

Contrary to popular belief, it is quite possible to swim in piranha-infested waters. The variety of piranha found in Ecuador will only ever turn nasty on large mammals, such as humans and horses, if there is a large quantity of blood in the water. Even so, such is the reputation of the fish that swimming here is rather unnerving, and many prefer to endure the Amazonian heat rather than test the murky waters.

Another unforgettable Oriente experience is night-time caiman-watching. Slip out on a canoe at night and shine a flashlight into the reeds by the lakeside: hundreds of red eyes stare back, the reflections from caimans' retinas (rather like the "red eye" effect in flash photography). The more adventurous guides will take the boat right in among these reptiles; an experience that can feel a little too adventurous if you happen to be in an unstable dugout canoe. Some guides will even grab a small caiman by the tail, to bring it alongside the canoe and give everyone a closer look.

BELOW:
caimans may look vicious but are harmless.

TIP

Contact Aves y Conservación (the Ecuadorian Ornithology Foundation), for more information on birds and their habitats. *See Travel Tips, page 346 for details.*

A lime lake and a museum of curiosities

If you have a few days to spare it is possible to visit **Limoncocha** (Lime Lake) downriver from the jungle town of Coca. Oil production has had some impact on the area, but parts of the swamp and surrounding forest remain intact. This unique ecosystem harbors white caiman and over 400 species of bird. Boat trips can be made at the park headquarters of the **Reserva Biológica Limoncocha ❹** near the town of Limoncocha. Although there is no formal lodge, an extended stay can be arranged at the SEK University research station or in the Limoncocha community.

About 8km (5 miles) from Limoncocha is the Capuchin mission of **Pompeya**. Among the houses built on wooden stilts is an altar with a crucifix above a colored canoe, as well as a curious museum. Here you can handle the various blowpipes used by Amazonian peoples to hunt – many are surprisingly long and heavy – and often used to shoot directly upward into the trees with a dart coated with natural venom that paralyzes the prey. Opposite Pompeya is **Isla de los Monos** (Monkey Island), where you can wander freely and spot wooly monkeys high in the trees above. You will need a little patience, but you should be well rewarded. There have been regrettable changes, however: not long ago the island was literally packed with monkeys, but the Ecuadorian Army chose this location as the site for survival training, and hundreds of these creatures ended up in the soldiers' stews.

Amazon lodges on the Río Napo

Not every visitor to the Oriente wants to bathe in a jungle river and sleep on the floor of a native hut at the end of a hard day of hiking in the jungle. For those wishing to visit the virgin rainforest, yet return to a comfortable room with a private shower at night, there are several options.

La Selva Jungle Lodge ❺, off the Río Napo, is perhaps the best known of the lodges. The journey there is half the adventure: first by aircraft to Coca, then a motorized dugout canoe for 2½ hours followed by a rough board-

BELOW: a wooly monkey.
BELOW RIGHT: the heliconia is also called the false-bird-of-paradise.

walk through the rainforest to Laguna Garzacocha and finally a dugout canoe to the lodge. The buildings at La Selva, up on stilts and with thatched roofs, have been constructed from secondary rainforest materials to withstand the extremes of jungle climate. Rooms are lit with kerosene lamps, and the lack of a thumping generator outside the cabins ensures that guests are able to hear the myriad sounds of the rainforest. La Selva is a magnet for birdwatchers: parrots, tanagers, toucans, and numerous other species can all be seen. Expert naturalists, many of them English-speaking, can guide visitors on jungle walks and canoe rides, and there is a new observation tower.

Sacha Lodge is another excellent option offering plenty of creature comforts (including electricity and hot water) and a great variety of trails and trips. Just north of the Río Napo, it is reached by a 3-hour motorized canoe trip from Coca. The lodge's observation tower enables you to climb 40 meters (130ft) into the canopy for an unobstructed view of miles and miles of intact rainforest, close-up views of plants and birds, and maybe the occasional sloth hanging from a treetop. After a long day exploring the magic of the rainforest, a dip in the Pilchicocha Lagoon in front of the lodge may be a welcome form of relaxation.

Also on the Río Napo is the award-winning **Napo Wildlife Center**. This luxury lodge with 12 large individual *cabañas*, located by Lago Ananguco-cha, within the ancestral territory of the Anangu Quichua Community, and part of the Parque Nacional Yasuní. In its beginnings in the early 1990s, Napo was one of the pioneering community-built lodges in the Ecuadorian Amazon. Private investment allowed the early rudimentary lodge to develop into the luxurious enclave it is today. Napo is particularly known for the quality of its guiding and for its two freestanding canopy towers.

If you are short of time, on a budget, and just want a taste of the rainforest, there are plenty of trips on offer starting from the small town of **Misahuallí** ❻ in the headwaters of the Río Napo. Here guides can be hired for about

There are English-speaking guides available at Sacha Lodge to make your tour more informative.

BELOW: tourists surveying the rainforest from a viewing platform in the tree canopy.

The large owl butterfly is most active at dusk and takes its name from its wing spots, which resemble owls' eyes.

BELOW: a 70-year-old Huaorani man hunting with a blow gun.

$30–40 a day. The area has been colonized and the forest here is secondary growth. The large mammals and birds have mainly been hunted close to extinction, but a short trip will give you an experience of the jungle and a look at a variety of plants, insects, and smaller birds.

Near Misahuallí, on the Río Napo, is **Reserva Biológica Jatún Sacha**, a center dedicated to conservation, education, and research, where a number of unknown species have been discovered. Next door are the **Cabañas Aliñahui** (also known as the Butterfly Lodge) offering comfortable cabins, canoe trips, visits to indigenous communities, and walks along a great variety of trails in the area. Tourists can visit the reserve and see fieldwork in progress. For butterfly-lovers this area is paradise: besides hundreds of birds and plants, an astonishing 765 butterfly species have been identified at Jatún Sacha.

One aspect of forest life that can be observed around Misahuallí is colonization: small coffee *fincas* (estates), oil-palm plantations, cattle ranches, and

yucca plots are prevalent. As you journey down the nearby river, you may occasionally notice workers washing and sifting material. They are panning for gold – modern descendants of the long line of settlers obsessed with dreams of El Dorado. A little farther down the Río Napo is **Yachana Lodge**, run by the Yachana Foundation, a not-for-profit organization that funds innovative community projects through profits made by the lodge. The foundation runs a Technical High School, health projects, an organic farming operation, and several other microenterprises. Yachana Lodge and the foundation are much awarded and regarded as one of the most best and most effective examples of eco-tourism in Ecuador. Visitors who stay here comment on the meaningful interactions possible with local indigenous people, and this is one of the lodge's highlights.

Going remote

Kapawi Ecolodge, on the Río Pastaza near the border with Peru, is one of the most highly regarded lodges in the world. Perhaps the best thing about

Environmental Lawsuit

A gargantuan environmental battle has long been raging over Ecuador's Oriente. A multibillion-dollar case against oil company Chevron has been ongoing since 1993. Brought by a group of US-based trial lawyers led by Ecuadorian environmental lawyer Pablo Fajardo, the case is on behalf of 48 plaintiffs and thousands of indigenous people living in oil-contaminated areas. The suit is expected to result in the biggest ever payout by an oil company for environmental damages: up to $27 billion dollars. In a report compiled by a court-appointed team in 2008, it was concluded that oil spilling and deliberate, uncontained dumping of petrochemical waste by Chevron (previously Texaco) had lead to 1,401 cancer deaths in the Ecuadorian Amazon and countless other long-term health effects including birth defects and miscarriage, disability, and chronic disease. Chevron used unlined pits to dump oil sludge in the jungle, which resulted in contaminants entering water sources and the food chain. The oil giant (then Texaco) was forced to pay $40 million in a clean-up operation in 1993, but a subsequent change in Ecuadorian law has allowed this new case to be brought. The damages that the company is expected to have to pay will likely make this the most expensive environmental clean-up case ever, dwarfing the $3.9 billion awarded against ExxonMobil for its 1989 oil spill in Alaska.

Kapawi is that it is so remote: it's accessible only by a 90-minute flight by small plane from the jungle's-edge hamlet of Shell, some two hours' drive east of Baños, and then by motor canoe to the lodge itself. Kapawi is set deep in some 681,218 hectares (1,683,326 acres) of jungle that is the territory of the Achuar people, where some 6,000 indigenous people live in 64 communities. Kapawi was set up as a partnership between the Achuar people and an Ecuadorian tourism enterprise with the idea of providing the Achuar with a sustainable income to remain in their ancestral land and defend themselves against oil exploration and exploitation. The project has been a resounding success and the beautiful lodge – built in traditional Achuar style – is highly lauded. The area also supports abundant wildlife, including pink river dolphins and 570 species of birds, but one of the best things is the close interaction with the Achuar people, who will soon take over and run the lodge completely independently.

Fragile balance

It is imperative that anyone thinking of visiting the Oriente region ask themselves whether they are harming the environment and the lifestyles they are so keen to see and to preserve. This is a particularly pertinent question when it comes to visiting indigenous communities. One group that has so far resisted significant contact with outsiders is the Huaorani, who live in relative isolation in an area around the Río Cononoco. The political organization ONHAE is working to protect the Huaorani from colonization, following the discovery of oil in the region, but it is difficult to predict whether Ecuador will be able to walk the tightrope between economic development and protecting the Huaorani and the rainforest ecosystem. Most of the Huaorani people, who maintain a hunter-gatherer way of life, do not welcome tourist visits to their communities and it is advisable to respect their wishes, but conversely,

some Huaorani are turning to ecotourism to protect their culture, and it is possible to spend time with the Huaorani community of the village of Quehueri'ono by prior arrangement.

Living along the Río Aguarico, a small group of Cofan natives work with the help of US-born Randy Borman to encourage tourists to visit their village of **Zabalo** on carefully organized tours. Once there, visitors experience the Cofan lifestyle, traveling in dugout canoes and hiking into the jungle in search of medicinal plants. The ideal behind the enterprise is not just to safeguard the jungle, but also to allow the Cofan people to control the rate of change, so that they can retain their language and their sense of themselves as a people. Some people feel that bringing tourism to a region in need of preservation is self-defeating, but Borman and the village leaders disagree. All the money generated goes to the Cofan, who are able to use and display their traditional knowledge of the Oriente, both for personal survival and as their singular contribution to a changing world.   ❏

BELOW: a Cofan woman passes the Guanta oil production site, which has contaminated the river where her community fetches water and bathes.

ORIENTE WILDLIFE

Everyone wants to see the armadillos and tapirs, the big cats, and the prolific birdlife. But the armies of insects that most people try to avoid are no less interesting

The Oriente has such a diverse variety of wildlife that for many people, the chance to see some of it in its natural habitat is reason enough to travel to Ecuador. Whether your interest is in birds, beasts, reptiles, or insects, you will find fascinating species in the Amazonian forest.

Fantastic birdlife

Some 550 species of birds have been recorded in the Napo region alone, and ornithologists and bird-watchers flock to the area to see species with such exotic names as green and gold tanager, greater yellow-headed vulture, purple-throated fruitcrow, puffbird, and toucan. One of the highlights in a trip to an Amazon lodge is the opportunity to see birdlife gather at patches of soil – often along riverbanks – laden with mineral salts. At dawn, bird-watchers can witness a magnificent display of hundreds of squawking, squabbling parrots feeding at the *saladeros*, as the salt licks are known. Species that need the mineral in their diet such as the blue-headed, orange-cheeked, and yellow-crowned parrot as well as the dusky-headed parakeet and scarlet-shouldered parrotlet are amongst the colorful species one can observe.

Mammals of the rainforest

The salt licks also attract a variety of jungle mammals. Most of these feed at night and leave only footprints for the curious visitor to observe in daylight.

An adventurous person could spend the night by a salt lick and perhaps be rewarded with moonlit glimpses of a variety of mammals. These may include the nine-banded armadillo, or a rodent called the paca which has spotted fur, weighs up to 9kg (20lb) and is considered excellent food by local hunters. The capybara, the world's largest rodent, weighing around 64kg (140lb), is another animal that you might see.

Some salt licks attract a huge, strange mammal, the South American tapir. The largest land mammals in

Main attractions
WATCHING PARROTS AT A SALT LICK
SPOTTING A SHY TAPIR
CHANCING ON AN ELUSIVE SPECTACLED BEAR
SPYING SLOTHS IN THE TREETOPS
GOING MACRO ON THE WORLD OF INSECTS

LEFT: shining sunbeam hummingbird.
BELOW: tapirs have prehensile snouts and are related to rhinoceroses.

The Scarlet Macaw is just one of many species of parrot found in the Ecuadorian Amazon.

Amazonia, tapirs can weigh in excess of 270kg (600lb). Their closest relatives are the other odd-toed ungulates, the rhinoceros and the horse. Members of the tapir family are among the most primitive large mammals in the world and are well adapted to life in the jungle. Their short sturdy legs, thick, strong necks, and barrel-like bodies covered with incredibly tough skin enable them to shove through the dense forest undergrowth like a living tank. One of their strangest features is a short trunk, which gives them an excellent sense of smell and is used to pull leaves off bushes and into their mouths.

Locally, tapirs are much sought-after game animals; one is enough to feed an entire village. Apart from the meat, the tapirs' fatty tissues yield an oil that is much prized for cooking, and the thick skin makes good-quality leather. The South American tapir lives in the Oriente lowlands and the mountain tapir inhabits the upper Amazonian basin and the Andean flanks. Hunting is not as much of a threat to the latter as habitat destruction, and the mountain tapir is regarded as an endangered species.

Apart from man, the tapir's greatest enemy is the big cat of Amazonia; the jaguar. A fully grown male can reach 113kg (250lb) in weight and, when hungry, will attack almost any large animal it comes across. Jaguars will leap onto tapirs' backs and attempt to kill them by breaking their necks in their powerful jaws. The tapirs' defense is twofold: the fact that the thick neck is protected by the tough, leathery skin and a bristly mane, and their habit of charging wildly through the dense undergrowth when threatened, thus making it difficult for a predator to hold on long enough to deliver the fatal bite.

Jaguars do not roar, as do most other big cats. Instead, they emit a low, coughing grunt, especially when courting. Generally, jaguars are afraid of humans and only the luckiest of visitors catches a glimpse of them in the wild.

You are also unlikely to see another shy resident, the endangered spectacled bear: fewer than 2,000 individuals are thought to exist in the wild. The only bear found in South America,

BELOW: a young puma.
BELOW RIGHT: a red howler monkey.

its habitat ranges from 200 meters (650ft) to 4,200 meters (13,800ft) on the heavily forested subtropical slopes. It is mainly vegetarian, often climbing trees in search of succulent fruits. The bear's habitat is increasingly being encroached upon by colonists, and it is protected by Ecuadorian law.

A multitude of monkeys

The mammals that visitors most often get to see, however, are the monkeys. The most vocal of these is the very aptly named howler monkey. Male howler monkeys have a specialized, hollow, and much enlarged hyoid bone in the throat. Air is passed through the hyoid cavity producing an ear-splitting call, which can easily carry for well over a kilometer in the rainforest. This is an astounding feat when one remembers that the forest vegetation has a damping effect on sound. When heard in the distance, the call has been variously described as sounding like the wind moaning through the trees or like a human baby crying. Close up, the call can be quite terrifying to the uninitiated visitor.

The purpose of the call is to advertize a troop's presence in a particular patch of rainforest. This enables troops to space themselves out in the canopy and thus avoid competing as they forage for succulent young leaves. Occasionally, troops do meet in the treetops and the result is often chaotic with howling, chasing, threatening, and even fighting. The energy used in these meetings is better expended in feeding, and thus it pays for a troop to make its presence known by frequent howling.

Several other species of monkey are frequently seen, including wooly, squirrel, spider, and tamarin monkeys. Often, the best way to observe monkeys is from a dugout canoe floating down a jungle river. A local, trained guide will spot a troop of monkeys early enough to stop the boat in a position that offers a clear view of the animals foraging in trees along the banks. From within the rainforest, on the other hand, animals may be difficult to see in the treetops. In addition, monkeys may display their displeasure at human intrusion by hurling sticks, fruit, and even feces down on the unfortunate visitor's head.

The sloth is one of the most remarkable animals of the Ecuadorian rainforest. This slow-moving creature can often be spotted sitting motionless in tree branches or inching at a glacial pace toward its next meal of fruits, nuts, berries, or bark. Sloths have an extremely slow metabolism and may only descend to the ground to defecate once a month.

BELOW: a stunning blue butterfly.

Wildlife beneath your feet

Many people come to the Oriente hoping to see exotic birds and mammals, while trying to avoid the myriad insects. Yet it is the insects that are the most common and, in many ways, most fascinating creatures of the rainforest. Some are simply beautiful, such as the breathtaking blue morpho butterflies whose huge wings flash a dazzling electric blue. Other species have such complex life cycles that they are still not fully understood by tropical ecologists. Among these are hundreds of ant species, particularly the ubiquitous army and leafcutter ants.

Colonies of leafcutter ants numbering hundreds of thousands live in huge nests dug deep into the ground. Foragers search the vegetation for particular types of leaves, cut out small sections and, holding the leaf segments above their heads like small umbrellas, take them back to the nest. The ants can be quite experimental, bringing back a variety of leaves and even pieces of discarded plastic wrappers. Workers within the nest sort out the kinds of leaves which will mulch down into a type of compost; unsuitable material is ejected from the nest after a few days. The composted leaves form a mulch on which a fungus grows. Ants tend these fungal gardens with care, for they provide the main diet for both the adult ants and for the young that are being raised inside the nest.

The story does not end there. When a particularly good source of leaves has been located, ants lay down a trail of chemical markers, or pheromones, linking the nest with the leaf source, often 100 meters (330ft) or more away in the forest. People frequently come across these trails in the jungle, with hundreds of ants scurrying along carrying leaf sections back to the nest, or returning empty-handed for another load.

Other species, for example army ants, prey on this ready and constant supply of foragers. To combat this the leafcutter ants are morphologically separated by size and jaw structure into different castes. Some specialize in tending the fungal gardens; others have jaws designed for cutting; and yet others are soldiers, armed with huge mandibles, that accompany the foragers and protect them from attackers. Close observation of the foragers will sometimes reveal yet another caste, a tiny ant that can ride on the leaf segments without disturbing the foragers and are thought to act as protection against parasitical wasps, which may try to lay their eggs on the ants.

A colony of leafcutter ants may last for a decade or more. New colonies are founded by the emergence of a number of potential queens, who mate and then fly off to found another nest, carrying some of the fungus used for food. This is essential to "seed" the new nest. The rest of the new queen's life is spent laying tens of thousands of eggs, destined to become gardeners, foragers, soldiers, riders, or even queens.

Such complex interactions make the rainforest interesting to biologists and tourists alike. A day with a trained guide will bring to light many such stories about the habits of the forest's vast population of creatures great and small. ❏

BELOW: a tree boa, ready to strike.

The Vanishing Rainforest

Satellite images show it shrinking: closer up, it is obscured under palls of slash-and-burn smoke. We see it drenched in oil, cut and devastated. And yet still the decimation of the world's rainforests is a daily reality.

The plight of the planet's tropical forests has been well publicized. Huge areas of forest are being logged or burned every day; so much deforestation is occurring that, at the present rate, with more than 25,900 sq km (10,000 sq miles) being destroyed for ranching, farming, and logging each year in Brazil alone, some scientists have predicted that 40 percent of the rainforest will disappear by 2050. Of the almost 2 million known species of plants and animals, about half live only in the rainforest. Estimates of species yet to be discovered are numbered in millions. Most of these unknown species live in the tropical forests, which have by far the greatest biodiversity of any region on the globe. Thus deforestation is causing countless extinctions, with many of the plants and animals as yet unknown.

The value of rainforests

Numerous medicines have been extracted from forest plants, ranging from malarial prophylactics to anesthetics, from antibiotics to contraceptives. Many more useful drugs will undoubtedly be discovered in the forests, if they are not destroyed first.

The diversity of species growing in the rainforests also comprises a storehouse of new strains of agriculturally important plants that may be destroyed by disease or drought. For example, if banana crops were to be seriously threatened by disease, scientists could search the rainforests for disease-resistant strains to cross with the commercially grown varieties and eradicate the problem.

The forests are also essential for the survival of indigenous peoples. Hundreds of discrete communities living in the jungles of Latin America (and in Africa and Asia) are threatened by rainforest loss.

On a worldwide scale, the moderating effect of the rainforest on global climate patterns is only recently being understood. Deforestation could cause severe

global warming, leading to melting ice caps, rising ocean levels, and flooding of coastal regions. Climates would be altered to the extent that some major crops, such as wheat, would no longer grow.

One of the chief reasons the rainforests are being destroyed is the displacement of poor *campesinos* who migrate from other parts of the country looking for free land on which to make a living. Generally the soils are not well suited for agriculture and are quickly depleted of scarce nutrients. The short-sighted colonization policies causing this damage are now at last being re-evaluated and solutions being sought, but the forest is still being cleared at an alarming rate. Illegal timber-poaching by large forestry companies and clearing of land for large-scale industrial animal farming are other major factors in the disappearance of rainforests.

Debt-for-nature swaps, whereby foreign debts are paid off by the lenders in return for protection of the rainforest, are a move in the right direction, but the developed countries that lend the money must ensure that such incentives reflect the full value of the forests.

Sustainable use, such as rubber-tapping, brazil-nut-harvesting and tourism also help to a certain extent. Rainforests such as the Oriente are vital for the planet's survival. Whatever the methods used, protection of the planet's green lung should be regarded as an urgent, global priority. ❑

RIGHT: Oriente settlers.

THE WESTERN LOWLANDS

Agriculture has become vitally important in this region. As you travel south from Santo Domingo, you'll find rice on the roads, bananas in bags, and houses on stilts

Map on page 244

The road from Quito to **Santo Domingo** is one of the most dramatic in the country. In a matter of hours the elevation dips a jaw-dropping 3,000 meters (10,000ft) down the western slopes of the Andes. The 2½-hour drive is one of the most terrifying bus journeys in Ecuador. Truck and bus drivers rely on headlights and horns as they hurtle down the road, paying scant attention to the poor visibility (the roads are often shrouded in fog, especially in the afternoons) or oncoming traffic. Surprisingly, accidents are rare, but it is not without some sense of relief that the traveler finally arrives.

Home for healers

The capital of Santo Domingo province is **Santo Domingo de los Colorados ❶**, after the Colorado people, also known as the Tsáchilas, who once dominated the area. Their appearance was distinctive: both sexes painted their faces with black stripes and the men plastered down their bowl-shaped haircuts with the brilliant red dye from *achiote*, a local plant (*see picture, left*). *Achiote* is thought to have been brought from the mountains by a group of shamans many generations ago who said that the dye would help protect the tribe from yellow fever and other diseases. Some of the men built up a nationwide reputation as *curanderos* (medicine men). People still come from all over Ecuador to be treated for

a variety of illnesses, a custom that has seen a resurgence in recent years with the growing trend for alternative and natural medicines.

Many travelers visit Santo Domingo in the hope of seeing the Colorados in their authentic finery or perhaps witnessing or partaking in a curing ceremony. Some are lucky, for the traditions do still exist, but many are disappointed to find that most of the 2,000 or so remaining Colorados now wear Western dress, no longer paint their faces, and have largely abandoned their

Main attractions

SPECTACULAR QUITO–SANTO DOMINGO ROAD JOURNEY
TSÁCHILA CULTURE IN SANTO DOMINGO
GIANT BANANA AND TROPICAL FRUIT PLANTATIONS
VIEWING HOUSEBOATS ON THE RÍO BABAHOYO
BIRD-VIEWING AT TINALANDIA

PRECEDING PAGES: traditional weaving, Santo Domingo. **LEFT:** Tsáchila man. **BELOW:** *achiote*, used for hair dye.

TIP

It's important not to confuse the two Santo Domingos. Santo Domingo de los Tsáchilas is the name of the western lowland province created in October 2007 from territory previously in the province of Pichincha. The town of Santo Domingo de los Colorados is the provincial capital, but the name for the town and the province are sometimes used interchangeably.

BELOW: Tsáchila girl dancing.

traditional appearance and customs. The Colorados are spread out over eight areas between Santo Domingo and Quevedo, inhabiting a reserve of around 8,000 hectares (19,800 acres). The **Complejo Turístico Huapilú**, a museum and cultural center (charge) in a Colorado commune, is located about 10km (6 miles) from Santo Domingo, just off the road to Quevedo. A brief tour gives an introduction to the tribe's music, cooking, *curanderos*, and crafts.

Santo Domingo de los Colorados has a tropical climate and is the nearest place for Quiteños to come and enjoy the lowland heat. There are several small resort hotels nearby where visitors can relax next to a swimming pool in a tropical garden or try their luck in the casino. It is also the hub of a network of paved roads radiating out into the western lowlands.

Into banana lands

The road south of Santo Domingo leads through vast plantations of bananas and African oil palms. Until the discovery of petroleum in the Oriente in the late 1960s, Ecuador was the archetypal banana republic, with bananas being by far the most important export. Even today, Ecuador remains the largest exporter of bananas in the world, with annual exports averaging about 28 percent of the world's supply.

Bananas were not always so important. Friedrich Hassaurek, who served as US minister to Ecuador from 1860 to 1864, reported that the main export was cacao. This crop was grown along the rivers of the western lowlands, and floated down to Guayaquil for export. In the 1930s, cacao remained the principal export, followed by coffee, which was also grown in the western lowlands. After World War II, banana production became increasingly important, and by the 1970s, cacao had dropped to second place. Heavy floods during the El Niño phenomenon of the past two decades severely disrupted the cacao industry and, although it has since recovered, bananas and coffee are now the two most important export crops.

The banana trees in the plantations are arranged in regular rows for ease

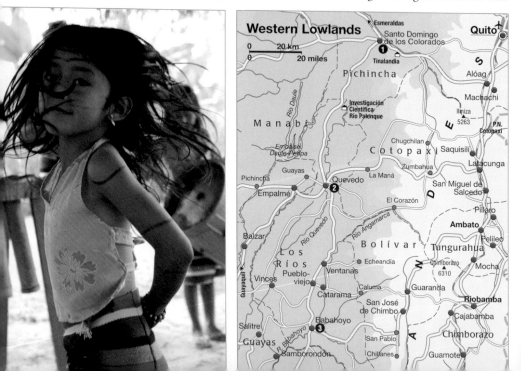

of harvesting, and travelers driving past are soon mesmerized by the endless lines of plants. The monotony is broken occasionally by the sight of workers collecting the ripe fruit with long-handled shears. Often bunches of bananas are sleeved in large blue plastic bags before harvesting; the polythene in the bags releases a chemical signal which hastens the fruits' ripening.

Market center

An hour and a half's drive south of Santo Domingo lies the largest market town of the western lowlands, **Quevedo ❷**. Not only bananas, but cacao, coffee, rice, sugar, African palm oil, and citrus and tropical fruits pass through this important center. Quevedo was founded in the mid-1800s and is thus a relatively modern town. You may sometimes hear the town referred to as "the Chinatown of Ecuador" because many Chinese immigrants, some of whom came to work on the railway construction around the turn of the 20th century, eventually settled here. Most of the better restaurants along Quevedo's main streets are *chifas*, as Chinese restaurants are called locally.

In the past, produce from the area was able to reach the coast at Guayaquil along the narrow and convoluted Río Quevedo, which runs a few blocks north of the city's downtown area. The journey was a difficult and hazardous one, with frequent sandbanks, log jams, and shallows to obstruct the unwary. Today, with the construction of a good paved road to Guayaquil, the river is used as a playground by the local children seeking relief from the tropical sun. Although the river port is no longer used, the accompanying street market is still found along the banks of the river.

South of Quevedo, a number of rivers dissect the land, which becomes increasingly subject to flooding during the rainy season, which lasts from January to April. It is after these rivers that the province **Los Ríos** is named.

This kind of low-lying terrain is admirably suited to the cultivation of rice, and paddy fields proliferate. The occasional trees between the fields serve as roosts for flocks of wading birds. White American egrets look especially pretty at sunset, when they gather like hundreds of huge white flowers, virtually blanketing the treetops.

During the dry months, rice is set out to dry on huge open-air platforms of concrete in the many commercial *piladoras* found along the road. *Piladora* is a local word meaning a drying and husking factory. Some of the poorer farmers are unable to afford the cost of using the *piladora* and so spread out their modest crops on the nearest available flat and dry surface. This may be the tarmac top of the highway, and drivers do their best to avoid running over the crops.

Rice and other agricultural products frequently make their way through **Babahoyo ❸**, the provincial capital of Los Ríos. The city is a modern one, but it has a long history. A settlement existed here before the arrival of the *conquistadores*, and Spanish records

Chifa (*Chinese restaurant*) *sign.*

BELOW:
women washing clothes near Santo Domingo.

Parque Nacional Podocarpus in southern Ecuador has one of the largest birding lists in this country of mega-diverse birding. Some 540 species have been recorded here so far, and, still relatively unexplored, it is may harbour over 800 species, which would make it second for bird diversity only to Peru's Parque Nacional Manu.

indicate the presence of a town here as early as 1576. The present city dates from 1867, after a catastrophic fire destroyed the previous town. Before the building of the road, Babahoyo was an important port known as Bodegas, meaning storehouses. There were frequent steamships linking the coast at Guayaquil with the inland river port of Bodegas, where goods were stored to await transport to the highlands and Quito by mule.

Houseboats and stilts

The city is a mere 7 meters (23ft) above sea level and flooding always seems to have been part of the way of life. Friedrich Hassaurek, in another of his observations made during his visit in 1860, noted how most of the houses were built on stilts to raise the sleeping rooms above the annual floodwaters. Today, some of the inhabitants live in a picturesque floating village of houseboats on the Río Babahoyo, while the Vinces district, nicknamed Little Paris, features a number of well-preserved colonial mansions once owned by wealthy cocoa merchants.

The western lowlands are an important part of Ecuador's agricultural and tropical life. The exotic crops, equatorial climate, gorgeous birds, and interesting people make this a fascinating area to visit. Yet it is very much off the beaten track. Most travelers pass through Babahoyo on their way to somewhere else.

Ancient forests

This region was not always rich in agriculture. At one time much of it was covered by dense tropical rainforest. The renowned British mountaineer, Edward Whymper, arrived in Guayaquil in December, 1879, with the aim of climbing Ecuador's major peaks. In his *Travels Amongst the Great Andes of the Equator* he describes his journey through the western lowlands, where he saw "forest-trees rising 150ft [46 meters] high, mast-like, without a branch, laden with a parasitic growth."

This terrain was very different from the Amazonian forests to the east of the Andean chain. The pronounced rainy and dry seasons produced a distinctive array of plants and animals that contributed to Ecuador's great variety of species. Ecuador holds the record for the highest biological diversity per unit of land of any Latin American country, but sadly much of the natural vegetation in this part of Ecuador was cleared long ago to make way for agriculture.

Some remaining vestiges of the western lowlands' original forest cover may be seen at **Tinalandia**, a lodge not far from Santo Domingo (on the turnoff 16km/90 miles east of Santo Domingo). More than 500 species of bird have been recorded within walking distance of the lodge by some of the world's most renowned birding experts. Accommodations are in a comfortable renovated hacienda, offering first-class service and a variety of outdoor activities from bird-watching to horseback riding, hiking, and swimming. *See Travel Tips, page 346 for contact details.* ❑

BELOW: cutting sugarcane.

Bird-Watching

One of the most remarkable things about Ecuador is that this relatively small country has such incredible biodiversity. Bird-spotters will be thrilled by the avian riches here.

Ecuador is a bird-watcher's paradise. The wide variety of habitats, from tropical rainforests to windswept highlands, from mangrove swamps to hilly forests, provide a wider range of species than any other country in the Americas. More than 1,500 bird species have been recorded here, twice as many as in the US and Canada combined.

In the *páramo* (high-altitude plateau) habitat of Cotopaxi National Park, one of the most surprising sights is a tiny hummingbird, the Andean hillstar, which survives the freezing nights by lowering its body temperature from about 40°C (104°F) in the daytime to about 15°C (59°F) at night, a remarkable feat for a warm-blooded creature. At the other end of the size scale is the Andean condor, which, with its 3-meter (10ft) wing span, is one of the largest flying birds in the world.

Other *páramo* species include the carunculated caracara, Andean lapwing, Andean gull, páramo pipit, great thrush, and bar-winged cinclodes. If you camp out, you may hear the loud hoot of the great horned owl as it searches for prey, or the eerie drumming of the Andean snipe's outer wing feathers as it careens by in the dark.

Hummingbirds aplenty

The Andes of Ecuador are split into two ranges between which lies the temperate central valley. The less extreme elevation of 2,800 meters (9,200ft) ensures a pleasant climate and attracts a variety of fascinating birds. Hummingbirds are great favorites. They begin to increase in number as the elevation drops and the climate becomes milder. More than one-fifth of Ecuador's 120 or so species of hummers are found in the central valley, and one of the best places to see them is the Pasochoa Nature Reserve, which is run by the Fundación Natura, Ecuador's leading conservation agency. In one of the last original stands of temperate forest in the central valley, 11 hummingbird species, plus a variety of doves, furnarids, tapaculos, tyrant fly-

catchers, honeycreepers, and tanagers can all be seen, just one hour's drive from the capital.

Spend a couple of days driving to Mindo down the Chiriboga and Nono roads, heading toward the western lowlands, looking for the cock-of-the-rock, plate-billed mountain toucans, and mountain tanagers.

On the eastern Andean slopes the road to Coca takes you over the Papallacta Pass through the *páramo*, dropping down through cloud forest, with its barred fruit eaters and gray-breasted mountain toucans, into the Amazon basin. Once there, bird-watching can get a little tricky as the lush vegetation hides a huge diversity of birds. You will need considerable patience and experience if you are to see them. Many people find that the best strategy is to take an organized tour or have a guide to point out some of the 550 bird species found in the area. Parrots, toucans, macaws, vultures, kingfishers, puffbirds, antbirds, herons, and hummingbirds are all there, waiting for the patient bird-watcher. Kapawi Lodge, Sacha Lodge and Napo Wildlife Center are some of the best options if you are looking for experienced guides. *(See Travel Tips, page 333 for more details.)*

The Galápagos, on the other hand, is a great place for bird-watching beginners to cut their teeth. Here, the 25 endemic species are relatively easy to spot, and there are many other fascinating species to interest even the most inexperienced twitcher. ❏

RIGHT: one of Ecuador's 120 species of hummingbirds.

THE PACIFIC COAST

Palm-fringed beaches are the main draw. But there's much more to a trip to the coast: marimba rhythms, mangrove swamps, the bustling port of Manta, and an echo of Africa all add to the fun

COLOMBIA
• Quito
ECUADOR
PERU

The north Pacific coast of Ecuador is one of the best places on the continent to take a break from the sometimes demanding rigors of travel. Much of this varied coastline consists of largely empty, palm-fringed beaches, which present the ideal opportunity to practice one of the foremost customs of ancient Ecuador: sun worship.

This area bore the brunt of the devastating floods of 1982–3 and 1998–9, brought about by the El Niño current, when roads, beaches, trees, crops, and a significant number of dwellings were washed away. Recovery has in many cases been slow, for in the tropical languor of a sweltering landscape, the tendency to consign things to *mañana* is pervasive.

As a string of holiday resorts springs up along the coast, however, the last signs of destruction fade. This development testifies to Ecuador's growing stature as a tourist destination, due partly to its own charms, and partly to its neighbors' ill fortunes. A holiday in parts of Colombia, with its cocaine-related civil disturbances, is not for the faint-hearted, while large sections of the Peruvian coastline are washed by the Humboldt Current that brings damp, misty weather and ice-cold waters. Because of this, Ecuador has cornered the market in tropical beaches along South America's west coast. However, the prevailing security situation should be checked before visiting. Ecuador's northern Pacific coast has also seen some of the armed violence that is prevalent across the Colombian border, and there has been an increase in kidnappings and armed violent crime in Esmeraldas province. Foreigners have been attacked on beaches, in popular tourist areas as well as in remote locations. The more touristy towns of Montañita and Manglaralto further south are safer, though it is still not a good idea to walk along the beaches at night.

Main attractions
LA TOLA–ESMERALDAS ROAD TRIP
THE BEACHES OF MUISNÉ
PANAMA HAT-MAKING IN MONTECRISTI
PARQUE NACIONAL MACHALILLA
WHALE-WATCHING AT PUERTO LÓPEZ

PRECEDING PAGES: landing the catch. **LEFT:** sunset, Puerto López. **BELOW:** juice stall.

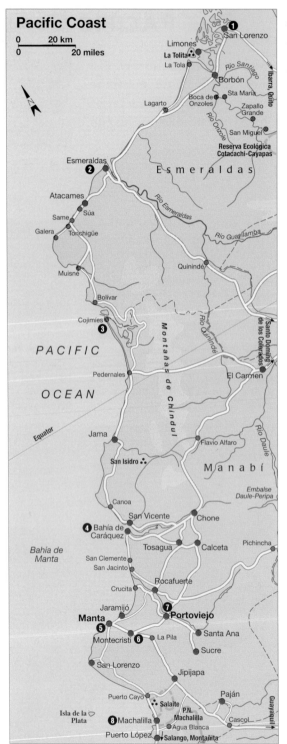

Pacific Coast

0   20 km

0   20 miles

Land of two seasons

The wet season on the Ecuadorian coast runs from December to June, the remainder of the year being dry – or perhaps, more accurately, not so wet. During the wet season, when flooding is commonplace and high levels of humidity make life uncomfortably sticky, the beaches – despite being below par – are well patronized. All things considered, August to October is the best time to visit this relaxed region.

The coastal topography consists of a thin lowland strip, which turns from forbidding mangroves in the north to dry scrubland on the Santa Elena Peninsula, west of Guayaquil. A short distance inland runs a range of low, rounded, crystalline hills. The region is cut by numerous rivers meandering down from the Andes, which regularly flood the alluvial plain that lies to the east of the hills. Huge alluvial fans, often consisting of porous volcanic ash eroded from highland basins, spread out from the major river mouths, providing very fertile soil.

The province of Esmeraldas is one of dense, luxuriant rainforest characterized by two main botanical strata: a high canopy of towering evergreen broadleaf species sprinkled with palms; and at eye level, clusters of giant ferns, shrubs, and vines. Among these are spectacular smaller plants such as orchids and bromeliads, which proliferate in the Amazonian forest.

South of Esmeraldas is a zone of deciduous scrub woodland that drops its leaves during the dry season. A narrow strip of tropical, semi-deciduous forest lies just north of Manta; and from here down to Guayaquil, this mangrove forest is broken only by the infertile scrubland of Santa Elena. Among the commercially used plants of the coastal forests are the balsa tree, source of the world's lightest timber; the ivory-nut palm (tagua), used to make buttons; and the toquilla reed, from which the renowned Panama hat is manufactured.

The coastal region, which contains almost half of Ecuador's 13 million people, is populated by a veritable melting pot of ethnic groups. Here, more than in the Sierra and the jungle, the trails of history incorporate all the colors of the rainbow. At the time of the Spaniards' arrival, the centers of coastal indigenous habitation were Esmeraldas, Manta, Huancavilca, and Puná; these peoples were either exterminated outright, or else they mixed to the point where the distinctness between groups was completely extinguished.

A century or so later, the Spanish-indigenous mixture (called mestizo) was infused with African blood as slaves were brought from West Africa, creating the mulatto (Afro-Hispanic mix) and *montubio* (indigenous-African mix) races. Indigenous Caribs were also shipped to Ecuador to work the plantations, adding a fourth element to this ethnic conglomeration. Mestizos comprise the majority of the coastal population, but the black influence is one of the region's most interesting features, pervading all aspects of life.

From the Colombian border

A journey that begins in **San Lorenzo** ❶, in Ecuador's northwestern corner, can only get drier. The sea is the town's *raison d'être*, and fresh, salty breezes fill the potholed streets. The land around San Lorenzo is mostly mangrove swamp, navigated by motorized dugout canoes, while the town itself is frequently sodden with rainwater that has nowhere to run off. A road was recently constructed, linking San Lorenzo to Ibarra and Quito, and there is a bus service. However, many travelers who find themselves here may have come up the coast by boat. San Lorenzo used to mark one end of the spectacular, day-long train trip from Ibarra; unfortunately this line currently only runs from Ibarra to Primer Paso.

Despite its isolation, San Lorenzo can generate a certain amount of bustle. It possesses the best natural harbor on the Ecuadorian coast, and a hinterland still largely untouched due to its inaccessibility. The population has grown from 2,000 in 1960 – when, in the days prior to the discovery of oil in the Oriente, this was Ecuador's El Dorado, the

A refreshing tropical fruit juice.

BELOW LEFT: boy enjoying the beach at Galera.
BELOW: house with wraparound veranda in Esmeraldas province.

alluring, untapped frontier – to 20,000 today. Timber traders have made profitable incursions into forests rich in mahogany, balsa, and rubber, creating industries and bringing itinerant laborers to this long-neglected outpost. However, illegal logging has put the forests under threat.

It should be noted that San Lorenzo has no immigration office, nor any official currency exchange, so crossing the Colombian border to Tumaco is near to impossible and, given the security risks in this part of Colombia, certainly not advisable.

African legacy

San Lorenzo has the feel of a town invented by Gabriel García Márquez. The descendants of people from distant continents have been washed up by history on this forbidding shore, and made the most of their displacement. African slaves transported in the 17th and 18th centuries were unloaded in Cartagena (Colombia) and marched southward to man the coffee, banana, and cacao plantations; less than half of this human cargo sur-

vived the privations of passage to reach their destinations.

The legacy of Africa lives on here today in the form of ancestor worship and the voodoo rituals of *macumba*, whereby spirits are summoned to cure and curse. Beneath the Latinized veneer of regular Sunday Mass lies an ancient belief in macabre spirits or *visiones* such as *La Tunda*, who frightens bad children to death and then steals their bodies, or *El Rivel*, who feasts on corpses.

African rhythms anchor the uptempo beat of marimba music, which can be heard in San Lorenzo. Esmeraldeña marimba retains purer links with its origins than does the Colombian style, which has borrowed heavily from the Caribbean jingles of salsa and often resembles Western pop music. Talented musicians and dancers of both marimba styles can be seen rehearsing on Wednesday nights, and when they hit the downtown bars, San Lorenzo starts jumping. Men are said to come of age when they begin to *andar y conocer*; literally, "to walk and to know," or "to travel and learn." In local idiom, this commonly used phrase

BELOW: bringing home the bamboo.

means "to strut," and is heavily loaded with sexual innuendo.

To get to the coast road you have to go by boat from San Lorenzo to **La Tola**. Services are cheap and regular and take about 2½ hours. En route to La Tola lies the island of **La Tolita**, an important ceremonial center from 500 to 100 BC. Tribal chiefs were buried here, their tombs filled with artifacts of gold, silver, platinum, and copper. In recognition of its historical significance, La Tolita has been declared an Archeological National Park and is undergoing extensive excavation. Like many such sites in South America, La Tolita has been savagely plundered by thieves, its treasures sold on the international black market. Fortunately, however, the government's attention was attracted in time to salvage a substantial portion of the relics, and another gap in the jigsaw puzzle of ancient Ecuador is slowly being filled. An archeological museum has been erected on the site, showcasing finds from the digs and recovered artifacts.

Frontier town

Opposite La Tolita at the mouth of the Río Santiago is **Limones** (which must also be reached by boat). It is a small town of some importance as the center of the local timber industry, but without a lot to offer tourists. Wood is floated downriver to the sawmill here, and processed for further distribution.

The timber camps, isolated in the dense, upriver jungle, were quite notorious in their early days during the 1960s for a form of outpost exploitation worthy of the author Joseph Conrad. The mestizo owners forbade their workers – mostly *morenos* (a generic term for dark-skinned people in Latin America) – to leave camp. Instead, prostitutes and alcohol were shipped in to the camps each pay day; a kind of slavery with overpriced and monopolistic fringe benefits.

This delta region is the home of the Cayapa or Chachi, who – along with the Tsáchilas of Santo Domingo – were

the only indigenous coastal tribe to evade extermination by the Spaniards. In both cases, survival was due to the inaccessibility of their homelands. Today, the Cayapa number approximately 4,000. They are sometimes seen selling their finely woven hammocks and basketwork in the markets of Limones and La Tola – and occasionally Esmeraldas – but they prefer the privacy of Borbón and the inhospitable upper reaches of the Río Cayapa. A turnoff on the La Tola–Esmeraldas road runs to **Borbón**, but this country is decidedly off the beaten track, and travel can be numbingly difficult, especially in the wet season.

A better option is to take a motorized dugout from El Bongo restaurant in Limones upriver to Borbón. From here expeditions continue up to **Boca de Onzoles**, at the confluence of the Cayapa and Onzoles rivers. In this far-flung village, a Hungarian émigré called Stefan Tarjany runs a comfortable lodge – Steve's Lodge (Casilla 187, Esmeraldas; no phone) and organizes trips to the mission stations of **Santa María** and **Zapallo Grande**. He also

BELOW: a quiet street in Puerto López.

arranges boat trips to the **Reserva Ecológica Cotacachi-Cayapas**, but the usual starting point for this trip is **San Miguel**, the last settlement on the river. It is advisable to check that these trips are still running before journeying to this remote location.

The reserve covers some 204,400 hectares (505,000 acres) and its habitat varies from lowland tropical forest, in this region, to cloud forest, to windswept plain, and accordingly has an enormous range of flora and fauna. It is also the home of the Cayapa, who continue to live in their traditional way, trying to avoid the encroachment of Western values and influences. The reserve receives protection from the Ecuadorian government and from international conservation organizations. Guided tours in dugout canoes can be arranged with the park rangers.

Travel in other parts of Ecuador is rarely as adventurous as in these alluring backwaters, which few visitors make the effort to explore. The Cayapa people's counterparts in the Oriente – Stone Age tribes such as the Jivaro and the Huaorani – have received far

greater international exposure, which in turn has attracted more tourists. This exposure may, however, prove beneficial as the search for oil in the Amazon basin is a much greater threat to indigenous lifestyles than anything the Cayapa are up against.

Difficult highways

The road from La Tola to **Esmeraldas** ❷ is rough and never ready: *rancheros*, which are open-sided trucks fitted with far too many wooden benches, take 5 hours to cover the 100km (60 miles); regular buses do the journey in 3 hours. The northern half of this road may suffer severe flooding during the wet season, but otherwise it is a carefree, breezy ride past cattle farms and swamps teeming with birdlife. A few small towns are strung out along the way, but offer little reason to pause.

It was near Esmeraldas that the *conquistador* Bartolomé Ruiz and company landed, the first Spaniards to set foot on Ecuadorian soil. Esmeraldas is named after the precious stone found in bountiful quantities in the like-named river, at whose mouth the city lies. The native Cara, who inhabited this area before migrating to the mountain basins around Otavalo during the 10th century, worshiped a huge emerald known as Umina. Today, the treasures are more industrial than geological: Esmeraldas is the major port of the north coast, whence timber, bananas, and cacao are shipped abroad. The 500km (300-mile) trans-Andean oil pipeline ends here, and the construction of an oil refinery has brought new jobs and money to the city.

The treatment of previously fatal tropical diseases has contributed significantly to the growth of Ecuadorian ports, notably Guayaquil, Manta, and Esmeraldas. The eradication of yellow fever from these towns early in the 20th century was the first step, followed by the discovery and availability of quinine as an antidote for malaria, which as recently as 1942 accounted for a quarter of all deaths in Ecuador.

BELOW: dancing the night away in Atacames.

theater is the venue for occasional performances, especially during the agriculture and tourism exposition held each October. **Playa Murciélago** is an unprotected surfing beach a few kilometers west of town, site of the comfortable Hotel Manta Imperial. In Tarqui, the Hotel Haddad Manabí, dating from 1931, offers central accommodations with a slight touch of faded grandeur.

Ecuador's "Panama" hat

Straddling the highway between Manta and Portoviejo is the deceptively nondescript town of **Montecristi** ❻, for more than a century the home of the renowned Panama hat. Until recently, the majority of Montecristi's 9,000-odd inhabitants were engaged in the weaving of these remarkable headpieces, made from the straw fronds of the *Carludovica palmata*. Large numbers of them still are, but Montecristi has had to move with the times, and some have switched to making fine wickerwork furniture and decorations. It is the quintessential cottage industry and many houses contain a rudimentary factory and showroom. The lack

of any signs of wealth in Montecristi is sad testimony to the inequitable distribution of the industry's hefty profits. Like Portoviejo, which we will come to next, Montecristi owes its existence to pillaging pirates: in 1628, a group of Manteños left the coast in search of an inland refuge following pirate raids. Their colonial-style houses, now in a state of chronic disrepair, line the quiet, dusty streets and, in combination with the non-mechanized weaving, this physical neglect creates the air of a town stuck in another time.

Montecristi's religious atmosphere is similarly dated: the beautiful church contains a famous statue of the Virgin to which several miracles were once attributed. And Montecristi's favorite son is now long dead: Eloy Alfaro, president of Ecuador at the turn of the 20th century and a committed liberal reformist, was born here. His statue overlooks the main plaza, and his house is now a mausoleum, with his library and many personal effects on display. Almost alone among towns in coastal Ecuador, Montecristi survives as a relic, an impression heightened by

Weaving a good-quality Panama hat can take two months or more.

BELOW: the cathedral at Montecristi contains a statue of the Virgin that has supposedly worked several miracles.

the sight of modern-day tourists and Panama hat dealers roaring into town in search of a bargain.

Portoviejo's memories

From Montecristi it is only 24km (15 miles) to **Portoviejo** ❼, a town with a long history. In fact, it was one of the earliest Spanish settlements in Ecuador, founded on March 12, 1535, just three months after Benalcázar re-founded Quito atop abandoned Inca ruins. Guayaquil *(see pages 273–80)*, founded in January 1535, was the first Spanish coastal community, but the local people, based on the nearby island of Puná, repeatedly launched marauding raids of such ferocity that alternative sites were sought.

The original settlement, founded by Francisco Pacheco on the orders of Francisco Pizarro and Diego de Almagro, was, as its name ("Old Port") suggests, located on the coast. The omens, however, were far from auspicious: in 1541, a fire destroyed the town, and 50 years later the local indigenous population staged a fearsome uprising. Finally, when English pirates ravaged the port

in 1628, it was decided that a spot further inland would be out of harm's way. Since then, Portoviejo has existed in the shadow of Manta, though as capital of Manabí province it remains an important administrative and educational center. Its population has recently topped the 170,000 mark, most of which is engaged in commerce, industry, and the rich agricultural pickings of the hinterland. Portoviejo's bustling streets are prettily bordered with rows of trees and flowering shrubs, and a stroll through the **Parque Eloy Alfaro** is perhaps the most pleasing pastime. Opposite the park is one of Ecuador's starkest modern cathedrals; beside it stands a statue of Pacheco, the city's founder.

There are two museums: the **Casa de la Cultura Ecuatoriana**, with a collection of traditional musical instruments; and the **Museo Arqueológico**, which is not as good as its counterpart in Manta. Portoviejo has a few old colonial buildings still standing, but otherwise little testimony to its long and tumultuous history.

Leaving Portoviejo, go back the way you came for 14km (8 miles), then

BELOW: playing pool in Puerto López.

turn off the Guayaquil road to the village of **La Pila**, which is an interesting stop-off. In the wake of the discovery of exquisite pre-Columbian ceramics in the area, the resourceful inhabitants of La Pila began producing indistinguishable imitations to cash in on their forebears' artistry. Nowadays they have embraced originality and appear to have inherited not only the enterprise but also the considerable artistic skill of their ancestors.

In contrast, **Jipijapa** – a town of 30,000 inhabitants situated another 40km (25 miles) along the highway to Guayaquil – appears to have been swallowed up by Ecuador's flourishing agricultural industries, particularly coffee and cotton. At Jipijapa, a side road climbs into the damp, luxuriant hills of southern Manabí before descending to the coast near **Puerto Cayo**, a fishing village with pristine beaches.

A large tract of the surrounding area was designated the **Parque Nacional Machalilla** in 1979. It protects a 55,000-hectare (135,910-acre) expanse of tropical dry forest, which is home to a wide variety of bird and animal life,

as well as a stretch of coast and two islands. Some 15km (9 miles) offshore is **Isla de la Plata**, an ancient Manteño ceremonial center currently undergoing excavation. The island is named for an incident in the late 16th century, when Sir Francis Drake captured a silver-laden galleon and made camp on the island to tally his spoils. Recently, there have been a number of archeological finds from pre-Columbian times. Today it is inhabited only by sea turtles, blue-footed boobies, and a number of frigate birds such as the albatross, and can be reached by hired motorboat from Puerto Cayo; a trip of two hours. Look out for shells of the spondylus oyster, which in pre-Columbian times served as a unit of currency, and as such was regularly interred in the tombs of tribal chieftains. There is good diving and snorkeling here as well, and a number of agencies in Puerto López (*see below*) can provide gear and transportation.

You can enter the park from the coast road, or from the Manta to Guayaquil highway south of Jipijapa. Park admission costs $12 for the mainland parks,

Tourist trinkets and souvenirs for sale in Puerto López.

BELOW: strolling along a Pacific coast beach.

Whale-Watching

Dusty, sleepy Puerto López is at first glance perhaps not a typical visitors' paradise. That all changes between June and September, however, when the waters offshore fill with frolicking whales, and Puerto López becomes the whale-watching capital of Ecuador. During these months, humpback whales (*Megaptera novaeangliae*) migrate with the Humboldt Current from the Antarctic to mate and give birth to their calves in the warm, shallow waters around Machalilla National Park. Humpback whales, which can reach 16 meters (53ft) in length and weigh 30–40 tonnes, are the most acrobatic of the bigger whales, often breaching out of the water and slapping the water's surface dramatically with their large pectoral fins and tail flukes. The excitement becomes palpable in town during whale-watching season when many professional – and some fly-by-night – operators open up shop and loudly tout their tours to make the best of the short, but lucrative, season. Most operators offer whale-watching tours with snorkeling or diving and park excursions. Book well ahead. Recommended operators include: Exploratur, with 8–12-person boats and PADI divemasters (tel: 05-230 0123), and Mantaraya, which also has an excellent lodge (tel: 02-244 8985; www.mantarayalodge.com). Puerto Cayo is also becoming another centre for whale-watching along this part of the coast and has a handful of operators that offer good boat tours.

Map on
page 252

Parque Nacional
Machalilla is the only
coastal park in Ecuador,
and it protects varied
habitats including
tropical beaches and
coastline, cloud forests,
and tropical dry forests,
as well as over 350
species of bird together
with monkeys,
anteaters, lizards,
iguanas, and deer.

BELOW: mouth-
watering ceviche.
RIGHT: surfer in
Montañita.

$15 for Isla de la Plata, or $20 for both (ticket valid for five days), and tickets can be purchased at the park office in Puerto López (Alvaro and Moreno; daily 7am–6pm) or at the park.

Continuing south, the well-worn coast road passes through **Machalilla** ❽, the center of the culture of the same name that flourished between 1800 and 1500 BC. It is rich in archeological remains, especially in the vicinity of **Salaite** and **Agua Blanca**, where there is a small archeological museum. A pleasant 45-minute walk from Machalilla brings you to the deserted horseshoe beach called **Los Frailes** (the Friars). About 10km (6 miles) further south, fleets of heavily laden fishing boats dock in the village of **Puerto López** each afternoon at about 4pm, and the skippers sell their catch there and then.

Digging for the past

About 5km (3 miles) south of Puerto López is **Salango**, a small fishing village close to a site where dozens of people took part in the largest archeological dig in the country, providing insights into the fragmentary history of pre-Columbian Ecuador. The relics of a host of successive cultures – Valdivia, Machalilla, Chorrera, Engoroy, Bahía, Guangala, and Manteño – that inhabited this fertile stretch of coastline as early as 2000 BC were painstakingly recovered. A museum here is filled with artifacts found in the area.

Some 6km (4 miles) south of Salango is an interesting ecological resort, called the **Centro Turístico Ecológico Alandaluz** (tel: 04-278 0690; www.alandaluzhosteria.com), with buildings constructed of locally grown, easily replenishable bamboo and palm-leaf thatch. The accommodations and observation towers are set within organic gardens overlooking the sea. The gardens produce much of the food that is served in the restaurant, water and rubbish are recycled, and innovative organic bathroom facilities convert human waste into fertilizers for the land.

Further south from here **Montañita**, which for many years was simply a locally known surf spot, has blossomed into the largest surf resort in the country, one of Ecuador's largest backpacker hangouts and very much part of the hip traveler "scene." Many cheap hotels, jewelry stands, restaurants, and bars and clubs line the cluster of streets. The town is a good base for arranging tours into Machalilla National Park, Isla de Plata, and for whale-watching, paragliding, or kite-surfing. The beach is crowded during the summer months and filled with umbrellas, beer vendors, surfers, and carts selling *ceviche de ostra* (oyster ceviche). More upmarket accommodations can be found at the north end of the beach, known as Baja Montañita, and in the town of Olon a few kilometers north. Some 3km (2 miles) south of Montañita is **Manglaralto**, which is a small, cozy town with several small yet decent hotels offering great value for money, such as Hotel Manglaralto just off the beach beside the central park. ❏

GUAYAQUIL AND THE SOUTH COAST

The vibrant port city of Guayaquil and the beach resorts of the Santa Elena peninsula show a different side of Ecuadorian life

Map on page 280

Many visitors to Ecuador are surprised to learn that the seaport of **Guayaquil ❶** is the country's largest city, with an unofficial population of close to 3 million, nearly half as large again as Quito. This bustling commercial city offers the nation's finest hotels, restaurants, and shopping, along with plenty of mosquitoes. Guayaquil is not for the meek. Situated on the west bank of the busy Río Guayas, navigable for the biggest of ocean vessels heading in from the Pacific via the Golfo de Guayaquil, this city handles 90 percent of Ecuador's imports and 50 percent of its exports. Having previously lacked tourist attractions, the city has redefined itself amid a flurry of building projects and investments in several districts. The regenerated Malecón 2000, formerly Malecón Simón Bolívar, now has parks, malls, restaurants, museums, and markets. The faded Las Peñas district has been completely restored and become a much friendlier place.

During the rainy season, January to April, the heat and humidity are oppressive, but from May to December the climate is pleasant, with little or no rain and cool nights. And Guayaquil, with its new image, is dotted with wide concrete boulevards, spacious parks, and colorful gardens, as well as beautiful monuments, attractive residential neighborhoods, museums with rich archeological and art collections, and excellent restaurants. Its most obvi-

ous attraction is the **Guayas** itself. The chocolate-colored river teems with ships, small boats, dugout canoes, and rafts loaded with produce from the inland villages and plantations. Considered one of the cleanest deepwater ports in this part of the world, it is also a controversial spot. Although Ecuador is not considered a major drug-trafficking country, Guayaquil figured prominently in a drug scandal several years ago when 3 tonnes of cocaine in boxes labeled "Ecuadorian cocoa" were shipped from here to the United

Main attractions
GUAYAQUIL FESTIVALS
IGUANA-VIEWING IN
   PARQUE BOLÍVAR
MALECÓN 2000
BUQUE GUAYAS
CERRO SANTA ANA AND
   LAS PEÑAS
SALINAS
RESERVA ECOLÓGICA
   MANGLARES CHURUTE

PRECEDING PAGES:
Cerro Santa Ana.
LEFT: MAAC.
BELOW: Parque del
Centenario.

Cerro del Carmen

Cerro Santa Ana
LAS PEÑAS

Cementerio General

Julian Coronel

Vernaza

Puerto
Santa Ana

Julian Coronel

Centro Cultural Libertador
Simón Bolívar   G

Loja

Baquerizo Moreno

Piscina
Municipal

Avenida Boyacá

Quito

Galecio

Avenida

Riobamba

Jimena

Lorenzo de Garaicoa

Chimborazo

Avenida Rocafuerte

Galecio

Durán

TARQUI

Alejo Lascano

Pedro Moncayo

General Córdova

Padre   Solano

Escobedo

Malecón Simón Bolívar

Mendiburo

Rumichaca

Luis Urdaneta

ROCA

Avenida Rocafuerte

Luis Urdaneta

Riobamba

Roca

Junín

Dock 4

Casa de
Cultura
Ecuatoriana   D

Victor Manuel Rendón

La Merced

PARQUE
DEL
CENTENARIO

Plaza
La Merced

Hotel
Oro Verde

Vélez

Bulevar   9 de Octubre

Panamá

Piscina Olímpica

C

Aviles

ROCAFUERTE

San Francisco

La Rotonda

Avenida Boyacá

B

H

Aguirre

Luque

Vélez

Clemente Ballén

Chile

Pedro Carbo

Aguirre

Francis

Unicentro

Malecón Simón Bolívar

Catedral   A

PARQUE
BOLÍVAR
(PARQUE
SEMINARIO)

Museo
Nahim
Isaías

E

Palacio de
Gobierno

Malecón 2000

10 de Agosto

6 de Marzo

Rumichaca

Palacio
Municipal

Torre
Morisca

i

Sucre

Museo
Municipal

Pichincha

I

Alcedo

F

Buque Guayas   J

BOLÍVAR

Fco. Campos

Avenida Boyacá

Chimborazo

Pedro Carbo

Colón

Torres de Aire, Agua, Tierra y Fuego   K

Benalcazar

Ayacucho

Avenida Olmedo

Chile

Mercado
La Bahía

Lavayen

Luzarraga

Pirate Ship Morgan   L

Lorenzo de Garaicoa

Franco Dávila

Noguchi

Malecón 2000

Simón Bolívar

Villamil

OLMEDO

Avenida Olmedo

Río Guayas

Manabí

Chimborazo

Huancavilca

Huayna Cápac

Departure Point of
Bus Panorámico Guayaquil Vision

M

N

Capitán Nájera

Malecón

Palacio de Cristal   N

Guayaquil

| 0 | 200 m |
| 0 | 200 yds |

States. But the so-called Great Chocolate Cocaine Caper was an exception to the mostly legitimate traffic that moves on the Río Guayas. In Guayaquil, a number of travel agencies offer river tours, taking visitors past small settlements, farms, and cattle ranches along this lush tropical river and through locks into the Salado estuary where the city's seaport area is located.

A name inspired by tragedy

Although Spanish explorer Francisco de Orellana – credited with discovering the Amazon River – claimed to have founded Guayaquil, it was inhabited long before the Spanish arrived. The Valdivia people flourished in the area around 2000 BC, followed by the Huancavilcas. Legend has it that the Huancavilca chieftain, Guayas, killed his beautiful wife Quil then drowned himself so that the Spaniards would not capture them. The tragedy of this doomed couple is allegedly what inspired the city's name.

While fairly calm and conventional Quito was worrying only about infrequent earthquakes, Guayaquil spent its first 400 years fending fires. The last major blaze, in 1896, destroyed a large number of Guayaquil's charming wooden houses. The different natures of Quito and Guayaquil – one a sophisticated center for art and culture, the other a center of commerce occupied by tattooed sailors and hard-working, hard-drinking laborers – bred a rivalry between the cities. It is common for competing presidential candidates to be from one or the other, and while Quiteños think the Guayaquil residents rough and unrefined, Guayaquil dwellers think the residents of the capital are dull and backward, not to mention foolish for living in a city with no nightlife and no beaches. Guayaquileños claim that they make the country's money and the Quiteños spend it.

Brassy wealth

Despite its development problems Guayaquil is a growth area, a center of industry with oil and sugar refineries, cement mills, breweries, and all types of manufacturing. Few visitors see Guayaquil as a tourist destination, but with a little effort and dedication, you

When some of Guayaquil's most beautiful early 20th-century buildings were threatened with demoltion, far-sighted developers had the inspired idea to move them to a safe location outside the city. The result is the Parque Histórico Guayaquil (www.parquehistorico guayaquil.com), which showcases local architecture, culture, and traditions. The park is in Samborondón, across the Durán bridge from the city.

BELOW: Guyaquil's Las Peñas district has plenty of pretty colonial buildings.

The new Malecón del Salado on the west side of Guayaquil's Downtown has followed the Malecón 2000 as an attempt at urban renewal on the city's waterfronts. The large, manicured Parque Baquerizo Moreno, and the long waterfront walkways on the Estero Salado, make a pleasant refuge from the buzz of the city.

can find some luxurious hotels, fine restaurants, clubs for tennis, golf, yachting, and swimming, exciting nightclubs and upscale shopping, including a bevy of duty-free stores. While the once high crime rate has been drastically reduced in many areas of the city, Guayaquil still has a well-deserved reputation for being dangerous. The Malecón and Las Peñas district are generally quite safe during the day, but Guayaquileños warn that care should be taken anywhere else around town, and to be particularly circumspect at night: muggings and armed robbery are common. Taxi-hijackings have become rife in the city of late, so it is advisable to order your taxi by phone from a hotel or through a reputable taxi service, rather than hailing one in the street. Leave valuables and your hotel room key behind when you go out.

There is no straightforward way to see the sights of Guayaquil, but a suggested route is to visit the scattered downtown places of interest first, then follow the extensively refurbished *malecón* along the water's edge, past the docks to Las Peñas and Cerro

Party Town

Guayaquileños like to party. They will take any opportunity the year's calendar presents and turn it into a city-wide celebration that can go on for days. The biggest events in Guayaquil's calendar are the anniversaries of Símon Bolívar's birthday and the day of the founding of the city: July 24 and 25. The city goes crazy with parades and pageants, exuberant dancing, and fireworks, much of it fueled by liberal amounts of drinking. People dress up, take to the streets, book out restaurants, and party hard day and night. Hotel rooms are hard to come by on these (and surrounding) dates, so be sure to book well ahead if you visit at this time.

The other main holidays are celebrated in October: Independence Day on October 9 and Día de la Raza on October 12, the celebration of the Hispanic heritage of Latin America. The holiday usually stretches into the 10th and 11th as well, with colorful parades on the *malecón*, and the party crowds out in force. Carnival is held on the days before Ash Wednesday in the run-up to Easter, and is another excuse for dressing up and parading. Watch out on the streets at this time though, as townspeople enthusiastically defend the tradition of throwing water, and other less innocuous liquids, as part of this celebration. You might fall victim to water bombs, eggs, or flour: but take it all in the fun spirit in which it is meant; you might even prepare some Carnival missiles of your own.

Santa Ana. Start with a visit to the neo-Gothic **cathedral** Ⓐ on the west side of Parque Bolívar, on Calle Chile between 10 de Agosto and Clemente Ballén. The cathedral was built in 1948, with lovely stained-glass windows and a Cuenca marble altar. Its side altars are overwhelmed by innumerable votive candles lit by the devout; some people even hold candles in their hands while walking around the church praying. The original wooden cathedral, built in 1547, burned down in one of the city's many fires.

Parque Bolívar (officially known as Parque Seminario) is perhaps the most interesting park in the city, The old, well-maintained botanical garden earned its nickname from its equestrian statue of Bolívar; around the statue's base are bas-relief depictions of that mysterious Guayaquil meeting between Bolívar and San Martín (*see page 278*). The pavilion and gates in this century-old park came from France. The park is best known, however, for the hundreds of green tree iguanas – some of them a meter in length – that roam freely. A small pond is home to several species of turtles and tortoises.

On the other side of the park is the **Unicentro Shopping Center**. The **Unihotel** at this sparkling indoor gallery of shops and services has gained a reputation for its cocktails, including its *jipijapa*, a blend of orange *aguardiente*, grenadine, and lemon served with a slice of pineapple.

From here, walk two blocks along Calle Chile to the plaza and church of **San Francisco** Ⓑ. The church was built in 1603 and beautifully restored in 1968. You will also see that many streets in the central district preserve porticoes protecting pedestrians from the elements. Going west along Bulevar 9 de Octubre you will come to the **Parque del Centenario**, the city's largest plaza, covering four city blocks. It is filled with monuments, the most important being the patriotic liberty monument with the likenesses of Ecuador's heroes, and smaller statues

representing history, justice, patriotism, and heroism. Five blocks further west on Bulevar 9 de Octubre is the **Hotel Oro Verde**, the best spot in town for a gringo breakfast. Go south from here down Calle García Moreno, and you will find the **Piscina Olímpica ⓒ** (Olympic Swimming Pool).

Pre-Columbian artifacts

Just outside Parque del Centenario on 9 de Octubre and Moncayo is the **Casa de Cultura Ecuatoriana ⓓ** (Tue–Fri 10am–6pm; charge) with a display of pre-Columbian artifacts found in archeological digs on the country's coast. This museum once had an impressive collection of gold items – reported to be Ecuador's most valuable pre-colonial gold collection – but many of them mysteriously disappeared; those that remain at the museum are not publicly displayed. Current exhibits range from clay whistles known as *ocarines* to molds for casting gold masks and colonial art. Other artifacts – including ceramics, textiles, gold, and ceremonial masks – are located at the **Museo Nahim Isaías ⓔ** (Pichincha

and Clemente Ballén; tel: 232 4182; Tue–Sat 9am–5pm, Sun and holidays 10am–3pm; charge, free Sun). Perhaps the most intriguing museum in town is the nearby **Museo Municipal ⓕ** (Tue–Sat 9am–5.30pm; free with ID) on Calle Sucre. There are pre-Hispanic artifacts from the Huancavilca and Valdivia peoples, colonial art, and a gallery of paintings of the presidents of Ecuador here. The museum also contains the Act of Independence document, but its real treasures are a collection of shrunken heads – *tzantzas* – prepared by jungle tribes using secret processes that shrink them with their features still perfectly intact, to the size of a fist. The heads are only on display in February, however, when the museum celebrates the culture of the peoples of the Ecuadorian Oriente. Tourists in Ecuador are occasionally offered *tzantzas* for sale, although authorities say these are not only illegal but are almost certainly monkey – not human – heads.

On the waterfront

Running along the Río Guayas from Las Peñas at the north end to the very

Green tree iguana at home in Parque Bolívar.

BELOW LEFT:
iguana takes a pose in Parque Bolívar.
BELOW:
strolling allong Malecón 2000.

The glass plaques of the Donations Pavilion (next to the Centro Cultural Simón Bolívar) feature the names of the businesses and individuals who contributed to the Malécon 2000 project.

exclusive Club de la Unión is the tourist-friendly promenade Malecón 2000, or Malecón Simón Bolívar. The tree-lined boardwalk is filled with restaurants, roaming vendors, parks, monuments, and activities for families. At the Las Peñas end is the recently built **Centro Cultural Simón Bolívar** (Wed–Sat 10am–6pm, Sun and holidays 10am–4pm; charge, free Sun), which combines the ancient and the new with more than 50,000 archeological pieces and 3,000 works of modern art. There is an independent movie and IMAX theater next door.

Heading south down the *malecón*, at the foot of Bulevar 9 de Octobre, you will see the semicircle of **La Rotonda** Ⓗ. This statue commemorates the historical but mysterious meeting between the continent's two great liberators, Venezuelan Simón Bolívar and Argentine General José de San Martín. Bolívar had freed the countries to the north and San Martín was responsible for the independence of Argentina and Chile but their final plans differed; Bolívar wanted the countries united under a democ-

racy with an elected president, while San Martín envisioned a monarchy. The meeting resulted in the Acuerdo de Guayaquil (Guayaquil Accord), which established the short-lived Gran Colombia, uniting Venezuela, Colombia, and Ecuador. There was no witness to the exchange between the two men and the only thing that is known for sure is that when the meeting ended, Bolívar remained and San Martín went into exile in France. La Rotonda is built so that people can stand on either side of the statue, whisper, and hear one another, though these days that may be difficult above the noise of the traffic. From here you can enjoy impressive views to the north of the hill known as Cerro del Carmen and, far beyond, the Guayaquil–Durán bridge, the country's longest at 4km (2½ miles) long.

Continuing south from La Rotonda, one comes to the **Torre Morisca** Ⓘ, a Moorish clock tower dating from 1770. The clock tower's gardens are a favorite meeting spot for young couples in the early evening. Across the street is the stately colonial **Palacio Municipal**, which is separated from the severe

Palacio de Gobierno by a plaza with a statue dedicated to General Sucre, hero of Ecuador's war of independence.

Just south of here, moored at the end of a riverside pier is the **Buque Guayas** ❶ (Mon–Thur 4.30–6pm, Fri 2–6pm, and Sat–Sun 10am–6pm; free) a glorious four-masted tall ship belonging to the Ecuadorian Navy, on which it trains its cadets. The vessel is open for inspection.

Close by are the four postmodern monuments known as the **Torres de Aire, Agua, Tierra y Fuego** ❶ (Air, Water, Earth, and Fire), built as part of the refurbishment of the *malecón*, and a landmark waterfront meeting place.

Just south again the **Pirate Ship Morgan** ❶ is a replica of the type of ship that once plied the Ecuadorian coast. The ship runs hour-long river cruises (Tue–Sun afternoons and evenings), which are a great way to get a different perspective on the city. Alternatively, for a land-side view, catch the **Bus Panorámico Guayaquil Vision** ❶ (departs corner of Malecón and Avenida 11 SE (Villamil); five times a day 10.40am–10pm; charge).

This journey takes about two hours, with five stops at places of interest, including the attractive new park and waterways development at the **Malecón del Salado** in the west of the city. There's a good commentary in several languages.

At the very far southern end of the new *malecón* at Plaza de la Integración, you will find the Eiffel-designed Antiguo Mercado Sur de 1907, now known as the **Palacio de Cristal** ❶, or Crystal Palace. This serves as an exhibition hall and gallery displaying temporary exhibits, but is worth a visit for its graceful architecture alone.

Riverside heights

Back at the northern end of the *malecón*, past restaurant boats, working docks, and the Durán ferry exit, Calle Numa Pompilio Lloma mounts the side of **Cerro Santa Ana** and enters the picturesque bohemian district of **Las Peñas**. The area's romantic 19th-century neoclassical houses are today inhabited by many artistically minded Guayaquileños, and many are filled with craft shops, cafés, bars, and galleries. On the

BELOW LEFT:
Torre Morisca, an 18th-century clock tower.
BELOW:
the district of Las Peñas on Cerro Santa Ana.

small **Plaza Colón**, two cannons commemorate the defense of the city against pirate invasions. Continued investment in the area has paid off, and Las Peñas is now filled with tourists who climb the scenic 444 steps from the *malécon* up through the district to the *mirador* above for spectacular views. At the top there is a small fortress with cannons and naval artifacts, as well as a church. For refreshments, there's the very touristy Pirate Bar, or you could walk back down to Las Peñas and choose from the many, much more authentic, bars and restaurants. The security situation is much improved on Cerro Santa Ana these days, but climbing the hill late at night is not recommended.

The Las Peñas area also has an open-air theater – Teatro Bogotá – and, just behind it, the oldest church in Guayaquil, **Santo Domingo**, founded in 1548 and undergoing extensive restoration. A patio at the left-hand side of the church's nave contains a spring credited with miraculous healing powers. From here, stairs to the right of the church and the steep Buitron Street lead to **Cerro del Carmen**, topped by the Cristo del Consuelo monument. At the foot of the hill is the dazzling white cemetery, the **Cementerio General**, with its avenue of royal palms leading to the grave of 19th-century President Vicente Rocafuerte, elaborate marble sculptures, and imposing Greco-Roman mausoleums. Because of problems with crime, it is not recommended that tourists visit Cerro del Carmen independently. Go with a local or join a tour.

Beaches of the south

Guayaquil is an important meeting city for business executives but rarely the sole destination of tourists. Rather, it is the jumping-off point for the Galápagos Islands and the beaches of Ecuador's southern coast. There has been a surge of development on the coast from Guayaquil to Manta and resorts have appeared where once there was only dirt road. Endless stretches of sandy beaches are lapped by warm water and toasted by the tropical sun. People with fair skin should take precautions under these burning rays; sometimes less than half

BELOW: the steep steps up the side of Cerro Santa Ana.

South Coast

0   20 km
0   20 miles

an hour of sun can cause severe sunburn on uprotected skin. Although weekends and the December to April vacation season see much beach activity, the area is all but deserted during the week. The road southwest from Guayaquil passes through dry scrubland, with the scenery undergoing an astonishing change from wet fields of rice and bananas to an arid – but attractive – landscape with strange bottle-shaped kapok trees and scattered bright flowers.

Traffic on the coastal road, which passes the busy villages of **Cerecita** and **Progreso** about 70km (42 miles) outside of Guayaquil, is heavy from January to April during local vacation months, and on weekends. In Progreso (officially called Gómez Rendón), the road forks off to the right to Salinas and Santa Elena. A left-hand fork leads to the popular beach resort of **Playas** ❷ (officially known as General Villamil), also an important fishing village. Old balsa rafts, similar to craft used in pre-Inca times, line the beaches and are still used by some of the fishermen who bring in their catch every

afternoon. However, the main focus of this little town is tourism, and the sandy beaches are the lure for weekend crowds. An alternative to the main beach with its hotels, including the popular Playas and Rey David, and the villas used as escape destinations for Guayaquil residents, is the beautiful beach to the north, called the Pelado. It is a long and lonely stretch set against the backdrop of a cliff. For overnight stays in Playas, the best lodgings are to be found in the more expensive *hostería* Bellavista (tel: 04-276 0600; www.hosteria bellavista.net) just outside the village on the main road to Data.

About 14km (8 miles) south along the coast from Playas is **Data de Villamil**, notable for its traditional wooden shipbuilding industry. An inland road from here passes the old village of El Morro with its huge wooden church, and farther along is the fishing village of Posorja with commercial boats and hundreds of seabirds wheeling around the **Canal de Morro**, that is used by overseas vessels bound for Guayaquil. Shrimp farming produced an economic boom in the village,

The design of the balsa rafts still used by fishermen off the south coast has not changed much since before the time of the Incas.

BELOW:
traditional balsa raft on the beach at Playas.

Shellfish and lime are two key ingredients for making ceviche.

which has grown rapidly over the past few years. This is a pleasant stop on a day trip, even though the beaches are not really good for swimming.

Opposite Posorja is the large island of **Puná**, which was already inhabited in pre-Inca times as evidenced by the traces of two settlements from the Valdivia culture that archeologists have found there. The island is quite difficult to reach as there is no public transport, although boats can be hired for the trip in Guayaquil some 50km (31 miles) to the north: contact the Capitanía del Puerto or the Yacht Club for details.

Cactus and tuna

To get to Salinas, Ecuador's most fashionable resort town, you must go back to Progreso, and take the left-hand road through an increasingly dry, cactus-covered landscape. At Km 35.6 outside Progreso is the road to the fishing village of **Chanduy**, a mecca for archeologists who have made important discoveries while excavating the remains of Valdivia, Machalilla, and Chorrera indigenous settlements. This is considered to be the oldest

agricultural settlement on the continent where ceramics were made, and may have been a ceremonial center. Nowadays, as at all the fishing villages along this route, the biggest fish, such as tuna and marlin, are brought close to the shore with the cold Antarctic-born Humboldt Current to feed on smaller, warm-current fish.

Just before reaching Chanduy is the **Museo Real Alto** (daily 10am–5pm; charge), which takes the form of two giant huts covered with straw roofs. Poorly marked, it is to the left of a directional sign reading *Fábrica Portuguesa*. Among the exhibits at this museum is one demonstrating how the local inhabitants live.

Back to the main roadway, at Km 49.5, a right-hand deviation in the road leads to the **Baños de San Vicente**, a large complex in which water is channeled into swimming pools and mud baths that are said to have curative powers. Farther down the main road is **Santa Elena**, interesting only for its church and usually bypassed in favor of La Libertad and Salinas. However, on the outskirts of the town near a Mormon temple with a small tower is the **Museo Los Amantes de Zumba** (The Lovers of Zumba) archeological site. Two human skeletons estimated to be 3,500 years old are entwined in an after-life embrace in the grave, which falls under the auspices of the Archeological Department of the Banco Central in Guayaquil. **La Libertad**, the largest town on the peninsula, with over 70,000 inhabitants, is a busy port with a market and serves as the hub for bus services farther north.

To travel north along the coast toward Manglaralto, take the right-hand fork in the road from La Libertad. There are several fishing villages along this stretch of coast, where Guayaquileños have vacation homes, but there are no restaurants or hotels. **Punta Blanca** has an exquisite, isolated beach that attracts shell collectors. **Ayangue**, 45km (28 miles) farther north, has white, gently sloping beaches, and no

BELOW: gaily painted fishermen's boats on a south coast beach.

big waves, making it ideal for children. **Valdivia ❸**, 5km (3 miles) up the coast, is the center of Ecuador's oldest culture, established around 3000 BC, and has an interesting museum of local finds (although its best pieces are in museums in Quito and Guayaquil).

Summer beach mecca

Salinas ❹ lies on a half-moon bay at the tip of the **Santa Elena peninsula**, a total of 150km (90 miles) from Guayaquil. It has pleasant beaches, excellent hotels, good restaurants, a casino, and a yacht club, all of which lure throngs of swimmers and sun-worshippers. It is also the site of a naval base.

Lined with new hotels and resorts, and countless seafood restaurants, the stretch of road heading north from Salinas to Manta is known as the Ruta del Sol (the Sun Route). About 9km (5 miles) from Salinas is **Punta Carnero** with a beach several kilometers long. From the Hotel Punta Carnero (tel: 04-294 8477), situated on a cliff, you have a marvelous view of the ocean and the hotel has a good restaurant. Fishing charters can be arranged from here, and it's also a great vantage point to see whales (July–September) and wading birds.

The deep south

To get to the next destination you must return to Guayaquil and take the road to Azogues, turning off after about 20km (12 miles) onto the Pan-American Highway toward Machala in **El Oro**, the southernmost of Ecuador's provinces, which owes its name to the rich gold deposits mined here during the 16th century. It is now Ecuador's leading shrimp- and banana-producing region, its fields blanketed by massive banana plantations, and the ripening fruit protected by plastic bags. **Machala ❺**, the main city, is known as the "World Banana Capital." The International Banana and Agricultural Festival is held here every year in late September and draws large crowds. With 200,000 inhabitants, Machala is Ecuador's fourth-largest city. Although not particularly attractive, it is a thriving city with some comfortable hotels and an international port, **Puerto Bolívar** (near the popular **El Coco** beach),

BELOW: just-caught, deep-fried *camerones* make a perfect beachside meal.

Mangrove Reserve

Just off the Pan-American Highway, between Guayaquil and Machala, is one of the south coast's most interesting reserves, the Reserva Ecológica Manglares Churute, which protects the largest remaining area of mangroves in the country. As well as safeguarding other endangered native vegetation – many species of trees and shrubs can adapt to saline conditions and be found in mangrove swamps – 70 percent of the reserve is occupied by ancient mangrove forests, growing up to 30 meters (99ft) high, and with spectacular tangles of roots. The mangrove ecosystem is important in protecting against erosion and offers a safe environment for young marine organisms. The reserve is also home to 270 species of bird, various species of monkey, three-toed sloths, ocelot, armadillo, and otters.

Off the coast dolphins, pelicans, flamingos, and fish eagles can often be seen, and the highly endangered coastal crocodile is also found here. The reserve's information centre is located close to the highway 46km (28 miles) south of Guayaquil, and here park rangers can arrange boat trips that allow you to see the mangroves in close-up. There are also various good hiking trails in the park. Buses plying the highway between Guayaquil and Machala will usually drop off and pick up visitors at the park entrance (www.ambiente.gov.ec/paginas_espanol/4ecuador/docs/areas/churute.htm).

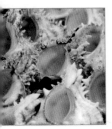

South coast beaches, such as the one at Punta Blanca, are the source of pretty shells that are sold to tourists.

BELOW: Machala is the "World Banana Capital."
RIGHT: Guayaquil's Malecón 2000 is one of the city's top tourist attractions.

from where around 1 million tonnes of banana and shrimp are exported annually. From its boat pier, motorized dugouts can be taken to the archipelago of **Jambelí**, an extraordinarily beautiful area that is little explored by visitors to the region.

Other side trips are available from Machala, including a journey to the pleasant farming center of **Santa Rosa**, on the Loja road, and then on to the beautiful old coffee-growing town of **Piñas** (take a left-hand turn about 20km/12 miles from Santa Rosa). The road is flanked by banana, coffee, and cacao plantations.

Town among the ruins

The road from Piñas continues to **Portovelo**, from where you can see the town of **Zaruma** ❻ stuck to the mountainside like a swallow's nest. This mining town of 8,000 inhabitants was founded during the colonial-era gold boom and recently attracted renewed interest with the discovery of pre-Columbian ruins at Chepel, Trencillas, Payama, and Pocto. Although the ruins have not yet been fully excavated,

they have led archeologists to conclude that the area was densely populated in pre-Inca times.

The town conserves much of its colonial past: its wooden houses, elaborately decorated balconies and church are well worth seeing. From the main plaza, there is a fantastic view of the surrounding valley. A stop at the **Museo Municipal** (Wed–Fri 8am–noon and 2–6pm, Sat 8am–3pm, Sun 8am–noon), with displays of archeological artifacts, colonial art, and Zaruma's history, is recommended, and interesting visits to abandoned gold and silver mines can be arranged through the city council, the Consejo Municipal, or with local travel agents.

Southeast of Machala, 50km (31 miles) farther on, the route ends at **Huaquillas** ❼, right on the border with Peru. Most maps have been reprinted to show the new border along the Cordillera del Condor, which was agreed on in 1998. Since the signing of the peace treaty, relations between the two countries have been cordial. This border not only marks the beginning of Peruvian coastal desert, but is one of the continent's main cross-border commercial centers – although much of what is bought and sold is contraband.

Huaquillas is a busy, dusty, and unattractive town with stagnant water lying on its rutted roads and a reputation for pickpockets – who generally seek out tourists, sometimes returning stolen passports if a reward is proffered and no charges are pressed. The only decent hotel is the government-run Parador Turístico, north of town, with a restaurant and swimming pool, the latter being a welcome relief from the insufferable heat and dust, but most people stay overnight in Machala.

The main street of Huaquillas leads to the **International Bridge** into Peru and is lined with street vendors, money-changers, police and border officers, and people offering to carry luggage. Travelers must cross the bridge on foot unless they are driving their own car or on a direct bus to Tumbes, Peru. ❏

THE GALÁPAGOS ISLANDS

For ever associated with Charles Darwin and giant
tortoises, the Galápagos archipelago is without
doubt one of Ecuador's greatest attractions

The Galápagos Islands had their fame guaranteed in 1835 when the 26-year-old naturalist Charles Darwin landed on one of their black volcanic coasts. No other place would prove to be quite as fertile for his work as the Galápagos. In 1859, Darwin published *On the Origin of Species*, making the creatures of the Galápagos a cornerstone of his theory of evolution by natural selection, and in one stroke overturning the whole train of Western scientific thought. Wildlife is still the main reason why visitors fly the 960km (570 miles) from mainland Ecuador to the Galápagos archipelago, which was designated a World Heritage Site in 1979 and subsequently a World Biosphere Reserve by Unesco in 1985.

The islands are the ultimate natural zoo, where bizarre fauna exist totally free and fearless of man. Giant lumbering tortoises, blue-footed boobies, and equatorial penguins carry on their daily routine, indifferent to their audience of human visitors only feet away. Baby sea lions play with swimmers in the water and perform somersaults. Come as close as you like, and the marine iguanas sunning themselves on black rocks will just sit and stare blankly back.

Until recently, permanent human settlement had been kept to a minimum. In 1959, the Ecuadorian government declared the islands a national  park and restricted human settlement to the small outposts already established, however enforcement has been poor. Today the Charles Darwin Research Station on Santa Cruz, founded in 1964, and the Marine Research Reserve, created in 1986, have their hands full trying to restore the Galápagos ecosystem to that of the days before humans began to upset the delicate ecological balance. In December 2001, Unesco also declared the Marine Reserve around the islands a World Natural Heritage Site in an attempt to stop illegal fishing and in recognition of the conservation issues it faces. But the sad fact is that however hard the conservationists, scientists, and authorities work together, it seems the only way the islands and their inhabitants will be preserved unharmed is by severely reducing the numbers of tourist visits. ❑

PRECEDING PAGES: volcanic eruption on Isla Isabela; sunbathing sea lions; once in the water, sea lions become extremely agile. **LEFT:** volcanic landscape. **ABOVE LEFT:** colorful Sally Lightfoot crab. **ABOVE RIGHT:** brown pelican.

THE GALÁPAGOS ISLANDS: DARWIN'S LABORATORY

The volcanic archipelago teems with rare bird and marine life that can be seen nowhere else in the world

The "living laboratory" of the Galápagos archipelago is set in the Pacific Ocean some 960km (570 miles) west of the Ecuadorian coast. It consists of 13 major islands, six small ones, and 42 islets that are barely more than large rocks. All are of volcanic origin and spread over roughly 80,000 sq km (30,000 sq miles) of ocean. Their highest point is Volcán Wolf, at 1,707 meters (5,600ft) on Isabela, which, at 4,600 sq km (1,800 sq miles), is by far the largest island.

Visited at different times by explorers from around the world, most of the islands have two or even three different names. British pirates gave them solid, English names like Jervis and Chatham; the Spanish dubbed them from their standard stock of place names, such as Santa Cruz and Santa Fe; while the Ecuadorian government in 1892 tried to clear up the confusion by giving the islands official titles, so now each usually has at least two names still in use.

An eccentric climate

The Galápagos year can be divided into two seasons: the "hot" or "wet" season lasts from January to early May with an average temperature of 28°C (82°F), while the "cool" or "dry" season from May to December has an average of 18°C (64°F). The cooler period is also referred to as the *garúa* season, named after the bank of clouds that generally settles over the islands at this time.

Altitude also has an effect on the climate: it can be hot and dry in the low-lying parts of the islands, and almost cold and humid in the highlands (above 22 meters/72ft). The winds, the marine currents, and the geological formation of the soil can alter the climatic conditions considerably generally speaking, the beaches with white sands are cooler on the feet, while stretches of black lava can reach temperatures of up to 50°C (120°F).

Two marine currents pass along the archipelago. The cold Humboldt

Main attractions

VOLCANIC LANDSCAPES
ARID ZONE VEGETATION
BLUE-FOOTED BOOBIES
GALÁPAGOS PENGUINS
GALÁPAGOS FLIGHTLESS
  CORMORANTS
MARINE IGUANAS
GIANT TORTOISES
SEA LIONS

LEFT: marine iguanas. **BELOW:** Charles Darwin visited the islands in the early 1830s.

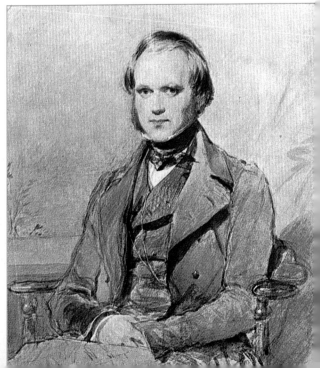

Steps and walkways on the islands help to avoid soil erosion and preserve vegetation.

Current originates in the south of Chile and brings the *garua* with it in May. It has a moderating effect on the whole climate of the Galápagos, which should be more punishing than it actually is, given the islands' position directly on the equator.

The other current is the warm northern stream called El Niño, "the boy child," because it arrives around Christmas time, although its effects are rarely welcome: it brings heavy rains and – on occasion – floods and tidal waves to the Ecuadorian mainland, and also affects global weather patterns.

Geology of the islands

What we see of the Galápagos Islands is the tips of various gigantic "shield volcanoes" poking up some 10,000 meters (30,000ft) from the ocean floor and composed entirely of basalt. It is widely accepted that the archipelago was formed mainly by the accumulation of lava from successive underwater volcanic eruptions.

BELOW: cactus thrives on lava flows.

It appears that the earliest of the islands were formed roughly 4 to 5 million years ago, and that some of the western islands, such as Fernandina and Isabela, are only 1 million years old. The process of island formation is still going on as the Galápagos lie on the northern edge of the Nazca tectonic plate.

Over time, its gradual continental drift heads toward the southeast – precisely over one of the world's so-called "hotspots." These volatile, unmoving points beneath the tectonic plates build up heat over time to create a volcanic eruption that will rise above the ocean's surface. The southeastern islands of the Galápagos were the first formed in this way, and the more recent, western islands still have active volcanoes; Fernandina's La Cumbre erupted as recently as April 2009.

Relatively fresh basalt lava flows can still be seen around Isabela, often making fascinating patterns. They include pahoehoe or "ropy" lava – where the skin of the lava flow has been wrinkled by the heat of the still-flowing lava beneath. Another type is aa – pronounced "aah aah" – that looks like twisted black toffee.

Animal colonization

The volcanic lumps that first burst forth from the Pacific 4 million years ago were utterly devoid of life. Yet now the islands are teeming with plants and animals. Somehow they must have made their way from South America, and, since the islands were never connected to the continent, this fauna and flora must have crossed the 1,000km (620-mile) stretch of water.

Only certain types of creatures could survive the journey: this explains the present-day predominance of seabirds (that could fly), sea mammals (that could swim) and reptiles (that apparently floated across from the American coast on accidentally formed vegetation rafts and, unlike amphibians and land mammals, could survive for long periods without food or water). Meanwhile, plant seeds and insects could have come across stuck to birds' wings or in animals' stomach contents. Once they had landed on the bleak islands, only certain animals could survive. Those that did found that their traditional predators had been left behind on the South American coast. The ani-

mals' lack of timidity probably stems from this general absence of predators; a fact that also explains why recently introduced domestic goats and pigs are able to wreak havoc so easily.

Charles Darwin was the first to observe how each arriving species had adapted over time in order to thrive and survive. The most famous case is "Darwin's finches," the 13 similar species of finches that probably descended from one original species. Each modern species has differences that suit its particular environment: some have short, thick beaks so that they can split seeds; others have long, thin bills to catch insects.

Many years after his visit to the Galápagos, Darwin attributed the process to natural selection. After their arrival on the Galápagos, each finch produced offspring that were imperceptibly different from the parent. In this strange new environment, some chicks were better able to survive. They were the ones that reached maturity and produced young, passing on new genetic traits to their offspring. Over thousands of generations, some

Compared with those on the mainland, the volcanoes on the Galápagos are much lower; however, their craters are excellent destinations for hiking or horseback excursions. Sierra Negra volcano on Isabela has one of the world's widest craters, measuring 10km (6 miles) at its widest point. Camping is permitted nearby.

BELOW: Sullivan Bay and Pinnacle Rock, Bartolomé Island.

Thor Heyerdahl is among those who believed that the Inca Tupac Yupanqui organized an expedition to the islands in the 15th century, but there is no evidence to support this theory.

traits were thus "selected" as fitting the finches' new home, until the differences between the new creature and the original qualified it to be renamed as a new species.

Darwin propounded this theory in his classic work *The Origin of Species*. It became particularly controversial when applied to man, not only suggesting that the animal kingdom did not spring ready-made from the hand of God, but that man is in many respects no different from other forms of animal life.

Human history

While it is possible that there was settlement by Manteño people and that the Inca Tupac Yupanqui organized an expedition to the Galápagos during his rule in the 1400s, most historians accept that the islands were first discovered by accident in 1535 by the Spanish cleric Fray Tomás de Berlanga, bishop of Panama. On the way to Peru, his boat was becalmed and drifted to the Galápagos. The cleric landed in search of water but "found nothing but seals and tortoises, and such big tortoises that each could carry a man on top of itself" and birds "so silly that they do not know to flee." He dubbed the islands "Las Encantadas," the Bewitched Ones, because they tricked his navigator's eyes and seemed to appear and disappear in clouds of mist.

For the next two centuries, the islands, far from the Spanish trade routes, were a hideaway for Dutch and English buccaneers. They began the practice of killing large numbers of giant tortoises for their meat, having found that the creatures could be stacked upside down in their ships' holds without food and water for over a year and still be turned into fine soup. This practice was taken up most devastatingly by 19th-century whalers. Between 1811 and 1844 there were said to be more than 700 whaling ships in the Pacific, and many of them called into the Galápagos Islands to stock up on tortoise meat.

The first permanent colonist on the Galápagos was an Irishman named Patrick Watkins, who arrived at Floreana in 1812. His story is included in a

BELOW: tourists marvel at the islands' giant tortoises.

series of sketches called *The Encantadas* by Herman Melville. Melville's portrait of the islands was not a flattering one: "Take five and twenty heaps of cinders dumped here and there in an outside lot; imagine some of them magnified into mountains, and the vacant lot the sea; and you will have a fit idea of the general aspect of the Encantadas."

When the Ecuadorian government claimed the islands in 1832, Floreana was given as a reward for bravery to a local Creole officer. He brought 80 people from the mainland and kept them enslaved using giant dogs. But the so-called "Dog King of Charles Island" was forced to flee when his slaves rebelled. A brutal penal colony was set up on San Cristóbal in the 1880s, with the prisoners worked hard, flogged mercilessly, and marooned on desert islands to die slowly of thirst as punishment for misdemeanors.

When the United States entered World War II, it chose the Galápagos as a defense base against attacks on the Panama Canal. An airstrip was built on Baltra Island that is still in use today. In 1958, the last convict colony was closed, and in the 1960s regular passenger flights began to operate. Since then, tourism has been ever-increasing. In September 1995, the islands' tourist trade was brought to a halt when locals, led by a Galápagos legislator, Eduardo Véliz, seized San Cristóbal airport, the National Park office and the Charles Darwin Center, demanding more control of and benefits from tourism. Some kind of peace was secured, but only after two weeks of fierce protesting, complete suspension of all visits, and intense negotiations in Quito.

Concern for conservation

Scientists have been observing the Galápagos periodically ever since Darwin's work in the mid-19th century. In the 20th century, it became obvious that many of the animals introduced by man had turned feral and were devastating the natural ecology of the islands. Everything from goats to pigs, rats, dogs, and cats were breeding furiously. They were taking other animals' food, devouring turtle eggs and baby land iguanas, eroding the soil, and destroying the plants.

Charles Darwin (1809–82) visited the Galápagos Islands from September 15 to October 20, 1835 as a young naturalist onboard The Beagle. *Never setting foot on the Ecuadorian mainland, on his visits to Chatham, Charles, Albermarle, and James Islands he noted the similarity of the finches to those he had seen earlier in Chile. His interest lay mainly in researching the birds, plants, and geology of the island, while the tortoises provided fresh meat for the onward journey to Tahiti.*

BELOW: the Galápagos penguin.

About 20 percent of locals work in agriculture, ranging from ranching to growing of bananas, sugarcane, and coffee. Along with fishing, most of this activity is highly problematic. On San Cristóbal, Hacienda El Cafetal produces 100 percent organically grown coffee on 400 hectares (1,000 acres). A wind farm nearby produces clean electricity, reducing demand for diesel fuel.

BELOW: great frigate male with fully inflated pouch.

In 1930 an expedition led by Gifford Pinchot from the USA suggested creating a wildlife sanctuary in the archipelago. Five years later, laws were passed to protect the fauna of the islands, but it was not until 1959 that the Galápagos were declared a national park, with the aim of protecting the islands and encouraging scientific research.

Also created in 1959 was the Charles Darwin Foundation for the Galápagos Islands, an international organization under the auspices of Unesco and the International Union for the Conservation of Nature. In 1964 the foundation established the Charles Darwin Research Station, with scientific, educational, and protective objectives. The scientific program provides assistance for experts and biology students who visit the islands. The educational program is aimed at improving environmental awareness, particularly among students. And the protective program attempts to overcome the negative effects of introduced animals, and prevent other manmade disasters.

Various protective programs have been undertaken in cooperation with the national park administration. So far, they have been successful in eliminating black rats on Bartolomé and wild goats on Santa Fe, Española (Hood), and Rábida. A campaign against dogs, which attack young tortoises and land iguanas, started recently.

A law has been passed restricting human colonization. Only residents and their children are allowed to live permanently in the Galápagos Islands. This has slowed the tide, but illegal migration does continue and the islands have a resident population of over 20,000.

Tourism takes off

Before the 1960s, a visit to the Galápagos involved a long and uncomfortable sea voyage on the old ship *Cristóbal Carrier*, which ran once a month from Guayaquil to the archipelago. Travel between the islands was often nearly impossible. Not surprisingly, most visitors were wealthy and could afford their own yachts and cruise the islands at leisure. All this changed when regularly scheduled air transportation was made available

Economic Boom

Booming tourism, the dominant industry on the islands, has helped the Galápagos become one of the world's fastest-growing economies. From 1999 to 2006, it grew 78 percent, drawing in new settlers from the mainland including Ecuador's neighbors, Colombia and Peru. The impact of the influx has been very negative and imperils the islands' status as a Unesco World Heritage Site. New residents have taken up agriculture and fishing, pressuring the islands' flora and fauna along with imported goats, cats, dogs, and rats. Many Galapagueños have little or no interest in the unique environment, preferring to make a profit and hoping the islands will one day become mostly a beach resort destination, with all the money-making opportunities that would offer.

to the public, and passenger ships run by Ecuadorian tourist agencies started to make the journey. In 1970, an estimated 4,500 tourists arrived; in 1978 the figure was 12,000; in 1990, it was 66,000; and today, more than 100,000 visitors a year are estimated to come to the islands each year. Although tourism is tightly controlled, more must be done to preserve the islands. There are some 56 visitor sites and 62 marine sites where tourists are allowed outside of towns, and then only in the company of trained guides. Trails are marked with small stakes painted in white to stop you crushing plants and animals underfoot, and also to keep crowds away from crater borders, where serious erosion can occur. *(See page 318 for guidelines on responsible tourism in the islands).*

A range of plant life

Every island in the Galápagos is unique. Many are virtual deserts. Others, more mountainous, are relatively lush. Thanks to the icy Humboldt Current, the islands are not as hot as you would expect, but the sun can still be pun-

ishing, and few can stand more than a few hours hiking steep trails. There are six different vegetation zones on the Galápagos, beginning with the shoreline and ending with the highlands. The low islands are the driest, as clouds pass by here without discharging. Meanwhile, the mountainous islands often block clouds, which turn into fog, drizzle, or rain showers and help flora to thrive.

The shoreline is populated by plants that can tolerate high levels of salt, such as mangrove, saltbush, myrtle, and other minor aquatic plants. Next comes the arid zone, characterized by thorny plants with small flowers: different types of cactus (particularly *opuntia* and *cereus*), brushwood *(matorrales)*, the ghostly-looking *palos santos*, carob trees *(algarrobos)*, and lichens *(líquenes)*. In the transition zone, perennial herbs and smaller shrubs are dominant, among them the *matazarnos* and the pega pega *(Pisonia floribunda)*.

The high humid area – called scalesia after the zone's dominant tree, typically covered with brome-

Santa Cruz (Indefatigable), San Cristóbal (Chatham), and Isabela (Albermarle) are the only islands with human settlements, with more than 20,000 people living on the islands permanently, a quarter of them in Puerto Baquerizo Moreno, the archipelago's provincial capital, and more than 10,000 in booming Puerto Ayora. Residence permits, however, are restricted, and voluntary return to the mainland is encouraged by soft government loans.

BELOW: *opuntia* cactus grows in the arid zone.

Brachycereus
nesioticus *or lava
cactus is unique to
Bartolomé island.*

liads, ferns, and orchids – extends between 200 and 500 meters (650 and 1,650ft) above sea level. Several typical plants are found in this zone: locust and guava trees, *passiflora* and fungus. Above 500 meters (1,650ft) is the miconia zone, which is also the main area used for cultivation and pasture on the inhabited islands, where coffee, vegetables, oranges, and pineapples are planted. In the highest zone, called fern-sedge, grow mainly ferns and grasses, including the giant Galápagos fern tree, which can sometimes reach 3 meters (10ft) in height. Of the 875 plant species so far recorded on the islands, 228 are endemic.

Fascinating wildlife

Fifty-eight resident bird species have been recorded here, of which 28 are endemic. The remainder are either found in other parts of the world or are migratory, spending some part of the year living or breeding away from the islands. They can be classified into seabirds and land birds: among the latter are the famous Darwin finches, mockingbirds (distinguished

BELOW:
waved albatrosses
nest on Española.

by their gray and brown streaks), the Galápagos dove, and the endemic Galápagos hawk.

Seabirds tend to be more impressive for non-naturalist visitors. The world's entire population of 12,000 pairs of yellow-billed, waved albatrosses nest on the single island of Española (Hood). These magnificent creatures are famous for their extraordinary courtship displays, dancing about and "fencing" with their beaks – literally, standing face to face and clicking their beaks together at a great rate.

One of the most common birds is the blue-footed booby, which is not endemic. They are an unforgettable sight, as their feet really are a bold, striking blue. They were named "boobies" after the Spanish word *bobo* (dunce) by early sailors, who were amazed that the birds would not fly away when men approached. The boobies have a somewhat comical courtship ritual: they "dance" toward one another, plodding about with blue feet working up and down, "sky-point" (pushing their wings up to the heavens) and give one another twigs

as presents. They are often seen diving into the water from heights of 20 meters (65ft) to catch fish.

Another common seabird is the frigate. They can look quite sinister when hovering overhead, and are not above preying on other birds' young. The males' puffed scarlet chest sack makes an impressive sight when they are mating. With only 400 pairs still alive, the Galápagos lava gull is said to be the rarest bird species on earth. The Galápagos also have the world's only two flightless seabirds: the Galápagos penguin and the flightless cormorant.

The penguin is a big favorite on the islands, clumsily waddling about on land but speeding like a bullet under the waves. They are the most northerly penguin species, probably first coming up from the south with the icy Humboldt Current. They are mostly found on Isabela and Fernandina, although they can also easily be seen on Bartolomé. Like the penguin, the endemic flightless cormorant makes an entertaining sight – if you are lucky enough to spot one, since there

are only 700 pairs in existence – on the remote, far coasts of Isabela and Fernandina. The flightless cormorant has no enemies to fear, so does not suffer from its inability to fly – it scampers along flapping what look like the shreds of lost wings. It is, however, a good diver and can easily catch the fish it needs for its food.

Prehistoric creatures

It was Darwin who called the Galápagos "a paradise for reptiles." Most common are the endemic black marine iguanas, often found sunning themselves on cliffs and shorelines. Darwin himself found their dragon-like appearance rather horrifying: he called them "imps of darkness… of a dirty black color, stupid and sluggish in [their] movements." They are probably relatives of a land-going reptile species that died out 100 million years ago. But these creatures have adapted themselves to the ocean to feed on seaweed, often diving to 12-meter (40ft) depths. They have developed unusual glands connected to their breathing systems that accumulate the excess of

The flightless cormorant cannot fly because it lost the keel of its breastbone long ago. Its aquatic mating dance routine can last for 40 days.

BELOW: flightless cormorant drying its wings, Fernandina.

salt in their bodies. Every so often the salt is snorted out through the nose; not an attractive sight. While they are usually black, the males change color during mating to orange, red, and blue.

The rarer-to-spot land iguanas are yellow in color and often larger than their seagoing relatives. They are one of the species that was hardest hit by the animals introduced by man. Tiny lava lizards can be found on all the Galápagos Islands, frequently seen doing somewhat absurd "push-ups" on pathways, which is a sign that they are marking out their territory against intruders.

Slow-moving giants

The most famous of the Galápagos reptiles is the giant tortoise. Countless thousands were killed for their flesh by whalers during the 18th and 19th centuries, and now only an estimated 15,000 remain. There were 14 subspecies of giant tortoise here – distinguished most easily by the different shell shapes – but three are now extinct (the last example of one

species was found at the turn of the 20th century by an expedition from a San Francisco museum: the scientists promptly dispatched the creature in order to study its shell).

The giant tortoise is one of the most ancient of reptiles, but also among the rarest – it exists only here and on the island of Aldabra in the Indian Ocean. Weighing up to 250kg (550lb), it has two types of shell: the dome-shaped type is found in humid environments such as Santa Cruz, where vegetation is low and abundant; this type of tortoise has a short neck and short legs. The second type has a shell that resembles a horse's harness and lives on islands with uneven soil and no low grass, such as Española (Hood). These tortoises are more agile (relatively speaking) and have long legs and necks in order to feed themselves. The shell indentation allows them to protrude their necks further.

Legend has it that these tortoises can live for centuries. One, given to the Queen of Tonga by Captain Cook in the 1770s, is said to have survived until 1966, but there is no certain evi-

dence for them living for more than 100 years.

Saving these magnificent creatures has been a major task of the Darwin Research Station: a program of breeding seems to be successful. On Española, only 10 males and two females of a subspecies were still alive until, after years of breeding in captivity, some 100 healthy specimens were returned to the island. But the tortoise population is still at risk: on Santa Cruz a mysterious disease killed several of them in 1996 and for a while visitors were banned.

There is only one survivor, however, of one subspecies from the island of Pinta, and he goes by the name of Lonesome George. He was discovered on the island of Pinta in 1971, during a period of goat removal, and was transferred to the captive breeding program at the Charles Darwin Research Station soon after. He is estimated to be 70–80 years old. Despite a $10,000 reward for a female of the species, no mate has been found for him. Attempts have been made to interbreed George with similar species. Eggs laid by two females of a related species have been found in their enclosure, however none have so far been fertile. Considering their lifetime it will take generations to breed a species close to that of the original Pinta tortoise.

Easier to spot in the wild is the Pacific green sea turtle, which snorkelers can often observe underwater.

Playful sea lions and dolphins

There are fewer land mammals than there are birds or reptiles in the Galápagos because they were much less likely to survive the journey across from coastal South America. Storms may have blown the hoary bat to the Galápagos, while the rice rat may have made it across on a vegetation raft. Sea mammals, however, simply followed the currents to the islands, and these days they make up some of the Galápagos' most popular creatures with visitors.

Topping the list is the sea lion. The young are incredibly cute and playful; they will swim about snorkelers and tease them, even staring into your

BELOW: a giant tortoise under attack by a Galápagos hawk.

BELOW: swimming with sea lions.
RIGHT: snapping marine iguanas.

goggles and pretending to charge you before turning away. The *machos*, or older males, do, however, stake out their territory very jealously. They can turn aggressive and have been known to bite swimmers, so a degree of caution should be used in their presence (guides will know which areas are the preserve of the bull lions).

Fur seals have more hair than sea lions, and are smaller and very shy: they prefer to live in colonies, on distant cliffs. Bottle-nosed dolphins are often seen surfing the bow spray of boats, while no fewer than seven whale species have been sighted at or near the Galápagos archipelago, although getting a close look at them is a fairly unlikely prospect.

An underwater world

Under the waves, snorkelers will be constantly surrounded by many of the 307 species of fish recorded in the Galápagos, and more are being discovered every year. Schools of brightly colored tropical fish pass over the sea floor and around rocks, making a spellbinding sight.

Hammerhead and white-tipped Galápagos sharks can also be seen in the waters around the islands, but they are not dangerous. The grace of these creatures is particularly impressive. Non-native sharks, however, possibly arriving due to climate change, attacked one swimmer each in 2007 and 2008.

Keep an eye out for the different types of rays that glide majestically along the ocean floor. The giant manta ray can sometimes be spotted leaping out of the sea and landing with a loud slap on the waves. None of the rays are dangerous except for the stingray – on some beaches they lie in shallow water beneath a layer of sand, and can give quite a sting if trodden on. When you enter the water, it's worth giving the sand a shuffle with your feet to scare off any basking rays.

Invertebrates such as jellyfish, sponges, mollusks, and crabs, proliferate. The most commonly seen of these is the bright yellow and orange Sally Lightfoot crab, which can be found on almost every rock in the Galápagos. ❑

BIRDS OF THE GALÁPAGOS

From the marbled godwit to the black-necked stilt, the birdlife on the Galápagos Islands, which taught us about evolution, is still rich, rare, and rewarding

Where else in the world will birds practically come out to greet you? Life without predators has made the birds of the Galápagos fearless, which means that many of them are easy to spot. There are 58 resident species, of which 28 are endemic, as well as about 30 migratory birds. The seabirds are the most frequently seen: in the dry coastal areas you are likely to spot three species of the booby family, the waved albatross – found nowhere in the world except on the Galápagos island of Española, which supports a nesting colony of 12,000 pairs – and the world's only flightless seabirds, the Galápagos penguin and the flightless cormorant. The best time for bird-watching is in winter (October to February) when most migrants are visiting, and birds are reproducing. Then, a serious ornithologist might see 50 species in a week, and even a dilettante should be able to spot two dozen.

There are dangers in paradise, however: the introduction of mainland animals brought over by economic migrants to the islands has been disastrous. Cats and rats prey on the birds, while goats destroy the birds' habitats. Farming on the inhabited islands also destroys habitats (agriculture supports 20 percent of the locals), and a natural phenomenon, the El Niño current, brings mosquito-carried disease and disrupts the food chain.

TOP LEFT: the endangered peregrine falcon *(Falco peregrinus)* winters in South America and is frequently seen on the islands of Española, Isabela, Baltra, and Santa Cruz. The world's swiftest bird, this falcon can reach speeds of 320km/h (199mph) when it is swooping to attack prey.

LEFT: waved albatrosses perform their elaborate courtship dance.

ABOVE: unlike much of other local birdlife, the greater flamingo – mostly found on Floreana, Isabela, and Rábida islands – is quite s

THE SECRET OF DARWIN'S FINCHES

The finches of the Galápagos were vitally important in the development of Charles Darwin's ideas about evolution and the formation of species. When he set off on his voyage around the world on HMS *Beagle* (1831–6), he believed, like most people of his time, in the fixity of species. But on the Galápagos he observed that 13 different species of the finch had evolved from a single ancestral group, and it was this (together with his observations of the islands' tortoises) which led to his contention that species could evolve over time, with those most suited to their natural environment surviving and passing on their characteristics to the next generation.

The main differences he noted between the finches was the size and shape of their beaks, leading him to conclude that the birds which survived were those whose beaks enabled them to eat the available food.

The 13 species of finch are divided into two groups: ground finches (pictured above is the large ground finch, *Geospiza magnirostris*) and tree finches, of which the mangrove finch, found only in the swamps of Isabela Island, is the most rare. You are unlikely to see all of them on a short visit, but it's a challenge to see how many you can spot.

ABOVE: the magnificent frigate bird (*Fregata magnificens magnificens*) and its close relation the great frigate bird, can be seen near the coasts of many islands. The male is remarkable for the red gular pouch which puffs in the mating season.

LEFT: the lava gull *(Larus fuliginosus)* is believed to be the rarest species in the world. It roosts on the shores of saltwater lagoons and builds solitary nests along the coast.

BELOW: the blue-footed booby *(Sula nebouxii excisa)* lays two or three eggs and both of the parents share the task of incubating them. Once they have become independent, the young birds leave the islands and do not return to breed until some three years later.

LEFT: the female Galápagos hawk (*Buteo galapagoensis*) is larger than the male of the species. Males are monogamous but females will mate with up to seven males per season to ensure that breeding will be successful.

BELOW: the vermillion flycatcher (*Pyrocephalus rubinus*) has a high-pitched, musical song and builds a distinctive cup-shaped nest.

VISITING THE ISLANDS

Uncontrolled, tourism could destroy this
Pacific paradise. The hundreds of thousands
of visitors who follow in Darwin's footsteps
must follow strict rules if the wildlife of
the archipelago is to survive

Main attractions
CHARLES DARWIN
 RESEARCH STATION
TORTOISE RESERVE
PLAZA SUR
ISLA SEYMOUR
PUERTO EGAS
CERRO BARTOLOMÉ
TAGUS COVE
ESPAÑOLA'S WAVED
 ALBATROSS

PRECEDING PAGES:
Isla Bartolomé. **LEFT:**
candelabra cactus.
BELOW: setting off
on a boat trip.

Most travelers to the Galápagos arrive by air, except for a few who have pre-arranged trips on one of the larger cruisers that occasionally depart from Guayaquil. Flights from Quito connect through Guayaquil. TAME flies daily to the island of Baltra, from where a bus and ferry will take you across to Puerto Ayora on Santa Cruz, and three times a week to San Cristóbal. Aerogal offers thrice-weekly flights to San Cristóbal and Baltra. On arrival, you must have your passport ready and $100 entrance tax to the Galápagos; without these two essentials, you will not be able to enter the islands.

Many travelers will have pre-arranged their cruise around the islands on one of the larger luxury ships. Two of the best on offer are the *Galápagos Explorer II*, a liner operated by Canodros, which leaves from Baltra; and the *Santa Cruz*, run by Metropolitan Touring, which leaves from San Cristóbal (*see Travel Tips, pages 353–4 for tour operators*). Both offer all the comforts of a five-star hotel, with excellent food, swimming pools, evening slide shows, and the like. They also have English-speaking guides who are all qualified naturalists. Although the capacity of these ships is 90 people, they operate with groups of no more than 20, landing them by small dinghies called *pangas* for twice-daily excursions. The large boats have the advantage of covering a lot of territory by night, easily reaching the more

remote islands without unduly rough passages. Smaller luxury boats carrying 16–20 passengers, such as the *Beluga* run by Angermeyers, offer a more intimate experience.

Independent and budget travelers may organize their own cruise on one of the dozens of smaller boats on the islands. This can be arranged in Quito or Guayaquil, but is cheapest when done in Puerto Ayora on Santa Cruz, though a few small boats also operate from San Cristóbal. Take your time, meet up with other like-minded

Dried lava patterns.

travelers, find a captain, and agree a price. This usually takes two or three days, but if you have more time than money it's worth doing. The main advantage of organizing your own trip is flexibility: you can choose which islands you want to visit, for how long, and when. However, the guides often do not speak English, and rough weather conditions can make night journeys on these boats difficult for those with delicate stomachs. For younger, independent travelers, this is an experience not to miss.

A guide to the visitor sites

The only places where boats may land on the islands are at the 56 designated visitor sites, and even then visitors must be accompanied by a guide. Some of the more fragile sites are further restricted so that only small groups are allowed to visit, or limits are imposed on the numbers each month. The landing by *panga* is either wet or dry; your guide will tell you which to expect. Wet landings simply mean that you leap into the water up to your ankles (sometimes up to your knees), so keep your shoes aside; dry landings are at natural or manmade jetties, where you should keep your shoes on.

The most densely populated island in the Galápagos, as well as its second-largest (at 986 sq km/380 sq miles), is **Santa Cruz ❶**. Most tours start here at the township of **Puerto Ayora**, and even those that begin at San Cristóbal call here to visit the **Charles Darwin Research Station ❷**.

Puerto Ayora has grown in size and population in recent years. The wide, turquoise **Academy Bay** is full of small boats and makes a picturesque sight, while the town docks are usually crowded with small children running, swimming, and playing with sea lions. Ayora has plenty of small hotels and restaurants, the most eccentric being the Sol y Mar (*see Travel Tips, page 341*). It sits right on the waterline and its porch is always crowded with marine iguanas (they may walk over your feet while you are having breakfast, which can be something of a surprise until you get used to it).

The main attraction is the research station. This is the classic place to have

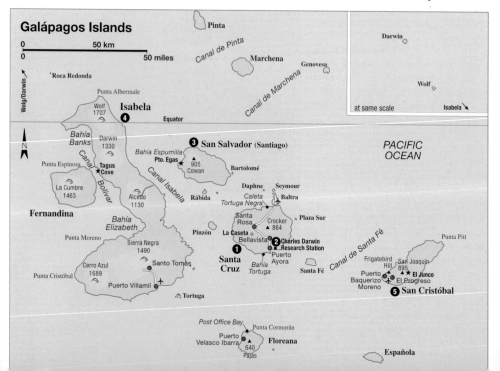

your photo taken with one of the giant tortoises: mature specimens of several subspecies are kept in pens here. While you often see pictures of tourists riding tortoises, this can damage their shells and is prohibited. The station has a tortoise breeding house, where the young can be seen, and a small museum and information center.

There are several trails from Puerto Ayora that are worth exploring. Some 7km (4 miles) westward is **Bahía Tortuga** (Turtle Bay), with fine white sand and waters rich in lobsters. You can go there to swim and relax without a guide, although the fish and animals are still protected. The highland interior of Santa Cruz, in the national park, offers several attractions: the lava tubes are long underground tunnels made when lava solidified on the surface of a flow but kept going underneath. Climbing **Cerro Crocker**, an 860-meter (2,800ft) high hill, shows the range of vegetation zones on the island. And a day excursion can be made to the **Tortoise Reserve**, which is one of the few places to see giant tortoises in the wild; organize your trip beforehand with a tour guide in the town or visit independently: you need to hire a jeep and then take a two-hour walk to see these creatures wallowing in the mud.

The central islands

The islands close to Santa Cruz are the most visited, although not necessarily the most interesting for naturalists. Day trips are run by various agencies from Puerto Ayora: this means a lot of traveling time on the water if you want to visit more than one. It is more fun and – if properly organized – only slightly more expensive to visit several on your own cruise.

Only 24km (15 miles) from Puerto Ayora is **Isla Santa Fe** (also known as Barrington). A compulsory wet landing is the start of a short trail into a dry landscape crowded with opuntia cacti. Santa Fe is one of the best places to see the shy land iguana, but the steep path is one of the more difficult on the Galápagos, so a swim from the beach near the landing site comes as a welcome relief.

On the northeastern coast of Santa Cruz is the tiny island of **Plaza Sur**.

TIP

While last-minute booking is possible in Puerto Ayora, visitors are unlikely to succeed in securing berths on ships during the July and August holiday months as well as around Christmas and New Year. Beyond hiking, snorkeling, and diving, other sports on the islands include biking, kayaking, surfing, and windsurfing. Active tours can be booked at tour operator Lonesome George in Puerto Ayora (Avenida Baltra and Enrique Fuentes; tel: 05-252 6245).

BELOW: getting to know a giant tortoise.

BELOW: sea lions provide an underwater photo opportunity.

Only 13 hectares (32 acres) in area, its coast is so crowded with sea lions that everyone on the *panga* needs to clap and shout to clear a landing space. Swimming is not encouraged here, since the *macho* or bull sea lions are particularly aggressive. Plaza Sur is unusually crowded with animal life; there are plenty of land iguanas and the impressive black cliffs are populated with seabirds, as well as the rare Galápagos hawk. Nearby is a "convalescent home" for bachelor *macho* sea lions: after losing a brawl over territory, they come here to recuperate before returning to the fray.

Isla Seymour is separated from the larger island of **Baltra** by a channel. Baltra has little to interest a visitor, whereas Seymour is one of the Galápagos' best breeding grounds for seabirds: blue-footed boobies are so common that visitors have to be careful not to step on any of the nests that may have been built on the trails.

The strange, block-shaped island of **Daphne** is 10km (6 miles) away. Access is restricted to only a few boats a month. Landing here is difficult, with a leap onto nearly sheer rocks that becomes somewhat hair-raising in rough weather. But it is worth the effort: at the end of a trail, a large crater is dotted with hundreds of blue-footed booby nests, making a decidedly surreal sight.

Volcanic rock and iguanas

One of the larger islands, relatively close to Santa Cruz, is known as either **Santiago** or **James**, although its official title is **San Salvador ❸**. It has a number of landing sites, by far the most popular being **Puerto Egas** on the west coast. This is one of the best places to see hundreds of marine iguanas sunning themselves on black volcanic rocks, while fur seals can be spotted swimming nearby. The **Sugarloaf Volcano** dominates the horizon here. Swimming is good at Espumilla Beach and Buccaneer Cove. If you are in a small group, try snorkeling at the **fur seals' grotto**. You can swim with these characters for hours through the pools that have formed under natural stone archways.

Sitting off the east coast of San Salvador, the small 120-hectare (300-

acre) island of **Bartolomé** is one of the most photographed in the Galápagos. The centerpiece of a visit is the steep climb up **Cerro Bartolomé**: the view is spectacular, looking over lunar fields of dried lava, craters, and out over the jutting, honeycombed **Pinnacle Rock**. The heat is also quite intense, so after working up a sweat, transfer to the second landing site, one of the most pleasant beaches on the islands. The snorkeling is excellent, especially around Pinnacle Rock itself: apart from the tropical fish moving in formation, you have a chance of spotting teams of penguins hunting underwater. A path leads over to the other side of the island, where dozens of reef sharks patrol only meters from the edge of the water.

South of San Salvador is the island of **Rábida** (Jervis), which has a dark-red sand beach (due to its high iron-oxide content) along which lounge hundreds of bloated sea lions. Indolent and clumsy on land, they are surprisingly energetic in the water: this is a great place to observe the baby sea lions.

A path into the interior of the island passes a marshy lake full of bright pink flamingos (the pinker the flamingo, the healthier it is; the feather color comes from the diet of shrimps they sieve through their beaks). In the trees by the beach are a large number of brown pelicans.

Another unusual point on Rábida that is well worth visiting is **Caleta Tortuga Negra** (Black Turtle Cove). This tidal lagoon leads into a maze of mangroves: it can be visited only by *panga*, cutting the motor and paddling quietly through the natural tunnels made by trees. The brackish waters of the area are full of white-tipped sharks and mustard rays. But it is most famous as a mating spot for the green Pacific turtles. With luck, you can spot the two heads coming up for air during copulation, which lasts for many hours.

When cruising the south coast of San Salvador, keep an eye out for **Sombrero Chino**, literally "Chinese Hat," named for the island's sweeping conical shape. One of the more recent islands, it has a 400-meter (1,300ft) long path around its circumference, along which sea lions relax in abandonment.

BELOW: it is thought the Galápagos land iguana can live for around 50 years.

Diving

Not to be outdone by the unique life above ground, the Galápagos Islands are one of the world's premier diving areas. At 133,000 sq km (51,350 sq miles), it's the biggest marine preserve in Latin America. Some 300 species of fish have been catalogued. Diving tours on yachts are the best way to reach remote diving spots such as Darwin and Wolf islands at the northwest end of the archipelago; both are excellent locations to see schools of endemic Galápagos, white-tipped, or black-tipped sharks, hammerheads, and even gigantic whale sharks. These, the largest species of fish in the world, can be seen June through December. Manta rays are common off Cabo Marshall on Isabela. High quantities of nutrients in the water, however, can limit underwater visibility.

Preserving the Islands

Tourism is a mixed blessing for the Galápagos: follow these guidelines to ensure that the islands will be left unaltered by your visit.

• No natural object – plant, animal, shell, bone, stone, or scrap of wood – should be removed or disturbed. It is illegal and alters the islands' ecological conditions.

• Be careful not to transport any live material to the islands, or from island to island. Before leaving the boat, check your shoe soles for dried mud, as it may contain plant seeds and animal spores. Inadvertent transport of these materials represents a special danger to the Galápagos: each island has its own unique fauna and flora, and introduced plants and animals can quickly destroy them. Obviously no other animals or plants should be brought to the islands.

• For the same reason, do not take any food to the uninhabited islands. Along with the food may come insects or other organisms that might threaten the fragile island ecosystems. Fresh fruits and vegetables are especially dangerous: a dropped orange pip, for example, may become a tree.

• Animals may not be touched or handled. Young animals that have been handled may be rejected by their mothers because of their smell. They soon die as a result.

• Animals may not be fed. Not only can it be dangerous but in the long run it can destroy the animals' social structure and affect their reproduction.

• Do not startle or chase any animal from its resting or nesting spot. Exercise extreme caution among the breeding colonies of seabirds. These birds will fly from their nests if they are startled, often knocking the egg or chick to the ground or leaving it exposed to the sun. (A recently hatched booby chick will die in 20 to 30 minutes if it is exposed to the sun; frigate birds will also eat any unguarded chick.)

• Do not leave the designated visiting sites. Where trails to points of interest are marked with wooden stakes, you should remain within the stakes.

• Litter of all types must be kept off the islands. Disposal at sea must be limited to certain types of garbage which can be thrown overboard in selected areas. Keep all rubbish in a bag or pocket, to be disposed of on your boat. The crew of your vessel is responsible to the national park for proper trash disposal. Never throw anything overboard.

• Do not buy souvenirs or objects made from plants or animals. Black coral is now endangered by islanders' carvings. If anyone offers you any of these souvenirs, please advise the national park. Camping anywhere within the Galápagos without a permit is against the law. Camping is permitted only in certain sites designated by the national park. Contact any of the national park offices (see below) to get a camping permit.

• All groups visiting the national park must be accompanied by an approved, qualified guide. The visitor must follow the guide's instructions, while the guide must ensure compliance with the national park regulations.

• Notify the national park service if you see any serious damage being done. You may be a decisive factor in the preservation of the islands. The head office is a 10-minute walk east of the main town of Puerto Ayora (tel: 05-252 6511; Mon–Fri 7am–12.15pm and 1.45–4.30pm), but there are also offices on San Cristóbal (Puerto Baquerizo Moreno; tel: 05-252 0497), Floreana (Puerto Velasco Ibarra; tel: 05-252 9509), and Isabela (Puerto Villamil; tel: 05-252 9178). ❑

LEFT: visitors to the Galápagos Islands must not stray off the designated visiting sites.

The western islands

Some 120km (75 miles) in length and shaped like a seahorse, **Isabela ➍** is the largest of the Galápagos Islands. It is still recovering from fires that blazed across the island in 1994. The fires were eventually extinguished, but not without a severe impact on vegetation. One of the island's main attractions, the giant tortoises, were rescued by helicopter and taken to the other side of the island to the safety of a breeding center. Isabela is one of the islands that still has volcanic activity, and there are five cones still visible: **Wolf** at 1,707 meters (5,395ft); **Alcedo** at 1,130 (3,600); **Sierra Negra** (also called Santo Tomás) at 1,490 (4,885); **Cerro Azul** at 1,689 (5,540), and **Darwin** at 1,330 (4,200).

Some 1,600 people live on Isabela, mostly in and around **Puerto Villamil** on the south coast. Cruise ships rarely visit since it is difficult to enter the bay, especially when the sea is rough. It does, however, have a fine sandy beach and several basic hotels and restaurants. About 18km (11 miles) away is the village of **Santo Tomás** and the "Wall of Tears," built of lava stone in the convict colony that was closed in 1959. The crater Santo Tomás has a diameter of 10km (6 miles), making it the second-largest in the world, while Alcedo has a still-steaming fumarole and scores of giant tortoises living at its rim.

Most of the visitor sites on Isabela are on the west side of the island. Probably the most popular is **Tagus Cove**. Here you can climb up a path to see the lava fields. A *panga* ride along the cliffs reveals colonies of penguins and other seabirds. It is probably also the best place to see the unique, but difficult to sight, flightless cormorant. Other landings can be made at **Urbina Bay**, **Elizabeth Bay**, and **Punta Moreno**.

On the other side of Isabela is **Fernandina**, one of the least visited islands because it is so remote; the island is the most westerly in the Galápagos. It has one visitor site at **Punta Espinosa**, with some impressive lava flows (this was probably the

most recently formed major island, and still has some volcanic activity). Along its shores are more penguins and hordes of marine iguanas.

A whalers' post box

Of historical interest on **Isla Floreana**, to the south of the archipelago, is the post box at **Post Office Bay**, where whalers used to leave mail in the late 18th century. Having been replaced several times, the box is still in use. It is the custom to look through the mail and take anything addressed to your home country, putting a local stamp on it when you arrive there and sending it on its way.

Of the visitor sites on Isla Floreana, **Punta Cormorán** is a sandy beach with a greenish tinge from the tiny crystals of olivine, a mineral silicate. From here a trail leads to a lagoon, where occasionally pink flamingos nest. Nearby is a second beach called Stingray, which has glistening white sands. The **Devil's Crown** is a sunken crater that forms a semicircle of rocks: this is perhaps the best site for diving in the whole archipelago. Apart from

Charles Darwin called marine iguanas "imps of darkness."

BELOW: Nazca booby on Española.
RIGHT: inquisitive sea lions.

the schools of brilliant tropical fish, you will probably be joined by some baby sea lions that will race snorkelers through a natural underwater archway.

The outlying islands

The most southerly island in the Galápagos is **Española** (Hood). Española is famous for its seabirds, particularly the waved albatross. Twelve thousand pairs nest here, the world's entire population. During the mating season, they begin "fencing" by knocking their beaks together and waddling about "like drunken sailors," as one observer put it.

The whole astonishing range of seabirds can be seen on this island, as well as the beautiful beach of Gardner's Bay. Keep an eye out for the blowhole, which spouts water 50 meters (165ft) into the air whenever waves hit. At the eastern point of the archipelago lies **San Cristóbal ⑤** (Chatham), the second-largest human population center after Santa Cruz: some 5,000 people live in **Puerto Baquerizo Moreno,** the Galápagos' provincial capital. The introduction of flights

here caused a development boom, and several hotels and restaurants service the town. There is a small **museum** run by the Franciscan fathers, a monument to Darwin, and, at the entrance of the port, a rock called **León Dormido** (Sleeping Lion), which can be climbed for a good view of the island.

A road leads to the village of **El Progreso** and the 895-meter (2,935ft) high **Volcán San Joaquín** and **El Junco,** a freshwater crater lake. **Frigatebird Hill** is, as the name suggests, a good place to see frigate birds and only a short walk from the town. The nearby Galápagos National Park Visitor Center (tel: 05-252 1538; daily 7am–6pm), has a number of exhibits about the island's natural history and ecosystems. **La Lobería** is a beach crowded with sea lions and **Puerto Grande** a small cove particularly popular for swimming.

Other far-flung islands include **Marchena, Pinta,** and **Genovesa** (Tower), which is home to the main colony of red-footed boobies, three types of Darwin's finch, and everything from red-billed tropic-birds to storm petrels.   ❑

INSIGHT GUIDES TRAVEL TIPS
ECUADOR & GALÁPAGOS

T RANSPORTATION

GETTING THERE AND GETTING AROUND

GETTING THERE

By Air

Ecuador has two international airports, at Quito (Mariscal Sucre) and Guayaquil (José Joaquín de Olmedo). The largest planes cannot land at Mariscal Sucre airport, and some airlines fly only as far as Guayaquil, but that's all about to change with the opening of Quito's brand-new international airport. Due for inauguration in 2010, it will be the main point of air arrivals into the country. If Guayaquil is your entrance point into Ecuador, but you plan to head for the capital, make sure that your international ticket includes the onward connection, otherwise you will need to buy another ticket in Guayaquil airport. The flight time between Quito and Guayaquil is approximately 30 minutes.

Flights from the US and Canada

Travelers heading to Ecuador from the US can fly directly to Quito with **American Airlines** and **LAN** from Miami and via Guayaquil from New York. Continental also flies direct from New York to Guayaquil and Quito. **Delta Airlines** has flights via Atlanta. **TACA** operates flights from several US cities, including Dallas and New York. You can also fly to Quito with Avianca from various US cities via Bogotá; Taca via San José; LAN via Lima; and Copa via Panama City. AeroGal now also flies internationally, with routes to and from Miami, Bogotá and Medellín. Travelers from Canada will need to go via the US with Air Canada, American Airlines, or Continental.

American Airlines
Quito Hotel Hilton Colón, Av. Patria and Amazonas. Tel: 02-299 5000
Guayaquil Córdoba 1021 and 9 de Octubre. Tel: 04-259 8800
Cuenca Hermano Miguel 8-67. Tel: 07-283 1699

Avianca
Quito Av. Coruña 1311 and San Ignacio. Tel: 1-800-003 434
Guayaquil Av. Francisco de Orellana, Manzana 111. Tel: 1-800-003 434
Cuenca Presidente Córdoba 8-40 and Benigno Malo. Tel: 07-283 4484

Continental Airlines
Quito Av. 12 de Octubre 1830 and Cordero. Tel: 1-800-222 333
Guayaquil Av. 9 de Octubre and Malecón, Edificio Banco La Previsora, 25th Floor. Tel: 1-800-222 333
Cuenca Padre Aguirre 1096 and Mariscal Lamar. Tel: 1-800-222 333

Copa
Quito Av. República del Salvador 361 and Moscú. Tel: 02-226 9738
Guayaquil Av. 9 de Octubre and Malecón. Tel: 04-230 3000
Cuenca Mariscal Lamar 989 and Padre Aguirre. Tel: 07-284 2970

Delta Airlines
Quito Av. Los Shyris and Suecia Local 3, Edificio Renazzo Plaza. Tel: 02-333 1691
Guayaquil Hotel Hilton Colón, Av. Francisco de Orellana. Tel: 1-800-101 060

LAN
Quito Av. Amazonas and Pasaje Guayas E3-131. Tel: 1-800-101 075
Guayaquil Hotel Hilton Colón, Av. F. de Orellana. Tel: 1-800-101 075

TACA
Quito Av. República de El Salvador 1033 and Naciones Unidas. Tel: 1-800-008 222
Guayaquil Av. Pichincha 406 and Luque. Tel: 1-800-008 222
Cuenca Mariscal Sucre 7-70 and Luís Cordero. Tel: 1-800-008 222

Flights from Europe

Iberia flies direct from Madrid daily. **KLM** flies between Quito and Amsterdam via Curaçao, five days a week, or go via the US or South America.

Iberia
Quito Av. Eloy Alfaro 939 and Amazonas. Tel: 02-256 6009
Guayaquil Av. 9 de Octubre 101 and Malecón. Tel: 04-232 9558

KLM
Quito Av. 12 de Octubre N26-97 and A. Lincoln. Tel: 02-396 6728
Guayaquil José Joaquín de Olmedo Airport. Tel: 04-216 9068

Flights from Australia, New Zealand, and Asia

Travelers can take an **Aerolíneas Argentinas** flight from Sydney via

International Airlines

The following airlines operate flights to Quito and Guayaquil.
American Airlines www.aa.com
Avianca www.avianca.com
Continental www.continental.com
Copa www.copaair.com
Delta Airlines www.delta.com
Iberia www.iberia.com
KLM www.klm.com
LAN www.lan.com
TACA www.taca.com

Air Travel Taxes

• There is a 12 percent tax imposed on all air tickets bought within Ecuador.
• A $40.80 departure tax payable at the airport in cash is levied on international flights from Ecuador.

Auckland to Buenos Aires, with a connecting flight to Guayaquil; the **LAN** flight from Australia, also via Auckland to Santiago, then on to Ecuador; or fly to Los Angeles and take one of the several connecting flights from there.

Alternatively, **American Airlines** fly from Sydney to Los Angeles, from where you can fly to Miami for a connection to Guayaquil.

Getting to and from Airports

Mariscal Sucre International Airport (UIO) in Quito, tel: 02-294 4900, is located 8km (5 miles) north of the New Town. There are no luggage deposit boxes at the airport. Most of the large hotels have a shuttle service; otherwise a taxi to the New Town will cost about $6–8, and $8–10 to the Old Town.

The José Joaquín de Olmedo International Airport (GYE) is located 5km (3 miles) north of Guayaquil city center. If you already have a reservation, make arrangements with your hotel to pick you up. Otherwise, taxis marked "airport taxi" can be found to the left of the exit. There is no pre-pay stand, but the journey to the city center should not cost more than $6. There is a *casa de cambio* (bureau de change) at the airport as well as a small information office.

Cuenca's airport is a five-minute walk beyond the bus terminal and is easily accessible by city bus or taxi.

Upstream from Esmeraldas, there is a bridge over the river at San Mateo which connects with General Rivadeneira Airport, 25km (15½ miles) away for domestic flights. Taxis to the airport wait in front of the TAME office and will cost $5–6. Buses go to and from the Terminal Terrestre (Central Bus Terminal) every 30 minutes.

By Bus

It is common for backpackers to travel overland into Ecuador, crossing at either Huaquillas or Macará on the Peruvian border or Tulcán/Rumichaca on the Colombian side, although currently there are serious safety issues in this region due to increased drug-trafficking and the activities of illegal armed groups. At both borders,

minibuses and trucks run between bus centers on both sides for a small fee. The borders are usually open from around 8am to 6pm. Be sure to get an entry stamp and tourist card.

Several companies run comfortable buses on the longer routes, including **Panamericana Internacional**, **Ormeño** and **Rey Tours**, which run international services from Quito and Guayaquil to Lima (*see Buses from Quito, page 326*).

By Road

To drive a private car across a border into Ecuador, you are required to have a Carnet de Passage en Douane (CDP), an international customs document. These are normally obtained through the automobile club of the country where the car is registered. Motorbike and bicycle riders just need to show relevant registration papers.

GETTING AROUND

Until the 20th century, transport and communications in Ecuador were poorly developed. Most people got around by mule or donkey until the railway network was developed. The road network has expanded considerably since World War II, and the main roads are generally quite good, although many have been badly affected by landslides and flooding and have dangerous potholes. Of the 38,000km (23,560 miles) of highways, about 18,000km (11,160 miles) are open all year and about 7,000km (4,340 miles) are paved.

By Car

Traveling by private car is generally more convenient in Ecuador than in other Andean countries, because the main roads are in a comparatively better state, the running costs are economical, and the country is safer than in neighboring republics.

Nevertheless, beware of bus drivers, who often go very fast, and make sure that your car has good ground clearance. As insurance and rental costs become more prohibitive and incidents of ambushes at night increase in certain regions, more travelers tend to opt for buses rather than driving themselves.

Car Rental

Car rental is as expensive as in Europe or in the United States.

Charges start at about $55 a day, with mileage increments. Extra insurance costs may be charged, and most rental agencies prefer credit cards.

A valid driver's license from your home country is usually accepted, but some rental companies require an international license. It is worth applying for one before you leave if you plan to hire a car.

It is often more economical and less stressful to hire a taxi for several hours, which will take you to remote areas or to another town: be sure to agree the costs beforehand.

Automobile Club

The Asociación Nacional Ecuatoriana de Turismo y Automobilismo (**ANETA**) (Avenida Eloy Alfaro 218 and Berlin; tel: 02-250 4961; www.aneta.org.ec) offers an emergency breakdown towing and repair service to members and offers discounts to members of the AAA from Canada or the US.

By Bus

Local Buses

Local buses run frequently and are inexpensive. Destinations are shown on the front of the vehicle. All the main towns and cities are served by urban

Car Rental Agencies

In addition to the locations listed below, all of the following agencies have branches at the international airports in Quito and Guayaquil.
Avis
Av. Amazonas 4925 and Río Curay, Quito. Tel: 02-244 0270.
Av. de las Américas, Centro Comercial Olímpico, Guayaquil. Tel: 04-228 5498.
www.avis.com
Budget
Av. Amazonas and Colón, Quito. Tel: 02-223 7026.
Av. de las Américas 900 and Alejandro Andrade, Guayaquil. Tel: 04-228 4559.
www.budget.com
Hertz
Panamericana Norte 9900 and Murialdo, Quito. Tel: 02-241 1677.
Av. de las Américas and E. Arboleda, Guayaquil. Tel: 04-228 0910. www.hertz.com
Localiza
Av. de los Granados E11-26 y 6 de Diciembre, Quito. Tel: 02-225 9333.
Av. Francisco Boloña 713 (sector Policentro), Guayaquil. Tel: 04-239 5236.
www.localiza.com.ec

Taxis

Taxis are very cheap compared to developed countries, but meters are only used by taxi drivers in Quito, and often only on request. Tell the driver your destination and agree on a charge beforehand, or insist the *taxi-metro* (meter) is used. In Guayaquil, meters are installed by law but drivers do not use them: be sure to ascertain the fare beforehand, or you could be overcharged. In smaller towns, meters do not exist; at weekends and at night fares are 25–50 percent higher.

bus lines. The buses are mostly small and usually extremely overcrowded, especially at peak hours. The large *selectivo* buses running in Quito's New Town are a pleasant exception. Beware of pickpockets.

There is a smart trolley system operating between the north and south of Quito, but this, too, gets very crowded at peak hours. Pickpockets also work this network.

Since taxis are very cheap in Guayaquil, buses and *colectivos* are mostly avoided by foreign visitors, but *busetas* or minibuses are safe to ride. *Servicio especial* buses, marked with blue-and-white diagonal stripes, are slightly more expensive but relatively efficient. Take great care with taxis in Guayaquil, due to a spate of taxi-kidnappings of late. It is better to order one by phone from a company recommended by your hotel than to flag one down in the street.

BELOW: buses waiting to depart from Manta bus station.

If you want to get off a local bus, shout *¡baja!* (down!) or *¡esquina!* (corner!), when the driver will stop at the next corner.

Long-Distance Buses

Bus travel is not always comfortable, but the numerous companies connect all the main towns at frequent intervals, serve smaller localities, and the fares are incredibly low.

In general, buses leave from central bus terminals. The new, comfortable, luxury buses leave on time; regular buses may or may not. One can usually buy tickets one or two days in advance and choose the seat number; note that the front seats tend to have slightly more leg room than the back seats. During long holiday weekends or special fiestas, buses are generally booked up for several days in advance, so early booking is recommended.

Try to travel by daylight, as there are fewer road accidents and also less likelihood of being held up by bandits or armed gangs.

Four types of buses are used:
• small buses (*busetas*) for 22 passengers, which have cramped leg room and are not very comfortable;
• larger buses (*buses*), which have more space;
• luxury buses (*autobuses de lujo*), serving routes between major cities;
• trucks with roofs, open sides, and wooden plank seats, called *chivas* or *rancheros*, which are found mainly around the coast.

Buses from Quito

Long-distance buses leave mainly from the Terminal Terrestre in the

southern Villa Flora district, at Maldonado and Cumandá. There are about two dozen bus companies with offices at the terminal. It is worthwhile booking in advance. Take great care in this bus terminal, as it's a well-known spot for theft and confidence tricksters. There are also private companies that operate more comfortable buses from terminals in the New Town.

There are many buses a day to major destinations, including Ambato (3 hours), Bahía de Caráquez (8 hours), Baños (3½ hours), Coca (12 hours), Cuenca (9–14 hours), Guaranda (5 hours), Guayaquil (8 hours), Lago Agrio (10 hours), Latacunga (2 hours), Loja (14–18 hours), Machala (11 hours), Manta (8 hours), Portoviejo (8 hours), Puyo (7 hours), Riobamba (4 hours), Santo Domingo (2½ hours), Tena (9 hours), Esmeraldas (6 hours), Otavalo (2½ hours), Ibarra (2½ hours), and Tulcán (5½ hours).

There are no direct buses to Peru or Colombia. **Reytur** (E. Gangotena 158 and Orellana; tel: 02-256 5299/254 6674) runs an "international" bus to Lima, but this involves a change at the border. **Ormeño Internacional** (Los Shyris N34-432 and Portugal, opposite Parque la Carolina; tel: 02-246 0027) also offers services to Buenos Aires, Santiago, and Lima. It is cheaper to take a bus to Huaquillas, cross the border, and take a *taxi colectivo* to Tumbes in Peru, where regular buses connect with Lima.

Panamericana (Av. Colón and Reina Victoria; tel: 02-250 1585) operates a deluxe service from Quito to Huaquillas and other cities in Ecuador. Both Panamericana and Reytur offer services to Colombia, but this again involves changing buses at the border, and is not always the cheapest option.

Buses from Esmeraldas

There is no central bus terminal in Esmeraldas. **Aerotaxi**, the fastest line, leaves for Quito from the main plaza (journey time 5 hours, frequent departures); **Panamericana** has a luxury service to Quito once a day, leaving from Hotel Casino; **Transportes Occidentales** and **Trans-Esmeraldas**, Av. Piedrahita 200, operate slower buses (to Quito 7 hours, Santo Domingo 3½ hours, Guayaquil 9 hours, Machala 12 hours); **Cooperativa Sudamericana** runs buses to Ambato (8 hours), Reina del Camino to Portoviejo (9 hours), and Bahía de Caráquez (8 hours).

Provincial buses leave from La Costenita, or the waterfront area (Atacames and Súa 1 hour, Muisné 3½ hours). Frequent departures. Buses run also to La Tola (3 hours). The road is good until Río Verde; there is a combined bus/boat service to San Lorenzo.

Buses from Cuenca

All long-distance buses leave from the Terminal Terrestre on Avenida España, northwest of the city center. Destinations include Riobamba (5½ hours), Ambato (7½ hours), Quito (10½ hours), Loja (5–6 hours), Guayaquil (4 hours), Macas (10 hours), and Gualaquiza (6 hours).

Buses from Guayaquil

The Terminal Terrestre is near the airport and the bridge over the Río

Passport Checks

On buses, always carry your passport with you. There are police checks on all the roads leading out of main towns, and you can get into serious trouble if you are unable to present your documents when requested.

Guayas, and all long-distance buses leave from here. Destinations are: Quito (8½ hours), Cuenca (5 hours), Riobamba (5 hours), Santo Domingo de los Colorados (5 hours), Manta (3 hours), Esmeraldas (8 hours), Portoviejo (3½ hours), Bahía de Caráquez (5½ hours), Machala (3½ hours), Huaquillas (5 hours), Ambato (6½ hours), and Alausí (4 hours). There are also frequent buses to Salinas (2½ hours) and Playas/General Villamil (2 hours). There is a shared-taxi service to Machala (2½ hours) leaving from next door to the Hotel Rizzo, Downtown.

By Rail

When the Guayaquil–Quito railway line was completed in 1908, it cut the travel time between the two cities from 12 days to 12 hours. Today the rail system is more of a tourist attraction than a commercial link, as much of the network has fallen into disrepair because of mudslides, flooding, and lack of government funding. There are now four train journeys available in Ecuador: Quito–Latacunga–Quito; Riobamba–Alausí–Sibambe–Alausí; Ibarra–'Primer Paso'; and irregularly, San Lorenzo–El Progreso. For further information

on these, contact La Empresa de Ferrocarriles Ecuatorianos (EFE), tel: 02-258 5710; www.efe.gov.ec, or the local tourist information office.

The Devil's Nose section of the Riobamba–Sibambe route is one of the most spectacular train rides in the world, famous for its spectacular switchback. The train from Riobamba to Sibambe departs on Wednesday, Friday, and Sunday at 6.30am.

Metropolitan Touring (see page 353) operates its own Chiva Express service, a comfortable, converted bus with toilets, a bar, and space for 34 passengers. The Chiva Express (www.chivaexpress.com) runs one- and two-day tours departing from Quito.

Quito's train station is 2km (1 mile) south of the center, on Avenida P. Vicente Maldonado near Llanganates (tel: 02-265 6144). Trains run from here to Latacunga on Saturday and Sunday at 8am, returning at 6pm. Tickets cost $10 and can be bought in advance at Bolívar 443 and García Moreno (tel: 1-800-873 637) or on the day at the station.

By Air

Air transport is fairly well developed. The Oriente is the one area where airlines have virtually no competition from other forms of transport. There are many villages whose only contact with the rest of the country is by air; besides numerous small strips, 34 airports can handle bigger planes, some of them modern jet aircraft.

There are domestic flights between all the main cities. **LAN**, **AeroGal**, **Icaro**, and **TAME** connect Quito, Guayaquil, and Cuenca by jet service, with several flights daily each way. Flying time between Guayaquil and Quito is about 30 minutes. **TAME** flies from Quito to Esmeraldas, Manta, Portoviejo, Tulcan, and Loja (via Guayaquil), and from Guayaquil to

Domestic Airlines

AeroGal Av. Amazonas 7797 and Juan Holguín, Quito. Tel: 02-294 2800; Junin 440 and Córdova, Guayaquil. Tel: 04-231 0346; www.aerogal.com.ec
Icaro Palora 124 and Amazonas, Quito. Tel: 02-245 0928; José Joaquin de Olmedo Airport, Guayaquil. Tel: 04-263 0602.
TAME Av. Amazonas 1354 and Colón, Quito. Tel: 02-245 0928; Av. Fco de Orellana, Hotel Colón, Guayaquil. Tel: 04-269 2967; www.tame.com.ec

Machala. In the Amazon jungle Lago Agrio, Coca, and Macas are served.

There are military flights in the more remote Amazon areas but they are not generally available to foreign travelers. Air taxis (Cessnas or Bonanzas) can be rented. Small airlines' offices are found at the Guayaquil and Quito airports.

Flights to the Galápagos Islands are heavily booked, so you should confirm and reconfirm your seat and check in early at the airport, unless you have booked your cruise through an agency, in which case they will reconfirm for you.

TAME has two daily flights in the morning to Baltra, with connecting buses making the short trip to Puerto Ayora. Many cruises pick up their passengers directly at the airport and return them there. **TAME** and **AeroGal** both fly to San Cristóbal three times a week. Check carefully with the cruise operator which flight to book, as it can be quite difficult to travel between the islands.

All non-Ecuadorian travelers to the islands must pay a $110 entrance fee on arrival at the airport. Payment must be made in dollars and not by credit card. Keep the receipt: you may have to show it again.

There are also regular flights between some of the islands with **Emetebe**, a local airline, subject to demand. Tel: 05-252 0615. You will be restricted to luggage of 13kg (30lb) or less (non-negotiable). There are flights three times a week between Baltra and Isabela, as well as between Baltra and San Cristóbal.

With the exception of flying to the Galápagos Islands (which can cost $380–450 Quito–Galápagos return), domestic flights are fairly inexpensive (a return flight Quito–Guayaquil is about $80–100). Passengers are required to show up one hour before the departure of domestic flights, for baggage handling and check-in procedures. Many flights give marvelous views of the snow-capped Andes, so it is worth getting a window seat. Seats are given on a first-come, first-served basis.

By Boat

It is sometimes possible to travel some of the Pacific coast by boat. Check at the local capitanía del puerto (harbormaster's office) about boat departures (most often to Guayaquil and Manta).

Traveling by boat is the principal means of transport in the Amazon, and many lodges are only accessible by motorboat or canoe. The *Manatee Amazon Explorer* floating hotel (see page 223) offers a more luxurious way of visiting the area.

Cruises in the Galápagos

The Galápagos archipelago is almost entirely a national park, and no visitor is allowed to enter it without a qualified guide on an organized tour. There are a couple of ways that this can be done. Some travelers choose to take a series of different day trips from Puerto Ayora on Santa Cruz to the islands nearest that island, but, while this is cheap, it is not very satisfying (tour operators on the island will offer these kind of trips for about $50 a day). The great majority of visitors go on cruises around the islands, taking at least three nights; the more, the better. If you are going to spend the cash to come all this way, it is a pity to miss out or cut corners on one of the world's great travel experiences.

Large Cruises

For many, a trip on one of the largest cruisers is the most comfortable and convenient way to visit the islands. The *Galápagos Explorer II*, operated by **Canodros**, is the most luxurious of the boats touring the islands. Contact any travel agency that specializes in Latin America, or see www.canodros.com. The *Santa Cruz*, run by **Metropolitan Touring**, has all the comforts of a luxury liner, including excellent food. By traveling overnight, these cruisers can easily reach outer islands that smaller yachts sometimes struggle to get to. The going is smoother on a large ship as well.

Both boats are based in the Galápagos, taking around 90 passengers on three- or four-day cruises; one covers the northern islands, the other the southern. You can combine both trips to make a seven-day cruise. Passengers visit the islands in groups of 10 on motorboats (*pangas*) accompanied by English-speaking naturalist guides who all have university degrees in their fields.

The cost is between $300–400 per person per night on a twin-share basis (all inclusive, except for bar and air fare), depending on cabin and length of cruise.

Bookings for the *Santa Cruz* can be made at **Metropolitan Touring** in Quito or Guayaquil, or their US agents **Adventure Associates** (see page 353).

Smaller Yachts

Dozens of yachts carrying from eight to 20 people operate cruises around the islands. Most work out of Puerto Ayora, although a growing number are now based in Puerto Baquerizo Morena. The boats are categorized into five classes: luxury, first class, superior tourist, standard tourist, and economy class. Tours on them can be booked on the mainland from a number of agencies, or beforehand through a travel agency specializing in Latin America. **Quasar Naútica** (see page 353), for example, offers a selection of luxury yachts. These trips are more costly than on the larger cruises, but are also more intimate and allow more time on the islands. One of the most reliable companies offering both luxury small yachts and tourist-class yachts is **Enchanted Expeditions** (see page 353). They offer the *Beluga*, a luxury 16-person yacht and one cheaper option, the *Cachalote*.

Cheaper tours on small boats can also be arranged at places such as **Galasam Galápagos Tours** on 9 de Octubre 424 and Chile, Guayaquil, tel: 04-234 5446; www.galasam.com.ec. When booking in Quito or Guayaquil, expect to pay around $100–200 a day including food for a reasonable boat. Check with the South American Explorers Clubhouse in Quito (see page 123) for the latest reports on smaller operators to make sure you are not being ripped off.

Ecoventura operates a variety of cruises from three to seven nights, and can be booked in the US through **Galápagos Network**, 5805 Blue Lagoon Drive, Suite 160, Miami, FL 33126; tel: 305-262 6264; fax: 305-262 9609; www.ecoventura.com. One of the UK's leading dive specialists, **Scuba Safaris**, tel: 01342-851 196; www.scuba-safaris.com; have exclusive use of *Galápagos Aggressor I* and *II*.

Organizing Your Own Tour

There are many economy-class boats that can be booked in Quito quite cheaply or at the last minute. Dozens of backpackers turn up at Puerto Ayora and begin getting people together to charter a boat – if you look like a candidate, they are likely to stop you in the street and ask about your plans. The only drawback is that you need a few days to get the required number of people together and arrange a boat, so it's not a good idea to try to set it up in a hurry.

Boats take 8 or 12 people, and the cheapest cost from $60–80 a day with all meals but excluding tips for the crew. However, if your budget allows, it

Foreign Exchange

If you are flying to Quito or Guayaquil and straight on to the Galápagos Islands, and taking a tour on one of the large cruise ships, exchange facilities are available. Independent travelers can change foreign currency in Puerto Ayora, but at a poor rate, so bring whatever you need in dollars from the mainland.

is worth paying for a more expensive boat, as the cabins are likely to be bigger, the food better, and the guides more informed. The South American Explorers Club (see page 123) keeps lists of reports from travelers indicating which of the many boats are the best, and offers the following hints for travelers doing this:
• Boat owners like to fill their boats to capacity. The group is usually expected to share the cost of any unsold passenger space.
• When dealing directly with the boat owner, bargaining is expected.
• Bottled drinks are not included in the cost of the cruise. Bring as much mineral water as you think you will need; it is sold at the Puerto Ayora supermarket (at the docks).
• Boat travel to outer islands such as Española and Genovesa can be quite rough, especially from September to November.
• Make sure the boats have enough sets of snorkeling gear. The water is cold from July to December and wetsuits are recommended.

Traveling between the Islands

INGALA (Instituto Nacional de Galápagos) has official inter-island passenger services between Santa Cruz, San Cristóbal, Isabela, and Floreana, as well as services between Puerto Ayora and San Cristóbal. The INGALA office in Puerto Ayora is next to the hospital, tel: 05-252 6199. In Puerto Baquerizo Moreno on San Cristóbal, it is on the road leading inland at the edge of the town, tel: 05-252 0133.

Alternatively, if you can be flexible, check with the *capitanía del puerto* (harbormaster's office) for details of other boats, such as the converted cargo ship *Estrella de Mar*. This travels from Isabela to Santa Cruz. The trip takes between six and seven hours. To move from Santa Cruz to Isabela or San Cristóbal you can also pay a private speedboat to take you to the other islands. Try to negotiate a price, especially if there are several of you.

A CCOMMODATIONS

HOTELS, YOUTH HOSTELS, BED AND BREAKFAST

Hotels

The country has no shortage of hotels, but luxury options are limited to Quito, Guayaquil, Cuenca, the resort areas of Esmeraldas and Santa Elena, and first-class jungle lodges in the Oriente. Most other areas rely on more basic country inns *(hosterías)*, *pensiones*, or *residenciales*. In high season (June to September in the Sierra, December to January on the coast), during fiestas, and the night before market days (in Otavalo particularly), finding accommodations can be difficult, so it is worth making a reservation; at other times just turn up.

A room in a luxury hotel might cost $150–300 a night; in a first-class hotel, $60–150, while a double room with private bath in a comfortable *residencial* can be had for $20–35. Decent backpacker hotels with shared bathrooms are generally around $10 per person in even the remotest areas. In most places, apart from budget hotels and hostels, service (10 percent) and tax charges (12–14 percent) will be added to the bill.

If you have little Spanish, it may be easier to arrange accommodation as a package through a tour operator or local travel agency.

The rates for jungle lodges usually include room, meals, and all tours and activities. Such packages are usually from 3–7 days; per-day rates may range from $80, in the cheapest backpacker lodges, to $250 or more.

Camping

Camping is a cheap and popular option in many coastal areas, and most campsites provide access to bathrooms and running water. In the Galápagos, there are three official sites on the island of Santa Cruz: near the Darwin Research Station, at Tortuga Bay, and near the *caseta* in the tortoise reserve.

ACCOMMODATIONS LISTINGS

QUITO

Amaranta
Leónidas Plaza N20-32 and Jorge Washington; tel: 02-254 3619
Luxurious apartments with their own kitchens. On-site bar and restaurant.
Antinea Apart Hotel
Juan Rodríguez 175 and Diego de Almagro; tel: 02-250 6839
www.hotelantinea.com
Located on a quiet street in the Mariscal Sucre district, this delightful hotel offers individually decorated rooms and apartments, some of which have access to a terrace or private garden. It's filled with touches that make this feel more like a creative, stylish home than a hotel.

Café Cultura
Jorge Washington and Ulpiano Paez; tel: 02-222 4271
www.cafecultura.com
A converted mansion, surrounded by gardens, which mixes traditional English-style decor with trendy touches. Serves great breakfasts. **$$$**
El Cafecito
Luís Cordero 1124 and Reina Victoria; tel: 02-223 4862
www.cafecito.net
A friendly hotel with shared rooms in a great central location in the New Town. Excellent café downstairs, with live music on weekends.
$$

La Casa Sol
José Calama 127 and Av. 6 de Diciembre; tel: 02-223 0798
www.lacasasol.com
Beautiful Casa Sol has balconies, gardens, courtyards, and a warm, welcoming atmosphere. Internet and breakfast are included in the price of your cozy room with cheery Andean decor. Has a sister hotel in Otavalo. **$$–$$$**
Crossroads Cafe & Hostal
Mariscal Foch 678 (E5-23) and Juan León Mera; tel: 02-223 4735
www.crossroadshostal.com
This is one of the cheapest places to stay in Quito that's still quite salubrious. It's set in a remodeled house and

has a restaurant, use of kitchen, and terraces. **$**

PRICE CATEGORIES

Price categories are per night for a double room:
$ = under $35
$$ = $35–60
$$$ = $60–150
$$$$ = more than $150

ABOVE: refreshment served in the garden of the Café Cultura.

Hacienda Rumiloma
Obispo Díaz de la Madrid s/n;
tel: 02-254 8206
www.haciendarumiloma.com
Just a short taxi ride above
the heart of Quito, this
boutique hotel nestles in a
green gully overlooking the
city. Richly decorated rooms,
excellent food and friendly
service make this a
wonderful oasis. **$$$$**

Hilton Colón
Av. Amazonas and Patria;
tel: 02-256 3903
www.hilton.com
A typically luxurious Hilton
with five good restaurants,
shops, all business
services, and top-notch
sports/fitness facilities.
Some suites have wide
mountain views. All rooms
have cable TV and wireless
internet. Good disabled
facilities. **$$$$**

Hotel Caiman
Juan Rodríguez 270 and Reina
Victoria; tel: 02-256 7616
www.hotelcaymanquito.com
This is a clean, quiet haven
with a lovely garden, great
breakfasts, wireless internet
and friendly staff, situated
on one of the prettiest tree-
lined streets of La Mariscal
Sucre. **$$**

Hotel Patio Andaluz
García Moreno 652;
tel: 02-228 0830
www.hotelpatioandaluz.com
Located in the Old Town,
this beautiful colonial hotel
feels historic and yet has

mod-cons like wireless
internet. **$$$$**

Hotel Plaza Grande
García Moreno and Chile;
tel: 02-251 0777
www.plazagrandequito.com
This grand 16th-century
converted mansion
overlooks the Plaza de la
Independencia, and
everything about it is first
class. Suites are elegant
and luxurious; many
consider it to be the
country's best hotel. **$$$$**

Hotel Quito
Av. González Suárez 27-142;
tel: 02-254 4600
www.hotelquito.com.ec
Large but quiet hotel with
splendid views and pleasant
gardens, this classic old
Quito establishment
includes several restaurants
and bars, a nightclub, and a
heated pool. **$$$**

Hotel San Francisco
de Quito
Sucre 217 and Guayaquil;
tel: 02-295 1241
www.sanfranciscodequito.com.ec
In the heart of the Old Town,
this attractive hotel's split-
level rooms give onto a
central courtyard with a
fountain, so most are very
peaceful. Breakfast is
included. **$$**

Hotel Sebastián
Diego de Almagro 822 and Luís
Cordero; tel: 02-222 2400
www.hotelsebastian.com
This hotel's architecture
resembles a Swiss ski

chalet, which feels odd in
modern downtown Quito.
Rooms are comfortable, and
the restaurant good. **$$$**

Hotel Spas Termas
de Papallacta
Km 67, Vía Quito–Baeza;
tel: 02-256 8989
www.papallacta.com.ec
A range of cabins and rooms
set in the most luxurious
spa in the country, near a
popular hot spring 67km
(41½ miles) east of Quito.
$$$$

Magic Bean
Mariscal Foch 681 and Juan León
Mera; tel: 02-256 6181
www.themagicbeanquito.com
An attractive house in
Mariscal Sucre with a
choice of shared or private
rooms and an excellent
restaurant downstairs.
Breakfasts are included. **$**

Mansión del Ángel
Wilson ES-29 and Juan León Mera;
tel: 02-255 7721
The most elegant option in
Quito's New Town, this
gorgeous boutique hotel is
all antique furnishings,
lavish bedding and
polished wood floors, but
modern necessities like
wireless internet and
endless hot water have not
been forgotten. The
restaurant is excellent.
$$$–$$$$

Marriott
Av. Orellana 1172 and Av.
Amazonas; tel: 02-297 2040
www.marriott.com

City and volcano views add
to the resort feel of this very
large hotel. Rooms boast
the finest cotton bedding
and goose-feather quilts.
There is a choice of
Ecuadorian and inter-
national cuisine in the
restaurants. **$$$$**

Nü House Hotel
Plaza del Quinde; tel: 02-223 0567
This boutique hotel has
transformed the area
around Plaza del Quinde
(often known as Plaza Foch)
and offers style and modern
amenities for a reasonable
price. Modern Quito's most
popular restaurants, bars,
lounges, and discos are on
the doorstep. **$$$**

Le Parc
Av. República de El Salvador 34-348
and Irlanda; tel: 02-227 6800
www.leparc.com.ec
A cool hotel close to Parque
Carolina that is the hottest
spot for contemporary style
in the city. **$$$$**

Posada del Maple
Juan Rodríguez E8-49 and Av.6 de
Diciembre; tel: 02-254 4507
www.posadadelmaple.com
One of Quito's nicest backpacker hostels occupies this
rambling old house set on a
leafy Mariscal Sucre street.
Service and atmosphere are
very friendly, a big breakfast
is included, there is endless
hot water, and even wireless
internet. **$$**

La Rábida
La Rábida 227 and Santa María;
tel: 02-222 1720
www.hostalrabida.com
This old Quito home has
been converted into a small,
stylish boutique hotel with
just 11 rooms, friendly
service, and a homey feel.
There is wireless internet in
the common areas and staff
are multilingual. Breakfasts
included. **$$–$$$**

Sheraton Four Points
Av. Naciones Unidas and Av.
República del Salvador;
tel: 02-297 0002
www.sheraton.com
Very modern and
comfortable hotel with all
the necessary amenities.
Popular with business
travelers. There's wireless
internet in every room and a
good menu on offer. **$$$**

THE NORTH

Otavalo

Casa Mojanda
Near Lagunas de Mojanda;
tel: 09-973 1737
www.casamojanda.com
This family-friendly homestead has a peaceful countryside setting, 10 minutes' drive – or one hour's walk – from Otavalo. Accommodation is homely and comfortable, meals are taken together with the family and other guests, and there's bike or horse riding, endless hiking, or visits to the nearby *lagunas* to keep you occupied. **$$**

La Casa Sol
Cascada de Peguche, 3km (2 miles) northeast of Otavalo; tel: 02-223 0798 (Quito)
www.lacasaandina.com
Charming Andean-style hotel built with clay tiles, volcanic stones, and plenty of color, located near the Cascada de Peguche protected forest, at Peguche, 3km (2 miles) north of Otavalo. **$$**

Hacienda Cusín
San Pablo de Lago, Imbabura (15 minutes south of Otavalo); tel: 06-291 8013
www.haciendacusin.com
A historic hotel set in beautiful grounds in rural surroundings with stunning views of the Imbabura volcano, this gorgeous place has been decorated with incredible attention to detail. There are various styles of room and suite, as well as garden cottages. A whole constellation of activities are on offer for guests here: from riding to rose farm visits to volcano climbing. **$$$**

Hacienda Pinsaquí
Panamericana Norte, Km 5; tel: 06-294 6116
www.haciendapinsaqui.com
From the moment you pull up at the grand, tree-bordered turning circle of this 1790 estate, you feel like you have stepped back to the colonial era. Pinsaquí offers luxurious guest accommodation in classily decorated suites – most with fireplaces – and

the house is still furnished with its original antiques. There's excellent horseback riding on the estate and farther afield. **$$$**

Hacienda Zuleta
Angochagua, near Otavalo; tel: 06-266 2182
www.zuleta.com
Surely one of the most exquisite haciendas in the Andes, Zuleta absorbs guests in nearly 500 years of history and a welcoming family atmosphere. But this is no ordinary family: it's produced two much-loved presidents of Ecuador. The historic hacienda is set in its own secluded valley where guests can walk, ride horses, spot condors, and participate in the life of this working farm. **$$$**

Cotacachi

Polylepis Lodge
El Ángel, Ibarra; tel: 06-295 4009
www.polylepislodge.com
Stay in rustic stone and timber cottages, set in a

secluded valley thick with ancient polylepis forest. The lodge is on the doorstep of the Reserva Ecológica El Ángel, where you can hike and horseback-ride to your heart's content. **$**

La Mirage Garden Hotel and Spa
Cotacachi; tel: 06-291 5237
www.mirage.com.ec
This is a stylish, contemporary resort built on the grounds of a 200-year-old hacienda. Set in lovely gardens filled with hummingbirds, the hotel has excellent facilities including a spa, pool, gym, fine dining, and luxurious rooms. **$$$$**

CENTRAL HIGHLANDS

Cotopaxi

Hacienda El Porvenir
Machachi, Cotopaxi; tel: 02-223 1806 (Quito)
www.tierradelvolcan.com
A high-altitude hacienda with both simple rooms with shared bathroom, and more luxurious accommodation with en suites. Activities range from volcano climbs to zip-lining over a nearby canyon. **$–$$$**

Quilotoa Crater Lake Lodge
Lake Quilotoa, 10km (6 miles) north of Zumbahua; tel: 09-717 5780
Amazing location on the edge of the the Quilotoa volcano crater. The lodge has a cozy, rustic feel with log fires, wooden furniture, and candles. Rooms are clean and warm and all have private bathrooms. **$$**

San Augustín de Callao
Lasso, Cotopaxi; tel: 03-271 9160
www.incahacienda.com
This incredible hotel is partly built within the walls of an Inca temple; has pretty, historic rooms; an excellent restaurant; and all sorts of outdoor activities. **$$$**

Ambato

Ambato Hotel
Guayaquil 1801 and Rocafuerte; tel: 03-242 1791
www.hotelambato.com
This modern hotel in the city center is popular for its casino. Rooms are clean and comfortable, the restaurant and bar are bustling, and there's 24-hour room service. **$$**

Hacienda Leito
Km 8 on the road to Baños; tel: 03-285 9329
www.haciendaleito.com

A beautifully restored Jesuit hacienda that has stunning views of Tungurahua; spacious, elegant rooms; a pool and spa set in lovely grounds; and a host of activities, like white-water rafting, on offer. **$$$**

Baños

Hostal La Posada del Arte
Calle Ibarra and Av. Montalvo; tel: 03-274 0083
www.posadadelarte.com
Decorated with great flare and sense of color, this sweet little hotel has cozy rooms, fantastic food, and is close to Baños's thermal baths, but out of the noisy center. **$$–$$$**

Luna Runtun
Caserío Runtun, Km 6; tel: 03-274 0882
www.lunaruntun.com
Swiss-run luxury spa hotel that is hands down the best

in Baños, set on a steep hillside above the town; it's bathed in a real sense of tranquillity. You can soak in the miraculous thermal waters here in private luxury, while you also soak up the incredible views. **$$$$**

PRICE CATEGORIES

Price categories are per night for a double room:
$ = under $35
$$ = $35–60
$$$ = $60–150
$$$$ = more than $150

TRANSPORTATION

ACCOMMODATIONS

EATING OUT

ACTIVITIES

A – Z

LANGUAGE

La Petite Auberge
16 de Diciembre 240 and Montalvo; tel: 03-274 0936
http://banios.com/lepetit/hotel2.htm
Set back off the street in pretty gardens, this hotel has neat and simple rooms, plenty of hot water, and an on-site French restaurant that is said to be the best in Baños. This option is a great, central retreat from the noisy downtown Baños. **$$**

Sangay Spa-Hotel
Plazoleta Isidro Ayora 100; tel: 03-274 0490
www.sangayspahotel.com
This is an old Baños favorite that has had a good modern upgrade. Choose from accommodation in cheaper cabins or fancier executive rooms. There's a private swimming pool in the spa, but the temperature is much cooler than the

steaming public pools across the road. **$$–$$$**

Riobamba

Hacienda Abraspungo
Km 3.5 Vía Riobamba–Guano; tel: 03-294 0820
www.haciendaabraspungo.com
There are comfortable, modern rooms at this converted country estate in pretty countryside close to Riobamba. All sorts of activi-

ties are on offer: volcano climbing, naturally, but where else can you take polo or bullfighting classes? **$$$**

La Estación
Unidad Nacional 29-15 and Carabobo; tel: 03-295 5226
Excellent colonial building with all modern amenities just beside the train station. There's a good restaurant downstairs and the helpful staff can arrange tours. **$**

SOUTHERN SIERRA

Cuenca

Casa del Barranco
Calle Larga 841 and Luís Cordero; tel: 07-283 9763
Basic rooms with private baths and cable TV set around a garden-filled courtyard in a restored colonial house overlooking the Río Tomebamba. **$**

El Conquistador
Gran Colombia 6-65; tel: 07-284 2888
www.hotelconquistador.com.ec
Located in the historical and commercial part of Cuenca, this hotel represents good value with basic but comfortable rooms that are all noise-protected. **$$–$$$**

El Dorado
Gran Colombia 787 and Luís Cordero; tel: 07-283 1390
This is a modern, slick business hotel with recently renovated rooms; smart public areas; and a disco, sauna, cafeteria; as well as an excellent restaurant. You can tap into wireless internet throughout. **$$$**

Hotel Crespo
Calle Larga 7-93; tel: 07-284 2571
www.hotel-crespo.com
Great variety of rooms, all very clean and cozy, with private bath, color TV, and central heating. Some rooms overlook the Río Tomebamba. The restaurant has an excellent reputation. **$$$**

Hotel Santa Lucía
Antonio Borrero 844 and Sucre; tel: 07-282 8000
www.santaluciahotel.com
This gorgeous boutique hotel set around an interior

courtyard in a converted republican-era home is perfect in every way. Beautifully furnished with antiques, it has all the comforts of a first-class establishment with the personalized service and relaxed feel of a small hotel. **$$$–$$$$**

Posada del Angel
Bolívar 14-011 and Estévez de Toral; tel: 07-284 2695
www.hostalposadadelangel.com
Set around central courtyards in a restored colonial house, this delightful hotel is surely one of the nicest places to stay in Cuenca. The rooms are immaculately clean and comfortable, the common areas bright and inviting, and the family that runs it endlessly helpful. Breakfasts are included, and there's an excellent Italian restaurant on site. Highly recommended. **$$**

Mansión Alcázar
Bolívar 12-55 and Tarquí; tel: 07-282 3918
www.mansionalcazar.com
Sophisticated boutique hotel set in a colonial building with exquisite Republican-era furniture and decor. Each room is furnished uniquely. A truly elegant and luxurious small hotel with an upscale restaurant and service to match. **$$$–$$$$**

Oro Verde
Av. Ordóñez Lazo s/n; tel: 07-409 0000
www.oroverdehotels.com
This is a smart, first-class hotel situated on the banks

of the Río Tomebamba, out of town, by a lake with rowing boats. A large hotel, it has an excellent restaurant, La Cabaña Suiza. There is also a heated open-air swimming pool, gymnasium, Turkish bath, and massage room. **$$$**

Around Cuenca

Hostería Durán
Av. Ricardo Durán; tel: 07-283 2069
www.hosteriaduran.com
An inviting spa hotel in the suburb of Baños just outside Cuenca, this establishment has comfortable rooms set around thermal pools and Turkish steam baths. The restaurant is top-notch. **$$–$$$**

Hostería Uzhupud
32km (20 miles) from Cuenca on the Via Paute; tel: 07-225 0339
This beautiful colonial building under a pantile roof has a wonderful setting has luxurious rooms. They also serve excellent food. A 45-minute journey from Cuenca by taxi. **$$$**

Ingapirca

Posada Ingapirca
Next to the site of the Ingapirca ruins, west of Cañar; tel: 07-283 1120
This is a beautifully peaceful spot outside the village of Ingapirca and a short stroll from the ruins. Enjoy relaxing in the sunny garden, where hummingbirds fly, and

the sumptuous, fireside breakfasts in the colonial homestead. **$$–$$$**

Loja

Hotel Libertador
Colón 14-30 and Bolívar; tel: 07-257 8278
www.hotellibertador.com.ec
The best hotel in Loja's city center, with comfortable modern rooms, a swimming pool and the good La Castellana Restaurant. **$$–$$$**

Vilcabamba

Hostería Izhcayluma
2km (1 mile) out of town on Zumba road; tel: 07-264 0095
www.izhcayluma.com
This friendly hotel and restaurant are on a hillside just out of town and have a gorgeous panoramic view of the Vilcabamba Valley. They offer all kinds of accommodation, from backpacker to lovely private cabins with balconies, hammocks, and views. The restaurant is also excellent and the helpful staff can arrange activities including horseback riding and bike trips. **$–$$**

ORIENTE

For more information on jungle lodges and destinations in the Oriente, see pages 223–233.

Baeza

Cabañas San isidro
Contact: Carrión N21-01 and Juan León Mera, Quito;
tel: 02-254 7403
www.sanisidrolodge.com
Surrounded by its own forest reserve, this beautiful lodge has modern amenities in rustic but comfortable cabins. Equally good territory for serious birders and wildlife enthusiasts, as those just looking for some deep-forest relaxation. **$$$$**

Lago Agrio

Gran Hotel del Lago
Via Quito, Km 1.5;
tel: 06-283 2415
Attractive hotel with a swimming pool, gardens, and a decent restaurant. **$$**

Reserva Cuyabeno

Jamu Lodge
Calama E6-19 and Reina Victoria;
tel: 02-222 0614
www.cabanasjamu.com
The name Jamu is derived from the Siona word for armadillo, and this is just one of the species that you may see here in the heart of

the Cuyabeno Reserve. There are nine cabins at this lodge, built in traditional rustic style and lit with kerosene lamps. The ethos is very eco-friendly and the surrounding wildlife is keen to be spotted. **$$$**

Around Tena

Cabañas Aliñahui
Contact: Inglaterra 1373 and Av. Amazonas, Edificio Centro Ejecutivo, 7th floor, Quito;
tel: 02-227 4510
www.ecuadoramazonlodge.com
Comfortable lodge on the Río Napo in 200 hectares (500 acres) of primary and secondary forest with well-marked trails. Also known as the Butterfly Lodge due to the abundance of butterfly species in the area. **$$**

Cofán Village
Contact: Fundación para la Sobrevivencia del Pueblo Cofán, Mariano Cardenal N74 and Joaquín Mancheno, Quito;
tel: 02-247 0946
www.cofan.org
Conservation-friendly accommodation in traditional thatched cabins in a village of the Cofán indigenous group. **$**

Jatun Sacha
Contact: Pasaje Eugenio de Santillán and Maurián, Quito;
tel: 02-243 2240
www.jatunsacha.org
Eight conservation-friendly

cabins that use solar energy, overlooking the Río Napo. **$$$**

Sacha Lodge
Contact: Julio Zaldumbide 375 and Valladolid, Quito;
tel: 02-250 9504/8872
www.sachalodge.com
Beautiful 26-room lodge set on a 2,000-hectare (5,000-acre) private reserve near Lago Pilchicocha. The lodge has an aerial walkway where you can get spectacular views above the treetops, or you can watch the jungle world pass by from your hammock. **$$$$**

La Selva
Contact: Av. Mariana de Jesús E7-211 and La Pradera, Quito;
tel: 02-254 5425
www.laselvajunglelodge.com
Rustic yet cozy lodge made of secondary forest materials and set amid primary rainforest. A good option for families. They do four- to six-day packages. **$$$$**

Yachana Lodge
Contact: Vicente Solano E1261 and Av. Oriental, Quito;
tel: 02-252 3777
www.yachana.com
Lovely lodge two hours downriver from the town of Coca (see below). Stays help fund community development projects organized by the Yachuna Foundation in the local area. Packages vary from four or five days.

Community visits are a highlight here. **$$$**

Coca

El Auca
Napo and García Moreno;
tel: 06-288 0600
This is the best hotel in Coca and has a variety of accommodations, ranging from basic wooden cabins to quite luxurious modern rooms, all, importantly, with air conditioning. **$$**

Around Shell

Kapawi Ecolodge
Edificio Reina Victoria, Oficina 1 Mariscal Foch E7-38 y Reina Victoria;
tel: 02-600 9333
www.kapawi.com
One of the most isolated and stunning eco-lodges in the world, set on the Río Pastaza on the border with Peru. Here you will not only experience the jungle, but also the culture of the Achuar people in whose territory the lodge lies. **$$$$**

WESTERN LOWLANDS

Santo Domingo de los Colorados

Diana Real
29 de Mayo and Loja;
tel: 02-275 1380;
fax: 02-275 4091

PRICE CATEGORIES

Price categories are per night for a double room:
$ = under $35
$$ = $35–60
$$$ = $60–150
$$$$ = more than $150

Despite a rather noisy location on a principal street, this hotel has clean, modern rooms with private bathrooms, hot water, and cable TV. **$**

Tinalandia
Contact: Urbanización El Bosque, Segunda Etapa, Av. del Parque, Calle Tercera, Quito;
tel/fax: 02-244 9028
www.tinalandia.com
Hacienda with small chalets and modern amenities. The surrounding

area is one of the best places in Ecuador for bird- and butterfly-watching. **$$$**

Quevedo

Río Palenque
45km (30 miles) from Santo Domingo on the Quevedo Road;
tel: 04-220 8680 (Guayaquil)
The research station here has a charming lodge with room for 20 guests. The surrounding area has

superb lowland scenery with great opportunities for bird-watching and botanizing. **$$$**

PACIFIC COAST

Esmeraldas

Apart Hotel Esmeraldas
Av. Libertad 407 and Tello;
tel: 06-272 8700
Apartments here have
private bathrooms with
plentiful hot water, air
conditioning, and TV. There
is also a good restaurant,
and the establishment is
centrally located. **$$**

Costa Verde
Luís Tello 809 and Hilda Padilla,
Las Palmas; tel: 06-272 8714
This high-rise establishment
on the beach offers
comfortable, modern suites.
There is air conditioning, a
pool, and a pleasant res-
taurant. Recommended. **$$**

Hostería Pura Vida
Vía Palestina, just south of Río
Verde; tel: 06-274 4274
This is a peaceful budget
hostel on a deserted beach,
with a restaurant and bar.
Fishing tours on offer. **$**

Hotel Cayapas
Av. Kennedy 401 and Váldez;
tel: 06-272 1318
This hotel is set in a
transformed colonial
mansion, filled with paintings
by local artists. Rooms are
sunny and comfortable, and
the restaurant serves great
seafood. **$$**

Atacames

Hotel Club del Sol
Av. Universitaria Oe5-284 and
18 de Septiembre;
tel: 06-731 281/730 140
www.hotelclubdelsol.com
This hotel is a comfortable
beachfront resort with a large
pool area and a number of
restaurants and bars. Rooms

are brightly colored and well
looked after. **$$$**

Villas Arco Iris
Tel: 06-273 1069
The villas are a collection of
slightly rustic, whitewashed
and thatched *cabañas*, set
in a lush tropical garden
with a pool close by. The
restaurant serves excellent
seafood. **$$$**

Same

**Casablanca Beach Hotel
and Golf Club**
Contact: Club Casablanca, Av.
República del Salvador 780 and
Portugal, Quito; tel: 02-225 2077
This is a smart golf club
resort, built in "Greek villa"
style. There are other
sporting facilites apart from
golf, including a pool and
tennis courts. **$$$**

Bahía de Caráquez

Hotel Italia
Bolívar and Checa; tel: 05-269 1137
A good mid-range option
with air conditioning and hot
water, a few streets back
from the bay. **$$**

Hotel La Piedra
Circunvalación and Bolívar;
tel: 1 888 790 5264
Set right on the beachfront,
this hotel has great ocean
views, a nice pool, and easy
access to the beach. **$$$**

Río Muchacho
Río Muchacho Valley, north of Bahía
de Caráquez; Contact: Guacamayo
Bahía Tours, Bolívar 902, and
Arenas, Bahía de Caráquez; tel:
05-269 1107/1412 (tel/fax)
Family-run organic farm with
cabin accommodation. A
host of activities are on offer,

including horseback riding,
chocolate-harvesting, and
talks on permaculture. You
can also feed the resident
sloth at night. Most guests
arrive on horseback. **$$**

Manta

Hotel Las Gaviotas
Malecón de Tarquí 1109;
tel: 05-262 0140
The ocean-view rooms are
the best ones at this clean,
pleasant hotel set around a
pool on the *malecón* at
Tarquí. There's a tennis
court and a good
restaurant/bar. **$$-$$$**

Hotel Manta Imperial
Malecón and Playa Murciélago;
tel: 05-621 955; fax: 05-623 016
There is a popular disco and
casino at this sprawling
beachfront hotel with
modern amenities. **$$$**

Oro Verde
Malecón and Calle 23; tel: 05-262
9200; www.oroverdehotels.com
This luxurious hotel – the
best in Manta – has a resort
atmosphere with a beach-
front location, pool, air
conditioned rooms, and
wireless internet. You can
order cocktails on the beach
or play the casino. **$$$**

Machalilla

Hostería Alandaluz
Ruta del Sol, Comunidad de Puerto
Rico; tel: 04-278 0690
www.alandaluz.com
Built mostly of bamboo and
palms, this hotel has a
serene setting with a village
feel, set just back from a
clean beach and surrounded
by gardens. Very eco-friendly

and has a great restaurant
and organic gardens. **$$**

Montañita

Baja Montañita
At the north end of the beach;
tel: 04-290 1107
www.bajamontanita.com.ec
A neat, whitewashed, resort
with spa facilities just a
stone's throw from the
beach. The smartest place
to stay in Montañita. **$$$**

Charo's Hostel
On the Malecón; tel: 04-319 2222
www.charoshostal.com
In the heart of all the action,
this is the best-value choice
in the town center. This
hostel is built like a mini-
resort, set around a pool and
Jacuzzi, with hammocks in
the garden. **$$**

Manglaralto

Hotel Manglaralto
1 block from the plaza;
tel: 04-290 1369
Good-value hotel with ocean
views in a tranquil setting.

Hotel Manglaralto Sunset
Next door to Hotel Manglaralto;
tel: 04-244 0797
A few clean, quiet rooms
with small patios and
hammocks, just away from
the beach. **$**

SOUTH COAST

Guayaquil

Dreamkapture
Sixto Juan Bernal, Manzana 2, and
Benjamín Carrión; tel: 04-224 2909
www.dreamkapture.com
Canadian/Ecuadorian-run
hostal with a variety of
rooms and helpful, friendly
staff. There are cooking

facilities, wireless internet, a
safe storeroom for left
luggage, and a free info desk
that gives advice on trips in
and around the city. **$**

Four Points Sheraton
Av. Constitución and Plaza del Sol;
tel: 04-269 1888
www.sheraton.com
A large, business-oriented

hotel in a convenient
location beside the Mall del
Sol and a few minutes from
the airport. **$$$**

Hilton Colón
Av. Francisco Orellana Manzana
111; tel: 04-268 9000
www.hilton.com
Largest and most luxurious
hotel in the area, close to

Guayaquil's airport. There are elegant rooms, three restaurants and a coffee shop, gym, pool, and spa. **$$$$**

Hotel Palace
Av. 9 de Octubre and García Moreno; tel: 04-232 7999
www.oroverdehotels.com
The cavernous marble lobby sets the elegant tone of this smart, award-winning hotel. Very comfortable rooms with air conditioning, TV, and minibar. There are several restaurants serving international cuisine and Swiss dishes, plus a swimming pool and fitness center. **$$$$**

Hotel Orilla del Rio
Ciudadela Entrerios, Calle Septima 8 and Av. Río Guayas; tel: 04-283 5394
www.orilladelrio.com.ec
A beautiful boutique hotel set around a peaceful courtyard with an excellent restaurant. The spotless rooms have crisp, white sheets, and tasteful decoration. Helpful staff man this quiet, safe haven away from the bustle of the city. **$$–$$$**

Oro Verde
Chile 214, between Vélez and Luque; tel: 04-231 1080
www.hotelpalaceguayaquil.com.ec

Centrally located hotel with clean, air-conditioned rooms, a restaurant, laundry, and travel agency. **$$$**

Ramada
Malecón 606; tel: 04-256 5555
www.hotelramada.com
Very nice rooms, some with view of the Guayas River. Excellent restaurant, indoor swimming pool, discotheque, and casino. **$$$**

Tangara Guest House
Block F, House 1, Mañuela Sáenz and O'Leary; tel: 04-228 2828
www.tangara-ecuador.com
Friendly, family-run guesthouse situated between the airport and bus terminal in Ciudadela Bolivariana. A peaceful retreat from Downtown. **$$**

Playas

Hostería Bellavista
Data Highway, Km 2; tel: 04-276 0600
www.hosteriabellavista.net
Swiss-run hotel with air conditioning, swimming pool, and beachfront bungalow suites. **$$$**

La Libertad

Puerto Lucía Yacht Club
Av. Puerto Lucía; tel: 04-278 3180

www.puertolucia.com.ec
Large-scale resort and yacht club with pools, tennis courts, restaurants, water sports, hotels, and condos. You hardly need to leave the hotel, except to saunter down to the beach. **$$$**

Samarina Hotel
9 de Octubre and 10 de Agosto; tel: 04-278 5167; fax: 04-784 100
Basic bungalows with clean, comfortable rooms within walking distance of the beach. Pleasant swimming pool area. **$$**

Salinas

Barceló Colón Miramar
Malecón, between la 38 and la 40; tel: 04-277 1610
www.barcelocolonmiramar.com
A high-rise resort hotel on the beach with a wide range of amenities. One of the leading hotels on South America's Pacific coast. **$$$$**

El Carruaje
Malecón 517; tel: 04-277 0214
Great mid-range hotel located on the *malecón*, close to the best of Salinas's restaurants and nightlife. The rooms are clean and classy with air conditioning, cable TV, hot water, and a good restaurant. Ocean-view

rooms cost more, but breakfast is included. **$$**

Hotel Francisco I
Calle Enríquez and Rumiñahui; tel: 04-277 4106
A pleasant small hotel one block back from the beach, set around a courtyard with a pool. Rooms are simple but clean, and there is a good café on site. **$**

Hotel Punta Carnero
Malecón, between la 20 and la 22; tel: 04-294 8477
Nice mid-range choice, close to the beach with air conditioning, pool, good restaurant, and a resort feel without a high price. **$$$**

Yulee
Av. Segunda and Calle 14; tel: 04-277 2028
Basic hotel with a range of rooms in a good location at Diagonal Iglesia Central. There's a pleasant courtyard where you can sit in the sun, and a good restaurant is attached. **$**

Zaruma

Fina Gálvez
About 3km (2 miles) outside of Zaruma
Set on a coffee plantation with an orchid garden. A good place to stay. **$$$**

THE GALÁPAGOS ISLANDS

Santa Cruz

Fernandina
Av. 18 de Febrero and Marchena, Puerto Ayora; tel: 05-252 6499
Reasonable prices, friendly management. **$**

Finch Bay Eco Hotel
Barrio Punta Estrada s/n; tel: 05-252 6297; www.finchbayhotel.com
Situated at the opposite side of Academy Bay and accessible only by boat. First-class eco-hotel near the beach. **$$$$**

Hotel Red Booby
Av. Plazas and Charles Binford, Puerto Ayora; tel: 05-252 6485
www.hotelredbooby.com.ec
A beautiful hotel with spacious rooms and modern amenities. Staff can arrange boat tours and a number of water sports. **$$$$**

Hotel Silberstein
Av. Charles Darwin and Piqueros, Puerto Ayora; tel: 05-252 6066
www.hotelsilberstein.com
Comfortable hotel with good facilities. Only five minutes' walk from the Charles Darwin Research Station. **$$$**

Hotel Sol y Mar
Av. Charles Darwin and Binford, Puerto Ayora; tel: 05-252 6281
One of the best-known hotels in Puerto Ayora, where you share the terrace with iguanas. **$$**

Red Mangrove Adventure Inn
Av. Charles Darwin and Las Fragatas, Puerto Ayora; tel/fax: 05-252 6564/524 475
www.redmangrove.com
Quirky lodge with good rooms and interesting activities including

mountain biking and horseback riding. **$$$$**

Royal Palm Hotel
Via Baltra, Km 18; tel/fax: 05-252 7408/9
www.royalpalmgalapagos.com
This exclusive hideaway is set in the highlands of Santa Cruz and has 10 villas, eight studios, and three suites. Fine dining, spa treatments, and luxurious facilities in Ecuador's most expensive hotel. **$$$$**

Salinas
Islas Plaza, between Av. Charles Darwin and Tomas de Berlanga, Puerto Ayora; tel: 05-252 6107; fax: 05-526 072
Cheap and clean. **$**

Isabela

La Casa de Marita

Puerto Villamil; tel: 05-252 9238
www.galapagosisabela.com
Stylish boutique hotel with modern amenities on a very secluded island. **$$$$**

PRICE CATEGORIES

Prices categories are per night for a double room:
$ = under $35
$$ = $35–60
$$$ = $60–150
$$$$ = more than $150

TRANSPORTAION

ACCOMMODATIONS

EATING OUT

ACTIVITIES

A – Z

LANGUAGE

E ATING OUT

RECOMMENDED RESTAURANTS, CAFÉS, AND BARS

What to Eat

Ecuador has a rich and varied gastronomic culture, different from that of other Latin American countries. Ingredients and seasonings from other parts of South America and from Europe have blended to create some exciting tastes. The following local dishes are well worth trying:

Asado ("roasted"): generally means whole roasted pig.

Ceviche: raw seafood marinated in lemon, orange, and tomato juice and served with popcorn and sliced onions. Types of seafood include fish, shrimp, mussels, oysters, lobster, or octopus. Very popular on the coast and usually only eaten at lunchtime.

Cuy: whole roasted guinea pig is a traditional food dating back to Inca times. Not always served in fancy restaurants, but quite commonly at markets and street stands.

Empanadas de morocho: a delicious small pie stuffed with pork, fried, and served with hot sauce.

Empanadas de verde: a pie of green plantain, filled with cheese or meat.

Fanesca: a rich fish soup with beans, lentils, and corn. Eaten mainly during Easter week.

Humitas: a pastry (sweet or savory) made from *choclo* (corn), crumbled cheese, egg, and butter and wrapped in a corn husk.

Lechón hornado: roast suckling pig; a specialty of Sangolquí, near Quito.

Llapingachos: potato and cheese pancakes usually served with *fritada* (scraps of roast pork) and salad.

Locro: a yellow soup prepared from milk, stewed potatoes, and cheese, topped with an avocado. It may also contain watercress, meat, lentils, and pork skin.

Seco (stew): it can be based on *gallina* (hen), *chivo* (goat), or *cordero* (lamb) and is usually served with plenty of rice.

Tamales: a pastry dough made from toasted corn flour or wheat flour and filled with chicken, pork, or beef, wrapped in a leaf and steamed.

Tortillas de maíz: fried corn pancakes filled with mashed potato and cheese.

At the coast, seafood is very good. The most common fish are *corvina* (white sea bass), *camarones* (shrimp), and *langostas* (lobster). Look out for *encocada* (coconut) dishes, and the *sal prieta* of Manabí, a sauce of peanut butter and corn flour.

A surprisingly tasty dessert *(postre)* is *helados de paila*, ice cream made with fruit juice and beaten in a large brass pot *(paila)*, which is rotated in another pot filled with ice.

Where to Eat

Quito has a very good selection of restaurants, serving everything from local dishes to international cuisine. Surprisingly, there are few good restaurants in Guayaquil, apart from in the bigger hotels. In the provinces it is possible to eat well at reasonable prices. A restaurant need not be fancy to serve delicious and healthy food. Most of the best restaurants in Quito are in the New Town, around Amazonas, Colón, and 6 de Diciembre. There are several outdoor cafés along Amazonas where you can take in the sun and street life during the day.

In Quito and Guayaquil there are some very expensive restaurants, but in a good restaurant you can have a full meal for approximately $10–15 plus 20 percent service charge and tax. If you order a bottle of wine, however, the bill will be much higher,

because wine is imported. It is customary to leave an additional tip of 5–10 percent for the waiter if you have had especially good service.

Restaurants are open for lunch from noon until about 3pm. They often offer inexpensive "executive lunches." Many local *comedores* serve good, set three-course lunches *(menu del día)* for as little as $2.50. Dinner is from 7pm until midnight. In the evening, ordering is à la carte. Most restaurants are closed on Sunday or Monday, but hotel restaurants are open every day.

Drinking Notes

There is an amazing choice of juices *(jugos)* such as *mora* (blackberry), *naranja* (orange), *maracuya* (passion fruit), *naranjilla* (a local fruit tasting like bitter orange), and papaya. Beers like Pilsener, Club, and Loewenbrau are quite drinkable; all other beers are imported and rather expensive. The usual soft drinks are known as *gaseosas*, and the local brands are very sweet. The excellent mineral water is called Güitig (pronounced "gweetig") after the best-known brand.

Coffee is often served after meals. A favorite Ecuadorian way of preparing it is to boil it for hours until only a thick syrup remains. This is then diluted with milk and water. Instant coffee is common. Espresso machines are found only in the better hotels and in a very few restaurants and cafeterias.

Finally a word about alcoholic beverages: rum is cheap and good (often drunk with Coca-Cola in a *cuba libre*); tequila is also cheap; whiskey is fairly expensive; and imported wines (from Chile and Argentina) cost much more than they do in their country of origin. Local wines cannot be recommended.

RESTAURANT LISTINGS

QUITO

Cuban

La Bodeguita de Cuba
Reina Victoria 1721 and La Pinta;
tel: 02-254 2476
Good Cuban food served in
a pleasant atmosphere. $$

Ecuadorian and Fusion

La Boca del Lobo
José Calama 284 and Reina
Victoria; tel: 02-223 4083
Chic, fashionable vibes,
bright decor, Ecuadorian
and international fusion
dishes and a crowd of
beautiful people. $$

Café del Fraile
Pasaje Arzobispal, 2nd floor
(off the Plaza de Independencia);
tel: 02-251 0113
Highly recommended for
both lunch and dinner, this
excellent, welcoming
restaurant is set around an
interior courtyard just off the
Plaza de Independencia.
Their *locro* is a specialty. $$

Ceuce Wine Bar
Mall El Jardín, Av. Amazonas and
República; tel: 02-298 0259
Excellent fusion dishes in a
funky, elegant setting blank-
eted in white. The focus is
on the vast wine list. $$$

Mamá Clorinda
Reina Victoria 1144 and José
Calama; tel: 02-254 4362
One of the best choices in
Quito for traditional
Ecuadorian fare, this
restaurant often has live
music and is a good first
stop to familiarize yourself
with the local cuisine. $$

Su Cebiche
Juan León Mera 24-204 and José
Calama; tel: 02-252 6380
A great lunch spot serving
Manabí-style ceviches and
seafood in an unassuming
location in the Mariscal. $

Vista Hermosa
Calle Mejía 543 and García
Moreno; tel: 02-295 1401
www.vistahermosa.com.ec
This is the perfect place for
your first night's dinner in
the Old Town. The views are
spectacular, and the menu
and service are excellent.
Servings are large. $$

Zazu
Mariano Aguilera 331 and La
Pradera; tel: 02-254 3559
www.zazuquito.com
One of the leading New
Andean restaurants in
Ecuador, with a global wine
list. This is the ultra-hip
meeting place of Quito's
coolest. $$$

French

Rincón de Francia
General Roca 779 and 9 de Octubre;
tel: 02-255 4668/222 5053
www.rincondefrancia.com
This French restaurant has
been part of the Quito dining
establishment for a quarter
of a century and has an
excellent reputation for the
finest cuisine. Reservation
necessary. $$$

Greek

Café El Mosaico
Manuel Samaniego 8-95 and
Antepara, Itchimbía;
tel: 02-254 2871
This restaurant serves all
the regular Greek specialties
and has an extensive menu
of cocktails, but the real draw
here is the astounding view
from the hillside terrace
which seems to hang right
out over Quito's Old Town.
This is the perfect place to
sip an early-evening drink as
the lights begin to sparkle in
the valley below. $$

International

Magic Bean
Mariscal Foch 681 and Juan León
Mera; tel: 02-256 6181
Café/restaurant serving
coffee, brownies, pancakes,
felafel, salads, kebabs, and
pizzas. Great meeting place
with a pleasant, relaxed
atmosphere. $$

Magic Wrap and Garden Grill
Corner Mariscal Foch 476 and
Diego de Almagro;
tel: 02-252 7190
Same owners as the ever-
popular Magic Bean. Serves
wraps and *empanadas*, and
there's an outdoor Garden
Grill that is open in the evenings. They serve excellently
strong espresso. $

Mea Culpa
Palacio Arzobispal, Plaza de la
Independencia; tel: 02-295 1190
Perhaps the best and most
expensive restaurant in the
city, overlooking Plaza de
Independencia from the
Palacio Arzobispal, which
was constructed in 1545.
Serves an array of inter-
national and Mediterranean
dishes. $$$

Theatrum
Manabí, between Guayaquil and
Juan José Flores; tel: 02-257 1011
www.theatrum.com.ec
Set inside the Teatro
Nacional Sucre, this is one
of the hottest new
restaurants in the city, with
numerous creatively
prepared, contemporary
international dishes. $$$

Zocalo
José Calama 469 and Juan León
Mera; tel: 02-223 3929
Inexpensive terrace
restaurant and bar with a
wide menu of international
food and pleasantly
attentive service. $

Italian

Il Pizzaiolo
Juan León Mera 1012 and Mariscal
Foch; tel: 02-254 3900
Italian restaurant serving
delicious, inexpensive pasta
dishes and pizzas. A popular
spot that often gets quite
lively later in the evening. $

Il Risotto
Pinto 209 and Diego de Almagro;
tel: 02-222 0400
Authentic Italian cooking in
a pleasingly casual
atmosphere. They serve
great homemade pasta and
good tiramisu. $$

Local Dishes

Café del Tianguez
Sucre and Cuenca, below the
Iglesia de San Francisco;

PRICE CATEGORIES
Categories are based on the
cost of a meal for two
people, excluding wine:
$ = under $10
$$ = $10–30
$$$ = more than $30

BELOW: Mea Culpa overlooks the Plaza de la Independencia.

ABOVE: El Maíz restaurant, Cuenca.

tel: 02-257 0233
Ecuadorian specialities served in a casual, cozy atmosphere under dimmed lights and with an interesting ethnographic collection for decoration. **$**

Café Cultura
Robles 513 and Reina Victoria; tel: 02-222 4271
www.cafecultura.com
A beautiful hotel serving delicious breakfasts, with a dining room that is also open for lunch and afternoon English tea. Fireside dinners by reservation. **$$**

La Choza
12 de Octubre 1821 and Luís Cordero; tel: 02-223 0839
Among typical, rustic decoration from the Sierra, you can enjoy the best of traditional Ecuadorian cuisine. This restaurant has been in business for over 30 years, and is known as one of the best for Ecuadorian food in Quito.

El Cebiche
Juan León Mera 1232 and José Calama; tel: 02-252 6380
This elegant restaurant serves at least seven delicious varieties of ceviche and an array of seafood temptations. Lunchtime only. **$$**

El Pobre Diablo
Corner of Isabel la Católica E12-06 and Galavis; tel: 02-223 5194
www.elpobrediablo.com
A cool jazz bar/restaurant that serves an excellent

menú del día at lunchtime, and also has a good à la carte menu. Delicious Ecuadorian specialties cooked incredibly well, and several sorts of *piqueos* (snacks). **$$**

Las Redes
Av. Amazonas 845 and Veintimilla; tel: 02-252 5691
Las Redes – the nets (referring to the fishing nets used in the decoration) – serves some of the best seafood in Quito. Delicious ceviche and other seafood specialties are served by friendly staff in informal surroundings. Be sure to book: this is a small restaurant that often fills up. **$$**

Taberna Quiteña
Av. Amazonas 1259 and Luís Cordero; tel: 02-223 0009
There is a wide menu of good Ecuadorian food here, served in a lively atmosphere. The restaurant also hosts live entertainment. **$$ $$–$$$**

Oriental

Sake
Paul Rivet N30-166 and Whymper; tel: 02-252 4818
Very hip, upscale Japanese restaurant with a creative selection of sushi rolls, sashimi, and other Japanese dishes. Said to be the best sushi in Quito. Certainly a place to see and be seen amongst the smart Quito crowd. **$$$**

Siam
José Calama E5-10 and Juan León Mera; tel: 02-379 2035
This is a popular Thai eatery with cool East Asian decor and a terrace overlooking the center of the Mariscal. There is a wide selection of dishes, though beware the Thai/Ecuadorian penchant for über-spicyness. **$$**

Peruvian

Astrid y Gastón
Av. Coruña N32-302 and Av. González Suárez; tel: 02-250 6621
www.astridygaston.com
A clone of the enormously popular restaurant in Lima, Peru, which pairs South American dishes with a contemporary touch and a hip, elegant setting. Somewhere to spoil yourself for a special dinner out. **$$$**

Steakhouses

Adam's Rib
José Calama 329 and Reina Victoria; tel: 02-256 3196
Excellent steakhouse serving large portions of down-to-earth meaty fare. Conveniently located in the heart of the Mariscal Sucre district. The desserts are divine. **$$$**

Shorton Grill
José Calama 216 and Diego de Almagro; tel: 02-252 3645
This great Argentine steak-house serves some of the

city's best steaks, a variety of *parilladas*, and has a large wine list. For those who do not fancy steak, the menu also includes a number of fish, seafood, and international dishes. **$$$**

Vegetarian

El Marqués
José Calama 443 and Av. Amazonas
Inexpensive vegetarian restaurant which is particularly popular at lunchtimes. **$**

CAFÉS

Cafecito
Luís Cordero and Reina Victoria; tel: 02-223 4862
www.cafecito.net
Popular café with good service and atmosphere. Great light meals, cocktails, and scrumptious homemade deserts.

Café Sutra
José Calama 380 and Juan León Mera; tel: 02-250 9106
Trendy internet café/bar serving a wide range of coffees and sweet snacks.

Coffee Tree
Plaza del Quinde (Plaza Foch)
Enormously popular café with good coffee, juices, sandwiches, and snacks.

Crepes & Waffles
Quicentro Shopping Center, La Rábida 461 and Francisco de Orellana; tel: 02-243 6058
Clean and modern Colombian chain that specializes in sweet and savory crêpes, waffles, and ice creams.

Kallari
Wilson E4-266 and Juan León Mera; tel: 02-223 6009
www.kallari.com
A coffee shop and handicraft gallery specializing in fairtrade and organic coffee, which it serves with some fine cakes and brownies. Breakfasts here are excellent. Profits benefit farmers and artisans in Napo province, who grow the cacao for the chocolate that is also sold here. **$**

THE NORTH AND THE CENTRAL HIGHLANDS

Otavalo

Alli Alpa
Plaza de Ponchos
Local dishes such as *trucha* (trout) prepared in a number of ways, plus reasonable set meals. **$$**

Shenandoah Pie Shop
Plaza de Ponchos
Tourists rave about the excellent pies at this shop on the plaza. It also serves milkshakes and desserts, plus a decent breakfast. Just the place to fortify yourself before some serious handicraft shopping. **$**

Cotacachi

El Colibri
End of Calle 10 de Agosto; tel: 06-291 5237
Gourmet restaurant set in the gardens of the lavish La Mirage hotel and spa. It's worth making the hour-and-a-half drive from Quito just for lunch. **$$$**

Ibarra

Café Floral
Bolivar and Gómez de la Torre
Friendly café serving a number of dishes including crêpes and fondue. The Swiss owners make their own cheese. **$$**

Ambato

El Alamo Chalet
Cevallos 1179
Another Swiss-owned restaurant, this place serves a variety of tasty Ecuadorian and international dishes. Open late. **$$**

Baños

Asadero Dulce Carbon
12 de Noviembre 558 and Oriente; tel: 03-274 0353
A great traditional, meaty grill. They do what they do excellently, and that is grilled meat, so not an option for vegetarians. **$$**

Café Blah Blah
Ambato and Haflants

Small sidewalk café serving light meals and coffees. **$**

Casa de la Abuela
Ambato and 16 de Diciembre; tel: 03-274 2962
A variety of traditional dishes, such as *llapingacho*, plus international fare. **$$**

Mama Inés
Ambato and Halflants; tel: 03-274 2912
This is down-home style cooking in a friendly atmosphere with good service. Ecuadorian specialities, as well as pizzas and pasta. **$$**

Pancho Villa
Montalvo and 16 de Diciembre
Good variety of Mexican food in a pleasant atmosphere. Makes a nice change from the other places in town. **$$**

Le Petit Restaurant
16 de Diciembre and Montalvo; tel: 03-274 0936
www.lepetit.banios.com
With a great garden setting and Parisian owners, this is the best restaurant in the city. Serves a variety of

international dishes as well as French cuisine that could not be faulted on the streets of Paris. **$$$**

Restaurant Regine's Café Alemän
Caserío Chamana-Ulba; tel: 03-274 2671
It is not just German specialties on offer here, as the menu is quite international, but you would be silly not to try the excellent strudel. **$$**

Riobamba

D'Baggio Pizzeria
Av. Borja and Miguel Angel León; tel: 03-296 1832
Wood-fired, Neopolitan-style pizza in a modern setting; also serves excellent pasta, delicious salads, and there's even tiramisu for afters. **$$**

La Gran Havana
Borja 42–52 and Duchicela
Good-value Cuban restaurant serving sandwiches, rice, and beans, plus a number of international dishes. **$**

SOUTHERN SIERRA

Cuenca

Aguacolla Café
Bajada de Todos Santos; tel: 07-282 4029
Great-value and great-tasting vegetarian lunches are served here. There's also a climbing wall on site, but climb before you fill up on a big, healthy lunch. **$**

Café Austria
Benigno Malo 5-99; tel: 07-284 0899
Excellent corner café/restaurant serving hot drinks, cocktails, pastries, and light meals. It's a popular choice with locals and tourists, and has a pleasantly lively, but relaxed, atmosphere. A wonderful place to while away a Cuenca evening or two. **$**

Café Eucalyptus
Gran Colombia 9-41 and Benigno Malo; tel: 07-284 9157

Sparkling, colonial-style bar and restaurant that has been visited by presidents and celebrities. They serve excellent international cuisine, and there is a lengthy sushi menu and cocktail list. Hosts a lively salsa night on a Saturday. **$$$**

El Cafecito
Honorato Vásquez 736 and Luís Cordero; tel: 07-283 2337
Popular place for a light meal, coffee, or beer, particularly with the younger crowd. **$**

Goda Restaurant and Delicatessen
Gran Colombia 7-87 and Luís Cordero; tel: 07-283 1390
Situated in the El Dorado Hotel, this place has two sections; a good deli for soups and sandwiches, and a trendy, modern eatery with some of the most cutting-edge dishes in town. **$$**

Guajibamba
Luís Cordero 12-32; tel: 07-283 1016
If you want to try *cuy* (guinea pig), this is one of the best places in Ecuador to do so. They get the skin just perfectly crispy, and serve this dish with all the traditional accompaniments. *Cuy* takes an hour to prepare, so call in your order unless you don't mind waiting that long. **$$**

El Jardín
Calle Larga 6-93 and Presidente Borrero (in Hotel Victoria); tel: 07-282 7401
This is one of Cuenca's best restaurants; pricey but worth it. Serves a variety of international dishes. **$$$**

El Jordán
Larga 6-111 and Presidente Borrero; tel: 07-285 0517
www.eljordanrestaurante.com
Arabian dishes are paired with a few Ecuadorian ones

and served in an elegant setting with hand-painted murals on the walls and views over the Río Tomebamba. The lamb moussaka mahshi is said to be legendary. There are live shows with Arabian belly dancing every Friday night. **$$$**

El Maíz
Calle Larga 1-279 and Calle de los Molinos; tel: 07-284 0224
Set in historic El Barranco, close to the Pumapungo ruins, El Maíz presents itself as the true bastion of Cuencaña cuisine. Serves typical Andean delicacies such as alpaca, *cuy*,

PRICE CATEGORIES

Categories are based on the cost of a meal for two people, excluding wine:
$ = under $10
$$ = $10–30
$$$ = more than $30

tamales, and *humitas*. Salubrious surroundings and great service too. **$$$**

New York Pizza Restaurant
Gran Columbia 10-43
Tel: 07-284 2792
This fun and funky place is a good, value-for-money option serving enormous pizzas and filling *calzones*. **$**

Poncho
Larga 579; tel: 07-580 4075
Excellent American-owned, Californian-style café serving tacos, burritos, and other fast, but somewhat healthy, goodies. **$**

Raymipampa Café
Benigno Malo 859;
tel: 07-282 7435

Best budget restaurant in Cuenca, this institution is popular with locals, and serves inexpensive steaks and braised chicken and chips. The chocolate milkshakes are to die for. **$$**

Restaurante Mangiare Bene
Bolívar 14-011 and Estévez de Toral; tel: 07-282 6233
You really do eat exceptionally well at this stylish but informal little restaurant attached to the Posada del Ángel. Their homemade artesanal pastas are melt-in-the-mouth delicious, and they also do good meat dishes with an Italian flair. Definitely one of the best meals out in Cuenca. **$$**

Sankt Florian
Larga 7-119 and Luís Cordero;
tel: 07-883 3359
Casual restaurant/bar on the Barranco, popular with a young crowd, serving tasty international dishes. The steak with green pepper is a speciality. There's often live music here at night. **$$**

Loja

Mi Tierra
10 de Agosto 1144;
tel: 07-420-431
This restaurant serves typical regional dishes and staple Ecuadorian fare in a pleasant rustic setting. It's great value for money and has friendly service. **$$**

Salon Lolita
Salvado Bustamente Celi at Guayaquil, La Valle;
tel: 07-257 5603
This is the best place in town to try local specialties including *cuy* and *cecina* (salty fried pork). The portions are vast, so go on an empty stomach. Located north of the city center in the La Valle district. **$$**

Vilcabamba

La Terraza
Vega y Bolívar
Occupying a sidewalk setting on the main plaza with good Mexican and international dishes. Popular with backpackers. **$**

ORIENTE AND THE PACIFIC COAST

Puyo

El Alcázar
10 de Agosto 936; tel: 03-288 5330
Great Spanish restaurant with good-value set meals. The house specialty – when it's available – is paella and is recommended. **$$**

Coca

Parrilladas Argentinas
Cnr Inés and Cuenca
This Argentine-style grill/steakhouse is considered the best restaurant in town, with plenty of cuts to tempt meat-lovers. **$$**

Tena

Café Tortuga
Orellana s/n; tel: 06-529 5419

With a great location on the *malecón* (waterfront), this Swiss-owned café is a breezy place to hang out and drink delicious fruit frappes, while you browse the enticing, international menu. **$**

Esmeraldas

Chifa Asiático
Mañizares and Bolívar
The best of the *chifas* (Chinese restaurants) in Esmeraldas. **$**

Las Redes
Bolívar, on the main plaza;
tel: 06-272 3151
A tiny but popular café/restaurant serving inexpensive fish dishes. It is open only for lunch. **$**

Restaurant El Manglar
Quito 303; tel: 06-272 7112

Serving a wide menu of seafood, steaks, pizzas, and pastas, this is deservedly the most popular restaurant in Esmeraldas. **$**

Bahía de Caráquez

Arena Bar
Bolívar and Arenas
Great and wildly popular place for pizza. **$$**

Muelle Uno
On the pier for the San Vicente boats
The best grill and seafood restaurant in town, with a number of wonderfully prepared dishes to choose from. **$$**

Manta

El Marinero
Malecón and Calle 110

In Tarquí, this is one of the better typical Manabí seafood restaurants. The menu offers a choice of good ceviches and other seafood dishes. **$$**

Montañita

Tiburón
In the town
Well-run restaurant serving ceviche, fish dishes, and seafood *empanadas*. Also good for drinks and cocktails. **$$**

Zoociedad
In the town
The town's most sophisticated restaurant: pastas, meats, and a nice wine list. The *lomo de pimienta verde* is highly recommended. **$$**

SOUTH COAST

Guayaquil

Aroma Café
Jardines del Malecón 2000;
tel: 04-239 1328
Pleasant café on the *malecón* overlooking a small pool and gardens. The kitchen serves mostly Ecuadorian food and also has a children's menu. **$$**

Asia de Cuba
Datiles 205 and Calle Primera (Urdesa); tel: 04-600 9999
This Latin-influenced Asian restaurant serves Japanese-Thai-Chinese-Indian-Cuban-Peruvian fusion food amidst super-stylish decor. There's also an extensive wine list. **$$**

Blu Restaurant
Víctor Emilio Estrada 707 and Ficus, Urdesa; tel: 04-288 4954
Blu serves up Mediterranean and international dishes together with a wine list that hails from Chile, Argentina, California, France, Spain, and Italy. Low lighting and candles on the tables add a romantic ambience. **$$$**

El Cantonés
Av. Guillermo Pareja and Calle 43, La Garzota; tel: 04-223 6333
Reasonably priced *chifa* (Chinese restaurant) with the usual bright decor and a pleasant atmosphere. **$**

El Caracol Azul
9 de Octubre and Los Ríos;
tel: 04-228 0461
This smart, white-tablecloth

ABOVE: a rosy ceviche makes a delicious light and refreshing meal.

place with a Peruvian chef at the helm is popular with the business crowd. The menu sports fusion Peruvian-French haute cuisine: mostly seafood, though there are also meat dishes on offer. **$$**

La Casa del Cangrejo
Av. Plaza Dañín
If you are keen on eating crab, then this is the place to come. They serve all sorts of imaginative crab dishes and other seafood to complement it. **$$**

Ciao Restaurant
Samborondón Centro Comercial Piazza, Local 4C; tel: 04-283 7349
Many Guayaquileños say that this is the best Italian restaurant in town. It serves eclectic contemporary dishes, and brilliant deserts including the "vulcano di cioccolato". Leave room. **$$**

Escalón 69
Cerro Santa Ana; tel: 04-230 9828
This is a welcoming local spot which serves delicious Ecuadorian specialities just off the steps of Las Peñas. It is decorated with bright indigenous textiles and hammocks, and feels suitably exotic. **$**

Guayaquil Club Naval de Yacht
Malecón Simón Bolívar and Aguirre; tel: 04-244 6366
A nice place for the happy hour or sunset. Serves international dishes and seafood. There is also a smaller, but less atmospheric, restaurant on the first floor with very economical menus. **$$$**

Lo Nuestro
Víctor Emilio Estrada 903 and Higueras, Urdesa; tel: 04-238 6398
Guayaquil's best Ecuadorian restaurant is a place for a long, slow repast

rather than a quick meal. They serve excellent seafood but also meat; the seco de chivo (goat meat stew) is a house specialty. **$$$**

La Parrillada del Ñato
Víctor Emilio Estrada 1217 and Laureles; tel: 04-238 7098
This is a popular Argentine-style grill which serves up huge portions of meat in a friendly, down-to-earth atmosphere. It's also a child-friendly restaurant and offers small portions for little ones. **$$**

Restaurant Nuvó
Av. Alzibar and Edificio Torres del Norte Torre B, Local 7; tel: 04-268 7758
Very modern, elegant restaurant with hip decor, and a menu that it describes as vanguardista. The cuisine is international fusion, accompanied by a suitably extensive wine list. **$$**

Sion Lung
Víctor Emilio Estrada 619 and Ficus, Urdesa; tel: 04-228 7949
Great chifa (Chinese restaurant) that will even deliver to your hotel room. **$**

Trattoria da Enrico
Bálsamos 504; tel: 04-238 7079
This is a friendly, rustic Italian eatery with a menu that is big on seafood, but also includes excellent pastas. Try the Spagetti Pirata (Pirate's Spaghetti) or pulpo a la brasa (grilled octopus). **$$**

Tsuji
Víctor Emilio Estrada 813 and Guayacanes, Urdesa; tel: 04-288 1183
Exquisite Japanese food served in a stylish atmosphere. Specialties are sushi, sashimi, noodle, and tempura dishes. **$$**

Salinas

Mar y Tierra
Malecón and Valverde; tel: 04-288 4954
Perhaps the best seafood restaurant in Salinas. The ceviches are a delight, and the menu offers a number of good meat dishes as well. **$$$**

La Bella Italia
Malecón and Calle 17; tel: 04-288 4954
As well as great pizzas and pasta, the menu here has a good selection of international dishes and is of course big on seafood. Very popular. **$$**

THE GALÁPAGOS ISLANDS

Santa Cruz

The main area for restaurants and cafés in the Galápagos is along Avenida Charles Darwin in Puerto Ayora on the island of Santa Cruz.

PRICE CATEGORIES

Categories are based on the cost of a meal for two people, excluding wine:
$ = under $10
$$ = $10–30
$$$ = more than $30

Angermeyer Point
Punta Estrada, Puerto Ayora; tel: 05-252 7007
www.angermeyerpoint.com
Directly overlooking the water, this restaurant can only be reached by water taxi across Academy Bay. It serves fine international cuisine leaning towards Thai and Japanese, offering freshly caught fish and seafood. **$$$**

El Chocolate Galápagos
Av. Charles Darwin, opposite fishermens' dock, Puerto Ayora;

tel: 05-252 6993
Recommended for snacks and delicious chocolate cake. **$**

La Garrapata
Av. Charles Darwin, Puerto Ayora; tel: 05-252 6264
Popular meeting place for travelers serving sandwiches and main dishes and à la carte dishes, lunch and dinner. **$$$**

Hotel Sol y Mar
Av. Charles Darwin and Binford, Puerto Ayora; tel: 05-252 6281

Good place for breakfast on terrace with iguanas. **$$**

Limón y Café
Av. Charles Darwin, Puerto Ayora
Popular thatched bar serving drinks and snacks. Open evenings only. **$$**

Red Sushi Bar & Restaurant
At the Red Mangrove Inn, Av. Charles Darwin, Puerto Ayora; tel: 05-252 7011
Japanese restaurant with a long sushi and sashimi list. They will also deliver to your hotel or yacht. **$$$**

A CTIVITIES

THE ARTS, NIGHTLIFE, FESTIVALS AND EVENTS, SHOPPING, AND SPORTS

THE ARTS

In Ecuador, it seems that almost everyone is an artist. Music, dance, and folk art are part of every Ecuadorian's life from an early age, and the country is proud of its strong artistic heritage. Quito considers itself a particularly artistically sophisticated city, and justifiably so: as well as all the wonderful architecture and museums, there are scores of private galleries and artisan markets, as well as world-class theaters and orchestras. Guayaquil has recently embarked on an artistic renaissance and boasts a couple of excellent theaters.

Art Galleries

Quito
Artists display their works in the Parque El Ejido, near the big arch on Av. Patria, at weekends.
Centro de Arte Viteri
Juncal 64-196 and Ambrosí;
tel: 02-247 4114
Exhibition of Oswaldo Viteri's work.
El Centro Cultural Mexicano
Suiza 343 and República del El Salvador; tel: 02-225 5149.
Often shows Ecuadorian and Latin American artists.
Centro de Promoción de Artistas, Casa Blanca, Parque del Ejido;
tel: 02-252 2410.
Fundación Posada de las Artes Kingman
Diego de Almagro 1550 and Pradera;
tel: 02-222 0610
Exhibitions and cultural events. Exhibits of Eduardo Kingman's work.
Galería Mina Álvarez
Carrión 243; tel: 02-252 0347

Permanent exhibition of the artist's most outstanding works, and others to buy.

Cuenca
Ariel Dawi
Borrero 7-40; tel: 07-282 2935.
Galería de Arte Contemporáneo Illescas
Calle Alvear 1-91 and Solano;
tel: 07-283 5764.

Theaters

Quito
Casa de la Música
Valderrama s/n and Av. Mariana de Jesús; tel: 02-226 7093
Home of Ecuador's philarmonic orchestra and venue for the best classical concerts.
Humanizarte
Leónidas Plaza N24–226 and Lizardo García; tel: 02-222 6116
www.humanizarte.org
A theater and dance group showing contemporary Andean dance performances.
Teatro Bolívar
Flores 421 and Junín;
tel: 02-258 2486.
www.teatrobolivar.org
A variety of festivals and events are held in this colonial gem of a building.
Teatro Prometeo (Teatro de la Casa de la Cultura)
6 de Diciembre and Tarqui;
tel: 02-290 2272.
Adjoining the Casa de la Cultura Ecuatoriana, this theater most often shows plays and dance.
Teatro Sucre
Calle Flores and Guayaquil;
tel: 02-257 2823.
www.teatrosucre.com
Ecuador's national theatre, this is the

most upscale and traditional of the theaters for plays, concerts, ballets, and shows.

Guayaquil
Centro Cultural Sarao
Calle Primera Oeste and Av. del Periodista, Cuidadela Kennedy Vieja;
tel: 09-229 5118
Avant-garde theatre and dance as well as more traditional shows.
Teatro del Ángel
Bálsamos 620 and Las Monjas, Urdesa; tel: 09-238 0585
Live theatre, and often comedy on weekends.

NIGHTLIFE

The Latino penchant for partying is not absent in Ecuador. People here love to socialize over a drink or three, and they're always ready to get up and dance. Nightclubs, bars, and live music venues keep Quito's Mariscal Sucre area jumping into the early hours, while in Guayaquil some of the most pleasant places to drink and dance are along the *malecón* waterfront. A big night out starts later in Ecuador than in many countries: people rarely get started before 10pm. Clubs and live music venues tend to have a cover charge, pubs and bars do not.

Cinemas

Quito
Some of the larger shopping centers around the city have a few screens that show (usually dubbed) American blockbusters. The best cinemas in the city include:

Cinemark
Plaza de las Américas, República and Naciones Unidas, Quito; tel: 02-226 2026
www.cinemark.com.ec
Popular multiplex showing Hollywood blockbusters.

Multicines
CCI Shopping Mall, Amazonas and Naciones Unidas, Quito;
tel: 02-225 9677
www.multicines.com.ec
Eight screens, good sound quality, and the latest movies.

Ocho y Medio
Valladolid N24-353 and Vizcaya; tel: 02-290 4720
www.ochoymedio.net
Shows more arty, offbeat, and international films.

Guayaquil
There are many cinemas in Guayaquil that show English-language movies with Spanish subtitles. Look in the local newspapers or at the reception desks of the more expensive hotels to see what is going on. *El Universo* has information on movies and events.

IMAX
Malecón and Loja, Guayaquil;
tel: 04-230 9400
www.imaxmalecon2000.com
IMAX and movie theater right on Malecón 2000. Also on the same site is MAAC Cine, which shows indie films.

Cinemark
Mall del Sol, Guayaquil;
tel: 04-208 5106, www.cinemark.com.ec

Live Music

Quito

La Casa de la Peña
García Moreno 11-13;
tel: 02-228 4179.
Atmospheric setting in the Centro Histórico. Has live Ecuadorian folk music most nights.

Nucanchi
Av. Universitaria and Armero;
tel: 02-254 0967.
One of the best *peñas* in town where you can hear live local folk music.

El Pobre Diablo
La Católica and Galavis; tel: 02-223 5194.
Frequent live jazz nights ($5–8 entrance) with a pleasant atmosphere and excellent food.

Vox Populi
Eugenio Espejo Oeste 2-12 and Flores; tel: 228 2263.
Slick bar/nighclub with live Latin and jazz Thursday to Sunday.

Baños

Amenitay
16 de Diciembre and Espejo;
tel: 03-274 1713.
Decades-old *peña* with live music every night of the year.

Cuenca

Bar San Angel
Corner Hermano Miguel and Presidente Córdova; tel: 07-283 9090.
There's live music here from Thursday to Saturday. A popular locals' hangout.

Guayaquil

Rincón Folklórico
Malecón 208 and Montalvo.
Popular *peña* that stays open late on the weekends.

Nightclubs

Quito

Huaina
Foch E5-12.
An often crowded bar and dance hall with cheap drinks and loud music.

Mayo 68
García 662.
This salsa joint is so popular, it's often splitting at the seams. Great atmosphere.

No Bar
Calama 380.
Young crowd with popular music and a lively dance floor.

Vulcano Bar
base of the Teleférico;
tel: 02-223 5195.
One of the "it" clubs of the moment, with high covers and pricey drinks.

Cuenca

Café Eucalyptus
Colombia 9-41 and Benigno Malo;
tel: 07-284 9157.
Salsa night on Saturdays is the liveliest place in Cuenca. Ladies' night on a Thursday is also popular.

Guayaquil

Bla, Bla, Bla Mykonos Café,
Imbabura 229 and Rocafuerte.
A loud, rowdy disco that gets thumping pretty much any night of the week.

Pubs and Bars

Quito

The Lounge
Foch E5-25
Glitzy lounge with Victorian furniture and a laidback atmosphere.

Naranjilla Mecánica
Tamayo and Veintimilla. Trendy, with a labyrinthine layout and good cocktails. They also serve an extensive food menu.

Reina Victoria Pub
Reina Victoria and Roca;
tel: 02-222 6369.
British pub with a good selection of imported beers and microbrews. Serves classic British dishes such as fish and chips, and curry.

Sport Planet
Av. Naciones Unidas and América;
tel: 02-226 7790.
Sports bar with a full menu. The best place to catch a game away from home.

BELOW: Atacames, on the Pacific Coast, has a reputation for being a party town.

Calendar of Festivals and Events

Each month sees numerous festivals take place in Ecuador. Typical festivities involve fireworks, processions, masquerades, and folkloric dancing. Bullfights and horse racing are common in rural areas. Here is a calendar of Ecuador's principal festivals, including national holidays and any particularly good places to see them.

January

1 – National holiday: New Year's festivities.
6 – National holiday: Epiphany.
Ambato (Tungurahua) and **Cuenca** (Azuay): Children's Mass (masa de niños), processions, carols.
Gatazo Grande (Chimborazo) and **Lican** (Chimborazo): Fireworks, hymns, election of the prioste (Steward of the Festival) and kings.
Montecristi (Manabí): Bands, dances.
Tisalleo (Tungurahua): High Mass, paying homage to the Christ Child in the crib.
15 – Quito-Chillogallo (Pichincha): Dances of the Innocent, bands, masquerades.
Calpi (Chimborazo): Marimbas, processions with "La Mamá Negra."

February

1 – Mira (Carchi): Festival of the Virgin of Charity (Virgen de la Caridad); fireworks, dances, glove ball games (pelota nacional), vaca loca (crazy cow) rodeos.
12 – (All Ecuador): Anniversary of the "discovery" of the Amazon River (Día del Oriente) – Fairs in Puyo, Tena, Macas, and Zamora; day of the province of Galápagos – civic events.
27 – (All Ecuador): Patriotism and National Unity day to commemorate the battle of Tarqui in 1829.
Changeable date – (All Ecuador): Carnival preceding Lent.

March

2–5 – Atuntaqui (Imbabura): Sugar-cane and Craftsmanship Festival, verbenas (open-air dances).

April

19–21 – Riobamba (Chimborazo): Farming, cattle, handicraft, and industrial fair.
Changeable date – (All Ecuador): Holy Week. Celebrations on Good Friday and Easter Sunday.

May

1 – (All Ecuador): Labor day – workers' parades.

2 – Quito: Festival of Las Cruzes at La Cruz Verde quarter (corner of Bolívar and Imbabura streets).
3 – Quito: Festival of La Cruz at Champicruz (Avenidas Prensa and Sumaco).
11–14 – Puyo (Pastaza): Farming and industrial exhibition and fair in the Amazon region.
24 – (All Ecuador): National civic festivity to commemorate the Battle of Pichincha in 1822.

June

23 – Indigenous communities all over Ecuadorian highlands: Inti Raymi (Inca Festival of the Sun)
23/24 – Otavalo (Imbabura), **Tabacundo** (Pichincha), **Guamote** (Chimborazo): Festival of Saint John (San Juan).
24 – Sangolquí (Pichincha): Corn and tourism festivities.
24 – Calpi (Chimborazo): Gallo Compadre and vaca loca (crazy cow) rodeos.
28–29 – Santo Domingo de los Colorados (Pichincha): Canonization anniversary.
29 – Cotacahi and Cayambe (Imbabura), and other communities: Festival of saints Peter and Paul (San Pedro y San Pablo).
Changeable date – (All Ecuador): Corpus Christi.

July

16 – Ibarra (Imbabura): Celebration of Virgen del Carmen.
22 – Pelileo (Tungurahua): Canonization anniversary.
23–25 – Guayaquil: Guayaquil's foundation anniversary.
24 – National Holiday: Simón Bolívar's birthday.
29 – Pillaro (Tungurahua): Celebration day of the Apostle Santiago the Elder.

August

3–5 – Esmeraldas: Independence Day.
5–7 – Sicalpa (Chimborazo): Festival of the Virgin of the Snow (Virgen de las Nieves).
10 – National Holiday: Commemoration of independence in 1809.
Pillaro (Tungurahua): San Lorenzo festivities.
Yaguachi (Guayas): San Jacinto Festival, with popular pilgrimages.
25 – Santa Rosa (El Oro): Agricultural Fair.

September

2–15 – Otavalo (Imbabura): Yamor festivities.
5–12 – Loja: Festival of Virgen del Cisne, the patron saint.
6–14 – Cotacachi (Imbabura): Jora festival.
8–9 – Macara (Loja): Agricultural fair.
8–9 – Sangolquí (Pichincha): Bullfights, dances, processions.
11–16 – Milagro (Guayas): Agricultural fair.
20–26 – Machala (El Oro): International Banana Festival.
23–24 – Quito and **Latacunga** (Cotopaxi): Festival of Virgen de las Mercedes, the patron saint.
24 – Piñas (El Oro): Product fair.
24–28 – Ibarra (Imbabura): Festivals of the Lakes.
27 – Espejo (Imbabura): Indigenous handicrafts fair.
29 – Gonzanama (Loja): Agricultural and industrial exhibition.

October

9–12 – Guayaquil: National civic festival to commemorate the independence of Guayaquil.
12 – National Holiday: Columbus Day (Día de la Raza).
14–18 – Portoviejo (Manabí): Agricultural and industrial exhibition. Many attractions.

November

1 – National Holiday: All Saints' Day.
2 – (All Ecuador): All Souls' Day (Día de los Difuntos).
3 – Cuenca (Azuay): Commemoratation of Cuenca's independence.
4 – Manta (Manabí): Manta Day.
11 – Latacunga (Cotopaxi): Independence of Latacunga.
21 – El Quinche (Pichincha): Day of the Virgen of El Quinche, the patron saint.

December

1–6 – Quito (Pichincha): Anniversary of the Foundation of San Francisco de Quito.
25 – National Holiday: Christmas Day.
28 – All Fools' Day.
31 – (All Ecuador): New Year's Eve celebrations. Parades and dances culminate in burning of life-size dolls representing politicians, artists, and el año viejo (the old year). Celebrations are particularly active the larger cities of Quito, Guayaquil, and Esmeraldas on the Pacific coast.

Baños
Jack Rock Café
Eloy Alfaro 541
Longtime travelers' favorite, with great mixed drinks and a pool table.
Mocambo
Eloy Alfaro and Ambato.
Sprawling bar with lounge areas and small dance floors over three levels.

Cuenca
Wunderbar
Hermano Miguel 3-43 and Larga; tel: 07-283 1724.
Pasta, sandwiches, and a few German dishes round out this friendly restaurant-cum-bar with a few pool tables.

Guayaquil
DADA
Calle Numa Pompilio 117, Las Peñas; tel: 09-230 2828.
A friendly and cultivated place to drink. Open every day but Monday until the early hours.
Proa
Malecón 2000, next to the IMAX cinema; tel: 09-426 7061.
A sophisticated, minimalist bar with wide river views playing hip music and serving equally stylish food and drinks.

SHOPPING

Dedicated shoppers will love Ecuador for its huge range of well-priced, hand-crafted souvenirs. Embroidered cotton clothing, richly colored textiles, uniquely patterned carpets, art – both folk and fine – and a great range of ceramics and jewelry are to be had from both street markets and retail outlets. Bargaining is standard at markets, not shops – but don't be merciless: think of what an item is worth to you considering all the hours of work that have gone into it. Books – particularly the glossy, photographic kind – are also a good buy as souvenirs. Quito and Guayaquil both have shiny malls where you can buy the latest fashions, at international prices.

Bookstores
Quito
Confederate Books
Calama 410; tel: 02-252 7890
www.confederatebooks.com
Good for books in Spanish on Ecuadorian culture, and also English-language titles.
Ediciones Abya Yala
12 de Octubre 1430 and Wilson; tel: 02-250 6251/250 6247

ABOVE: colorful, delicate bead necklaces are popular souvenirs.

www.abyayala.org
Good for books in Spanish on Ecuadorian culture.
Libri Mundi
Juan León Mera N23-83 and Wilson; tel: 02-223 4791/252 9587
Also at the QuiCentro Shopping Mall; tel: 02-246 4z473
www.librimundi.com (in Spanish)
Books in English, German, French, and Spanish; large selection of maps, international magazines, and records.
Mr Books
Mall El Jardin, 3rd floor; tel: 02-298 0281
Wide range of books in Spanish and English.
Nuevos Horizontes
6 de Marzo 924
Book exchange.
Selecciones
Albán Borja Mall
Books and magazines in English.

Handicrafts
Quito
There are dozens of *artesanía* stores and kiosks in Quito, especially in the area around Avenida Amazonas. Several have outstanding selections of high-quality folk art and clothing. They include:
La Bodega
Calle Juan León Mera 614
Selling a huge range of high-quality crafts for over 30 years.
Centro Artesanal
Calle Juan León Mera 804; tel: 02-254 8235
This shop has high quality crafts and paintings by local artists.
Exedra
Carrión 243 and Plaza; tel: 02-222 4001
A not-for-profit community store that sells quality *artesanías* and supports scholarships for poor children.

Folklore Olga Fisch
Av. Colón E-10-53 and Calle Caamaño; tel: 02-254 1315
www.olgafisch.com
There's also a branch in the Patio Andaluz Hotel in the Historic Center.
Galería Latina
Calle Juan León Mera 833 and Veintimilla; tel: 02-222 1098
www.galerialatina-quito.com
Exquisite Andean folk art.
Mercado Artesanal La Mariscal
Calle Juan León Mera and Jorge Washington
The best artisan market in downtown Quito, with dozens of stalls.
Mindalae
Calle Reina Victoria and La Niña; tel: 02-223 0609
This museum has a fairtrade shop filled with the finest quality handicrafts, at a price.

Cuenca
There are several handicraft shops along Gran Colombia, near the El Dorado Hotel.
Artesa
Luís Cordero 10–31 and Gran Colombia
Ecuadorian ceramics (including Vega designs).
Artes Artesanías y Antigüedades
Borrero and Córdova
Textiles, jewelry, and antiques.
Homero Ortega
Av. Gil Ramírez Davalos 3–86; tel: 07-280 1288
www.homeroortega.com
High-quality Panama hats; the factory near the bus station is open for tours, where you can see these famed and misnamed straw hats being made.

Guayaquil
Mercado Artesanal
Calle Baquerizo Moreno
Not far from the waterfront. A large indoor artisan's market that takes up a whole city block.

TRANSPORTATION
ACCOMMODATIONS
EATING OUT
ACTIVITIES
A – Z
LANGUAGE

Shopping Centers

Quito

Most of the large malls in Quito are open daily from 10am–8pm or later.

Centro Commercial El Jardín
Av. Amazonas and Av. de la Republica; tel: 02-298 0300
Has many Ecuadorian and international chain stores. There is a handy alteration service on the lower level and a Supermaxi Supermarket.

Centro Commercial Quicentro
Av. 6 de Diciembre and Naciones Unidas; tel: 02-246 4512
Large, classy centre containing clothes and jewelry shops, hardressers, and eateries.

El Recreo Commercial City
Av. Pedro Vicente Maldonado 14-205, La Magdalena
Large mall with entertainment as well as shopping opportunities.

Guayaquil

Guayaquil has several smart shopping centers, including:

Centro Comercial Malécon
Malecón 2000, between Olmedo and Colón; tel: 04-232 0245.
Large mall on the waterfront with over 200 stores and a range of international restaurants.
Shopping at the Bahía (street market), along calles Pinchincha and Olmedo, is very popular. Watch out for pickpockets.

Mall del Sol
Av. Marengo and Orrantia; tel: 04-269 0100
Mall and entertainment complex with many international shops, restaurants, and bars.

Mall del Sur-
Av. 25 de Julio, between Cuadra and Albán; tel: 04-208 5000
Large mall with many European and North American shops.

SPORTS

Ecuador is an outdoor enthusiast's paradise. From climbing and trekking in high-altitude environments to diving mysterious underwater worlds, and zip-lining over canyons and through tree canopies, this country has it all. Choose an organised trip or an independent adventure; whatever your approach, there is a plethora of activities to keep sports and outdoor-lovers busy. Even the big cities have good recreational facilities, as well as decent sports clubs, while outside the cities, it is all about getting out into the wilds.

Diving

Galápagos Sub-Aqua
Guayaquil office: tel/fax: 04-230 5514
Galápagos office: Av. Charles Darwin, Puerto Ayora, Isla Santa Cruz; tel/fax: 05-252 6350/252 6633
www.galapagos-sub-aqua.com
Offers scuba and diving tours and diving instruction.

Scuba Iguana
Av. Charles Darwin, Puerto Ayora, Isla Santa Cruz; tel/fax: 05-252 6497
www.scubaiguana.com
Offers a wide choice of scuba-diving courses and dives.

Fishing

The Guayas and Manabí provinces hold some of the world's best sport fishing; dolphinfish, barracuda, blue and black marlin, and yellow-finned tuna are all found there. Andean rivers and lakes are filled with trout and popular with fly-fishermen, while fishing for piranha in the rivers of the Oriente is a popular activity at jungle lodges.

Pescatours
Comín 135 and El Oro, Guayaquil; tel/fax: 04-244 3365;
Salinas office; tel: 04-277 2391
www.pescatours.com.ec
For fishing trips on the Pacific Coast.

Golf

Quito

Quito Tenis y Golf Club
Av. A N73-154 and Calle B, El Condado; tel: 02-249 1420)
Offering an 18-hole, par-72 golf course (as well as extensive tennis and gym facilities and a pool).

Los Arrayanes Country Club
Tel: 02-239 2000
This club has a par-71, 18-hole course just outside Quito.

Guayaquil

Guayaquil Country Club
Km 22, Vía a Daule, Guayas; tel: 04-226 7026
Guayaquil's best 18-hole course (along with an extensive range of recreational facilities including clay tennis courts, swimming pool, and gymnasium).

Horseback Riding

Horseback-riding trips can be arranged from most major tourist destinations (see also page 121). Most of the haciendas also have a good stable of horses and skilled riding guides who can take you out for a few hours or a few days. In Guayaquil, the Guayaquil Country Club offers horseback riding.

The Green Horse Ranch
Casilla 17-12-602, Quito; tel: 086 125 4333 (mobile)
www.horseranch.de
Offers one- to nine-day trips for all levels of rider.

Monta Runa Tours
Gran Colombia 10-29 and General Torres, Cuenca; tel: 07-846 395
Horseback riding around Cuenca, and particularly in Parque Nacional Cajas.
The following UK-based operator runs a variety of excellent tours all over Ecuador: www.rideandes.com

Mountain Biking

Biking tours can be booked through specialist tour agencies, such as the ones listed here. It is also possible to hire bikes in major destinations including Quito, Cuenca, Riobamba, and Baños.

Bird-watching

Andean cloud forest and the Amazonian lowlands are extremely diverse and are home to many rare and endemic avian species. Some of the country's ornithological highlights include the area around Mindo northeast of Quito and Parque Nacional Podocarpus, near Vilcabamba. In the Galápagos you can see Darwin's finches, various boobies, and numerous frigate birds. The following organizations can provide information on bird-watching in Ecuador.

Andean Birding
Salazar Gómez E-1482 and Eloy Alfaro, Quito;
tel/fax: 02-224 4426
www.andeanbirding.com
Arranges custom tours to Ecuador's richest birding destinations.

Aves & Conservación
(Ecuadorian Ornithology Foundation), Pasaje Joaquín Tinajero E3-05 and Jorge Drom; tel/fax: 02-227 1800/224 9968
www.avesconservacion.org

Fundácion Natura
See National Parks box, opposite.

Tinalandia Ornithological Reserve
Urbanización el Bosque, Calle Tercera 43-78, Quito;
tel/fax: 02-244 9028
www.tinalandia.com

Biking Dutchman
Foch 714 and Juan León Mera, Quito;
tel: 02-256 8323/254 2806
www.bikingdutchman.com

ProBici
Primera Constituyente 23-51 and
Larrea, Riobamba; tel: 03-295 1760
www.probici.com
The original operator of the
spectacular Chimborazo downhill, as
well as other tours in the Riobamba
area.

SurTrek
Avenida Amazonas 897 and Wilson,
Quito; tel: 02-223 1534
www.surtrek.com
Offers all sorts of mountain-biking
trips from one to 13 days in length.

Sports Clubs

Quito
Many of the best hotels have
gymnasiums, often with access to
tennis and squash courts. The Hotel
Hilton Colón often has special
discount rates for its gym. Even if you
are not a guest at one of the smarter
hotels, you can join some of the top
hotel gym clubs if staying in the city
for a while. Membership is about
$100 a month.

Guayaquil
Guests of the Hotel Oro Verde can use
the facilities of the Tennis Club
Guayaquil on request. Guests of the
Gran Hotel Guayaquil can use the
facilities of the Terraza Racquet Club
(with two squash courts, gymnasium,
and sauna). There are many sports
clubs in Guayaquil, so even if you are

not staying at one of these fancier
hotels, there are plenty of gyms to
choose from. Ask for a temporary
membership.

Swimming

Quito
There is a public pool at Av.
Universitaria and Nicaragua and also
one at Cochapata, near Villarroel and
6 de Diciembre.

Guayaquil
Most of the pools in Guayaquil are in
private clubs, but you can visit the
Piscina Olímpica on Calle García
Moreno if you want to do laps. There
is also a swimming pool at Malecón
Simón Bolívar 116. There is a heated
swimming pool at the Guayaquil
Country Club.

Trekking and Mountaineering

Compañía de Guías
Tel: 02-920 1551
www.companiadeguias.com.ec
Works only with guides certified by the
Ecuadorian Association of Mountain
Guides, and takes would-be climbers
all over Ecuador, specializing in two-
day Cotopaxi trips.

Moggely Tours
Calama E4-54 and Av. Amazonas,
Quito; tel: 02-255 4984
www.moggely.com

Terranovatrek
Av. Portugal 585 and 6 de Diciembre;
tel: 02-225 3327
www.terranovatrek.com

National Parks

For information on Ecuador's
national parks contact:
Ministerio del Ambiente y
Turismo (Parks Section:
ex-INEFAN), 8th Floor, Av.
Amazonas and Eloy Alfaro, Quito;
tel: 02-256 3429
www.ambiente.gov.ec
The main conservation
organization is:
Fundación Natura
Calle Elia Liut N45-10 and El
Telégrafo Primero, Quito;
tel: 02-227 2863.
www.fnatura.org

Terranovatrek offers guided volcano
climbs and mountain treks (as well as
arranging rafting, jungle trips, and
paragliding).

White-Water Rafting
With the Andes and one of the
highest concentrations of rivers in
any country, it's no wonder rafting in
Ecuador is world class. Baños, Tena,
and Puyo are great bases for rafting
class III and IV rapids, including the
Upper Río Napo (Class III) and Río
Misahuallí (Class IV and IV+). The Río
Toachi (Class III–III+) is also popular
due to its proximity to Quito. The
following agencies specialize in
rafting trips.

Explorandes Ecuador
Presidente Wilson 537 and Diego de
Almagro, Quito; tel: 02-222 2699
www.explorandes.com.ec
Day trips on the Class IV Toachi River
and longer trips on the Jondachi-
Yatunyacu.

Geo Tours
Ambato and Haflants, Baños;
tel: 03-274 1344
www.geotoursbanios.com
Seventeen years' experience on the
white water around Baños.

Ríos Ecuador
Foch 746 and Juan León Mera, Quito;
tel: 02-290 4054
Tarqui 230 and Días de Pineda, Tena;
tel: 06-288 6727
www.riosecuador.com
One of the top rafting agencies, with
offices in Quito and Tena.

Row Expediciones
Pablo Suárez 151, Quito;
tel: 02-223 9224
www.rowexpediciones.com

Yacu Amu Rafting
Foch 746 and Juan León Mera, Quito;
tel: 02-290 4054
www.yacuamu.com
Rafting and other sporting experiences.

BELOW: biking in the Parque Metropolitano, Quito.

A – Z

A HANDY SUMMARY OF PRACTICAL INFORMATION, ARRANGED ALPHABETICALLY

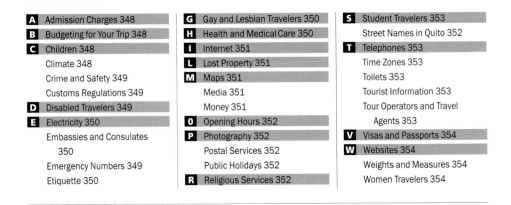

A dmission Charges

Charges for museums are usually more than a few dollars; children often pay less. National park entrance fees are more costly, around $10 for several of the popular national parks and reserves like Cotopaxi.

B udgeting for Your Trip

Ecuador falls into the middle when comparing prices to other Latin American countries. Since dollarization in 2000, prices have climbed. Cities such as Quito and Guayaquil remain more expensive than other places. The difference is mainly noticeable in accommodation and food prices, as well as taxi fares.

In the large cities and major tourist destinations budget accommodation will run from as little as $8 per night, but a top hotel will charge several hundred dollars for a room (*see also page 329*). Getting around by bus is fairly cheap, and journeys are never more than a few hours due to the size of the country.

Transportation by bus averages about $1 per hour, depending on the level of comfort. Trains are also economical, although less reliable. Within cities, taxis are cheap and ubiquitous, and rarely will a ride within a city – even Quito or Guayaquil – cost more than a few dollars. Some locations in the Oriente, as well as the Galápagos, can only be reached by airplane, which can be expensive. A round-trip plane ticket to the Galápagos will cost about $450.

The cost of food varies heavily. In large cities, and especially the Galápagos, rarely will you be able to eat out for less than $5, and meals can cost as much as $40 per person for a top restaurant. In rural areas, small local restaurants will serve set menus, usually including several hearty courses, for a couple of dollars. Drinks tend to be relatively cheap, as a beer will generally cost just over a dollar in most bars and pubs, although in a large club in a place such as

Quito, you will likely have to triple that price. Cover charges at clubs tend to be anywhere between $3–15.

C hildren

Ecuador is a great place to travel with children: it's sufficiently adventurous to be exotic, but not the kind of country where you'd feel you're putting your children in danger. Ecuadorians are very child-focused, and traveling with your children is a great way to break the ice. Some tourist attractions and transport offer children's entrance fees and fares. Take a good medical kit when traveling with a child and know how to use its contents. Anti-diarrhea drugs are a must, as are electrolytic salts to combat dehydration, which are rapid in children.

Climate

Because it is on the equator, Ecuador has only two seasons: wet and dry.

A – Z ◆ 349

TRANSPORTATION
ACCOMMODATIONS
EATING OUT
ACTIVITIES
A – Z
LANGUAGE

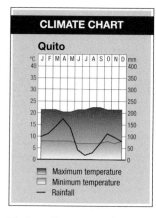

CLIMATE CHART

Quito

- Maximum temperature
- Minimum temperature
- Rainfall

Weather patterns vary greatly between the different geographical regions, however.

In the inhabited inter-mountain basin of the Sierra, the temperature changes little between seasons. However, mornings are generally sunny and fresh, becoming warmer toward midday; in the afternoon it often rains, and toward the evenings it gets chilly, and the nights are cold. This means that in Quito the daily range of temperature is generally around 8° to 21°C (46° to 70°F). Above 3,800 meters (11,400ft) temperatures reach freezing during the night. Occasional snowstorms also occur. There is one rainy season in the Sierra, from November to May, when there is frequent rainfall during the afternoon and evening. However, it rains quite often during the dry season too, and the sun shines in the rainy season for at least a couple of hours every day.

The coastal lowlands and Amazon basin are very hot year-round, with temperatures ranging from 22°C (73°F) at night to 33°C (100°F) during the day. Humidity is extremely high. The rainy season in both areas is from May to December, although tropical downpours are regular in the dry season also. In the Galápagos Islands, there are also two seasons, produced by the ocean currents: the rainy (warm) and dry (cool) seasons. During the rainy season, from January through June, the weather is warm and sunny, while the water temperature is a comfortable 23°C (75°F); heavy tropical showers occur occasionally. This is the best time to visit. For the rest of the year, a mist called the *garua* settles over the islands and makes the day cloudy, and the water begins to cool. It rarely rains, but it can be windy.

What to Wear

Ecuador has three very different climatic zones, so what you wear depends completely on where you are headed.

The Sierra is where most travelers begin. Quito is called the "City of Eternal Spring," although "eternal fall" (autumn) might be more accurate. When the sun is shining, Sierran days are warm and pleasant, but when the clouds roll in and winds begin to blow, you need a sweater. Nights can be quite cold, so a warm overcoat or parka is recommended.

Ecuadorians, like most Latin Americans, like to dress up and look their best when they go out, even at more casual restaurants and nightspots. Note that Quito tends to have more conservative dress standards than the rest of the country.

Of course, this doesn't apply to many backpacker hangouts, and even in the ritzier establishments traveling gringos are forgiven for a more laidback appearance than Ecuadorians. But remember that a night out in a restaurant is more of a big deal for an Ecuadorian, and dressing too unkemptly can seem like an insult to the other clients. If in doubt, err on the side of smartness.

The coast and Galápagos Islands are tropical regions, so dress for the heat. Guayaquil and the coast are very casual, so shorts for men are widely accepted for many social situations (not so widely for women; a light dress is more appropriate). Remember to use sun protection.

Dress in the Oriente is even more functional. All clothes should be light, because of the stifling heat, but long trousers and long-sleeved shirts are recommended to guard against insects. Bring some sneakers for walking.

Rain can strike in any part of Ecuador, whether it is the rainy season or not, so bring protection.

What to Bring

What you bring depends on where you are going to go and what you are going to do. A few recommended items: antibacterial handsoap or gel, hand wipes, personal stereo, basic first aid kit, sunscreen, sunglasses, Swiss Army knife, and Spanish dictionary. Basic necessities can be found throughout the country, and in the larger cities nearly all the same products can be found that you would find in your own country.

If you intend to partake in any adventure activities, check with your tour operator ahead of time to see what exactly you will need. Often for

Emergency Numbers

Ambulance/Red Cross 131
Fire 102
Police 101 (911 in Quito)
Police Radio Patrol 101
Policía de Turismo, Quito
Reina Victoria and Roca, Quito; tel: 02-254 3983
This is where to make a declaration if you are robbed in Quito. An official police report will be required by your travel insurer.

more technical activities such as climbing it is best to bring your own equipment. You can buy equipment for a number of sports in many towns such as Baños. However, prices tend to be much higher than they would be in the US or Europe.

Crime and Safety

Most of Ecuador is relatively safe, although petty theft does occur in large cities. Armed robberies can occur on isolated mountain trails, but this is somewhat rare. In major cities it is best only to go in marked taxis. Guayaquil has recently seen a spate of taxi-hijackings. It is best to order a taxi by phone from a reputable company here, rather than stop one in the street. Don't walk alone at night and avoid poorly lit streets. In hostels, particularly dorms, secure your belongings in a locker. Take extra precautions along the border with Colombia, and check the current situation in the area to which you plan to travel. Although drugs such as marijuana may seem common in areas where many travelers visit, use or purchase is punishable by up to 16 years in prison, where a number of foreigners now reside.

Customs Regulations

Each traveler may bring a liter of spirits, several bottles (a "reasonable amount") of perfume, and 300 cigarettes into Ecuador duty-free.

D isabled Travelers

In large cities and major tourist areas, most large hotels and attractions are equipped with ramps and/or elevators. Elsewhere there are few services for the disabled traveler. Most areas of the Galápagos Islands tend to be quite untouched by development for conservation reasons and therefore lack proper facilities for wheelchair-users. Consult

Electricity

110V/60Hz is the standard current throughout the country. Ecuador uses the North American flat-pronged plug. Travelers from other countries will need to bring an adapter with them.

a tour operator to see what types of activities may be accessible.

E mbassies and Consulates

Quito

British Embassy
Av. Naciones Unidas and República del Salvador, Edificio Citiplaza, 14th Floor; tel: 02-297 0800
ukinecuador.fco.gov.uk/en
Canadian Embassy
Av. Amazonas 4153 and Unión Nacional de Periodistas, Eurocenter Building, 3rd Floor; tel: 02-245 5499
www.canadainternational.gc.ca/ecuador-equateur
The Canadian Embassy also provides limited assistance to Australian nationals.
Honorary Consul of Ireland
Calle Yanacocha N72-64 and Juan Procel, Sector el Condado;
tel: 02-357 0156
US Embassy
Avigiras N12-170 and Eloy Alfaro;
tel: 02-398 5000
www.usembassy.org.ec

Guayaquil

British Embassy
Córdova 623 and Padre Solano;
tel: 04-256 0400
Canadian Honorary Consulate
Av. Juan Tanca Marengo and Av. J, Orrantea; tel: 04-229 6837
US Consulate
Av. 9 de Octubre and García Moreno;
tel: 04-232 3570
http://guayaquil.usconsulate.gov

Etiquette

Ecuadorians are polite to each other and respectful of authority and age. People shake hands when meeting for the first time. Men may embrace each other if they are good friends, and both men and women kiss once when they meet friends. It is impolite to point at someone, instead point by puckering or pursing the lips in the direction you want to indicate. There's no great value placed on punctuality in Ecuador. Arriving 15 to 20 minutes late is considered "on time" for social engagements, though business meetings do often

run more to schedule. Before you start eating, you may say *buen provecho* to your fellow diners, and it is also polite to do so to people you pass when you enter a restaurant, or seated near you.

G ay and Lesbian Travelers

As with most Catholic Latin American countries, homosexuality is often shunned in Ecuador. However, in large cities, particularly Quito, gay communities have developed, and homosexuality is slowly becoming more tolerated. The Mariscal Sucre district of Quito tends to be the center of Ecuador's gay scene. For more information for gay and lesbians in Ecuador visit: www.quitogay.net and www.gayecuador.com

H ealth and Medical Care

It is a good idea to consult a tropical medicine clinic before traveling. Vaccinations against diphtheria, polio, tetanus, typhoid, and hepatitis A are strongly recommended. A yellow fever certificate is compulsory if arriving from a tropical South American or African region. If traveling into the Amazon or the tropical lowlands, anti-malaria pills should be taken. Remember that, depending on what prophylactic you take, the course may start one or two weeks before your visit and should be continued for at least four weeks after you leave. Remember, too, to cover exposed areas of skin after dusk and use an insect repellent.

If you are hiking or cycling in rural areas, a rabies vaccination will mean more time to get to medical help and fewer post-bite shots if you get bitten by a rabid dog (rabies is not common).

The most common illness for tourists is, of course, mild diarrhea, which hits most visitors at some stage. Sufferers should have plenty of liquids (hot tea without milk is ideal, but definitely no coffee), avoid eggs and dairy products, and rest as much as they can. Rehydration products, such as Dioralyte and Rehidrat, taken regularly, will help prevent dehydration. Boiled water with a little sugar and salt added has a similar effect.

The symptoms of diarrhea can be stopped with medication like Imodium. This does not cure the ailment, and is really only useful if you have a long bus journey or flight and don't want a sudden attack. If the complaint continues for several days, consult a doctor. Also, if you suffer severe abdominal cramps, fever, or

nausea, or if blood or pus is evident in your stool, you need a test to see if you've caught amoebic dysentery. But in almost all cases, diarrhea is simply a matter of becoming accustomed to different bacteria and unfamiliar food, and the gut returns to normal after a couple of days.

To avoid diarrhea, do not drink the tap water in Ecuador. Ask instead for mineral water *con* or *sin gas* (with or without bubbles). Güitig (pronounced "gwee-tig") is the best brand. Stay clear of ice, uncooked vegetables, salads that haven't been properly treated, and unpeeled fruits.

Most food in the larger cities, or in the restaurants where most travelers eat, is perfectly safe. Hepatitis is a danger if you eat food prepared in dirty conditions, and it is advisable to have a gamma globulin shot to protect against this. There is also the drug Havirix, which gives 10-year protection, although you need a booster after the first year.

A more everyday health risk is the fierce equatorial sun, a danger even in the cold Sierra. Newcomers to Ecuador should not expose their skin to the sun for long periods, especially during the middle of the day. Bring strong sunscreen lotion. Wearing a hat is a good idea.

Altitude sickness (*soroche*) can sometimes affect travelers arriving in Quito by air. Most people will need a couple of days to get used to the thin Andean air, so take it easy at first: eat light meals, steer clear of excessive alcohol, and don't go on strenuous walks; a chocolate bar can sometimes help. Drink tea, relax, and let your body become accustomed to the height.

Mountain sickness is a more serious problem for climbers, who may be exerting themselves at altitudes over 5,000 meters (15,000ft). Symptoms can include headache, vomiting, rapid pulse, and failing blood pressure. The only real cure is to descend to a lower level. Before starting out, most climbers drink *mate de coca* (coca-leaf tea), which is the local preventative remedy.

There are several good private hospitals in Quito and Guayaquil, but they are expensive. Visitors are advised to take out travel insurance.

Drugstores

Regular medicine can be bought without a prescription in most pharmacies (*farmacias*). In major cities pharmacies carry a wide range of drugs, antibiotics, and treatments. It is recommended that you use well-known brands. The newspapers list *farmacias de turno*, which are open on Sunday or at night. In Quito a number are open 24 hours a day; look out for an illuminated "*Turno*" sign. Most drugstores will give injections as well as disposable serum needles (beware of non-disposable needles).

Medical Services, Quito
Ambulance
Tel: 02-911/131 for emergencies
Clínica Los Andes
Mariano Cueva 14-68 and Pio Bravo; tel: 02-284 2942
Clínica de la Mujer
Av. Amazonas N39-216 and Gaspar de Villaroel; tel: 02-245 8000
Women's clinic. Laboratory analysis for parasites.
Clínica Pichincha
Veintimilla E3-30 and Paez; tel: 02-256 2408
Clínica Santa Ana
Av. Manuel J. Calle 1-104; tel: 02-281 4068
Good medical center, 24-hour emergency service.
Hospital Metropolitano
Av. Mariana de Jesús and Occidental; tel: 02-226 5020
Best and most expensive hospital in Quito. English-speaking doctors available.
Hospital Voz Andes
Juan Villalengua 0E2-37 and Av. 10 de Agosto; tel: 02-226 2142
Run by HCJB, an American Christian organization. Has an emergency room. Most of the doctors speak some English.

Medical Services, Guayaquil
Clínica Guayaquil
Padre Aguirre 401 and Córdoba; tel: 04-256 3555.
Private clinic. Dr Roberto Gilbert speaks English.
Clínica Kennedy
Av. Periodista) Nueva Kennedy; tel: 04-228 9666/228 6963.
Best hospital in the city. English-speaking doctors, consulting rooms for external patients.

Medical Services, Galápagos
There is a basic hospital in Puerto Ayora. Consultations cost $10.

Internet

An extraordinary number of internet cafés have opened in Quito, especially in the Mariscal area around Calama/Juan León Mera/Reina Victoria. Elsewhere around the country, you shouldn't have a problem finding service, although speed may sometimes be an issue in rural areas.

Wireless internet is becoming more and more common in large hotels, resorts, luxury haciendas, and lodges.

Lost Property

Considering that many people in Ecuador live below the poverty line, the chances are that if you lose a bag or an item, you are unlikely to see it again. That said, if you leave an item on a bus, it is worth checking at the bus company's office.

Maps

The best selection of maps of Ecuador is produced by the Instituto Geográfico Militar (tel: 02-397 5100; www.igm.gove.ec) on top of the hill on Avenida T. Paz and Mino, off Avenida Colombia in Quito. Large-scale maps of the whole country, ranging from 1:1,000,000 one-sheet maps to 1:50,000 topographical maps, are available here. The Sierra has been covered in detail, but the Oriente and parts of the Western Lowlands are not well served. For a road map, pick up the *Guía Vial del Ecuador*, with 26 partial maps, by Nelson Gómez, Editorial Camino.

Media

In Quito, there are several good newspapers: *El Comercio, Hoy, Tiempo*, and *Ultimas Noticias* are the most established. In Guayaquil, you can choose from *Expreso, El Telégrafo, El Universo*, and *La Prensa*. There are also a few English-language publications, including the *Ecuador Times* and *Inside Ecuador*.

TV and Radio
Cable TV in Ecuador carries many of the same channels and shows as the United States. News channels, such as the BBC and CNN, and sports channels, such as ESPN and Fox Sports, are common in most cities, although rural areas may be limited to a few basic channels.

There are a plethora of local radio stations in nearly every part of the country, that you will no doubt hear blasting away on any rural bus. Most play a combination of popular and regional music and they are a great way to find out what each part of the country is listening to.

Money

Since September 2000, Ecuador's currency was legally changed from the sucre to the US dollar. Major credit cards (particularly Visa and MasterCard) are accepted in the larger hotels, restaurants, and tourist-oriented shops. Cards with a Visa sign are useful for withdrawing cash from ATMs which are now ubiquitous, even in small Ecuadorian towns. Only machines that accept Visa are widespread; those that accept MasterCard and Cirrus/Maestro cards are not so easy to find. ATMs are sometimes closed after 10pm for security reasons, and it is always good to be circumspect after withdrawing a wad of cash, particularly so in downtown Guayaquil. Try to find an ATM that is not on the street. Travelers' checks are not widely accepted except for in a few locations in Quito and Guayaquil. Getting change can be a problem, and in rural areas it is best to travel with small-denomination notes.

US dollars are by far the best currency to take to Ecuador, but other foreign currencies can be exchanged in banks and *casas de cambio* (currency exchange offices) in the business districts of Quito (Avenida Amazonas), Guayaquil, and Cuenca. Outside major city centers, however, it becomes difficult to exchange other currencies.On Sundays and holidays, when banks and *casas de cambio* are shut, you can always exchange money in the major hotels. Most people bring a certain amount

BELOW: colonial buildings, Cuenca.

Street Names in Quito

In 1998 a new street numbering system was introduced in Quito based on N (*norte*), S (*sud*), E (*este*), and O (*oeste*), followed by a street and building number. Many businesses still use the old street names, however, and maps of the city usually show both old and new street names.

of cash dollars in manageable denominations (say, $20 bills).

It is easy to have money transferred to Ecuador, through organizations such as Western Union. You can pick up the sum in US dollars and travelers' checks.

Banks in Quito

American Express
Av. Amazonas 329 and Jorge Washington; tel: 02-256 0488
Banco de Guayaquil
Colón and Reina Victoria;
tel: 02-256 6800
For cash advance on Visa and ATM.
Banco del Pacífico
Av. Amazonas N22-94 and Veintimilla;
tel: 02-250 0988
For cash advance on MasterCard.
Banco de Pichincha
Av. Amazonas and Colón;
tel: 02-254 7006
Visa ATM.
Western Union
Av. La Prensa 1463 and Zamora;
tel: 02-226 4353

Banks in Cuenca

Banco del Pacífico
Benigno Malo 9-75;
MasterCard ATM.
Banco del Austro
Sucre and Borrero; Visa ATM.

Banks in Esmeraldas

The **Banco del Austro** and **Banco del Pichincha** can change cash.

Banks in Guayaquil

Banco de Guayaquil
Pichincha and P. Icaza
Visa & AmEx ATM.
Banco del Pacífico
Fco P. Icaza 200 and Pichincha, 4th Floor; tel: 04-232 8333. MasterCard.

Tipping

In many restaurants 22 percent service and tax is added to the bill, but some cheaper establishments will leave it to your discretion. It is customary to leave a 10 percent tip for the waiter if you have received good service. Airport porters can be tipped about 50 US cents. Taxi drivers do not expect a tip.

O pening Hours

Government offices in Quito are open to the public Mon–Fri 8am–4.30pm. In Guayaquil, hours are Mon–Fri 9am–noon and 3.30–6pm, though many offices are now converting to the 9am–5pm working day.

Banks in Ecuador are open Mon–Fri 9am–5 or 6pm with some also open 9am–1pm on Sat. They are closed on public holidays. Private companies generally work weekdays 8am–5pm with an hour for lunch.

Stores are generally open Mon–Fri 9am–1pm and 3–7pm, then Sat 9am–1.30pm, with many now staying open during lunchtime. Shopping centers and small grocery stores stay open until 8pm. Drug stores (*farmacias*) are open Mon–Fri 9am–8pm, and some are listed "on duty" 24 hours a day (see local newspapers for the daily roster).

P hotography

If you plan to shoot with film rather than with a digital camera, bring sufficient film with you: buying camera gear within Ecuador is expensive, and the choice of film is limited. If you are stuck, try one of the photo stores on Quito's Avenida Amazonas and make sure the film date hasn't expired.

Equatorial shadows are very strong and come out almost black on photographs, so the best results are often achieved on overcast days.

Not surprisingly, Ecuadorian *indígenas* may resent having a camera thrust in their faces and often turn their backs on pushy photographers. Unless you are taking a shot from long distance, ask permission beforehand. Many will ask for a small fee or "tip" and it is often more pleasant to comply rather than trying to shoot people without being noticed.

Postal Services

Letters are often slow to be delivered and are sometimes lost. It is worth having your letters certified (*con certificado*) as you get a receipt, which won't do much practical good, but means that your letter's existence is recorded somewhere and, in theory, given safer treatment.

DHL, FedEx, and other international courier services can be found across the country.

Quito

The head post office is at Eloy Alfaro 354 and 9 de Octubre in the New Town, but many travelers use the main office in the Old Town at Espejo 935 and Guayaquil. This is where Poste Restante (*Lista de Correos*) is located. Also, the South American Explorers will hold mail for members.

Packages up to 2kg can be sent from any post office, but those over 2kg must be sent from the post office on the corner of Av. Cristóbal Colón and Reina Victoria. Residents at hotels Colón and Quito may drop letters at the reception desk for posting.

In addition to at post offices, stamps can be bought in many hotel bookshops or receptions as well as at some *librerías* (bookshops). Faxes can be sent from most hotels or – inexpensive, but less convenient – the Andinatel office at Avenida 10 de Agosto and Colón (daily 8am–10pm).

Guayaquil

Pacifictel and Correo Central (main post office) are side by side on Aguirre and Pedro Carbo; tel: 04-253 1713.

R eligious Services

Roman Catholic services are held regularly in Quito's churches. Other services are held at:
Carolina Adventist Church
Av. 10 de Agosto 3929;
tel: 02-223 9995.
Meetings on Saturdays at 9am.
Central Baptist Church
Ríos 1803.
Sunday services 9am and 6pm.

Public Holidays

Ecuador has numerous public holidays and festivals (*see page 344 for a comprehensive list*), and it is worth bearing in mind that shops, banks, and services may be closed around these dates.
• When an official public holiday falls at a weekend, offices may be closed on the Friday or Monday.
• When a public holiday falls midweek, it may be moved to the nearest Friday or Monday to create a long weekend.
• Major holidays are often celebrated for several days around the actual date.
• Banks and businesses are closed on official public holidays.
• If you plan to travel on a major holiday, book ahead if possible as transport can get very crowded.

Church of Jesus Christ of the Latter Day Saints
Almagro and Colón; tel: 02-252 9602.
Sunday service 9.30am.
Lutheran Church
Isabel la Católica 1431;
tel: 02-223 4391.
Sunday services: 9am in English;
10.15am in German; 11.30am in Spanish.
Synagogue
Versalles and 18 de Septiembre.
Services Friday 7pm.

S tudent Travelers

ISIC (International Student Identity Card) discounts are few and far between. At times you may be able to get airline and bus tickets for a reduced fair, but little else.

T elephones

There is a plethora of call centres in every city, town and village. You will rarely be stuck for a place to make a phone call. Local, long-distance and international telephone calls, as well as calls to mobile phones, can be made at a Centro de Llamadas (call centres, sometimes simply called cabinas). Charges are cheap: even international calls rarely exceed $1 per minute. This is much more cost-efficient than calling from hotel rooms where the per-minute call cost can be exorbitant. It is possible to purchase convenient, if more expensive, debit cards for public telephones, but these are not interchangeable between the different telephone networks.

Cellular phone SIM cards can be readily bought, however you will need a quad-band phone. It is also possible to hire a mobile phone for the duration of your stay in Ecuador. Phone company agents will likely approach you when you arrive off your international flight in Quito.

Some people prefer to make collect (reverse-charge) calls from their hotel or buy a charge card before leaving home. If using a hotel line, check tariffs carefully for hefty surcharges.

Many internet cafés in Quito, Guayaquil, and Cuenca offer a net phone service like Skype: the cheapest way to stay in touch.

Telephoning Ecuador
The country code for Ecuador is 593. To call a number in Ecuador from abroad, dial the international access code (011 from the US, 00 from Britain), the country code (593) the area code without the 0 (2, 3, 4, 5, 6, or 7, depending on the area) and the seven-digit local phone number. Area codes are divided by province. Examples of codes for popular destinations are:
Quito **02**; Cuenca **07**; Ambato **03**; Baños **03**; Riobamba **03**; Guayaquil **04**; Manta **05**; Galápagos Islands **05**; Esmeraldas **06**; Otavalo **06**. Mobile phone numbers begin with **09**.

Toilets

Most of the toilets in Ecuador are Western, although in some rural areas you may encounter a few that are little more than holes that use pails of water to flush. Regardless, you should never flush paper down the toilet. It should be disposed in the small wastebasket provided beside the toilet.

Tour Operators and Travel Agents

Tours can be arranged through tour operators and travel agents in Europe or the US, but it is simple to organize an itinerary on arrival in Ecuador.

Quito
There are many reliable travel agencies all along Avenida Amazonas and in the major hotels. Some of the best include:
Compañía de Guías de Montaña
Jorge Washington 425 and 6 de Diciembre; tel: 02-290 1551
www.companiadeguias.com.ec
Offering a range of climbing and trekking tours.

Tourist Information

The Ministry of Tourism has an excellent website (www.ecuador.travel), and its **iTur** tourist offices can be found throughout the country.

Quito
Cnr. Calle Venezuela and Espejo, Centro Histórico; tel: 02-257 0786.

Otavalo
Bolívar and Calderón;
tel: 06-284 4162.

Baños
Haflants and Rocafuerte;
tel: 03-284 4162.

Guaranda
Calle 10 de Agosto 2072 and García Moreno; tel: 03-294 1213.

Cuenca
Av. Mariscal Sucre, opposite Parque Calderón; tel: 07-282 1035.

Time Zones

Mainland 5 hours behind GMT, the Galápagos 6 hours behind.

Enchanted Expeditions
De las Alondras N45-102 and de los Lirios (Monteserrín), Floralp Building, Office 104; tel: 02-334 0525
www.enchantedexpeditions.com
Quality excursions throughout Ecuador at reasonable prices: Galápagos trips on the boats Angelito, Beluga, Cachalote, Galápagos Explorer II, and Santa Cruz.
Gala Cruises
N22-118 9 de Octubre and Veintimilla, Quito; tel: 02-250 9007
www.galacruises.com
Cruise agency for Galápagos boats and a number of other tours.
Metropolitan Touring
De las Palmeras Av. N45-74 and de las Orquideas; tel: 02-298 8200
www.metropolitan-touring.com
Oldest, largest, and most efficient travel agency network in Ecuador.
Nuevo Mundo Expediciones
18 de Septiembre E4-161 and Juan León Mera; tel: 02-250 9431
www.nuevomundotravel.com
Countrywide tours, including Manatee Amazon Explorer Cruises.
Quasar Naútica
José Jussieu N41-28 and Alonso de Torres; tel: 02-244 6996
www.quasarnautica.com
Excellent upmarket bespoke tours including boats in the Galápagos.

Loja
Bolívar 12-39, entrance on Mercadillo and Lourdes;
tel: 07-257 2964.

Tena
García Moreno and Calderón;
tel: 06-288 6536.

Esmeraldas
Cañizares and Bolívar;
tel: 06-271 1370.

Manta
Paseo José María Egas, between calles 10 and 11 near Av. 3;
tel: 05-262 2944.

Guayaquil
Plaza Icaza 203, between Pedro Carbo and Pichincha (opposite Banco Pacífico), 5th and 6th Floors; tel: 04-256 8764/256 0514.

Sangay Tours
Luís Cordero E4-358 and Amazonas;
tel: 02-255 0176
www.sangay.com
Range of tours from the Galápagos to
Amazon lodges and trekking.
Sierra Nevada
Pinto 637 and Amazonas;
tel: 02-255 3658
Email: snevada@accessinter.net

Baños

Geo Tours
Calles Ambato and Haflants;
tel: 03-274 1344
www.geotoursbanios.com
Rainforestur
Calles Ambato 800 and Maldonado;
tel: 03-274 0743
www.rainforestur.com

Cuenca
Eco Trek
Calle Larga 7-108 and Cordero;
tel: 07-283 4677
Email: ecotrek@az.pro.ec
Expediciones Río Arriba
Corner Hermano Miguel and Córdova;
tel: 07-283 0116
Email: negro@az.pro.ec
Metropolitan Touring
Mariscal Sucre 662; tel: 07-283 7340
www.metropolitan-touring.com
TerraDiversa Travel & Adventure
Hermano Miguel 4-46 and Calle
Larga; tel: 07-282 3782
www.terradiversa.com
Southland Touring
Calle Larga 5-24 and Mariano Cueva;
tel: 07-283 3126
www.southlandtouring.com

Bahía de Caráquez

Guacamayo Tours
Bolívar 902 and Arenas;
tel: 05-269 1107
www.guacamayotours.com

Guayaquil
To avoid disappointment, plan ahead
for your Galápagos trip; flights and
cruises get very heavily booked up.
Canodros Tours
Urbanización Santa Leonor, Manzana
5, Solar 10; tel: 04-228 5711
www.canodros.com
Excellent responsible tour operator
that operates luxury cruises in the
Galápagos Islands and the superb
Kapawi Ecological Reserve in the
country's Oriente province.
Macchiavello Tours
Antepara 802 and 9 de Octubre;
tel: 04-228 6079
Metropolitan Touring
Antepara 915 and 9 de Octubre;
tel: 04-232 0300
www.metropolitan-touring.com

Salinas
Guayatur
Av. General Enríquez Gallo and
Rumiñahui; tel: 04-232 2441
www.guayatur.com

Galápagos Islands
Moorise Travel Agency
Av. Charles Darwin, Puerto Ayora; tel:
05-252 6348

UK
For a useful list of some of the many
excellent companies offering trips in
Ecuador, check out www.lata.org, the
website of the **Latin American Travel
Association** in the United Kingdom.
They can also give impartial advice on
how to plan a trip to Ecuador.
Austral Tours, tel: 020-7233 5384.
www.latinamerica.co.uk
Crusader Travel, tel: 020-8744
0474. www.crusadertravel.com
Journey Latin America, tel: 020-
8747 8315. www.journeylatinamerica.co.uk
Select Latin America Ltd, tel: 020-
7407 1478. www.selectlatinamerica.co.uk
The director is a former naturalist
guide in the Galápagos.
South American Experience,
tel: 0845-277 3366. www.southamerican
experience.co.uk
The Ultimate Travel Company,
tel: 020-7386 4646. www.theultimate
travelcompany.co.uk
Quasar Naútica, which operates
bespoke tours in Ecuador and the
Galápagos (see page 353) is
represented in the UK by **Penelope
Kellie World Wide Yacht Charters &
Tours**, tel: 01962-779 317. www.
pkworldwide.com

US and Canada
Bookings for tours operated by
Metropolitan Touring can be made
in the US through **Adventure
Associates**, tel: 1-800-527 2500.
www.adventure-associates.com
eXito Travel, tel: 1-800-655 4053/
970-482 3019. www.exitotravel.com
Inti Travel, tel: 1-403-760 3565.
www.intitravel.com
Off-the-beaten-track hiking trips, climbing expeditions, and Galápagos tours.
Wilderness Travel, tel: 1-800-368
2794.

V isas and Passports

To visit Ecuador as a tourist, you need
a valid passport (valid for at least six
months before arrival) and a return
ticket. Visas are required by citizens of
some Central American and Middle
Eastern countries as well as China,
Cuba, India, North Korea, Pakistan,
and Vietnam. Check with the local

Websites

www.discoveringecuador.com
Independent site with hotel and
restaurant listings and numerous
articles on sites in the country.
www.quito.com.ec
Quito's municipal tourism site has
restaurant and hotel listings, and a
comprehensive list of things to do.
www.ecuador.travel
Ministry of Tourism website with
resources and articles.
www.turismoguayas.com
A Guayaquil-based site focusing on
things to do in Guayas province.
www.rutadelsol.com.ec
Information about surfing and
travel on the Ruta del Sol and
around the Pacific coast.
www.southamericaexplorers.org
South American Explorers club
(see page 123) site.

Consulate of Ecuador before
traveling. Ecuadorian Immigration
Police will give you a free T-3 Tourist
Card; keep this safe as you need it to
leave the country. It is usually given
for 30 days (unless you ask for more),
although you can easily extend it for
up to 90 days by visiting the local
immigration authority. Note that
tourists can only stay in the country
for a maximum of 90 days in any
calendar year, but sometimes a one-
month extension can be obtained for
a few dollars at the end of the 90-day
period. You must go to the Dirección
Nacional de Migración in Quito (Av.
Amazonas 171 and República). In
theory, Immigration Police can ask for
an onward ticket or proof of sufficient
funds ($20 a day) before allowing entry
to Ecuador, although they rarely do.
Carry your passport, or a photocopy
of it, at all times, as the police have the
power to arrest anyone without ID
should a check be made. Foreigners
are unlikely to be bothered in this way
in Quito, but it is important to have your
passport handy on bus trips in the
countryside, where checks may be
more common.

W eights and Measures

The metric system is used to calculate
distances and weights.

Women Travelers

Ecuador is safe for women as it lacks
the machismo of many other Latin
American countries. However, late at
night avoid flagging down taxis or
walking alone.

LANGUAGE

UNDERSTANDING THE LANGUAGE

Pronunciation

Anyone with a working knowledge of Spanish will have no trouble making themselves understood in Ecuador, but there are a few interesting local variations. In order to emphasize an adjective, the ending *-aso* is added: for example, something that is very good would be *buenaso*. An expression you will hear everywhere, and which is difficult to translate, is *no más*. *Siga no más*, for example, means "Hurry up (and get on the bus/move down the line, etc)." *Come no más* means "Just eat it/It'll get cold/it's nicer than it looks, etc." You will soon get the hang of it.

Indígenas almost all speak Spanish, but you will hear Quichua words which have crept into the language: *wambras* translates as "guys," and *cheveré* means "cool."

Vowels

a slightly longer than in cat
e as in bed
i as in police
o as in hot
u as in rude

Consonants

These are approximately like those in English, the main exceptions being: **c** is hard before **a**, **o**, or **u** (as in English), and is soft before **e** or **i**, when it sounds like **s** (as opposed to the Castilian pronunciation of **th** as in think). Thus, *censo* (census) sounds like senso.

g is hard before **a**, **o**, or **u** (as in English), but where English **g** sounds like **j** – before **e** or **i** – Spanish **g** sounds like a guttural **h**. **G** before **ua** is often soft or silent, so that *agua* sounds more like awa, and

Guadalajara like Wadalajara.
h is silent.
j sounds like a guttural English h.
ll sounds like y.
ñ sounds like ny, as in the familiar Spanish word *señor*.
q is followed by **u** as in English, but the combination sounds like **k** instead of like kw. *¿Qué quiere usted?* is pronounced: Keh kee-ehr-eh oostehd?
r is rolled, and more so for double r.
x between vowels sounds like a guttural **h**, e.g. in México or Oaxaca.
y alone, as the word meaning 'and', is pronounced **ee**.
Note that **ch** and **ll** are separate letters of the Spanish alphabet; if

Greetings

Hello *¡Hola!*
Good morning *Buenos días*
Good afternoon *Buenas tardes*
Goodnight *Buenas noches*
See you later *Hasta luego*
Goodbye *Adiós*
Welcome *Bienvenido*
How are you? (formal/informal)
¿Cómo está?/¿Qué tal?
Fine, thanks *Bien, gracias*
And you? (formal/informal)
¿Y usted?/¿Y tú?
What is your name? (formal)
¿Cómo se llama usted?
My name is... *Me llamo...*
Mr/Miss/Mrs *Señor/Señorita/Señora*
Pleased to meet you
¡Encantado(a)!/Mucho gusto
I am English/American/Canadian/Irish/Scottish/Australian *Soy inglés(a)/norteamericano(a)/canadiense/irlandés(a)/escocés(a)/australiano(a)*

looking in a phone book or dictionary for a word beginning with ch, you will find it after the final c entry. A name or word beginning with ll will be listed after the l entries.

Language Classes

Quito is considered one of the best places in Latin America to learn Spanish. There are dozens of cheap places offering classes: they advertise in the hotels, bars, and restaurants frequented by young gringos. Classes can be taken by the hour, by the day, or by the week. Also, many organizations offer intensive courses where you board with an Ecuadorian family and are usually taught on a one-to-one basis. Other places, including Otavalo, Tena, Baños, and Montañita, also offer language classes, and some schools offer college credit.

The following schools are recommended.

Quito

La Lengua
Av. Colón 1001 and Juan León Mera, Edificio Av. María;
tel/fax: 02-250 1271
www.la-lengua.com
Simón Bolívar
Leónidas Plaza 353 and Roca; tel/fax: 02-223 6688/250 4977
www.simon-bolivar.com

Otavalo

Mundo Andino
Salinas 509; tel: 06-292 5478
Email: andinoinn@hotmail.com

Baños

Baños Spanish Center
Cañar and Oriente; tel: 06-274 0632
Email: elizabasc@uio.satnet.net

International Spanish School
16 de Diciembre and Espejo;
tel: 06-274 0612

Cuenca

Sí Centro de Español y Inglés
Jaramillo 7-27; tel: 07-284 6932
www.sicentrospanishschool.com

Basics

Yes *Sí*
No *No*
Thank you *Gracias*
You're welcome *De nada*
Please *Por favor*
Excuse me (to get attention) *¡Perdón!*
Excuse me (to get through a crowd)
¡Permiso!
Excuse me (sorry) *Perdóneme*
I'm sorry *Lo siento/Perdone*
Wait a minute! *¡Un momento!*
Can you help me? *¿Me puede ayudar?*
Do you speak English? (formal)
¿Habla inglés?
Please speak more slowly *Hable más despacio, por favor*
Could you repeat that please
¿Podría repetírmelo, por favor?
I (don't) understand (No) entiendo
I don't know *No lo sé*
No problem *No hay problema*
Where is...? *¿Dónde está...?*
I am looking for... *Estoy buscando*
Here it is *Aquí está*
There it is *Allí está*
Let's go *Vámonos*
At what time? *¿A qué hora?*
Late *tarde*
Early *temprano*
Yesterday *ayer*
Today *hoy*
Tomorrow *mañana*

Finding Your Way

Where is the (men's/women's) lavatory? *¿Dónde está el baño (de caballeros/de damas)?*

Emergencies

Help! *¡Socorro! ¡Auxilio!*
Stop! *¡Pare!*
Call a doctor *Llame a un médico*
Call an ambulance *Llame una ambulancia*
Call the police *Llame a la policía*
Call the fire brigade *Llame a los bomberos*
Where is the nearest hospital?
¿Dónde queda el hospital más cercano?
I want to report an assault/a robbery *Quisiera reportar un asalto/un robo*

Where is (the tourist office)?
¿Dónde está (la oficina de turismo)?
town hall *ayuntamiento*
bank *banco*
currency exhange bureau *casa de cambio*
library *biblioteca*
post office *correos*
hotel *hotel*
youth hostel *albergue*
camping *camping*
parking *aparcamiento*
straight *derecho*
to the left *a la izquierda*
to the right *a la derecha*
street *calle*
square *plaza*
corner *esquina*
a block *un cuadra*

At the Hotel

Do you have a vacant room? *¿Tiene una habitación disponible?*
I have a reservation *Tengo una reserva*
I'd like... *Quisiera...*
a single/double (with double bed)/a room with twin beds *una habitación individual (sencilla)/una habitación matrimonial/una habitación doble*
for one night/two nights *por una noche/dos noches*
with a sea view *con vista al mar*
Does the room have a private bathroom or shared bathroom?
¿Tiene la habitación baño privado o baño compartido?
Does it have hot water? *¿Tiene agua caliente?*
Could you show me another room, please? *¿Puede mostrarme otra habitación, por favor?*
What time do you close (lock) the doors? *¿A qué hora se cierran las puertas?*
I would like to change rooms
Quisiera cambiar la habitación
How much is it? *¿Cuánto cuesta?/¿Cuánto sale?*
Do you accept credit cards/ travelers' checks/dollars? *¿Se aceptan tarjetas de crédito/cheques de viajeros/dólares?*
What time is breakfast/lunch/ dinner? *¿A qué hora es el desayuno/ el almuerzo/la cena?*
Please wake me at... *Por favor despertarme a...*
Come in! *¡Pase!/¡Adelante!*
I'd like to pay the bill now, please
Quisiera cancelar la cuenta ahora, por favor

In the Restaurant

I'd like to book a table *Quisiera reservar una mesa, por favor*

Do you have a table for...? *¿Tiene una mesa para...?*
breakfast/lunch/dinner *desayuno/ almuerzo/cena*
I'm a vegetarian *Soy vegetariano(a)*
May we have the menu? *¿Puede traernos la carta?*
wine list *la carta de vinos*
What would you recommend? *¿Qué recomienda?*
fixed-price menu *el menú fijo/la merienda*
special of the day *plato del día/ sugerencia del chef*
waiter *mozo*
What would you like to drink? *¿Qué quiere tomar?*
Is service included? *¿Incluye el servicio?*
The bill, please *La cuenta, por favor*

Menu Decoder

Entremeses/Primer Plato
(First Course)

ensalada mixta **mixed salad**
pan con ajo **garlic bread**
sopa/crema **soup/cream soup**
sopa de cebolla **onion soup**

La Carne (Meat)

a la brasa/a la parrilla **charcoal-grilled**
a la plancha **grilled**
a punto **medium**
ahumado(a) **smoked**
al horno **baked**
alas **wings**
albóndigas **meat balls**
aves **poultry**
bien hecho **well done**
cerdo/chancho/puerco **pork**
chivito **goat**
chuleta **chop**
conejo **rabbit**
cordero **lamb**
costillas **ribs**
crudo **raw**
empanizado(a)/apanado(a)
breaded
frito(a) **fried**
guisado(a) **stewed**
hamburguesa **hamburger**
hígado de res **beef liver**
jamón **ham**
jugoso(a) **rare**
lengua **tongue**
lomito **tenderloin**
milanesa **breaded and fried thin cut of meat**
morcilla **blood sausage**
pato **duck**
pavo **turkey**
pechuga **breast**
pernil **leg of pork**
piernas **legs**
pollo **chicken**
rebozado(a) **batter-fried**

riñones **kidneys**
salchichas/panchos **sausages or hot dogs**
término medio **medium rare**
ternera **veal**

Pescado/Mariscos (Fish/Seafood)

almejas **clams**
anchoa **anchovy**
atún **tuna**
bacalao **cod**
calamares **squid**
camarones **shrimp**
cangrejo **crab**
corvina **sea bass**
dorado **dolphinfish**
langosta **lobster**
langostinos **prawns**
lenguado **sole or flounder**
mariscos **shellfish**
mejillones **mussels**
ostiones/ostras **oysters**
pargo **snapper**
picudo **marlin**
pulpo **octopus**
sierra **mackerel**
trucha **trout**

Vegetales (Vegetables)

ajo **garlic**
alcaucil **artichoke**
arvejas **peas**
batata/camote **sweet potato**
berenjena **eggplant/aubergine**
brócoli **broccoli**
calabaza **pumpkin or yellow squash**
cebolla **onion**
chauchas **green beans**
choclo **corn (on the cob)**
coliflor **cauliflower**
espárrago **asparagus**
espinaca **spinach**
habas **broad beans**
hongos, champiñones **mushrooms**
lechuga **lettuce**
papa **potato**
pepino **cucumber**
pimentón **green (bell) pepper**
porotos **Lima beans**
puerro **leeks**
remolacha **beets/beetroot**
repollo **cabbage**
zanahorias **carrots**
zapallo **yellow squash**
zapallito **green squash**
zapallito largo **zucchini/courgette**

Frutas (Fruit)

aguacate **avocado**
banana/guineo **banana**
cereza **cherry**
ciruela **plum**
durazno **peach**
frambuesa **raspberry**
fresa **strawberry**
guayaba **guava**
higo **fig**
lima **lime**

limón **lemon**
maracuyá **passion fruit**
mandarina **tangerine**
manzana **apple**
mora **blackberry**
naranja **orange**
pera **pear**
piña **pineapple**
plátano **plantain**
pomelo **grapefruit**
sandía **watermelon**
uvas **grapes**

Drinks

agua mineral con/sin gas **carbonated/non-carbonated mineral water**
cerveza **beer**
chocolate caliente **hot chocolate**
coca **cola**
jugo de fruta **fruit juice**
mate de coca **coca-leaf tea**
té (con leche) **tea (with milk)**
té manzanilla **camomile tea**
vino blanco/tinto **white/red wine**

Miscellaneous

arroz **rice**
azúcar **sugar**
canguil **popcorn**
empanada **savory turnover**
fideos **spaghetti**
huevos (revueltos/fritos/hervidos) **eggs (scrambled/fried/boiled)**
ice cream **helado**
mantequilla **butter**
mermelada **jam**
mostaza **mustard**
pan **bread**
pan integral **wholewheat bread**
pan tostado/tostadas **toast**
panceta **bacon**
pimienta negra **black pepper**
queso **cheese**
sal **salt**
salsa picante **spicy sauce**
sandwich **sandwich**
tortilla **omelet**

Shopping

I'd like... *Quisiera...*
I'm just looking *Sólo estoy mirando, gracias*
How much is this? *¿Cuanto cuesta/sale?*
Do you have it in another color? *¿Tiene en otro color?*
Do you have it in another size? *¿Tiene en otro talle/número?*
smaller/larger *más pequeño/más grande*
trousers *pantalones*
skirt *falda*
dress *vestido*
shirt *camisa*
jacket *chaqueta*
suit *traje*

coat *abrigo*
underpants *calzoncillos*
socks *calcetines*
shoes *zapatos*
hat *sombrero*
swimsuit *traje de baño*
I would like some of that... *Quisiera un poco de eso...*
I would like a kilo of... *Quisiera un kilo de...*
I would like half a kilo of... *Quisiera un medio kilo de...*
A little more/less *Un poco más/menos*
That's enough/no more *Está bien/nada más*
Would you like anything else? *¿Quiere algo más?*
expensive *caro*
cheap *barato*
clothes store *tienda de ropa*
bookstore *librería*
hairdressers *peluquería*
bakery *panadería*
cake shop *pastelería*
butcher's *carnicería*
fishmonger's *pescadería*
green grocery *verdulería*
market *mercado*
grocery store *tienda de abarrotes*
newsstand *kiosco*
shopping center *centro comercial*

Tourist Attractions

tourist office *oficina de turismo*
postcard *postal*
handicrafts *artesanía*
market *mercado*
art gallery *sala de exposiciones*
indigenous community *comunidad indígena*
Old Town *ciudad vieja*
ruins *ruinas*
bridge *puente*
tower *torre*
monument *monumento*
statue *estatua*
fort *castillo/fuerte*
palace *palacio*
chapel *capilla*
church *iglesia*
cathedral *catedral*
convent *convento*
park *parque*
playground *parque infantil*
botanical garden *jardín botánico*
zoo *zoológico*
cable car *teleférico*
viewpoint *mirador*
hill *cerro*
mountain *montaña*
stream *quebrada*
river *río*
lagoon *laguna*
lake *lago*
sea *mar*
Pacific Ocean *Océano Pacífico*

TRANSPORTATION · ACCOMMODATIONS · EATING OUT · ACTIVITIES · A–Z · LANGUAGE

island *isla*
glacier *glaciar*
beach *playa*
hot springs *aguas termales*
swimming pool *piscina*
discotheque *discoteca*

Airport/Travel Agency

flight *vuelo*
arrivals *llegadas*
departures *salidas*
connection *conexión*
customs and immigration *aduana y migraciones*
travel/tour agency *agencia de viajes/de turismo*
ticket *boleto pasaje*
I would like to purchase a ticket for... *Quisiera comprar un boleto (pasaje) para...*
When is the next/last flight/departure for...? *¿Cuándo es el próximo/último vuelo/para...?*
How long is the flight? *¿Cuánto tiempo dura el vuelo?*
What time do I have to be at the airport? *¿A qué hora tengo que estar en el aeropuerto?*
Is the tax included? *¿Se incluye el impuesto?*
What is included in the price? *¿Qué está incluido en el precio?*
departure tax *el impuesto de salida*
I would like a seat in first class/business class/tourist class *Quisiera un asiento en primera clase/ejecutivo/clase de turista*
I need to change my ticket *Necesito cambiar mi boleto*
lost-luggage office *oficina de reclamos*
on time *a tiempo*
late *atrasado*

Transportation

luggage *equipaje*
bag(s) *valija(s)*

bus *colectivo (urban), autobús (long distance)*
bus stop *parada*
bus terminal *terminal de pasajeros*
first class *primera clase*
second class *segunda clase*
tourist class *clase de turista*
one-way ticket *boleto de ida*
round-trip, return ticket *boleto de ida y vuelta*
What time does the bus/boat/ferry (leave/return)? *¿A qué hora (sale/regresa) el autobús/la lancha/el ferry?*
Which is the stop closest to...? *¿Cuál es la parada más cerca de...?*
Is this seat taken? *¿Está ocupado este asiento?*
Could you please advise me when we reach/the stop for...? *¿Por favor, puede avisarme cuando llegamos a/a la parada para...?*
Is this the stop for...? *¿Es ésta la parada para...?*
Next stop please *La próxima parada, por favor*
train station *estación de tren*
platform *el andén*
sleeping car *coche cama*
car *coche/automóvil*
car rental *alquiler de coche*
dock for small boats/large boats *embarcadero/muelle*
ferry *ferry*
sailboat *velero*
yacht *yate*
ship *barco*

Health

(shift duty) pharmacy *farmacia (de turno)*
hospital/clinic *hospital/clínica*
I need a doctor/dentist *Necesito un médico/dentista (odontólogo)*
I don't feel well *Me siento mal*
I am sick *Estoy enfermo(a)*
It hurts here *Duele aquí*
I have a headache/stomach ache/

cramps *Tengo dolor de cabeza/de estómago/de vientre*
I feel dizzy *Me siento mareado(a)*
Do you have (something for)...? *¿Tiene (algo para)...?*
cold *resfrío*
flu *gripe*
cough *tos*
sore throat *dolor de garganta*
diarrhea *diarrea*
constipation *estreñimiento*
fever *fiebre*
heartburn *acidez*
aspirin *aspirina*
antiseptic cream *crema antiséptica*
insect/mosquito bites *picaduras de insectos/mosquitos*
insect repellent *repelente contra insectos*
sun block *bloqueador solar*
toothpaste *pasta de dientes*
toilet paper *papel higiénico*
tampons *tampones*
condoms *condones*

Days of the Week

Monday *lunes*
Tuesday *martes*
Wednesday *miércoles*
Thursday *jueves*
Friday *viernes*
Saturday *sábado*
Sunday *domingo*

Months of the Year

January *enero*
February *febrero*
March *marzo*
April *abril*
May *mayo*
June *junio*
July *julio*
August *agosto*
September *septiembre*
October *octubre*
November *noviembre*
December *diciembre*

Numbers

1 *uno*	16 *dieciséis*	101 *ciento uno*	first *primer(o)/a*
2 *dos*	17 *diecisiete*	200 *doscientos*	second *segund(o)/a*
3 *tres*	18 *dieciocho*	300 *trescientos*	third *tercer(o)/a*
4 *cuatro*	19 *diecinueve*	400 *cuatrocientos*	fourth *cuart(o)/a*
5 *cinco*	20 *veinte*	500 *quinientos*	
6 *seis*	21 *veintiuno*	600 *seiscientos*	**Note**
7 *siete*	25 *veinticinco*	700 *setecientos*	In Spanish, in numbers,
8 *ocho*	30 *treinta*	800 *ochocientos*	commas are used where
9 *nueve*	40 *cuarenta*	900 *novecientos*	decimal points are used
10 *diez*	50 *cincuenta*	1,000 *mil*	in English and vice versa.
11 *once*	60 *sesenta*	2,000 *dos mil*	For example:
12 *doce*	70 *setenta*	10,000 *diez mil*	**English** / **Spanish**
13 *trece*	80 *ochenta*	100,000 *cien mil*	$19.30 / $19,30
14 *catorce*	90 *noventa*	1,000,000 *un millón*	1,000m / 1.000m
15 *quince*	100 *cien*	2,000,000 *dos millones*	9.5 % / 9,5 %

FURTHER READING

Bird-Watching

The Birds of Ecuador by Ridgeley, R., and Greenfield, P. Christopher Helm Publishers, 2001.
A Guide to the Birds of Colombia by Hilty, Steven, and Brown, William. Princeton University Press, 1986.
A Guide to the Birds of the Galápagos Islands by Castro, Isabel, and Phillips, Antonia. Christopher Helm Publishers, 1996.

Crafts

Otavalo: Weaving, Costume, and the Market by Meisch, Lynn. Ediciones Libri Mundi, 1987. A good overview of the textile crafts of Otavalo.

The Galápagos

A Field Guide to the Fishes of the Galápagos by Merlen, G. Wilmot, 1988.
Galápagos by Vonnegut, Kurt. Dial Press, 1999. An apocalyptic satire of human evolution set in the Galápagos.
The Galápagos Affair by Treherne, John. Pimlico, 2002. An entertaining account of the scandals and murder occurring on Floreana in the 1930s.
Galápagos: A Natural History by Jackson, M.H. University of Calgary Press, 1988. Without doubt the best guide to the islands.
Galápagos, Islands Born of Fire. Tui De Roy, 2010. This tenth-anniversary edition of the Galápagos classic is a beautiful hard-cover photographic tour de force celebrating the landscapes, wildlife, and habitats of the Galápagos.
Galápagos Wildlife by Horwell, David, and Oxford, Pete. Bradt Travel Guides, 2005.
Galápagos, World's End. William Beebe, 1988. A wry, wonderfully evocative account of a 1924 scientific expedition. All the romance of science and adventure in this far-flung corner of the world.
The Voyage of the Beagle by Darwin, Charles. Penguin, 1989. Shortened journal of Darwin's five-year voyage around the world. A classic.

History and Society

The Conquest of the Incas by Hemming, John. Pan, 2004. The classic account of the Spanish conquest.
Indians, Oil, and Politics: A Recent History of Ecuador by Gerlach, Allen. Scholarly Resources, Wilmington, 2003. A study of Ecuadorian politics since the 1970s.
Savages by Kane, Joe. Vintage, 1996. First-hand account of the Huaorani people's struggle to preserve their way of life.

Travel Literature

Living Poor by Moritz, Thomsen. University of Washington Press, 1997. Life as a Peace Corps worker in 1960s Ecuador.
The Lost Lady of the Amazon by Smith, Anthony. Constable and Robinson, 2003. The story of Isabel Godin's harrowing journey through the Amazon in search of her husband.
Maíz y Coca-Cola by Terezakis, Diane. Xlibris, 2001. One woman's journey through Ecuador, from the Andes to the Amazon.
The Panama Hat Trail by Miller, Tom. National Geographic Books, 2002. The story behind the famous hats.
Personal Narrative of a Journey by Humbolt, Alexander von, abridged and translated by Jason Wilson. Penguin, 1996. The 19th-century scientist's account of his expedition to Ecuador.
Travels amongst the Great Andes of the Equator by Whymper, Edward. Rocky Limited, 2005. Memoirs of the famous 19th-century British mountaineer.

Other Guides

Among nearly 200 companion books to this one are several guides highlighting destinations in this region. Titles include Insight Guides to South America, Argentina, Brazil, Peru, Chile, and the Berlitz Guide to Buenos Aires.

Send Us Your Thoughts

We do our best to ensure the information in our books is as accurate and up-to-date as possible. The books are updated on a regular basis using local contacts, who painstakingly add, amend, and correct as required. However, some details (such as telephone numbers and opening times) are liable to change, and we are ultimately reliant on our readers to put us in the picture.

We welcome your feedback, especially your experience of using the book "on the road." Maybe we recommended a hotel that you liked (or another that you didn't), or you came across a great bar or new attraction we missed.

We will acknowledge all contributions, and we'll offer an Insight Guide to the best letters received.

Please write to us at:
**Insight Guides
PO Box 7910
London SE1 1WE**
Or email us at:
insight@apaguide.co.uk

ART AND PHOTO CREDITS

INDEX

Numbers in italics refer to photographs